Grace Jantzen was an internationally-renowned feminist philosopher of religion whose work has transformed the way we think about the interactions between religion, culture and gender in Western culture. Jantzen's aim was to 'redeem the present' via a critique and reconstruction of staple concepts of the Western imaginary.

This unique book brings together many of Grace Jantzen's colleagues and former students in a wide-ranging exploration of her enduring influence, ranging across philosophy of religion, to literature, psychoanalysis, theology, ethics and politics.

Part One assesses the ramifications of Jantzen's affirmation that Western culture must 'choose life' in preference to a prevailing symbolic of violence and death. Part Two explores some of the key voices which contributed to Jantzen's understanding of a culture of flourishing and natality: Quaker thought and practice, medieval mysticism and feminist spirituality. Further essays apply elements of Jantzen's work to the politics of disability, development and environmentalism, extending her range of influence into new and innovative areas.

Grace Jantzen
Redeeming the Present

Edited by

ELAINE L. GRAHAM
University of Chester, UK

ASHGATE

Published by
Ashgate Publishing Limited
Wey Court East
Union Road
Farnham
Surrey, GU9 7PT
England

Ashgate Publishing Company
Suite 420
101 Cherry Street
Burlington
VT 05401-4405
USA

www.ashgate.com

British Library Cataloguing in Publication Data
Grace Jantzen : redeeming the present.
 1. Jantzen, Grace. 2. Feminist theology. I. Graham, Elaine L.
 230'.092—dc22

Library of Congress Cataloging-in-Publication Data
Grace Jantzen : redeeming the present / [edited by] Elaine L Graham.
  p. cm.
 Includes bibliographical references and index.
  ISBN 978-0-7546-6823-7 (hardcover : alk. paper) — ISBN 978-0-7546-6824-4 (pbk. : alk. paper) 1. Religion—Philosophy. 2. Jantzen, Grace. 3. Christianity. 4. Philosophy. I. Graham, Elaine L.
 BL51.G719 2009
 210.92—dc22

2009017750

ISBN 9780754668237 (hbk)
ISBN 9780754668244 (pbk)
ISBN 9780754697350 (ebk)

Mixed Sources
Product group from well-managed forests and other controlled sources
www.fsc.org Cert no. SA-COC-1565
© 1996 Forest Stewardship Council
FSC

Printed and bound in Great Britain by
MPG Books Group, UK

Grace Jantzen

Contents

PART THREE   'CHOOSE LIFE!'

Notes on Contributors

Pamela Sue Anderson is Reader in Philosophy of Religion at the University of Oxford and Fellow in Philosophy and Ethics, Regent's Park College, Oxford.

Jeremy Carrette is Professor of Religion and Culture, University of Kent.

Elaine Graham is Grosvenor Research Professor of Practical Theology, University of Chester and was until October 2009 the Samuel Ferguson Professor of Social and Pastoral Theology, University of Manchester.

Claire Greer is a doctoral candidate in Religions and Theology, University of Manchester.

Mary Grey is Emeritus Professor of Theology, University of Wales, Lampeter and Research Fellow at St Mary's University, Twickenham.

Betty Hagglund is Research Fellow in English, Nottingham Trent University and a member of the Centre for Postgraduate Quaker Studies, Birmingham.

Nanci Hogan is a part-time doctoral student in international politics, University of Manchester and is involved in international advocacy on gender issues and political movements.

Morny Joy is University Professor in the Department of Religious Studies at the University of Calgary, Canada.

Ursula King is Professor Emerita of Theology and Religious Studies, University of Bristol.

Pam Lunn is a member of the Centre for Postgraduate Quaker Studies, Woodbrooke Quaker Study Centre, Birmingham.

Peter Manley Scott is Senior Lecturer in Christian Social Thought, University of Manchester and Director of the Lincoln Theological Institute.

Mary Elizabeth Moore is Professor of Religion and Education, Center for the Study of Law and Religion, Emory University, Atlanta, GA, USA.

Edwina Newman is a member of the Centre for Postgraduate Quaker Studies, Woodbrooke Quaker Study Centre, Birmingham.

Ben Pink Dandelion is Professor of Quaker Studies, Centre for Postgraduate Quaker Studies and an honorary professor at the University of Birmingham.

Kate Stogdon has been a Cenacle sister since 1989 and is a tutor on the Ignatian Spirituality Course, London Centre for Spirituality.

Frances Ward is a Residentiary Canon at Bradford Cathedral.

Graham Ward is Professor of Contextual Theology and Ethics, University of Manchester.

Acknowledgements

I should like to thank Clare Greer for her organizational assistance with the colloquium and Elisabeth Storrs for her work on preparing this manuscript.

My special thanks go to all participants in the Memorial Symposium, *Natality and Necrophilia* in Manchester in May 2007, and especially Tina Macrae, her partner; and to Professors George Brooke and Graham Ward for their support in making the event possible.

Chapter 1
Redeeming the Present

Elaine Graham

> What does it mean to do feminist moral philosophy with notions of utopia and transformation as points of reference? What characteristics are necessary for moral philosophy to address, criticize and ultimately redeem the present – a present whose constitutive ingredients include massive inequalities of gender, 'race', and economic and cultural resources?[1]

Grace Jantzen, in whose honour this volume has been assembled, was John Rylands Research Professor of Religion, Culture and Gender at the University of Manchester. Born in 1948 in Saskatchewan in Western Canada into a strict Mennonite farming family, she studied at the Universities of Saskatchewan and Calgary before moving to Oxford, where she completed a DPhil – her second doctoral degree – on *The Doctrine of Divine Incorporeality*. She taught Philosophy of Religion at King's College London for fifteen years until her move to Manchester in 1995. She remained there until her death from cancer in May 2006.

Her publications were many and distinguished, beginning with *God's World, God's Body*,[2] a development of her doctoral work on the doctrine of God and the enduring philosophical question of God's embodiment. Probably the most popular – in terms of best-selling and most widely-read – of her works was her study of the female medieval mystical writer and teacher, Julian of Norwich, as exemplar of a holistic, life-affirming theology. This contained many of the seeds of later work, brought especially to fruition in *Power, Gender and Christian Mysticism*[3] which argued that conventional characterizations of 'mysticism' (Grace always tried to avoid 'isms') as privatized, interior and ineffable were calculated to silence the distinctive voice of women mystics, for whom such experience offered a powerful source of religious authority. Whilst Grace was not concerned primarily to rehabilitate the Christian tradition, her work provided a powerful demonstration of how 'voices of dissent' against the predominant weight of patriarchy had always existed, albeit on the margins of the institutional Church, and how those seeking alternative patterns of belief and practice today might learn from them.

---

[1]   Grace Jantzen, 'Flourishing: Towards an Ethic of Natality', *Feminist Theory*, 2/2 (2001): pp. 219–32, p. 219.

[2]   Grace Jantzen, *God's World, God's Body* (Philadelphia, PA, 1984).

[3]   Grace Jantzen, *Power, Gender and Christian Mysticism* (Cambridge, 1995).

Her next major book, *Becoming Divine*[4] reflected her growing interest in the work of Luce Irigaray and the significance of continental philosophy and post-Lacanian psychoanalysis. She used these critical tools to develop a critique of Western modernity's preoccupation with death and violence and the envisioning of an alternative 'symbolic', as earlier interests, of God's corporeality and the possibilities of pantheism, fused with Irigaray's Feuerbachian positing of a 'divine horizon' towards which women in particular, denied autonomous identity within the Law of the Father, might thereby realize new models of human flourishing. Latterly, and up to the time of her final illness, Grace had embarked on an ambitious project of tracing the roots of violence in Western culture from the Greeks to the present day. *Foundations of Violence*,[5] volume 1 of the series *Death and the Displacement of Beauty*, was the only volume to be completed before her death, but further volumes, edited by Morny Joy and Jeremy Carrette, will be published posthumously. Yet the critical motif was, even to the end, complemented by the trajectory towards the articulation of an alternative: in *Foundations of Violence*, we see, alongside her customary exposure of Western symbolic of death and violence, the emergence of the articulation of a 'new imaginary of beauty'.[6]

At the heart of her work was a concern for the way in which a preoccupation with death and violence had distorted the Western cultural imagination, with corresponding pathological implications. She argued that the central symbolic of necrophilia – a morbid obsession with death, as much by its neurotic avoidance and displacement as its explicit veneration – infused virtually every aspect of Western thought. In particular, she regarded Christianity's veneration of a transcendent, disembodied, dispassionate God, its institutionalisation of a desire for other-worldly salvation as flight from immanent, material existence, serving as a major buttress to the 'moral imaginary' of death. Grace saw the exposure of the religious roots of violence as essential if Western culture was to come to a new understanding: a purely secular conception of culture, in which religion is 'bracketed out' of the public realm, would be incapable of addressing and rooting out the causes of the Western condition. Furthermore, the culture of death and violence was, in her view, implicitly but thoroughly gendered. An androcentric culture which defined its own exemplary understandings of virtue and human destiny around the assumption of violence and individualism as the norm, would inevitably determine such norms via the negation and subordination of their opposites – women, the feminine, nature – which represented to such a necrophilic culture the threat of contingency, embodiment and finitude. It was therefore appropriate that the title of Grace's post at Manchester should reflect her

---

[4]   Grace Jantzen, *Becoming Divine: Towards a Feminist Philosophy of Religion* (Manchester, 1998).

[5]   Grace Jantzen, *Foundations of Violence 1: Death and the Displacement of Beauty* (London and New York, 2004).

[6]   Jantzen, *Foundations of Violence*, p. 67.

insistence on the powerful triangulation of religion, culture and gender in shaping the distinctive contours of Western modernity.

In this introductory essay, I have chosen to take a thematic approach to Grace's work, complementing Morny Joy's more chronological treatment in Part One, in order to identify some of the major motifs of Grace's ground-breaking work. I once argued in the context of a discussion of Western feminist theology that it was characterized by a dynamic of 'critique' and 'reconstruction'.[7] It denotes an approach which exposes what is assumed to be taken for granted and objective knowledge as androcentric, before moving on to develop a more representative or authentic tradition, often founded on the inclusion of formerly excluded voices and experiences.[8] In re-reading Grace's work, and engaging with the essays collected in this volume, I am struck by her adoption of a similar approach, which she characterized as one of 'diagnosis' and 'transformation'.[9] This constitutes a strong thread throughout the various phases of her career: from her refusal of the inevitability of the *habitus* of necrophilia and the exposure of dualistic systems of thought, to the telling of alternative stories about women's religious experiences and voices and the celebration of the radical possibilities of life and beauty. Grace used the sharpest tools of philosophical critique to read against the grain of the present in order to 'redeem' it.[10] With its intention both to destabilize the present and to envisage radical alternatives, Grace's life-long intellectual endeavours did indeed resemble a kind of utopian thought, or as she put it, 'sketches towards a counterhistory'.[11]

We can perhaps begin to see how by the end of her life Grace felt the need to move to the foundational work of mapping the genealogy – the origins and inter-relationships – of the Western moral imaginary, as 'deeply rooted in competition, death and gendered violence'.[12] Yet it was its very constructedness and contingency that demanded its exposure; and the devices of psychoanalytic theory, continental philosophy and Foucauldian cultural history were consistently deployed in strategies of critique and reconstruction. I will return to this theme later when considering key elements of Grace's critical methodology.

This introductory chapter is therefore structured around a series of binary constructs which formed recurrent motifs in Grace's work, and seem to me to exemplify her strategy of diagnosis and transformation: Necrophilia and Natality;

---

[7]   Elaine Graham, 'Feminist Theology: Northern', in William Cavanaugh and Peter Scott (eds) *Blackwell Companion to Political Theology* (Oxford and New York, 2003), pp. 210–26.

[8]   Rosemary Ruether, *Sexism and God-Talk: Toward a Feminist Theology* (London, 1983; second edn, Boston, 1993).

[9]   Grace Jantzen, 'Before the Rooster Crows: The Betrayal of Knowledge in Modernity', *Literature and Theology*, 15/1 (2001): pp. 1–24, p. 3.

[10]   Jantzen, 'Flourishing: Towards an Ethic of Natality', *Feminist Theory*, 2/2 (2001): pp. 219–32.

[11]   Jantzen, 'Feminists, Philosophers and Mystics', *Hypatia*, 9/4 (1994): pp. 186–206, p. 188.

[12]   Jantzen, 'Flourishing: Towards an Ethic of Natality', p. 223.

God as Transcendence or Immanence; Salvation or Flourishing; and knowledge as dispassionate or transformative. Yet in taking this approach, I have no wish to portray her work as simply reinscribing the dualistic systems she sought to deconstruct. Thus, in my final section, I will focus on her adoption of key methodological tools, and argue that her use of Foucauldian cultural history, psychoanalysis and continental philosophy demonstrates how she sought to transcend such dualisms in favour of a truly dialectical approach. This rejection of binary thinking extended to her attempts to dissolve the dichotomy between theory and practice, since she also refused to allow her intellectual pursuits to become hide-bound by the relative security of the academy. Indeed, she regarded her intellectual endeavours as imperative if the grip of what she termed the 'moral imaginary' of the West was to be rooted out.

This culminated in *Foundations of Violence*, where the mapping of historical examples as indicative of the broader analytical framework of necrophilia/natality becomes central. As Jeremy Carrette points out in his essay, however, it was necessary to provide a full theoretical exposition of this task before embarking on the historical project. From her early forays into the nature of God as an embodied, immanent being, to her alliance of feminist and ecological thought in *God's World, God's Body*, through to the sustained engagement with Lacanian psychoanalysis and its feminist critics such as Luce Irigaray, to the final ambition of her last (and now continuing posthumously) project which seeks to put historical flesh on the theoretical bones, therefore, Grace's career was dedicated to a demonstration of the power of *thinking* differently in order to *act* differently.

Necrophilia/Natality

> Birth is the basis of every person's existence, which by that very fact is always already material, embodied, gendered, and connected with other human beings and with human history ... If anyone will become divine, it will be as an embodied, gendered, situated self: there can be no other selves than selves of woman born.[13]

At the heart of Grace's work, as we have seen, was the contention that Western culture is defined by what she termed the 'moral imaginary' which is grounded in death and gendered violence. Death is the 'guiding motif in the construction of rationality'[14] which shapes the logic of the Western moral imaginary.

The tradition of Western philosophy from Plato onwards has been to represent the human condition as one bounded by death. It reaches its epitome in the work of Martin Heidegger, who argues that death guarantees the authenticity of our lives. The anticipation of the rupture of death defines our individuality – but as Grace

---

[13]   Jantzen, *Becoming Divine*, p. 141.

[14]   Jantzen, 'Flourishing: Towards an Ethic of Natality', p. 227.

argued, this was a subjectivity founded in isolation and violence: psychoanalytically speaking, it evokes the separation from the mother that denotes the formation of the ego in the infant and ultimately the establishment of gender identity.

The motif of death as the defining event for our humanity is echoed elsewhere in Western culture. But Grace's question was why this resulted in a culture of anxiety and repression. Psychoanalytical theory is often deployed to demonstrate how the unspoken ubiquity of death is repressed and yet constantly threatens to disrupt our security. This cultural anxiety expresses itself in a moral imaginary that valorizes invulnerability, detachment, disembodied reason and longs for immortality, either in fantasies of escape to other worlds or in cults of youth and beauty. It also displaces itself into other fears, most notably fear of the maternal, the feminine, and of nature – all of which embody, literally, the things of contingency and materialism which serve as uncomfortable reminders of humanity's dependence and finitude. The doctrines of salvation and life after death are symptomatic of Western modernity's desire to long for a world and existence beyond the temporal and physical, with a resulting indifference to political transformation and material flourishing.[15] Similarly, fascination with other worlds and space flights, even consumer cults of eternal youth, reflect an implicit distaste for this world, embodiment and human finitude.[16]

Yet Grace's question is, consistently this: why should it be the prospect of our death – as mortals – and not the fact of our births – as natals – which so preoccupies the Western imaginary? Even if death were acknowledged as that which inevitably circumscribes human lives, why does this not translate into an ethic of recognising our fragility and thus our interdependence, rather than a means of effecting the formation of a subjectivity that reinforces the values of mastery, detachment and anxiety? It is this exposure of the hidden workings of the logic of necrophilia, a challenge to its inevitability as determining the human condition, and the articulation of an alternative ethic of natality, that characterises Grace's work.

The moral imaginary is described at one stage as equating with Bourdieu's 'cultural unconscious',[17] or the images, metaphors and narratives (including, as we shall see, the implicit anthropologies and soteriologies that define our assumptions about what it means to be human and what we must do to be saved) that help to construct our cultural values. But how does the 'moral imaginary' relate to other concepts Grace used, such as the 'symbolic', after Luce Irigaray, or Bourdieu's 'habitus' and Foucault's 'episteme'? Are they all loosely equivalent, meaning the language and thought patterns of a given civilization? Certainly, all these terms variously describe the taken-for-granted, inhabited reality of Western culture: the rules, or grammar, that guide and generate the logic of our moral reasoning. In later work, the influence of Pierre Bourdieu's notion of 'habitus', with its emphasis on

---

[15]   Grace Jantzen, 'The Gendered Politics of Flourishing and Salvation' in Vincent Brümmer and Marcel Sarot (eds) *Happiness, Well-Being and The Meaning of Life* (Kampen, 1996), pp. 58–75, p. 73.

[16]   Jantzen, *Foundations of Violence*, 1, p. 37; Jantzen, *Becoming Divine*, p. 274.

[17]   Jantzen, 'Feminism and Pantheism', *The Monist*, 80/2, (1997): pp. 266–85, p. 267.

reflexivity and lived experience, grew in significance. Thus, the moral imaginary constitutes 'that which is taken-for-granted, the space – literal and figurative – from which moral thinking is done.'[18] The moral imaginary is not an abstract theory or philosophical system, therefore, such as Kant's categorical imperative, but a common-sense world, rooted in the everyday practices of making sense of things: the 'central narratives, myths and icons of a society'.[19]

In some of the contributions that follow, this pairing of necrophilia and natality, so central to Grace's work, is developed in several directions. Morny Joy celebrates Grace's affirmation of life and love amidst the culture of death – a reminder of her enduring concern to read 'against the grain' of conventional readings in order to bring alternative interpretations into being. Frances Ward examines the poetry of John Donne, arguing that although his preoccupation with death appears to place him firmly within a necrophilic symbolic, the recurrent interplay of natality and necrophilia in his work suggests an altogether more complex relationship. This may begin to challenge the very dichotomy of Grace's diagnostic itself. The Woodbrooke Quaker collective offers detailed historical illustrations of the way in which these motifs played out in the religious and political witness of the Society of Friends. In considering how an ethic of natality would differ from one of necrophilia, Mary Elizabeth Moore's account of two inspirational women adds further historical substance to Grace's analysis. Nanci Hogan's paper highlights the implications of an ethic of natality for the discourse of human rights. Grace's perennial insistence on the vital need to engage with institutional religion as a potent well-spring of the moral imaginary of death is exonerated by Hogan's account of what happens when a lack of 'religious literacy' both fails to address the pathological influence of religion and inhibits an account of cultural difference that could facilitate women's agency.

Transcendence/Immanence

> The emphasis on the omnipotent, detached 'God out there' is … not unrelated to the ideal of neutral, detached reasoning, which is in turn part of the fantasy of an ungendered, non-embodied rational mind, separate from all else, living towards a world beyond, expressive, in short, of an imaginary of death.[20]

As I have already hinted, Grace believed that religious ideas were integral to the Western moral imaginary. Like many feminist scholars of religion, Grace was faced with the casual secularism of much Western academic feminism, which neither accounted for the phenomenon of religious feminism, nor (more importantly for Grace's concerns), considered how religious and theological concepts continued

---

[18]   Jantzen, 'Flourishing; Towards an Ethic of Natality', p. 221.

[19]   Jantzen, 'Flourishing; Towards an Ethic of Natality', p. 203.

[20]   Jantzen, *Becoming Divine*, p. 209.

to underpin the Western moral imaginary, despite the processes of secularization. Even in a post-Christian age, doctrines of God and notions of divinity are crucial to the logic of a necrophilic imaginary, providing key images of what it means to be human, the nature of reality, human relations with non-human nature, what constitutes virtue and fulfilment for humanity, and so on. Following Luce Irigaray, therefore, Grace argued that what is represented as divine, as ultimate, underwrites Western modernity's notion of exemplary personhood, 'a goal of human endeavour, that against which human thought and conduct must be measured'.[21] Alongside the pairing of necrophilia and natality, therefore, is a further set of oppositions to do with the nature of God, and how notions of a transcendent and dispassionate divinity form an essential underpinning of Western modernity's ideals of rationality, immortality and individualism.

Much of feminist theology of the 1980s and 1990s was concerned with the gender of God, or the relationship between Trinitarian theology and feminist thought; but this was not Grace's main focus. Perhaps this is indicative of her ability to step beyond the binary logic, such that she was not simply concerned to replace paternal imagery with that of a maternal God, but to expose the material, cultural and psychological effects of a particular way of thinking about God: to expose the real effects that our collective thought-forms have upon lived experience.

She believed that transformation required a shift from the dualism of Western monotheism towards the pluralism of pantheism. The binary system of dualism fosters the construction of a subjectivity founded on ontology as separation, which originates in constructions of subjectivity grounded upon the rupture of the maternal bond, the transcendence of nature, embodiment and the non-rational. In common with other feminist theologians such as Rosemary Ruether,[22] Grace argues that the elevation of God over creation sanctions other systems of domination and separation: male/female, colonizers/colonized, master/slave, humanity/nature. Such a masculinist and dualistic symbolic must therefore be dismantled, not reformed, and replaced by an alternative. Grace explores two models of divinity: pantheism,[23] and Irigaray's notion of 'becoming divine'.[24]

Grace developed Irigaray's contention that if women are to develop an autonomous subjectivity, they need an alternative divine symbolic to which to relate. 'Thus':

> although proceeding by way of critique carries the task that arguing on the same turf actually serves to reinforce it, there is no other place to begin than with the concept of 'good old God', the God who forms the onto-theological underpinning of the symbolic in which western women and men are constituted

---

[21] Jantzen, *Becoming Divine*, p. 12.

[22] Reuther, *Sexism and God-Talk* (1983), pp. 72–92.

[23] Jantzen, 'Feminists, Philosophers and Mystics'; Jantzen 'Feminism and Pantheism'.

[24] Jantzen, *Becoming Divine*.

as subjects. However, the recognition of the interaction of this divinity with the western masculinised psyche quickly opens doors to creative possibilities, not only of religious conceptualization but also of ethical engagement.[25]

For example, therefore, to move beyond the polarity of transcendence and immanence is not a question of simply reversing the hierarchy, but disputing the terms on which the fault-lines, or logic, of the distinction itself. As Grace argues, at the root of this is recognition that the privileged pair only achieves coherence via the repression of its other: 'Transcendence is not the opposite of immanence: indeed, immanence is a necessary condition of transcendence, since no-one can achieve intelligence or creativity without the requisite physical complexity'.[26] Some of this echoes models of emergent consciousness in evolutionary anthropology which argues that non-corporeal capacities such as language, imagination and even religious experience can be regarded as 'emergent' properties and thus thoroughly compatible with models of physiological development.[27] 'It is our actual physical embodiment and our bodily experiences out of which our conscious selves develop, and which constitute each of us as individuals.'[28]

Transcendence and immanence, consciousness and embodiment, mind and body, are thus interdependent, not polarised; but like classical Marxist ideology, the dominant half of each pairing conceals the circumstances of its own production by obscuring its dependence on its repressed other, which functions as 'the sign of an absence, an absence which is overcome by reason's access to a disembodied and mastering truth'.[29] Yet for Grace, 'transcendence' is that which surpasses and exceeds the material, not that which denies or suppresses; it is, more appropriately, the inverse of reductionism, as an expression of the irreducibility of being. It denotes that which is 'ever beyond present activity ... not reducible to the set of physical particulars of the material universe'.[30]

Thus, in a gesture forwards to a more comprehensive discussion of Irigaray's work in *Becoming Divine*, Grace calls upon her notion of the 'sensible transcendental' as the liberating concept of the divine against which those excluded from the privileges of Western moral imaginary can set their own aspirations.

The transcendent and the immanent are not to be seen as opposites. Rather, the sensible transcendental, the pantheistic projection of the female divine, opens out what has hitherto been seen as a set of polarities into a play of diversities, 'bringing the god to life through us'.[31] This needs to be pan/theism rather than secularism or

---

[25] Jantzen, 'Feminism and Pantheism', p. 270.

[26] Jantzen, 'Feminism and Pantheism', p. 275.

[27] J. Wentzel Van Huysteen, *Alone in the World? Human Uniqueness in Science and Theology* (Grand Rapids and Cambridge, 2006).

[28] Jantzen, 'Feminism and Pantheism', p. 282.

[29] Jantzen, 'Feminism and Pantheism', p. 282.

[30] Jantzen, *Becoming Divine*, p. 271.

[31] Jantzen, 'Feminism and Pantheism', p. 277.

humanism, however, since the power of the Western symbolic is still fuelled by its horizon of ontotheology. It requires the fluidity of a divine horizon of becoming rather than the reified notion of being. Clare Greer argues in her essay, however, that Grace's adoption of pantheism is a strategy for articulating a notion of divinity not modelled on absolute difference or otherness, what Greer refers to as the tension (or dialectic?) of univocity and equivocity. How is God 'other', both of and not of the world? Is it possible to speak of God as necessarily other, or transcendent, without reproducing the old devices of the dispassionate, Platonic divinity?

Salvation/Flourishing

> a symbolic that celebrates natality, makes for flourishing, prompts action for love of the world as contrasted with a symbolic which shuts down on flourishing for some or all people or for the earth.[32]

Another dimension of the distorted logic of the Western moral imaginary is, according to Grace, its grounding in a symbolic of salvation rather than that of flourishing. If 'becoming divine' was about identifying new horizons of becoming that ally oneself with *amor mundi*, love of the world and the realization of the ultimate preciousness of all natals, then a further concept, of flourishing, also articulated Grace's conviction that the Western moral imaginary needed re-orienting away from necrophilic values and towards more life-giving values. Grace was not alone in developing the concept of flourishing within ethics and moral philosophy, since a revival of interest in Aristotelian virtue ethics, pioneered by writers such as Elizabeth Anscombe and Martha Nussbaum, generated renewed interest in teleological accounts of the good as opposed to Kantian and utilitarian perspectives.

Yet Grace coupled discussion of the basic criteria of a life well-lived – the means by which we might aim towards an ethic that cultivated human flourishing – with her earlier convictions about the need to displace the logic of necrophilia with one of natality. The virtues by which one might cultivate the ultimate end of flourishing were those which promoted the values of life, creativity, diversity and justice, rather than death or fear of death; and in her discussion of a pantheistic world-view, and her plentiful use of organic and agricultural metaphors[33] she hints at a broader creation-centred appropriation of flourishing that might extend beyond human justice-making towards non-human animals, the environment and the planet as a whole. Indeed, in his essay, Peter Manley Scott takes this route, seeking an ethic which draws on the notion of 'posthuman nature' that appreciates the interdependence of humans, nature and technologies: one that desires the flourishing of all creation rather than bolstering a hierarchy of being. Mary Elizabeth Moore, too, discusses how for the author Beatrix Potter, beauty

---

[32]   Jantzen, *Becoming Divine*, p. 212.

[33]   Jantzen, 'The Gendered Politics of Flourishing and Salvation', p. 63ff.

and love of nature became the focus for her own spiritual journey. Like Grace, of course, this was expressed in particular in a love of the landscape of the English Lake District.

Unusually, Grace began by identifying the roots of flourishing in Biblical concepts,[34] and it is prefigured by the this-worldly theology of *God's World, God's Body*, which in turn builds on tentative forays in her early work into discussions of whether or not God could have a body.[35] Yet it was unusual for her to begin with the classic tradition of Christianity, since she was not particularly interested in the rehabilitation of Christian tradition, in the way of Rosemary Radford Ruether or Elizabeth Schüssler Fiorenza. This is perhaps the major difference between her strategy of 'transformation', rather than the feminist theological dynamic of critique and reconstruction, in that she speaks of a 'transformative moral imaginary' to succeed the destructive moral imaginary of death and violence.[36] Whilst flourishing is prefigured in the Biblical and classical tradition, therefore, it is of more interest to her to see how such concepts can be renewed for today.

She links her vision of flourishing with gendered concepts of well-being and salvation,[37] which underpins Western Christianity's dualistic understanding of nature, the self, and embodiment.[38] Later, she drew more on the notion of beauty as an essential device for envisaging an alternative aesthetics of flourishing,[39] once more echoing other voices in moral philosophy that link ethics and aesthetics. 'Flourishing' is thus related to the ontological privileging of natality: a model of absorption into 'life in all its fullness' rather than rescue from a world of corruption and death. It also signals a shift from an individualistic salvation to a collective enterprise of flourishing: 'The recognition that we are embodied, gendered selves and therefore socially situated means that it is within that social nexus, not as disembodied solitary thinkers, that we must become divine'.[40]

Mary Grey develops Grace's discussion of flourishing as a category for thinking in new ways about people with disabilities. She argues that it can function as a kind of ethical ideal or *telos* of well-being that avoids prescriptive models of perfection (which may themselves be rooted in a chronic fear of vulnerability and imperfection, akin to Jantzen's exposure of a moral imaginary of necrophilia founded on repression and fear of death). A flawed or differently-abled body reminds our culture of our bodily contingency and dependence, so we try to demonise or marginalise those who bear such reminders. Grey's analysis is further endorsement of the ubiquity of the norms of necrophilia in all aspects of Western culture.

---

[34]   Jantzen, 'The Gendered Politics of Flourishing and Salvation', pp. 58–9.

[35]   Jantzen, 'On Worshipping an Embodied God', *Canadian Journal of Philosophy*, VIII/3 (1978): pp. 511–19.

[36]   Jantzen, 'Flourishing: Towards an Ethic of Natality', p. 219.

[37]   Jantzen, 'The Gendered Politics of Flourishing and Salvation', p. 59.

[38]   Jantzen, 'The Gendered Politics of Flourishing and Salvation', p. 69.

[39]   Jantzen, *Foundations of Violence*, p. 41.

[40]   Jantzen, *Becoming Divine*, p. 209.

In her essay, Pamela Anderson notes resonances with Grace's work in the philosophy of Spinoza and Ricoeur. The philosopher nurtures that which is life-giving, which for Anderson are desire and yearning, the rejection of the dispassionate genderless disembodied God/deity, choosing instead to think from experience and draw upon an embodied sensuality in the work of a new kind of rationality. This is echoed by both Morny Joy and Ursula King in their respective considerations of Grace's account of women medieval mystics. The divinity of which these mystics speak is far from a traditional model of the 'unmoved mover', and Joy and King point out how the mystics articulated their religious experience in the language of sexual passion and sensual joy. I am reminded here, too, of the poster of the feminist critic and poet Audre Lorde that used to adorn Grace's living-room wall, and how Lorde's famous essay, 'Uses of the Erotic' might be applied to such divine encounters. In that respect, we can see a continuity between Grace's early work on divine embodiment and panentheism, and the necessity of a religious language that adopts the vernacular of sensuality rather than pure reason.

The Construction of 'Religion' and the Task of Philosophy of Religion

> A feminist philosophy of religion is ... one which must show the bias and sterility of masculinist (supposedly neutral) pursuits of the discipline. However, it must go on to the creative effort of developing a feminist imaginary which will enable the divine becoming of women.[41]

Grace was concerned not only with displacing a masculinist and necrophilic moral imaginary with a symbolic founded in natality, but also with the way in which a culture of necrophilia, with its elevation of disinterested, disembodied subjectivity and obsession with immortality and the denial of death also distorted our understanding of what it meant to be religious, and correspondingly how the study of religion should proceed. A consistent thread running throughout her work was a critique of the way in which Anglo-American philosophy of religion had defined the terms on which the West conceived of, and practised, religion. She was concerned with a critique of religion as rationality, God as transcendent and scholarship as disinterested, in favour of the religious life as one of 'becoming divine', of divinity as immanence, and the vocation of the intellectual as one of transformation, passion and engagement.

Thus, she begins *Becoming Divine* with questions about the ultimate aim of intellectual enquiry: 'why do they do it?' she asks.[42] 'What is the fundamental task of the philosophy of religion?'[43] Once again, she juxtaposes the alternatives as a binary pairing: whereas traditional philosophy of religion concerns itself with

---

[41]   Jantzen, *Becoming Divine*, p. 17.

[42]   Jantzen, *Becoming Divine*, p. 18.

[43]   Jantzen, *Becoming Divine*, p. 6.

questions of the existence of God, the truthfulness of doctrine, or the coherence of claims about the nature and being of God, she states her intention, along with Luce Irigaray, to chart a very different course: 'our fundamental moral obligation is to become divine; and the task of philosophy of religion must be to enable that becoming, or else it is ultimately useless'.[44]

This introduces two important strands: not only is she arguing for a different conception of the divine, but note also how this is a highly partisan understanding of the philosophy of religion. It is not about academic debate in some way abstracted from the concerns of everyday living, but knowledge generated in order to equip us for lives of virtue and wisdom. As Grace argues, this is probably closer to the traditional model of the ancient Greeks, but constituted something of a departure from conventions of value-neutrality favoured by the Western academy – although not, in general, amongst feminist scholars. Knowledge is to be put to work for the purposes of social justice. Grace's students and colleagues were familiar with her question, 'who benefits?'[45] Just as God is not dispassionate and unmoved by creation, neither is the academic to remain in his or her ivory tower without some thought for the relevance of their scholarship to the total sum of human flourishing.

> The struggle against suffering and injustice and towards flourishing takes precedence, beyond comparison, to the resolution of intellectual problems; and although it is important that the struggle is an intelligent one, there is no excuse for theory ever becoming a distraction from the struggle for justice itself.[46]

Grace regarded her work as no ivory tower theorising, but a project to put academic pursuits to work in the pursuit of transformation. This was in keeping with the contrast she drew between knowledge which pertained to be deductive, theoretical, universal and objective and that which – as she believed – more accurately reflected the origins of all knowledge and discourse in contingent lived experience. Echoing feminist moral philosophers such as Carol Gilligan and Nel Noddings[47] she argues for the inductive and experiential basis of all moral reasoning, an understanding that extends to her own commitment to scholarship that eschews pretensions of value-neutrality in favour of openly acknowledging its own partiality.

Grace was also exercised by what she saw as the necessity for privileged intellectuals to put scholarship to work in projects of critical transformation. Academics and intellectuals have a responsibility to foster transformative thinking 'in ways that open us to thinking and living to promote human flourishing'.[48] The problem was that by embracing value-neutrality in the name of disinterested objective scholarship, the academy had allowed 'intellectual endeavour [to be

---

[44]   Jantzen, *Becoming Divine*, p. 6.
[45]   Jantzen, *Becoming Divine*, p. 68.
[46]   Jantzen, *Becoming Divine*, p. 264.
[47]   Jantzen, 'Flourishing: Towards an Ethic of Natality', p. 203, n. 2.
[48]   Jantzen, 'Flourishing: Towards an Ethic of Natality', p. 227.

redefined] as no longer a threat, no longer in active engagement with public life'.[49] In contrast, Grace insisted both that knowledge always emanated from situated, embodied positions, and in turn such knowledge had a responsibility to return to and enrich, such real lives and contexts. The problem was that the 'big questions' of suffering, evil and the existence of God had become divorced from any kind of lived experience, with the result that they remained abstractions: 'if the philosophy of religion is to engage with ideas of suffering and salvation, these cannot be treated as abstract concepts but as occurring within actual narratable individual lives'.[50]

She thereby challenges the dispassionate stance of Anglo-American analytical philosophy of religion with its emphasis on 'the justification of truth-claims and the effort to assure believers of the credibility of their beliefs ... The idea that it might be part of the function of the philosophy of religion to project or imagine new religious ideas, a new God or gods as female, or as couple(s), or anything else hardly enters their pages'.[51] For practical theologians, this is familiar territory, reminiscent of the hierarchy of systematic theology over practical theology.[52] In reaction to models of theology as primarily a matter of propositional belief, or correspondence with revealed truth, however, liberation and contextual theologies insist on the primacy of *orthopraxis* over orthodoxy, in which 'talk about God' is regarded as a discourse intended to promote faithful praxis, in which 'truth' is performative, evaluated according to principles of justice and the doing of the divine will. There are many parallels in this to Grace's agenda: at the beginning of an article for the journal *Feminist Theory*, for example, she asks, 'What does it mean to do feminist moral philosophy with notions of utopia and transformation as points of reference?'[53] She seeks, like practical theologians, therefore, to re-conceive her discipline as a form of practical wisdom, directed towards the cultivation of virtue, justice and flourishing.

The traditional view, however, has been that religion is about belief, and philosophical theology is about justifying the coherence and credibility of such belief. Yet if Grace was not overtly interested in orthopraxis, she was interested in the role of religion in constructing and maintaining a particular symbolic, the images, narratives and values that determine Western culture. This is about who has the power to define the nature of authentic and authoritative religious experience; but this is contingent upon implicit understandings of the nature of God, knowledge and meaning. To refuse to uphold truth as correspondence with propositional belief also entails a break with 'good old God' and a break with an onto-theological tradition, into an alternative concept of the divine as yet to be

---

[49]   Jantzen, *Foundations of Violence*, p. 343.

[50]   Jantzen,'Necrophilia and Natality: What does it mean to be religious?', *The Scottish Journal of Religious Studies*, 19/1 (1998): pp. 101–21, p. 113.

[51]   Jantzen, *Becoming Divine*, p. 18.

[52]   Elaine Graham, Heather Walton and Frances Ward, *Theological Reflection: Methods* (London, 2005).

[53]   Jantzen, 'Flourishing: Towards an Ethic of Natality', p. 219.

Foucauldian tools were also a central part of her critical and reconstructive project. From Foucault's method of genealogy, she took on the task of 'a history of the present': of problematising the presuppositions of Western modernity, thereby questioning the inevitability of a moral imaginary of violence and death. Yet if Foucault's work is about exposing the episteme of modernity and the ways in which regimes of scientific enquiry and taxonomy plot the fault-lines that circumscribe our notions of normality and pathology, Grace turned also to deconstruction and psychoanalysis to trace the desires and repressions that inform the moral imaginary, and ultimately to expose its deeply gendered character. Thus, after Derrida, she asked what a dominant discourse might simultaneously repress and depend upon for its own stability and coherence, arguing that the 'death-dealing structures of modernity'[64] rested upon the repression of birth and natality. This is consistent with Bourdieu's notion of *habitus*, in terms of the moral imaginary as something that precedes our birth and yet is internalised in the process of our socialisation.

To excavate the roots of the present, however, is but a first step on the journey of transformation. If the current moral imaginary is not inevitable,[65] then the task becomes one of imagining new, life-giving alternatives; and this is where the creative task of philosophy, for Grace, comes into its own. The mapping of the contours of a different cultural imaginary, founded on natality, has many resonances with creative arts, such as the invention of forms of utopia.[66] This was perhaps one of the reasons why towards the end of her life Grace's thinking was focusing more on constructing an alternative 'new imaginary of beauty'[67] not simply as an object of aesthetic contemplation but in terms of its political, generative power.

The notion of utopia figures strongly in much feminist writing, and represents far more than functioning as a broad term of idealism. Rather, it performs much of the same task as envisaged by Grace's work: its positing of using refracted modes of thinking, such as alien cultures, or parallel universes, or alternative histories precisely harnesses our imaginations to render, as Mark Muesse has put it, 'the strange familiar and the familiar strange'.[68] Fantastic, speculative and utopian literature has long functioned as a form of social critique, which displaces or 'estranges' us from the familiar; and once it has been disrupted in this way, new possibilities can be fabricated. It is therefore no accident that much utopian thinking has functioned as radical social critique.[69] Yet, like Grace's philosophical method, its political character rests in its ability to emancipate the imagination as much

---

[64] Jantzen, 'Flourishing: Towards an Ethic of Natality', p. 229.

[65] Jantzen, *Foundations of Violence*, p. 21.

[66] Jantzen, *Foundations of Violence*, p. 67.

[67] Jantzen, *Foundations of Violence*.

[68] Mark W. Muesse, 'Religious Studies and "Heaven's Gate": Making the Strange Familiar and the Familiar Strange', in Russell T. McCutcheon (ed.) *The Insider/Outsider Problem in the Study of Religion* (London, 1999), pp. 390–94.

[69] Elaine Graham, *Representations of the Post/Human: Monsters Aliens and Others in Popular Culture* (Manchester, 2002) pp. 55–9.

as release material forces for change. In an essay published posthumously, Grace came closest to spelling out the strong connections between the critical, diagnostic excavation of a necrophilic imaginary and the cultivation of creative imagination in the pursuit of change. Drawing on Paul Ricoeur's work on utopia, she stresses the capacity of literature or narratives that deliberately abandons familiar territory, swims against the stream of inevitability or predictability and from its 'exterior' position, starts to imagine alternative futures.[70] The practice of 'reading against the grain' informs her use of Hannah Arendt's work. This is not to take her out of context or offer an anachronistic reading that attempts to edit or make apologies for her views. It is more to take the work in new, suggestive and creative directions even if they are not those the author herself would have foreseen.[71]

In representing the major themes of Grace's work via a series of oppositional pairings, I am aware of the risk that by stylising her work in terms of a series of dualisms, I simply collude in their reinforcement, rather than their deconstruction. Yet she was always concerned to resist this tendency, since there are plenty of references in her work to the dangers of this approach.[72] Whilst the dominant discourses of necrophilia that beset the Western moral imaginary are dependent on their repressed others, she is concerned to destabilise the entire structure of such binary thinking as well as their out-workings. It is not enough, she argued, to reverse hierarchies or valorise the subordinated or repressed categories of 'feminine' subjectivity, since this would be to commend categories that were themselves the products of distorted imaginary. 'What is needed instead is a strategy that overcomes the series of dualisms and offers scope for integration as well as for respect and honour of diversity'.[73] The intention is thus to construct transformative categories for a renewed moral imaginary that do not simply 'mirror' or invert the values of necrophilia. Yet the question is whether there is scope within the reconstructed categories for ambivalence or contradiction, a 'shadow' side to beauty or natality. Alyda Faber suggests this much in her review of *Death and the Displacement of Beauty* when she compares Grace's evocation of beauty with Kathleen Sands' more tragic representation of life and beauty as inherently fragile and ephemeral.[74] Certainly, as she always emphatically insisted, Grace's use of Arendt's natality is a long way from any kind of celebration of 'Mother God' or goddesses, or of the maternal as unimpeachable; but the tendency is, admittedly, to locate virtue entirely on one side of the binary divide, at the expense of an exploration of moral ambivalence.

---

[70]　Jantzen, 'On Philosophers (Not) Reading History: Narrative and Utopia', in Kevin Vanhoozer and Martin Warner (eds), *Transcending Boundaries in Philosophy and Theology: Reason, Meaning and Experience* (London, 2007), pp. 177–90, pp. 189–90.

[71]　Jantzen, *Power, Gender and Christian Mysticism*.

[72]　Jantzen, *Foundations of Violence*, p. 6.

[73]　Jantzen, 'Feminism and Pantheism', p. 275.

[74]　Alyda Faber, 'Review: *Foundations of Violence*', Ars Disputandi [http://www.ArsDisputandi.org] 5 (2005).

Graham Ward's essay in this volume provides us with an example of how binary thinking has infected both the moral and theological imaginary, but also how such a dualism might be transcended. Ward argues for the interdependence of matter and spirit, the material and metaphysical, despite attempts of Western philosophy and theology to divide and oppose them. This attains a particular expression in contemporary consumerist obsessions with body image and appearance – a corruption of beauty as classically conceived – when the substance of matter and flesh are reduced to superficial appearance. Ward stresses the metaphorical substance of the body amidst a thicker fabric of associations; in particular, he is concerned to rehabilitate the metaphysics of the 'body politic' and to remind us that the apparatuses of the State exercise tangible effects on the bodies, as much as the minds, of its citizens. Whilst Ward takes his argument into sacramental and ecclesiological territory into which Grace would not have ventured, there is a parallel with her work in his conviction to heal the separation of body and spirit in the interests of a renewed political vision. If the world is God's body, he argues, then human beings share in the redemption of the world by virtue of their participation in Christ's body. The positing of the Body of Christ as the organizing metaphor for the body politic locates the redeemed and transfigured human body as an artefact of the greater ecclesial body, but its origins in divine grace mean its political nature is irreducible to temporal norms.

I have stressed all along Grace's insistence that in order to act differently, we have to learn to think differently: but how exactly did she see the relationship between thought and action, between the worlds of the imaginary and material culture? Grace deployed several terms to describe the orientations of Western culture, by which she means the set of meanings and values informing a common way of life, or a system of symbols representing particular world-views by which people orientate their lives. For many, however, such a definition itself falls prey to idealism, in which it takes little account of material culture or the practices of labour by which people 'build worlds' not just of meaning but of physical artefacts and technologies and tangible social institutions – such as penitentiaries, asylums and clinics – which are both purveyors of value and disciplines of the body. It is in her use of Bourdieu's notion of *habitus*, underpinned by his robust conceptualisation of practice, that she perhaps comes closest to this more materialist concept. Certainly, one could claim that in her use of Foucauldian critique and in the constant subject matter of violence and death, her argument could not fail but to engage with material culture; but there is still a question as to whether the Western moral imaginary is theorised as effectively 'all in the mind' at the expense of a more thorough-going analysis of the material, economic and technological manifestations of culture.

In the introduction to one of her last essays, Grace asks, 'How does newness enter the world? How can such newness disrupt the violence of (post)modernity, violence whose perpetrators often invoke the names of God? And how can philosophers of religion and theologians help to change the world rather than be reduced to ineffectual hand-wringing, or worse, be complicit in the violence?'[75] These questions take us to the heart of her vocation as critical and transformative thinker. She consistently asked what it would mean to do feminist moral philosophy and philosophy of religion with the values of natality and flourishing, rather than violence and death, at their heart. Just as her concept of religion and the divine eschewed abstract and disinterested interpretations, so she extended that to an understanding of her own work as an intellectual. Her project was one which sought 'to address, criticize and ultimately *redeem* the present'[76] (my emphasis): an intriguing use of religious language, but consistent with her view that no knowledge is neutral and that part of the responsibility of the intellectual was to contribute constructively not only to a critique of the values of Western modernity but to its fundamental reorientation. Thus, her critical and reconstructive task was directed towards the articulation of a 'transformative moral imaginary',[77] one liberated from a preoccupation with mortality and violence, towards one grounded in flourishing and natality.

---

[75] Jantzen, 'On Philosophers (Not) Reading History: Narrative and Utopia', p. 177.
[76] Jantzen, 'Flourishing: Towards an Ethic of Natality', p. 219.
[77] Jantzen, 'Flourishing: Towards an Ethic of Natality', p. 219.

PART ONE
'The Gift of Life'

rather than encouraged. Yet it is precisely these that foster the development of loving subjects.[2]

Another term that Grace employed in order to convey her ideal of a loving subject is that of 'natal' – a modification of a term she found in Hannah Arendt – which is not necessarily gender specific. Grace nonetheless thought that, over the centuries, the prominence given to violence and destruction – particularly in the way it seemed endemic to Western civilization – had had an adverse and disproportionate impact on women. Grace herself was no essentialist, yet as a result of her urgency to rectify this unfortunate situation, sometimes her work has been interpreted as dualist. It has been interpreted so that men, mind, and violence are positioned on one side, in contrast to women, on the other, who are associated with body and natality. But I do not believe that this is the reading that Grace intended, and a careful scrutiny of her work on natals and the concept of natality would help to counter this impression. My own reading appreciates Grace's oeuvre as an impassioned plea to rearrange our priorities so as to insist on the wonder and beauty of this world. This move, she believed, would provide a corrective balance to the suffering and spectre of mortality that can so easily come to dominate our own worldview and existence.

In Grace's latest works, her evocations of creativity and beauty become particularly poignant, as she realised her own precarious hold on life. She never, however, ceased to extol the glories of nature, specifically in the Lake District, as well as the integrity and splendour of human friendship and love – erotic or otherwise. Her loving relationships with her partner, Tina, and her special bond with her canine companion, Button, were vital elements of this lived reality. In her work, the human body, in all its radiance, never ceased to be strongly affirmed. It was an extraordinarily moving experience to follow in the steps of Grace's own investigations and studies as she began to develop and express a life-affirming philosophical orientation. She believed that this orientation resonated with her own life in that it reflected the plenitude of a God who created the world out of an abundance of love. For Grace, this fostered an environment in which all human beings, by their own forms of flourishing in both the domain of creativity, and in the embrace of human love itself, could celebrate their god-given inheritance.

Grace was careful to claim she was not writing a theology, but her hope was that other women scholars, particularly feminist theologians, could build on the foundations she had established. So, in homage to Grace, I would like to elaborate what I understand to be the specific elements that illuminate the central concern of love in her thought. In this connection, I admit that I have no pretensions to making any constructive theological claims. I remain a philosopher of religion, tutored both by Grace and my other mentor, Paul Ricoeur, who unfortunately also died recently.

---

2   Jantzen, 'Birth and the Powers of Horror: Julia Kristeva on Gender, Religion and Death', in Phillip Goodchild (ed.), *Rethinking Philosophy of Religion: Approaches From Continental Philosophy* (New York, 2002): pp. 139–61, p. 160.

God's World, God's Body[3]

In her first book, Grace was quite adamant that in the light of both Jewish and Christian scriptures, a Christian anthropology could only be one where humanity was brought into being and blessed as part of a process of creation that God had confirmed as good. Even from the beginning, Grace was not going to concede anything to the Greek philosophic tradition that separated the mind/soul from the body and deemed that the former was superior to the latter.

> The actualizing of one's human potential is an actualizing of one's whole self in relation to God; reducing the idea of fulfillment of the person to fulfillment of the mind is excessively rationalistic.[4]

Another aspect of Grace's philosophical worldview that is first evident here is the on-going creative generativity by which God will continue to be manifest in creation.

> Creativity [of God], if it is an essential attribute and not an external insignificant activity, does not express itself only in one isolated act. If God is eternally a creative God, then his creativity would express itself eternally.[5]

This creative activity will also remain an emphasis throughout Grace's work, from this initial delineation, as a vital demonstration of God's magnanimous, even excessive love.

> The most telling point that God as portrayed in the Gospel accounts of Jesus' conception of him is above everything else a God of love ... [If] God is essentially and eternally love, then God must have loved eternally. He has not existed for endless ages in isolation ... Rather, he has poured himself out, and will continue to do so, in loving manifestations of himself, in ways which, doubtless, we cannot even guess.[6]

Grace orchestrated these diverse ideas in support of her own daring hypothesis – which has been variously reviewed as to its plausibility – that the world itself is actually a manifestation of God's body.

> Indeed, the model of the universe as God's embodiment provides a good way of thinking about God which sees his love as central, pouring himself out for individuals, with no limits on his self-giving. He is the One who is All, yet to whom the Many owe their freedom and their very selves.[7]

---

[3] Jantzen, *God's World, God's Body* (London, 1984).

[4] Jantzen, *God's World, God's Body*, p. 8.

[5] Jantzen, *God's World, God's Body*, p. 144.

[6] Jantzen, *God's World, God's Body*, p. 144.

[7] Jantzen, *God's World, God's Body*, p. 152.

This theological pronouncement marks a specific stage in Grace's own itinerary when she had moved from the Mennonite tradition of her Canadian prairie upbringing to the Anglican faith. This would, in turn, be replaced by the pacifist path of the Quakers. At this juncture in her journey, however, Grace was concerned primarily with establishing a view of the created world as not only essentially good, but as also suffused by a particular mode of God's voluntary self-expression that emanated from his own loving substance.

Julian of Norwich[8]

The next step, however, in Grace's development was not a theological one, in the sense of elaborating a system, though it continues to have theological resonances, especially in her sustained emphasis on the representation of God as love. Grace turned specifically to a certain female mystic, Julian of Norwich, who lived in the thirteenth century, as an exemplar of a current in Christianity that supported her views of the need to celebrate the wondrous beauty of the created world. In addition, Julian's rejection of the separation of the body and soul made her an especially congenial fellow-traveller.

> Julian's meditation on the loving creativity of God helps her to resolve a tension which had a long history in theology and spirituality before her time; and which is still with us. On the one hand, she took no part in disparaging or devaluing the created world, including our bodies and their functions; she does not share the suspicions of those strands of Christianized Platonic thought mediated by Augustine who saw his most important conversion as a conversion to chastity.[9]

Instead of divine love being understood as a dynamic that was confined to the interaction of the three persons of the Trinity, Julian appreciated God's love as inherently one that sought to disclose itself as a vibrant mode of connection that informed all his relationships with his creatures. Grace stressed the human potential for intimate engagement with God that was apparent in all of Julian's writings. This became apparent, on Grace's reading, in the fact that Julian, rather than regarding herself as especially privileged by unique divine revelations, understood her own charge as one of imparting the graciousness of God's love to her fellow humans. Her mission was to help them to both experience it and rejoice in it.

> The revelations in themselves do not single her out as special but are given for the good of her fellow Christians, not to prove to them by the fact of her vivid

---

[8] Jantzen, *Julian of Norwich: Mystic and Theologian* (New York, 1987).

[9] Jantzen, *Julian of Norwich*, p. 160.

experience that God exists or that religious doctrines are true, but to help them by her spiritual insights to proceed more deeply into the love of God.[10]

For Grace, Julian's major message was one that perceived God and humanity as linked in an embrace of love. 'Our essential selfhood, our substance is eternally united with God from whom it flows forth, though we are certainly not always aware of it, and can never be fully aware of it in this life'.[11]

Because of humanity's unfortunate lack of awareness, however, it was necessary to undertake a mode of spiritual cultivation so that such love could be realised and that God not remain an utterly remote mystery. As a result, Grace emphasises the principal intention of Julian's discussion of mystery as an assurance that, despite perhaps our finitude – including ignorance of our divine potential – God could be encountered in a loving relationship. 'All things were created and are preserved by the love of God immanent in them, and their natural state is to reciprocate that love as best they can'.[12] At this stage of her journey, Grace found in Julian a guide who helped her to deepen both her own spiritual searchings and assisted her to formulate her own discoveries more effectively. In the Preface to her book on Julian, Grace also stated that she felt Julian, with certain qualifications, could prove helpful to contemporary Christians in assisting their own spiritual growth.

> Though we must of course be careful not to transpose ideas without regard for the social and intellectual contexts that modify them ... this book is written with the presupposition that Julian's spirituality, and indeed all genuine spirituality, is not of merely antiquarian interest, but has a bearing on our own life before God. Here as elsewhere, scholarship and spiritual development must be colleagues not competitors.[13]

It was only in her next book, however, that Grace began to focus on certain problems that she discerned as constraining contemporary women in their spiritual search and their expressions of love.

Power, Gender and Christian Mysticism[14]

Grace's own effort at combining her scholarly and spiritual interests crystallised in *Power, Gender and Christian Mysticism*. In this book, she was deeply concerned with the way that the theological and philosophical projects of the Western world

---

[10] Jantzen, *Julian of Norwich*, p. 80.

[11] Jantzen, *Julian of Norwich*, p. 147.

[12] Jantzen, *Julian of Norwich*, p. 136.

[13] Jantzen, *Julian of Norwich*, p. ix.

[14] Jantzen, *Power, Gender and Christian Mysticism* (Cambridge, 1995).

come to focus on the textual tradition of religion which had, in turn, became reserved for an educated male elite.

> When those texts, that were only available only to a few, were read as having within them not only their obvious literal meaning but also a hidden mystical meaning accessible only to the purest of the inner circle, then those who were able to penetrate that meaning were powerful indeed.[15]

In carefully describing the emergence of the Western Christian mystical conventions, as they unfolded in the writings of the Church Fathers, Grace demonstrated their inherent bias against women. She did not deny that the love of God was the pivotal point of their attention, but she indicated her displeasure with the way that their 'emphasis on love often conjoined with an actual despising of bodiliness and sexuality, and inevitably of women'.[16] Indeed, the physical body and human love, whether in the affective strain of mysticism of Bernard of Clairvaux, or in the *via negativa* of Dionysius the Areopagite and Meister Eckhart, were viewed as distinct obstacles to what was depicted as the spiritual love of God. This went contrary to all of Grace's own affirmative instincts and convictions. Such a version of mysticism, while it may delight in the beauty of the created world, omitted the vital dimensions of human physical and erotic love. She observes that even the Church fathers' own use of erotic imagery:

> [W]as at the expense of the valuation of real sexual relations. It used the language of passion, but forbade any physical passion in an effort to channel all desire away from the body and towards God ... Since it was women's bodies that were identified throughout the centuries with passion and sexuality, women were part of the evil to be shunned or overcome by spiritual men.[17]

As if in defiant vindication of the body, Grace called upon other medieval women mystics, besides Julian of Norwich to come to the rescue. Many of these women mystics had exulted in employing explicit sexual imagery – with, as Grace notes, no indication that it should not be regarded as literal – to depict their amorous encounters with god. Grace describes this abandonment to the throes of divine love:

> With the women there is a direct, highly charged, passionate encounter between Christ and the writer ... There is no intellectualizing or spiritualizing, no climbing up into the head, or using the erotic as an allegory hedged about with warnings.[18]

---

[15]　Jantzen, *Power, Gender and Christian Mysticism*, p. 69.

[16]　Jantzen, *Julian of Norwich*, p. 124.

[17]　Jantzen, *Julian of Norwich*, p. 91.

[18]　Jantzen, *Julian of Norwich*, p. 133.

Grace examines in some detail the work of Hadewijch of Antwerp, another thirteenth-century mystic, as a representative of this mode of flagrant violation of accepted mystical boundaries. She also draws attention to another anomaly that first appears in the work of Hadewijch – and which is also conspicuous in the work of Julian. This is that God is given a female identity. Whereas Julian is content, however, to describe God as Mother – a maternal figure who cares for and loves his creatures – Hadewijch is not quite so restrained. She reverses the accepted comparison of God as the knight errant of medieval courtly love conventions who goes in quest of his reticent yet occasionally responsive Lady love. God now becomes the figure of Lady love herself, alternating between dispositions of intimacy and remoteness, thus representing the intense oscillations of emotions that characterise romantic love. Grace observes:

> On the one hand, we have here many of the standard themes which run throughout Western medieval mysticism: the sense of both the revelation and the hiddenness of God, the pain and the delight of divine encounter, the necessity of risking all for the spiritual quest. Yet although the themes are not new, they are presented in the radical new form of God the Lady Beloved who is Herself Love.[19]

Though this practice of appreciating God as female did not necessarily extend its influence beyond mystical expressions, it sowed a seed of possibility that Grace believed could be cultivated by later generations of women scholars. This, together with the female mystics' practice of affirming the body and sexuality as indispensable elements of any spiritual love affair, allowed Grace to affirm that 'it is precisely through actual eroticism that lessons of God are to be learned'.[20] Yet, though Grace believed that these medieval women could provide valuable resources for contemporary women scholars of religion, she again admonishes that they still remained very much inhabitants of their era – mostly cloistered within particular institutional traditions and belief structures – and thus should not be acclaimed anachronistically as nascent feminists.

Perhaps emboldened by her challenge to the Church Fathers and their dismissal of women as unsuitable for spiritual pursuits because of their wayward bodies, it is in this book that Grace takes her first passing shots at contemporary male philosophers of religion whom she views as being equally suspect as the medieval male philosophers and theologians in their treatment of women. She takes particular exception to the idea promoted by certain philosophers that mystical experience is ineffable, and thus cannot be communicated. This is because, as Grace demonstrates, the women mystics confounded such claims with their voluminous writings about their experiences.

---

[19] Jantzen, *Julian of Norwich*, p. 293.
[20] Jantzen, *Julian of Norwich*, p. 134.

always already constant process of renewal. In *The Human Condition*,[27] Arendt herself describes how she understands the term, which she does not describe from a spiritual perspective but aligns with the ability to undertake productive interventions in the world of the *polis*. 'The new beginning inherent in birth can make itself felt in the world only because the newcomer possesses the capacity of beginning something anew – that is of acting. In this sense of initiative, an element of action, and therefore of natality, is inherent in all human activities'.[28] She continues with a sentence that, I believe, is crucial for the development of Grace's thought. 'Moreover, since action is the political activity par excellence, natality, and not mortality, may be the central character of the political, as distinguished from metaphysics'.[29] In the sense that Arendt's understanding of 'political' was not confined to the contemporary narrow definition of it, but harked back to the Greek *polis* and the idea of acting for the good of the common weal, Grace finds in Arendt another kindred spirit in her concern to establish a solid base for the flourishing of a loving and just humanity. For though Arendt, as an non-practising Jew, was not preoccupied with religion *per se*, her own love of this world caused her to investigate the conditions that had so alienated certain human beings from their own creative potential that they had turned to its destructive opposite. That is, they instigated totalitarian regimes that prohibited people from exercising their freedom – the very kernel of natality – and inflicted a symbolic of a devastatingly lethal variety upon them. Grace perceived striking parallels in Arendt's work with her own search, and her attempts to provide a solution to the contemporary preoccupation with violence and destruction. She draws on one of these parallels, after she has first acknowledges Arendt's indictment of one of the principal intentions of totalitarian regimes. This was that their purpose was not only to destroy peoples' lives, but also to erase their life records, so that they disappeared from the annals of history. Grace relates:

> Though Arendt does not draw the comparison, many feminists will find in her emphasis on reclaiming the stories of victims of oppressive regimes resonances with the efforts to reclaim the 'dangerous memories' of women who have been silenced, oppressed, and consigned to the oblivion of the unrecorded past.[30]

Grace observes that while Arendt herself was not a feminist, her work lends itself to be interpreted in ways supportive of certain natal values that pertain specifically to women. She believes that these interpretations are not inimical to Arendt's thought.

Another area of common ground that Grace discovered in Arendt, related to natality, is her notion that though we are born into this world as strangers, we are welcomed into a community of life, which nourishes and provides the rich web of

---

[27] Hannah Arendt, *The Human Condition* (Chicago, 1958).

[28] Arendt, *The Human Condition*, pp. 10–11.

[29] Arendt, *The Human Condition*, p. 11.

[30] Jantzen, *Becoming* Divine, p. 48.

relationships so necessary for flourishing. This becomes a central focus for Grace as she begins to articulate a central tenet of her project.

> Human beings are already in relation to the world and in a human community, shaped by the symbolic and shaping it in their turn. 'Natals' are not isolated 'minds' or 'souls' beloved of traditional philosophers of religion ever since Descartes meditated in front of his stove.[31]

The adverse obsession with the soul at the expense of the body, of immortality and life after death at the expense of natality, is the precise site where Grace locates the source of the disregard, which she believes is at the root of the irreparable damage that has been inflicted on this world and its inhabitants. Grace shares with Arendt a profound sorrow at the losses thus incurred: 'of an estrangement' and 'detachment from community and cosmos' so that 'the world is perceived not as a home but as an alien reality to be fled from or conquered'.[32]

Grace then proposes her own remedial strategy, which differs somewhat from that of Arendt, so as to combat this destructive alienation and escapist delusions that have pervaded much philosophy and religion.

> If an obsession with death orients philosophers to a preoccupation with other worlds, by contrast taking birth as the centre of our imaginary will direct our attention to *this* (emphasis in the original) world, to our connection, through the maternal continuum, with all others who have been born.[33]

Grace is seeking nothing less than a reordering of this world. As she declares: 'What is at issue is nothing less than a transformation of the world from a self-perpetuating fixation on death to an opening on natality'.[34] She diverges from Arendt, however, in her attention to the specific problems of women and their bodies, because for Grace, natality is 'inconceivable' without recognizing its intimate involvement with the role of women – who are, both literally and metaphorically – the vessel of creation, by and through whom the original natality can occur. Grace notes that this is not a paean to actual motherhood, nor a simplistic appeal to maternal values, but a recognition of women as vital and necessary participants in the ultimate creative act of new life – birth.

All Grace's efforts, after presenting these remarkable insights, are concentrated on promoting and expanding the ways that a symbolic of natality can radically rearrange not only the manner in which human beings live and breathe, but can foster a harmonious co-exist in this earthly habitat. At the same time, Grace wants

---

[31] Jantzen, *Becoming Divine*, p. 149.

[32] Jantzen, *Becoming Divine*, p. 151 (Jantzen paraphrasing Arendt [1958: 248–57]).

[33] Jantzen, *Becoming Divine*, p. 150.

[34] Jantzen, 'A Reconfiguration of Desire', *Women's Philosophy Review*, 29 (2002): pp. 23–45, p. 44.

to re-envision the ways that they can reflect, even philosophies, so that the old negative, if not moribund patterns of thought, in accordance with the 'symbolic of death', can be slowly mitigated. Grace explains:

> The point is not to set up yet another binary for the subject as [the] fulcrum of reason, but to listen to what has been silenced [or repressed in Western culture] and enable the becoming of loving subjects who can recognise both death and birth.[35]

From this point on, earthly love becomes prominent. Thus, although Grace never accomplished her plan to write a book reconciling a philosophy of natality with the fulsome nature of divine love that affirms life in this world, drawn from her reading of the medieval mystics, she certainly prepares the ground by indicating the manner in which such a hybrid plant could be cultivated.

In *Becoming Divine*, Grace presents a number of compatible themes as preparatory gestures towards the emergence of this blending of modes of natality. This particular synthesis is, I believe, the most original contribution in Grace's entire work. To support her thesis, Grace presents Arendt's understanding of love of the world, specifically detailing Arendt's description of *amor mundi*:

> *Amor mundi* is not, for her, a romantic or sentimental attitude to a world where all is daffodils and songbirds, but rather respect for and fostering of the natality of all human beings and the world which is our home. A symbolic of natality is not in any sense a denial of death or a pretence that death does not matter. It is however, a love of life, and beyond our individual lives a love of the life of the world and the lives of those for whom it will be a home.[36]

While the fusion of Arendt's love of the world with that of the love of God's creation experienced by the medieval mystic might seem initially something of a stretch, Grace's grounds for so doing is her appreciation that natality and the notion of a divine inherence in the world do have a common concern. She alluded to this in the very first pages of *Becoming Divine* when she announced: 'The rest of the book will explore in much more detail what is involved in the aim of becoming divine, and how it resonates with a symbolic of natality'.[37] To this end, Grace depicts becoming divine not in traditional terms of mystical union, but by adaptation of Luce Irigaray's idea of becoming divine women. Grace understands Irigaray as proposing an exploration of new possibilities of self-awareness and self-healing, as well as mutual recognition of the integrity of all other human beings. Such a proposal has challenging implications for women if they are to restore their own divine inheritance. This involves in particular the task of mending

---

[35] Jantzen, 'Eros and the Abyss: Reading Medieval Mystics in Postmodernity', *Literature and Theology*, 17/3 (2003): pp. 244–64, p. 257.

[36] Jantzen, *Becoming Divine*, p. 152.

[37] Jantzen, *Becoming Divine*, pp. 6–7.

both themselves and the world. As a result: 'The divine, then, will not feature as a "God out there", beyond the realm of human love and action, but rather the divine as the horizon and constitution of ourselves and our world, within and between "natals"'.[38] Again, in this context, Grace provides explicit suggestions as to her intentions for integrating the medieval mystics with Arendt's natality. In discussing Hadewijch, Grace remarks: 'Since she speaks of God as Love, and Love in her writings is female, the baby is a little girl: here, indeed is a medieval precursor of a symbolic of natality'.[39] Such a vision of natality, grounded in love, has specific ethical implications for Grace that reflect the practical philosophy of Arendt. Grace's direction becomes particularly evident in a statement that she makes in the next to last chapter of *Becoming Divine*:

> A feminist symbolic whose source and criteria are found in woman's lives starts from the ethical, indeed from acting for love of the world, for love of the natal Others whose new and unexpected beginnings offer hope for the world. A symbolic of natality is therefore a symbolic yearning for a divine horizon. But that yearning is not just an ineffectual feeling, but a mode of action; and the horizon is a horizon of accountability and response to natals, a horizon of divinity 'defined through human relations and not the inverse'.[40]

Besides a Levinasian influence that can be identified in this ethically informed responsibility towards the other, there are a number of inferences made here. Though there is not exactly a leap of faith, there is definitely an assumption that love is fundamentally an ethical activity, grounded in a specific appreciation of the divine. This is realized, however, not by directing one's desires to otherworldly rewards, but by concentrating on a this-worldly responsiveness and responsibility. Such ethical activity is precisely a manifestation of love as natality. Grace will expand on this insight in a number of essays written subsequently to *Becoming Divine* where she both clarifies and refines this intimation and its direct links to the love portrayed by the medieval mystics.

Later Essays

In certain essays that she published between 2000–2003 Grace returns in delight to her earlier studies in medieval mysticism, particularly to two of her favourites, Julian and Hadewijch. She reengages with the invocations of desire and love that sustain their thought in the light of her more recent promotion of a symbolic of natality. In 'A Reconfiguration of Desire'[41] Grace reexamines in some depth Julian

---

38 Jantzen, *Becoming Divine*, p. 153.

39 Jantzen, *Becoming Divine*, p. 184.

40 Jantzen, *Becoming Divine*, p. 236.

41 Jantzen, 'A Reconfiguration of Desire'.

of Norwich's notion of desire. Grace depicts Julian as understanding desire not as a lack, a need, or a voracious appetite that cannot be appeased, but rather as a response to a divine longing. Yet this divine longing must never be construed as a lack. Grace recapitulates Julian's most significant mystical evocation: 'God is addressed as the one whose love and desire for humankind is an overflowing of generous plenitude. God is understood as wholly self-sufficient; and God's desire for the world and for humankind is sheer gift of divine abundance'.[42] Grace further reiterates how, for Julian, this fundamental human desire for God is indeed part and parcel of our created nature – that is, such desire is, as it were, a perfectly natural response.[43]

A further extrapolation Grace makes is that desire and creativity are inextricably interrelated, not just in the divine, but in the human scheme of things. Just as God's overflowing plenitude is manifested both as desire and creativity, humanity's own responsiveness to this love is mirrored in both wonder at the beauty of creation, and personal creativity.[44] From this perspective, Grace will argue that: 'creativity is related to natality, the birth of something that has not existed before'.[45] She then draws a comparison:

> The contrast between divine and human creation is not that only God can make the new, but that only God can make the new out of materials that did not already exist. Unlike God, human creators use existing materials, and are influenced by what has gone before. Nonetheless creation is not simply reflection; it is the emergence of the new.[46]

While human creativity is not exactly a replication of God's creative process, Grace appreciates that it is analogous. As such, human beings or natals introduce innovative ideas and devise splendid works of art as an expression of their own plenitude, inspired by the loveliness of the created world.

Such a vision of desire, as motivated by love of beauty, is a powerful repudiation of the received definition of desire, insofar as it has been predominantly depicted as an insatiable need since the time of Plato, by way of Hegel, to Lacan. It is also an incentive to revise attitudes toward the harmful, even destructive instincts that are encouraged when aggressive emotional outburst are regarded as endemic to the human species and, as such, inevitable. In such a fatalistic reading, there does not appear to be any human capacity that could balance, let alone moderate such congenital urges. Yet this is where Grace believes that a symbolic of natality can come to the rescue, not by eliminating such instincts, but by providing a measured intervention. In concluding this essay focused on recuperating Julian, Grace indicates what she hopes to achieve by her invocation of natality. 'It is

---

[42]   Jantzen, 'Birth and the Powers of Horror', p. 32.
[43]   Jantzen, 'Birth and the Powers of Horror', p. 36.
[44]   Jantzen, 'Birth and the Powers of Horror', p. 36.
[45]   Jantzen, 'Birth and the Powers of Horror', p. 37.
[46]   Jantzen, 'Birth and the Powers of Horror', p. 37.

through such engagement with beauty and natality that lack and death can be better understood, so that they stand not as binary opposites to plenitude and life, but as elements within them, never denied or without value, but taking their appropriate secondary place'.[47]

In another essay, 'Eros and the Abyss',[48] Grace depicts a reconciliation between a trope of medieval mysticism and natality. Here she surveys the changing symbolic connotations of the word abyss (*Abgrund*) as indicative of an epochal deterioration that has occurred since the medieval period. Grace describes the way that in Hadewijch's writings, the abyss featured as 'a place of ravishment, [of] erotic encounter with the divine Beloved'.[49] It also bespoke immeasurable depths, boundlessness, infinity – but it was not a place that aroused horror, or monstrous and unspeakable fears. In Grace's words: 'It is this immeasurable abyss into which Love hurls Hadewijch, an abyss which is Love itself'.[50] Hadewijch's abyss is in sharp contrast to today's postmodern abyss, where it becomes redolent with images of loss, of absence, of meaningless, and of hostile depths that express the void of nihilism. It is an understatement to assert that something has been irrevocably lost in the transition. Grace details this movement from an abundant love to deathly emptiness with scathing accuracy, principally because she does not believe that this development has taken place without invidious implications for women. As a counter-move, Grace retrieves Hadewijch's startling depiction of the abyss as similar to the womb: 'The womb is a place of nourishment and growth, a place whose darkness is not sinister but creative. And the child who is born of this womb is precious, is love – indeed is divine. It is not *geworfen* [random throwness] as Heidegger has it, but is gentle and joyfully received'.[51]

This description stands in stark contrast to the *Abgrund* of a shattered modernity where it figures as the emblematic marker of the death of God. In particular, Grace draws attention to its degradation in the guise of the fatal combination of womb as tomb, linked inevitably to women. Grace proposes Nietzsche be viewed as its original proponent.[52] It is this inversion in values that particularly exemplifies for Grace the desperation, even violation of love and creativity that appears to have marked the subsequent turn in postmodern thought to preoccupation with a certain morbid incapacity. This is a marker for Grace, as it was for Arendt, of desperate times, of a disenchantment with this world. But for Grace, as with Arendt, this is not a time for morose introspection, nor a retreat to former consolations, as these are inadequate for the new challenge that demands, as Arendt recommended, to think anew – that is, to think seriously in ways that speak specifically to the precise

---

47   Jantzen, 'Birth and the Powers of Horror', p. 43.

48   Jantzen, 'Eros and the Abyss'.

49   Jantzen, 'Eros and the Abyss', p. 244.

50   Jantzen, 'Eros and the Abyss', p. 247.

51   Jantzen, 'Eros and the Abyss', p. 260.

52   Jantzen, 'Eros and the Abyss', p. 275.

and previously unencountered crisis. To help in such thinking, Grace appeals to mystics for insights – but modifies them to address the contemporary situation.

Grace views Hadewijch as offering assistance specifically with her positive designation of the womb. 'While never minimizing the reality of death, Hadewijch places the stress rather on birth: on the importance of mortality but also of natality'.[53] From this perspective, Grace allows that Hadewijch can be of service in providing a reaffirmation of the womb so that, instead of being a space of repulsion, it can signify a place of natals, and of love – of loving subjects. In this sense, the association of women with the womb/abyss can be reassessed, even redeemed in ways that encourage an appreciation of the body and sexuality so that they no longer serve only as pawns in an exploitative and death-bound economy. Grace herself supplies a rationale for this undertaking.

> What I am suggesting is not a refutation of nihilism but a reconfiguration of its imagination. If the womb of the abyss is imagined not in misogynistic, hellish terms but rather in terms that value gender difference, embodiment, creativity and natality, then those aspects of the *Abgrund* which have been seen as implying the loss of all values are transformed into possibilities of new growth.[54]

Yet as Grace has previously cautioned, this new growth, with its creativity and symbolic regeneration, can only be fully implemented within an ethical framework that both seeks out and supports the welfare of fellow creatures and the world itself. It is here, in this ethical/political dimension of Grace's program with its stress on justice, that the legacy of Arendt's version of natality finds a resonance with the notion of natality Grace has attributed to the mystics. Grace will then place these envisaged ideals within a realistic philosophical perspective that is not a naive overturning, but is at once both subtle and serious reconfiguration of the way an ethics of love can be transformative.

> What I am not after is some new set of grounds for ethical propositions (or indeed religious beliefs). What I am after is the way in which our erotic imagination configures our response to the *Abgrund* acting not just as some kind of mental decoration but as a configuration of our behaviour and ethics.[55]

Grace's final words, however, are left for religion, and how, unfortunately, it has all too often been an accessory to the process of denial and destruction, in its mistrust of human physical love – of the body itself; and of many things deemed 'feminine'. Her hope is that religion too, may begin to examine its complicit ways and affirm that it also has a stake in natality, and not just of a virginal variety. In Grace's view, religion needs to abandon its close relation with a rarefied spirituality that longs

---

53 Jantzen, 'Eros and the Abyss', p. 260.
54 Jantzen, 'Eros and the Abyss', p. 262.
55 Jantzen, 'Eros and the Abyss', p. 261.

simply for eternity instead of advocating an entanglement and commitment to the wonders and beauty of creation.

> I believe that if religion is to have a role in the formation of loving subjects, it will need to focus much more on birth, on natality, as the source of creativity and potential, not a birth that sets aside our bodily beginnings, but precisely our bodily birth from our mothers, always already sexuate [sexual] in community connected to the web of life and to the earth.[56]

For Grace, natality opens up a gap that inspires us to think otherwise. I believe that it is up to those of us who are trying to find better ways of doing philosophy of religion to follow in the path where Grace has led the way. Our task is one to be taken as loving subjects, not disembodied and arid intellects, so that we can begin to qualify, refine, and expand on her life-giving body of work.

---

[56] Jantzen, 'Birth and the Powers of Horror', p. 161.

Chapter 3
The Urgent Wish ...
To Be More Life-Giving

Pamela Sue Anderson

Introduction

To begin, consider two quotations – one from Benedict de Spinoza and the other from Paul Ricoeur. Notice how their affirmations of life and of the power to act as responsible and autonomous thinking subjects resonate profoundly with the philosophical challenge of Grace M. Jantzen[1] that feminist philosophy of religion become 'more life-giving'. It is in an attempt to take up this challenge that I draw on the following words from Spinoza:

> A free man [sic] thinks of nothing less than of death, and his wisdom is a meditation, not on death, but on life.[2]

I also draw on these lines from Ricoeur:

> Power, I will say, affirms itself ... this connection between affirmation and power needs to be emphasized. It governs all the reflexive forms by which a subject can designate him – or herself as the one who can. ... [this] affirmation of a power to act already presents a noteworthy epistemological feature that cannot be proven, demonstrated, but can only be attested ... a confidence in one's own capacity, which can be confirmed only through being exercised and through the approbation others grant to it ... other people may encourage, accompany, assist by having confidence in us – by appeal to responsibility and autonomy.[3]

---

[1] From here I would like to refer to Grace by her Christian name, in order to stress the personal nature of my attempts to follow her passionate lead concerning life. For developing the two-fold idea of affirming life and acting responsibly also see Simone de Beauvoir, *The Ethics of Ambiguity*, trans. Bernard Frechtman (New York, 1948), pp. 74–155.

[2] Benedict de Spinoza, *Ethics*, ed. and trans. G. H. R. Parkinson (Oxford, [1661] 2000), p. 276: Part Four, prop. 67.

[3] Paul Ricoeur, 'Autonomy and Vulnerability', *Reflections on the Just*, trans. David Pellauer (Chicago, 2007), p. 75.

No doubt, Grace would have been intrigued by these quotations, even if she would have carefully qualified their philosophical significance for feminists. I will mainly expand on the first quotation with some appropriations of Spinoza's meditations on life, that is, on the power of life, including suggestions concerning confidence in life. Ricoeur's affinity to Spinoza appears in giving a highly significant role to power in both an individual's affirmation of life and the approbation of others: affirmation and approbation are required for the confidence to exercise this power to act. Some readers will have already noticed the post-Kantian dimension in the reflexive autonomy which Ricoeur stresses his appropriation of Spinoza. I will touch on these notions of affirmation, approbation and autonomy in the context of Grace's urgent wish for philosophy of religion to become life-giving and whole-making. In particular, I will raise questions about the relation between the individual and the collective in a Spinozist conception of corporate life.

In 2000, Grace and I began an open discussion of feminist philosophy of religion focusing on *A Feminist Philosophy of Religion*[4] and on *Becoming Divine*.[5] Our exchange was published as a correspondence in *Feminist Theology*[6] and in her first letter Grace writes: 'my book was in press when yours came out, and although we are different in approach we very much share the urgent wish for the discipline to be more life-giving and whole-making'.[7] Since her death, I have reflected upon Grace's words, especially her equally rational and passionate insistence that feminist philosophy of religion give life, not death, in a radical transformation of the Anglo-American discipline of philosophy of religion. Very much in the spirit of Grace, I urge us to move forward.

In particular, I have found new ways in which to be bold – that is more confident in acting rationally and passionately – by thinking more about the conception which intrigued Grace most in my own work, that is, yearning.[8] This conception can be significantly enhanced with an alternative form of rationality which is inspired by

---

[4]   Pamela Sue Anderson, *A Feminist Philosophy of Religion: The Rationality and Myths of Religious Belief* (Oxford, 1988).

[5]   Grace M. Jantzen, *Becoming Divine: Towards a Feminist Philosophy of Religion* (Manchester, 1988).

[6]   Unfortunately the open correspondence was published in the wrong order. Instead of Anderson's first letter appearing followed by Jantzen's response to this; and then, each of the replies to the other, Anderson's letter and her reply to Jantzen were published together in September 2000 before Jantzen's first letter to Anderson and her subsequent reply to Anderson's second letter. So the September 2000 issue of *Feminist Theology* (25) should be read alongside of the January 2001 issue (26) going from Anderson's first letter and then to Jantzen's and then back to Anderson's reply and Jantzen's. This chapter aims to take up crucial points from Jantzen's letter concerning *A Feminist Philosophy of Religion* (cf. Jantzen, 'Feminist Philosophy of Religion', *Feminist Theology*, 26 (2001): pp. 102–7).

[7]   Jantzen, 'Feminist Philosophy of Religion', p. 102.

[8]   For the account of 'yearning' as a rational passion for justice, informed by feminist accounts of injustice which can only be undone with the transformation of our lives, beliefs and passions, see Anderson, *A Feminist Philosophy of Religion*, pp. 22–3, 174 and 241.

contemporary philosophical appropriations of Spinoza's *conatus*. In other words, confidence can be generated from the very idea of (the) power which we each have to affirm our own existence at the same time as approving of another's. Of course, this form of power in approbation, or mutual recognition, would be risky if it was not wise in the sense of Spinoza's rationalist ethics (more on this below). To support this, let us try to imagine how Grace might have affected our appropriation of Spinoza. This exercise in imagination is absolutely essential for the corporate picture at the heart of Grace's vision for feminist philosophy of religion. Could this be Spinoza's imagination in the sense of free exercise of 'the affections of the human body'?[9] These affections would be 'ideas' in the sense of images of things, or corporeal traces which impinge on the affected body; and as such they would take on a highly positive role in the process of becoming, in Grace's terms, 'more whole-making'. Later I will refer to these affections in terms of the imagination's relation to bodily awareness. A critical question arises here: how with the help of Grace's philosophy do we ensure this optimism in corporate relations especially when we seem to have in 'imagining', in Spinoza's terms, 'inadequate ideas'?

Yearning for a Joyful Love of Life (not Death)

This section aims to follow closely Grace's encouragement to share actively with her in a love of life. This shared activity is most evident in the pursuit of a life-giving philosophy. Let us consider salient points which she made to me more than eight years ago. I list these here:

1. '[I]f we take seriously your emphasis on feminist standpoint epistemology and especially your very creative use of the concept of yearning, then the aim of feminist philosophy is radicalised in a way that I find highly insightful; and it's this that I find of most value in your book. ... I want to ask you to try to take it further'.[10]
2. 'Take for example your important and subversive idea of thinking from others' lives, "inventing ourselves as other":[11] the consequences for philosophy of religion are enormous. If we stop valorizing the disembodied "genderless" male subject then we also presumably stop valorizing the disembodied "genderless" male deity: what happens to the concept of God so beloved of the discipline'?[12]

---

9   Cf. Spinoza, *Ethics*, pp. 132–4, 139; Part Two, prop. 17 scholium.
10   Jantzen, 'Feminist Philosophy of Religion', pp. 102–3.
11   Anderson, *A Feminist Philosophy of Religion*, p. 165.
12   Jantzen, 'Feminist Philosophy of Religion', p. 104.

3. 'I think … that in fact your method of thinking from others' lives is far more radical than your stated aim of offering a supplement to the traditional idea of rationality'.[13]

4. 'To take masculinism … as you point out, men have historically identified themselves with rationality and have identified women with the body, passion, irrationality and madness. Now, to revision rationality so that it includes passion rather than sees passion as its other is indeed a huge epistemological shift; and I especially like your emphasis that one of its central categories is yearning. … your lifting up of yearning changes the whole epistemological landscape[14] … what you say about yearning actually destabilizes the [Anglo-American] emphasis on [justifying] beliefs rather than being a supplement to rationality'.[15]

5. '[J]ust think what a difference it would have made to the history of modernity if the philosophy of religion had taken as its emphasis and aim a yearning for beauty or goodness, and fostering their discernment'.[16] (106).

6. '[H]ow is yearning to be fostered, individually and collectively, and what forms of education of desire are appropriate?'[17]

With the above, Grace argues for the possibility that yearning could constitute a significantly new and radical conception; but this still needs to be pushed forward.

Grace's reading of *A Feminist Philosophy of Religion* has inspired me to enhance and develop my earlier conception of yearning. I have turned to a distinctive genealogy from Spinoza to Immanuel Kant, Paul Ricoeur, Gilles Deleuze, Michèle Le Doeuff, Genevieve Lloyd and Moira Gatens. Each of these philosophers guide the working out of an alternative form of rationality which has a critical role to play: it is to educate our emotions and passions. In fact, it now seems surprising that Grace herself had not drawn more significant content from Spinoza, Ricoeur, Deleuze, Le Doeuff, Lloyd or Gatens for affirming the power to persevere in being and, even more crucially for Grace, for meditation on life, not death.[18] Given more time, perhaps she would have explored Spinoza's *conatus*. But in any case Grace has pushed me in this direction wittingly or not; and for this, I am grateful.

---

[13]   Jantzen, 'Feminist Philosophy of Religion', p. 104.

[14]   Jantzen, 'Feminist Philosophy of Religion', p. 104.

[15]   Jantzen, 'Feminist Philosophy of Religion', p. 105.

[16]   Jantzen, 'Feminist Philosophy of Religion', p. 106.

[17]   Jantzen, 'Feminist Philosophy of Religion', p. 107.

[18]   In the concluding pages of *Becoming Divine*, Jantzen admits that she is willing to explore the possibilities in 'a pantheist symbolic' (p. 274). The present chapter is proposing one way in which to develop Jantzen's vision of 'a symbolic of natality' as 'a flourishing of the earth and those who dwell upon it' (*Becoming Divine*, p. 275; also see pp. 272–5). For more background on the theist's labelling of Spinoza as a 'pantheist,' see Michael Levine, 'Non-theistic conceptions of God', in Chad Meister and Paul Copans (eds) *The Routledge Companion to the Philosophy of Religion* (London, 2007), pp. 238–41.

Grace's passion for transformation keeps us on the move in philosophy. And we find that contemporary feminist and Continental appropriations of Spinoza's *conatus* not only shape an alternative form of rationality which can become life-giving and whole-making, but enhance Grace's passion for a radically new feminist ethics. What might she have said about Spinoza's *Ethics*?[19] Consistent with her suggestion to be bold in my treatment of yearning, I have not only suggested that yearning is the essence of religion but that a particular religious yearning could bind individuals together to create new corporate relations. In turn, this boldness finds support in what Spinoza's *Ethics* says about *conatus*: it is a rational striving of each individual body to exist fully; and this *conatus* becomes the essence of a rationalist ethics. Ultimately, I will suggest that not unlike a particular kind of religious yearning Spinoza's *conatus* binds bodies together in love. Human being is conceived as part of a dynamic and interconnected whole.

To go over some more ground in Spinoza's *Ethics*, *conatus* stands for a thing's endeavour to persevere in being against un-wise passions; and this perseverance becomes a thing's very essence. In the case of those individuals who are human bodies, *conatus* has an intimate connection with reason similar to what I have conceived in yearning. Instead of having reason serve, in turning away from harmful passion, as an alternative source of ethical motivation the virtuous mind achieves – according to Spinoza – freedom by bringing its understanding to bear on its own passions, transforming them into active, rational emotions. In Spinoza's terms, if we can be the 'adequate cause' of one of 'the affections of the body' by which the power of acting is 'increased or diminished, helped or hindered', then 'I understand by the emotion an action; otherwise, I understand it to be a passion'.[20]

Spinoza's technical term 'imagination' is like emotion in being driven by *conatus*. The activities of the imagination are caught up in the dynamics of *conatus*, that is, in the movement and impetus of the mind in its struggle to express its nature as 'a finite individual'. The mind's joys and sorrows, its loves and hates, are inseparable from the effort to imagine: 'The mind endeavours to imagine only those things which posit its power of acting'.[21] In his general definition of the emotions, Spinoza describes the passions of the mind as 'confused ideas': 'by which the mind affirms of its body, or of any part of its body, a greater or lesser force of existing than before, and which when being given, the mind itself is determined to thinking this rather than that'.[22] This definition incorporates his understanding of the natures: i) of pleasure as 'a man's [sic] transition from a lesser to a greater perfection',[23] ii) of pain as 'a man's transition from a greater to a lesser perfection',[24] and iii) of desire as 'the very essence of man, in so far as it is conceived as determined to

---

19   Spinoza, *Ethics*.

20   Spinoza, *Ethics*, p. 164ff.

21   Spinoza, *Ethics*, p. 205, Part Three, prop. 54.

22   Spinoza, *Ethics*, p. 223, Part Three, General Definition.

23   Spinoza, *Ethics*, p. 213.

24   Spinoza, *Ethics*, p. 213.

do something from some given affection of itself'.[25] So, pleasure or joy, pain or sadness, and desire are at the core of Spinoza's account of the emotions; pleasure, pain and desire are integrated into what it is to be a passion.

Genevieve Lloyd helpfully expands on Spinoza's definition of the emotions with her account of love, including sexual love. According to Lloyd, 'Spinoza's account makes it impossible to talk of the "pain" of love'.[26] Instead love is always 'joyful' in Spinoza's sense of this term. His parallel definition of the opposite of love, hate, integrates sadness: 'hate is "sadness associated with an idea of an external cause"'[27] (*ibid.*). Lloyd continues to expand on Spinoza, 'What we may see as the disturbance of love, Spinoza sees rather as our being torn by contrary passions'.[28] Understanding these distinctions must be part of what is meant by Spinoza's use of reason to 'educate' or transform the passions.

According to Lloyd's radical and, for some at least, provocative interpretation of Spinoza, to understand the operations of imagination and its interactions with the emotions is to learn to replace misleading and debilitating illusions with better fictions which help rather than hinder the actions of the mind in which freedom consists.[29] The capacity (*potestas*) to act and not merely to be acted on, to express one's own nature and not merely react to the nature of another is an expression of freedom, but equally of one's power (*potentia*) and so of *conatus*.[30] Spinoza's way to conquer (mis)fortune lies in the use of reason to understand the operations of the imagination and the passions. The power of reason rests in understanding the passions and increasing one's freedom. Again Spinoza's 'imagination' is a first kind of knowledge and as such constitutes a necessary step in the education of the passions. More adequate knowledge comes in understanding the errors or fictions which make up socially

---

[25] Spinoza, *Ethics*, p. 212.

[26] Genevieve Lloyd, 'What a Union!' *The Philosopher's Magazine*, (29) 2005: pp. 45–8, p. 48.

[27] Lloyd, 'What a Union!' p. 48.

[28] Lloyd, 'What a Union!' p. 48. For further, fascinating discussions of sexual love and the way in which bodily pleasures are for Spinoza as important for the well-being of the individual as the cultivation of reason, see Alexandre Matheron, 'Spinoza et la sexualité', *Giornale Critico della Filosofia Italiana*, 8/4 (1977): pp. 436–57, 454; Amelie Rorty, 'Spinoza on the Pathos of Idolatrous Love and the Hilarity of True Love', in Genevieve Lloyd (ed.) *Feminism and the History of Philosophy* (Oxford: Oxford University Press, 2002), pp. 204–26; Pamela S. Anderson, *A Feminist Philosophy of Religion*, pp. 214–20.

[29] For a different and more conservative reading of Spinoza's account of the imagination, see Roger Scruton, *Spinoza: A Very Short Introduction* (Oxford: Oxford University Press, 2002), pp. 74, 90–1 and 95ff.

[30] On the fine distinctions in Spinoza concerning *potentia* as act, active and actual, that is the essence of an individual mode and *potestas* as a capacity for being affected, see Gilles Deleuze, *Spinoza: Practical Philosophy*, trans. Robert Hurley (San Francisco CA, 1988) pp. 97–8.

embedded illusions.[31] Debilitating fictions are bound up with a lack of knowledge. For example, the fiction of a free will for Spinoza exhibits an awareness of one's actions but an ignorance of their causes. An ability to exercise an ongoing critique of illusion generates the highest exercise of philosophical thought: the mind's understanding of itself as 'eternal' with the love of God or nature as its cause. The latter becomes highly significant in the conclusions of Spinoza's *Ethics*.[32]

Yet the critical question for this chapter can be put crudely: Has Spinoza's core concept of *conatus* led us to a striving for greater self-understanding which, ultimately, remains self-interestedness and so incompatible with Grace's vision of a life-giving and whole-making philosophy? Is an individual's effort to persevere in being directed to a self-sufficiency and detachment from other bodies which would be incompatible with Grace's pursuit of whole-making in a feminist philosophy of religion? At a glance some readers might think that Spinoza's endeavour could not be compatible with 'a feminist standpoint epistemology' which aims to 'think from the lives of others', as I advocate in *A Feminist Philosophy of Religion* and Grace encourages.[33] And yet, is this to fail to understand how Spinoza explains the way in which individual bodies combine in order to create a new body and so a collective life? In order to begin to answer this line of critical questions, let us diverge a bit and try to *redeem* the crucial dimensions of Spinoza's account of *conatus* with certain feminist appropriations of his *Ethics* in the terms of individual bodies and gender politics.

Individuals, Bodies and Gender Politics

This section is bound to consider the relation of the individual and the corporate in Spinoza; but I will do this indirectly by considering the appropriation of Spinoza by feminist philosophers Michèle Le Doeuff, Genevieve Lloyd and Moira Gatens. The critical question already raised at the outset is: how can Spinoza and those who follow him ensure optimism, or joy? The answer has to do with negotiating reason so that rationality is shared; this in turn would increase power and so joy.

As already stated, Spinoza's concept of *conatus* is the very essence of finite individuals and closely connected to the imagination. For Spinoza, to be an individual is to be determined to act through the mediation of 'other finite modes', therefore 'that which is in something else and is conceived through something else',[34] and it is likewise to determine these others. According to his definition,

---

[31]   The critical question is: What, if any, role the imagination might play in striving for and achieving intellectual knowledge of God? Scruton, for one, assumes that the imagination indicates a lesser kind of knowledge only (Scruton, *Spinoza*, pp. 92, 97).

[32]   Especially Spinoza, *Ethics*, pp. 309–16; cf. Moira Gatens and Genevieve Lloyd, *Collective Imaginings: Spinoza Past and Present* (London, 1999), pp. 23–40.

[33]   See points 1 and 3 above. See also Jantzen, 'Feminist Philosophy of Religion', pp. 102–4; cf. Anderson, *A Feminist Philosophy of Religion*, p. 76ff.

[34]   Spinoza, *Ethics*, p. 75, Part One, Definition 5.

imagination assumes the awareness of our own bodies together with others;[35] so the interaction between bodies essentially involves imagination. Early in the present chapter, instead of awareness of our bodies I employed Spinoza's own terms, 'affections of the human body'. Here bodily awareness is not only readily understood as part of the nature of Spinoza's imagination, but we now recognize that it is also closely bound up with the impetus of *conatus*. It is the nature of bodies and minds, as finite individuals, to struggle in order to persevere in being. Our bodies are not just passively moved by external forces. They have their own motion, or movement in a certain relation to rest, which is their own characteristic force for existing. However, this force is not something that individuals exert of their own power alone. For an individual to persevere in existence is for it to act and be acted upon in a multiplicity of ways. The more *complex* the individual *body*, the more ways in which it can be *affected* by and *affecting* other things. The power of the imagination is integral to the continued existence and flourishing of the individual as corporeal. So, to define imagination in terms of bodily awareness is to place imagination at the heart of the story of human well-being and flourishing with one another. We approach the collective dimension of Spinoza's *Ethics* in light of the above understanding of *conatus*, imagination and bodily awareness.

We have returned to the crucial point about the nature of these individual bodies. We seek to understand the way(s) in which they make up a collective life. To repeat, Spinoza argues that each body, in fact each thing, has a *conatus* which constitutes its very essence and with which it 'endeavours to persevere in its being'.[36] This is as true of humans as it is of anything else. Yet in more exclusively masculine terms, Spinoza cautions men specifically to avoid pity,[37] since pity is an 'effeminate' or 'womanish' emotion.[38] In other words, pity is something undergone and as such obstructs the transition of passions to actions; it blocks the education of the emotions, and more generally, hinders life's *conatus*. Spinoza describes how each man (*sic*), by his very nature, is driven to preserve his own existence; his happiness consists in his being able to do just that. We might consider whether a man's (*sic*) essence is determined by his conatus; if so, according to A. W. Moore's reading, 'each man is driven to preserve his existence *as a* man who is driven to preserve his existence'.[39] The crucial point here is that the *conatus* for a human being is a drive to actualize the human essence to the greatest possible degree:

---

[35]   Another way to think of Spinoza's mode is a modification of the one substance which makes up all of Nature or 'God'; see the 'Editor's Introduction' in Spinoza, *Ethics*, pp. 19–26.

[36]   Spinoza, *Ethics*, p. 171, Part Three, Props, 6 and 7.

[37]   Spinoza, *Ethics*, pp. 185–7ff, 217.

[38]   Spinoza, *Ethics*, p. 253; Genevieve Lloyd, 'The Man of Reason', in Ann Garry and Marilyn Pearson (eds) *Women, Knowledge and Reality: Explorations in Feminist Philosophy* (London, 1996, second edn), pp. 157–9.

[39]   A. W. Moore, *Making Sense of Things: The Evolution of Modern Metaphysics* (Cambridge, forthcoming). Cf. Benedict de Spinoza, *Ethics*, pp. 230–33, Part Four, props 3–7.

this means a drive to maximise human activity and to minimize human passivity. To have this drive to maximize activity is the very essence, power and virtue of the human being.[40] This model of maximally active self-preservation and so perseverance in being is also Spinoza's model for freedom and salvation.[41] Thus, Spinoza returns us to the point that a thing is free when it 'exists solely from the necessity of its own nature, and is determined to action by itself alone'.[42] Yet this could sound like a non-relational autonomy. Moreover, it does not yet give us a gender-inclusive picture of both a corporeal and collective life.

Consider Lloyd's serious, feminist criticisms of Spinoza's attempt to transcend self-centredness for a corporate life. And I note that Grace would have made such critical assessment crucial to any feminist appropriation of Spinoza's power to exist and the affirmation of that power of existence. In addition, this critical assessment of Spinoza would apply equally to the quotation from Ricoeur on the affirmation of the power of the subject to act – with which I began. On the one hand, it is immediately attractive to a feminist philosopher that Spinoza rejects the dualism of mind and body where, crudely stated, the body had been given less value – especially in its symbolic association with women – than the mind in previous philosophy, notably in Descartes. On the other hand, as Lloyd recognizes, there remain problems implicit in the gender-bias in Spinoza's reference to a 'man' of reason.[43] Lloyd admits that 'there is indeed much that is appealing and impressive in the picture Spinoza presents ... the transcending of self-centred and hence dependent, jealous love; the pursuit of a detached perception of the truths of himself and his situation, transcending the distortions of his limited, unreflective perspective on things; the location of moral worth in a certain style of perception rather than in the will'.[44] Yet there remains the serious question of a man not only transcending selfish and obsessive love but any individual as the proper object of love. Moreover, the repudiation of pity as weak and effeminate might be an indication of a larger problem (for a Spinozist) with any ethics of compassion or care; and the latter is crucial today in forming a significant part of feminist ethics.

Michèle Le Doeuff has also voiced her strong objection to Spinoza's deliberate exclusion of women from government, and so the larger sphere of political life, on the basis of woman's natural inferiority and spiritual weakness.[45] Le Doeuff points out that in his very last, however unfinished political treatise, Spinoza makes absolutely clear that a woman's weakness and her potential (sexual) distraction of men from their rational emotional life provide definite grounds for Spinoza's

---

[40]   Moore, *Making Sense of Things*. Cf. Spinoza, *Ethics*, pp. 231–2, 241; Part Four, props 4 and 20.

[41]   Spinoza, *Ethics*, pp. 310–11, Part Five, prop. 36 and Scholium.

[42]   Spinoza, *Ethics*, p. 75 Part One, Definition 7.

[43]   Lloyd, 'The Man of Reason', pp. 155–60.

[44]   Lloyd, 'The Man of Reason', p. 159.

[45]   Michèle Le Doeuff, *Hipparchia's Choice: An Essay Concerning Women, Philosophy Etc.* trans. Trista Selous (New York, 1991, Second Edition, 2007), p. 168.

conscious exclusion of women from seventeenth-century political society.[46] In her biting words, 'Now according to [Spinoza] experience would tend to show that if women are excluded from government and subjected to male authority, it is because [of] a natural weakness of spirit';[47] and she cites Spinoza here: 'government by women "has nowhere happened, [therefore] I am fully entitled to assert that women have not the same right as men by nature, but are necessarily inferior to them"'.[48]

And yet, once women are seen to have the natural right[49] to cultivate knowledge and be part of any government, then we might find Le Doeuff applauding the education of emotions *à la* Spinoza. In other words, there is something deeply unwitting about Le Doeuff's own affinity with an ethics of joy: it seems close to Spinoza in terms of its affirmation of life and the power to act, while very critical of Spinoza in so far as he excludes women by conceiving them as weak and inferior. Basically, Le Doeuff exhibits her own pleasure in persevering in existence. Le Doeuff's writings are full of positive expressions (for women and men) which resonate powerfully with the seventeenth-century tradition of rationalism. Her form of rationality clearly embraces the power to act responsibly and autonomously, while also striving for a joyous contemplation of the life of Nature. Moreover, Le Doeuff's characteristic rationalist vision of a political community in which *women are united individually and collectively* – with the one-and-many metaphor of 'the corporate' – could not be that far from a modification of Spinoza's expression of *conatus* which would include women.[50] Basically Le Doeuff makes sure that gender is inclusive by turning a negative into a positive when it comes to Spinoza's womanish weakness. But can this help more generally our understanding of the relation of individual bodies to collective life, and so, to a new corporate body?

In fact Le Doeuff's favourite seventeenth-century female philosopher, Gabrielle Suchon, could have a great deal to do with her close affinity to what Spinoza would identify as 'intuitive' knowledge (*scientia intuitiva*) of 'God'.[51]

---

[46]   Michèle Le Doeuff, *The Sex of Knowing*, trans. Kathryn Hamer and Lorraine Code (London, 2003), pp. 104–6. Cf. Le Doeuff, *Hipparchia's Choice*, p. 206.

[47]   Le Doeuff, *Hipparchia's Choice*, p. 104.

[48]   Le Doeuff, *The Sex of Knowing*, p. 105; Benedict de Spinoza 'Tractatus Politicus', *The Political Works* (unfinished at his death) ed. and trans. by A. G. Wernham (Oxford, 1958): 443ff.

[49]   It is not clear what a 'natural right' might be in Spinozist's *Ethics*; perhaps the closest thing to this is the human capacity to act rather than merely be acted on or merely undergo such passions as 'pity'.

[50]   Le Doeuff, *The Sex of Knowing* pp. 138–41; Le Doeuff, *Hipparchia's Choice*, pp. 37–43, 168–70, 206–7, 243.

[51]   But here 'God' does not refer to any personal deity. Rather the divinity simply refers to the one substance: Nature in which bodies and minds are working as parts in accord (cf. Gilles Deleuze, *Spinoza*, pp. 86–91; Moira Gatens, *Imaginary Bodies: Ethics Power and Corporeality*, pp. 111–13, 117ff).

This kind of knowledge is far greater than the inadequate kind of knowledge which we have seen is due to the imagination; Spinoza himself calls the latter a 'first' kind of knowledge. Le Doeuff uncovers Suchon's philosophical writing in order to emphasize forcefully the ethical significance of both women and men in gaining knowledge and so freedom.[52] Similarly, Le Doeuff's preferred twentieth-century male philosopher, Gilles Deleuze, actively embraces a highly original reading of Spinoza's practical philosophy.[53] Instead of traditional theism we discover in the Spinozist dimensions of Le Doeuff's thinking a form of rationalism which has 'God or Nature' (*deus sive natura*) as its ground: no personal, male-gendered deity is implied yet a creative corporeality is.

It is helpful to present a final quotation – this time from Deleuze – on Spinoza. Notice Deleuze's unequivocal emphasis on life and the positive affirmation of the power of life, as a way of being, in his philosophical account of Spinoza:

> In the reproach that Hegel will make to Spinoza, that he ignored the negative and its power, lies the glory and innocence of Spinoza, his own discovery. In a world consumed by the negative, he has enough confidence in life, in the power of life, to challenge death, the murderous appetite of men, the rules of good and evil, of the just and the unjust. Enough confidence in life to denounce all the phantoms of the negative. Excommunication, war, tyranny, reaction, men who fight for their enslavement as if it were their freedom – this forms the world in which Spinoza lives.[54]

In Spinoza's thought, life is not an idea, a matter of theory. It is a way of being, one and the same eternal mode in all its attributes. And it is only from this perspective that the geometric method is fully comprehensible. In the *Ethics*, it is in opposition to what Spinoza calls satire; and satire is everything that takes pleasure in the powerlessness and distress of men, everything that feeds on accusations, on malice, on belittlement, on low interpretations, everything that breaks men's spirits ... People have asked whether the *Ethics* should be read in terms of thought or in terms of power (for example, are the attributes powers or concepts?). Actually, there is only one term, Life, that encompasses thought, but conversely this term is encompassed only by thought. Not that life is in thinking, but only the thinker has a potent life, free of guilt and hatred; and only life explains the thinker. Spinoza did not believe in hope or even in courage; he believed only in joy, and in vision. He let others live, provided that others let him live. He wanted only to inspire, to waken, to reveal.[55]

---

52   Michèle Le Doeuff, *The Sex of Knowing*, pp. 5–10, 15–24, 33–45.

53   Gilles Deleuze, *Spinoza*; Michèle Le Doeuff, *The Sex of Knowing*, pp. 217–20; Le Doeuff, *Hipparchia's Choice*, pp. 168, 319–21.

54   Gilles Deleuze, *Spinoza*, p. 13.

55   Deleuze, *Spinoza*, p. 14.

In the above debates about Spinoza's thought with its distinctive method, we find attractive the unequivocal confidence in a way of thinking and living, in a striving to increase or maximise the power of life. Much of Spinoza's positive vision depends on bodies acting together as a more and more complex body, and ultimately, making one whole (nature).[56] This vision exhibits a strong affinity to Grace's profoundly positive framework of life, including her crucial picture of natality,[57] of the new beginnings for women and men as 'natals', not mortals.[58] In Spinoza's terms, the human body needs for its preservation very many other bodies by which it is continually regenerated.[59] So, can we maintain this attractive picture for feminist philosophers of religion who follow after Spinoza, Le Doeuff, Lloyd and Jantzen? It is what we, our bodies with our minds, can do which determines what counts as our living well. The more we do rationally and corporately – as opposed to undergo – the better we live together. In particular, 'to love God' is no longer to trust in the benevolent purposes of a transcendent creator – the purposes for which we await satisfaction. Instead it is the mind's joyful recognition of itself as corporate, that is, as part of the unified whole of nature which expresses an intellectual love [of 'God']. Thus the core of love in all its forms is the joy of continued bodily existence. That joy is vulnerable, and yet it is a more sure grounding for our loves than the glorification of unsatisfied desire for a wholly transcendent and disembodied divine.[60]

Conclusion

This chapter is meant to recall the aims of feminist philosophy of religion which were discussed by Grace M. Jantzen in an exchange of published letters with me. These aims were originally discussed in relation to three questions – to which I can now offer brief answers. (1) How do we seek transformation? We continue to seek a radical transformation of Anglo-American philosophy of religion.[61] This transformation could come about with an alternative form of rationality which would generate a life-giving and whole-making philosophy.[62] (2) How do we carry

---

[56] For further discussion of *Spinoza's* notion of body, bodies and power, see Moira Gatens, *Imaginary Bodies*, pp. 102–13; cf. Spinoza, *Ethics*, pp. 131–2, Part Two, postulates on the body.

[57] Grace Jantzen, *Becoming Divine*, chaps 9 and 10.

[58] Cf. Harriet A. Harris, 'Feminism', in Chad Meister and Paul Copans (eds) *The Routledge Companion to Philosophy of Religion* (London, 2007), pp. 651–60.

[59] Cf. Spinoza, *Ethics*, p. 131ff.

[60] Cf. Spinoza, *Ethics*, pp. 106–12.

[61] Harris, 'Feminism', p. 640ff

[62] Michael Levine, 'Non-theistic conceptions of God', in Chad Meister and Paul Copans (eds) *The Routledge Companion to the Philosophy of Religion* (London, 2007), pp. 238–41.

out our critiques? Philosophers of religion in the mainstream are not seeking much that is new. So in the spirit of Grace and with the help of Ricoeur, Deleuze, Le Doeuff, Lloyd and others[63] who appropriate Spinoza's way of being, of preserving life and expressing one's nature as a finite individual mode acting with and upon others, feminist philosophers of religion could not do much better in affirming the power to act rationally, falsifying those contrary relations, of reason and passion, mind and body, men and women as illusions which undermine an(y) individual's power to act both responsibly-autonomously and with approbation. (3) What do we do with our sources? We seek to rethink our sources and not be afraid to reject that which is death-dealing and to embrace that which enhances our endeavours to persevere in being – and so in the life of God or Nature (*deus sive natura*).[64] Despite what the theists in the discipline of Anglo-American philosophy of religion have called the 'pantheism' of Spinoza's one substance, Grace encourages us to move beyond such labels to a more creative corporeality: to enable minds to affirm their bodies within an ever-greater perfection.[65] For each and every individual moves forward in striving for a joyful continuation of bodily existence which expresses, what we might agree is, an intellectual love of either God or Nature.

---

[63]   Here I would like to thank those others, including Adrian Moore, Jennifer Bunker, Daniel Whistler and Kathryn Bevis, who have helped me work through technical terms and ideas from Spinoza's *Ethics*, especially in our group discussions of 'Spileuze'.

[64]   Clearly there exists a significant theological issue: do we exclude 'God' and say, 'Nature' to avoid any confusion between Spinoza's one substance and the Christian theistic God? Feminist philosophers of religion might find Spinoza's alternative 'God or Nature' liberatory, since neither would be the personal God of masculinist theology.

[65]   For an European philosophical theologian who puts aside the label 'pantheist' in order to focus on Spinoza's *Ethics*, especially the ethical journey (*le trajet éthique*) of the finite mode towards recognition of being a particular individual within a larger whole (*la parcelle d'un grand tout*), see Paul Ricoeur, *L'unique et le singulier*. L'intégrale des entretiens 'Noms de dieux' d' Edmond Blattchen (Brussels Belgium, Alice Editions, 1999), pp. 43–7; cf. Rorty, 'Spinoza on the Pathos of Idolatrous Love and the Hilarity of True Love', pp. 204–24.

Chapter 4

Why I still read John Donne:
An Appraisal of Grace Jantzen's
Becoming Divine

Frances Ward

Introduction

If you want a past master in the business of constructing death, John Donne is your man. According to Izaak Walton, he waited fifteen days to die, and was conscious until the end, when he then arranged 'his hands and body into such a posture as required not the least alteration by those that came to shroud him'.[1] This dramatic deathbed scene occurred on 31 March 1631; but his death was anticipated long before (see Donne's *Devotions Upon Emergent Occasions*),[2] and then represented in effigy and sermon in the days immediately preceding. On 25 February Donne preached before Charles 1 a sermon that came to be entitled 'Death's Duel'. In it he dwelt on death, telling his congregation that '[w]e have a winding-sheet in our mother's womb which grows with us from our conception, and we come into the world wound up in that winding-sheet, for we come to seek a grave'.[3] And there's more:

> all our periods and transitions in this life, are so many passages from death to death. Our very birth and entrance into this life is *exitus a morte*, an issue from death, for in our mother's womb we are dead, so as that we do not know we live, not so much as we do in our sleep, neither is there any grave so close or so putrid a prison, as the womb would be unto us if we stayed in it beyond our time, or died there before our time. In the grave the worms do not kill us; we breed, and feed, and then kill those worms which we ourselves produced. In the womb the dead child kills the mother that conceived it, and is a murderer, nay, a parricide, even after it is dead. And if we be not dead so in the womb, so as that being dead we kill her that gave us our first life, our life of vegetation, yet we are dead so as David's idols are dead. In the womb we have eyes and see not, ears and hear not.

---

[1]   Izaak Walton, *Lives* (Oxford, London, New York, Toronto, [1670] 1932), p. 82.

[2]   John Donne, *Devotions Upon Emergent Occasions* (Anthony Raspa, ed.) (Oxford, London, New York, Toronto, 1975).

[3]   John Donne, *John Donne: The Major Works* (J. Carey, ed.) (Oxford, London, New York, Toronto, 1990), p. 404.

There in the womb we are fitted for works of darkness, all the while deprived of light; and there in the womb we are taught cruelty, by being fed with blood, and may be damned, though we be never born.[4]

This is a man who was well acquainted with death: his own mother had died just weeks before – hence so much reference to her (though it reads today as a strange way of expressing maternal grief); he had lost his wife Anne in 1617, whom he loved, when she was just 33, in childbirth after bearing him 13 children, of whom only six survived him. He was a man who made and kept friends, but many had died: the year 1627 saw the deaths of his own daughter Lucy before her eighteenth birthday; her godmother Lucy, Countess of Bedford, and Donne's close lifelong friend Magdalen, Lady Danvers, the mother of George Herbert. That year of grief and death, according to Edwards,[5] prompted Donne to write perhaps his most depressive poem, the 'Nocturnall upon S. Lucie's Day' in which he likened the shortest day of the year to the year's midnight. He asks his reader to:

> Study me then, you who shall lovers bee
> At the next world, that is, at the next Spring:
> For I am every dead thing,
> In whom love wrought new Alchimie.

He has become the essence of nothing:

> A quintessence even from nothingnesse,
> From dull privations, and leane emptinesse
> He ruin'd mee, and I am re-begot
> Of absence, darknesse, death; things which are not.

Saunders comments that in this poem Donne's misery pulls everything into itself: 'He is now the signifier of the death of death itself, the impossible epitaph written after the end of everything'.[6]

The effigy created at his death, which still stands in St Paul's Cathedral, having survived the 'great fire' of 1666 intact, captures this apprehension of 'nothingnesse', even as it witnesses to the hope of resurrection. Stubbs writes:

> A white marble statue depicts him rising in his graveclothes ... the image was taken while Donne was still alive, and he had designed it carefully himself. He orchestrated a masterly death. Throughout his many illnesses, his mind never

---

[4]   John Donne, (John Carey, ed.) *John Donne*, p. 403.

[5]   David L. Edwards, *John Donne: Man of Flesh and Spirit* (London and New York, 2001), p. 275.

[6]   Ben Saunders, *Desiring Donne: Poetry, Sexuality and Interpretation* (Cambridge, Mass. and London, 2006), p. 166.

tired: he could read and write from his sickbed. During his last days he felt strong enough to pose for one last portrait, and arranged a resurrection scene. He ordered charcoal fires to be lit in his official residence, a spacious house lying just to the south of the Cathedral itself. The braziers gave the scene a Purgatorial fog. With this stage set, the dying man stood facing east with his winding sheet about him, knotted at head and foot. The picture was drawn on a life-size wooden board, then copied for the coverpiece of Deaths Duel. Nicholas Stone, who carved the subsequent statue used this illustration as his guide. But he was kinder on Donne than Donne himself had allowed the first, unknown artist to be. The mason gave slightly more flesh to the cheekbones, tidied the beard and moustache, eased the drawn smile; relaxed the closed eyes.[7]

In John Donne we have someone who is the ultimate example of a lover of death, a necrophile, as Jantzen understands it.

In this chapter I pay tribute to her and especially her book *Becoming Divine* by engaging with the poet. I show how John Donne, in so many ways, is the epitome of the masculinist symbolic she describes and seeks to disrupt. Not just in his thorough preoccupation with death; in other ways too. After he turned to religion, he anticipated the other world of a bodily resurrection and union with Christ beyond death; and throughout his life he wrote of women's bodies in ways that betray the gendered imaginary that assumed the body of the woman was there to be dominated and subdued. When he thought of birth, or 'natality', it was intimately tied up with death – 'a winding sheet' as we have seen: a time of real danger which carried the reminder that 'we are born to die'.[8] In so many ways his poetry and sermons profoundly bear out Jantzen's words that this is a 'text' of Western theology and philosophy belonging to 'the Western intellectual tradition [which] is obsessed with death and other worlds, a violent obsession that is interwoven with a masculinist drive for mastery'.[9]

Jantzen's book *Becoming Divine* has had a real influence on me. It is a brave, intelligent book that sets its sights high to begin something new within a philosophical tradition that Jantzen knew well, and had struggled with throughout her academic career. It had such an influence, that when I first picked up John Donne's poetry after finishing *Becoming Divine* it was with a sense of unease, which quickly turned to the question: and so must I now not read such work again?

This chapter gives me the opportunity to explore my response to Jantzen's thesis as a woman working full time as a priest in the Church of England (have I learned to 'play men's roles by men's rules?'[10] and finding myself often struggling

---

[7]   John Stubbs, *Donne: The Reformed Soul* (London, New York and Toronto, 2006), p. xx.

[8]   Grace Jantzen, *Becoming Divine: Towards a Feminist Philosophy of Religion* (Manchester, 1988), p. 131ff.

[9]   Jantzen, *Becoming Divine*, p. 129.

[10]   Jantzen, *Becoming Divine*, p. 10.

within the very symbolic order that Jantzen seeks to dismantle – that she, following Lacan, describes as designating 'the broad conceptual patterns of civilization'[11] which shapes culture and life through art, through the discourses of law, science, economics, and religion.[12] And yet I am also captured by Donne's passion and the way he struggles to understand himself and his relationship with God and Jesus Christ. Much of his writing stirs me profoundly. In it I find a *jouissance*, a surfeit of desire that can only be represented through art – as he clearly understood himself. Ben Saunders has called him a theorist of desire par excellence, saying that '[w]hile his work cannot be approached in the manner of a philosophical treatise, Donne is one of the greatest theorists of desire to write in English, and he repays scrutiny as such'.[13]

Donne found his home within the contested world of the Christian church and ministry of his day – contested passionately and dangerously at the time. A poem entitled 'Show me deare Christ, thy Spouse, so bright and clear' (which Edwards comments is 'so unconventional that it must be kept almost entirely secret, surviving in a single copy')[14] hints at the fiercely conflictual changing ecclesiastical scene of Donne's day. And then there are his own changing desires in the light of his hope for eternal life, a hope that became more real as his life progressed. Jantzen's desire to 'become divine' means certain specific things; she envisages a goal and end very different to that imagined by Donne. For me it is a real dilemma. It would be wonderful to be able to discuss with her the ground I cover here. Her response in conversation would be as enjoyable as any real engagement with her ever was. Though I suspect Donne would get short shrift!

That is by way of an introduction. The chapter will be structured in this way: I will examine selected extracts from Donne's work to illustrate how he would be well within Jantzen's sights as confirming and extending the Western masculinist symbolic – in three different areas: his writing about love, sex and women; his preoccupation with death; his concern for the soul and anticipation of the after-life. He was a complex man and his writing is complex, stirring very different reactions in his critical audience – as Saunders comments, 'Donne has always divided his readers, and not just against one another but against themselves'.[15] There's a wide and diverse literature on him, and I've mainly drawn on the following: Ben Saunders, Catherine Belsey, David L. Edwards, J. C. Bald, and John Stubbs, and using Grierson and Carey for textual references.

---

[11]   Jantzen, *Becoming Divine*, p. 10.
[12]   Jantzen, *Becoming Divine*, p. 10.
[13]   Saunders, *Desiring Donne*, p. 2.
[14]   Edwards, *John Donne*, p. 242.
[15]   Saunders, *Desiring Donne*, p. 20.

Love, Sex and Women

> Licence my roaving hands, and let them go,
> Before, behind, between, above, below.
> O my America! My new-found-land,
> My kingdome, safeliest when with one man man'd,
> My Myne of precious stones, My Emperie,
> How blest am I in this discovering thee!
> To enter in these bonds, is to be free;
> Then where my hand is set, my seal shall be.

You can imagine the field day that Grace would have with this! Lines from the elegy 'Going to Bed',[16] which Donne wrote with Ovid's *Amores* I.5 in mind, and which is replete with imagery of the colonial realities of Donne's day. Grace discusses feminist standpoint epistemology[17] and draws on Patricia Hill Collins' concept of 'interlocking systems of oppression' which together form a 'matrix of domination', and how this has helped feminist analysts such as Schiebinger and Anne McClintock understand further the discourses and practices of imperialism as 'they are constitutive of the consciousness of European industrial modernity'.[18] A crucial element to this was the way in which lands were feminized 'virgin territory' as they were conquered. Donne's poem (and others, such as 'The Sunne Rising' in which he writes: '"She" is all States, and all Princes, I, / Nothing else is') betrays his gendered imagination where, sexually, the man conquers the land, penetrating the virgin new-found-land, exploiting its passive riches and precious stones. This is a man, standing in all his phallic glory, who 'discovers' and enters 'Rich Nature [who] hath in women wisely made / Two purses, and their mouths aversely laid' (from 'Loves Progress'), and who covers the woman when she is uncovered. And, moreover, in this lies freedom – 'To enter in these bonds, is to be free' – freedom from what? Well, Grace would argue that this bears out her comment: 'In this fantasy of omnipotence, and in particular in the claiming of mastery of his mother, lies a significant origin of the fantasy of male superiority over the female and all that can be identified with her: "mother" nature, most obviously, but also all "others" of race, sexuality, or class who are also often feminized'.[19]

The freedom that Donne claims (at the expense of women) is the freedom of the fantasy that structures the male desire to be omnipotent, free from the bonds of the material – the world, the flesh and the devil – all that prevents them, in short, from becoming immortal like God, from becoming divine.

---

[16]   John Donne, *The Poems of John Donne*, H. J. C. Grierson (ed.) (Oxford, London, New York, Toronto, 1933), p. 106.

[17]   Jantzen, *Becoming Divine*, p. 121ff.

[18]   Jantzen, *Becoming Divine*, p. 126.

[19]   Jantzen, *Becoming Divine*, p. 35.

Well, Grace – yes! It's difficult to disagree with you, when we consider the terrible cost to so many of the Western colonial civilization that caused (told and) untold destruction and suffering on so many since Donne's day. Who could argue when you write that divinity should be:

> that which is most to be respected and valued – *means* mutuality, bodiliness, diversity, and materiality, then … [i]nstead of the mastery over the earth which is rapidly bringing about its destruction there would be reverence and sensitivity; instead of seeing domination as godlike we would recognize it as utterly contrary to divinity. A symbolic in which what is divine, what is of ultimate value and worth, cannot be defined as separable from the material universe and its diversity but rather must be constitutive of it and constituted by it, would no longer permit the attitudes of domination fostered by a symbolic of cosmic dualism.[20]

Donne is guilty as charged. So why do I still read such poems? I find them dead sexy, that's why. I agree with Saunders that '[i]t is an awkward fact of Donne studies that while his representations of women have often been regarded as sexist, they have equally been praised as "extraordinarily self-reflexive in relation to gender", as protofeminist, and even as positively erotic: in short, not sexist, but sexy'.[21] These poems cannot be taken at face-value: they are not always what they seem. Donne revelled in his own cleverness, and was often pursuing a theme or subject that is not the one that is immediately obvious. There is humour here, too, in Donne, against the range of emotion and mood which incorporates the deep depression of the 'Nocturnall' and the flirtatious homo-erotic poem letters and sonnets he wrote to various young men.[22] Humour that leaves me delighted as Donne traces the anatomy of desire in poems such as 'Going to Bed'. Belsey, following Lacan, argues that unlike the Ovid poem with which Donne is engaging, 'Nothing, in short, *happens*: nothing sexual, that is'.[23] Donne is writing not about sex but about desire: '[w]hat is mapped by the text is not a body at all, not the fullness of a presence, but the unrepresented gaze as the symbol of an absence, the lack that precipitates desire'.[24] She shows how Donne's subject is not the body of the woman and sex (as it is in Ovid's poem) but his own wit as he claims mastery of the practice of desire.[25] Donne is presenting '… an intricate, knotty, difficult, dazzling formulation of desire'.[26] Saunders too highlights the way Donne explicitly works with the theme – he provocatively '[hopes] to demonstrate that

---

[20]   Jantzen, *Becoming Divine*, p. 269.

[21]   Saunders, *Desiring Donne*, p. 114.

[22]   Donne, *The Poems of John Donne*, p. 180ff.

[23]   Belsey, 'John Donne's Worlds of Desire', in Andrew Mousley (ed.) *John Donne*, Basingstoke and New York, 1999), pp. 63–80, p. 66, her emphasis.

[24]   Belsey, 'John Donne's Worlds of Desire', p. 67.

[25]   Belsey, 'John Donne's Worlds of Desire', p. 68.

[26]   Belsey, 'John Donne's Worlds of Desire', p. 70.

Donne's theorizations of desire are at least as sophisticated as those of the twentieth century and may even show up some of the limitations of Lacanian orthodoxy ... regarding the condition we call "love"'.[27] Whereas for Lacan, desire is premised on lack, Saunders argues that Donne confronts 'the impossibility of permanent satisfaction' more actively, exploring the creativity of fantasy.[28] Saunders says that Donne understood that 'all our joys are but fantasticall' (from 'The Dreame'); that fantasy structures desire. To give another example, at the end of the poem 'The Expostulation', after Donne has agonized about whether his female love object will be faithful or not in a highly complex exploration of the creation and sustaining of desire, the poet concludes with an assertion of the importance of art in generating and regenerating love:

> Loue was as subt'illy catch'd, as a disease;
> But being gott, it is a treasure sweete,
> Which to defend is harder then to get
> And ought not bee prophan'd on either part,
> For though t'is gott by chance, t'is kept by art.

Saunders comments on this poem: 'It is, I think, a perfect response to the psychoanalytic account of love as narcissistic fantasy to say ... that in that case love is an art form: the supreme fiction, indeed ... that falling in love constitutes the most creative use of nothing that anyone can make'.[29]

Becoming Divine is at heart an ethical book: Jantzen wants her readers to respond to a new herethics, a new way of relating to the world and to others; one not based on the necrophilic symbolic of the old world, but on natality. She writes with passion and you can hear her desire as she engages with the work of Levinas, Kristeva, Irigaray and others, drawing on them to find the psychoanalytic tools to dismantle and disrupt the masculinist imaginary, its necrophilic symbolic and social order which has such deep roots in dominant religion. Instead '[t]he symbolic of natality, with its insistence on embodied interdependence in a web of relationships and flourishing in diversity offers a way to think otherwise, a herethics in the face of the natals, becoming divine together'.[30] This ethical passion I share – and Jantzen's use of 'natality' captures my imagination. I want, though, to continue to explore desire with Donne – which is not an ethical enterprise at all but rather an aesthetic one, and does entail engaging with a range of emotion, triggered often by fear of death and loss, and by the pleasurable and painful relations of gender, sex and difference. I feel in me the urge to ask of Jantzen permission to do so, which is perhaps indicative of the strength of passion with which she advocates 'natality' as an ethical imperative, sometimes, it seems, to the exclusion of other approaches

---

27 Belsey, 'John Donne's Worlds of Desire', p. 77.
28 Belsey, 'John Donne's Worlds of Desire', p. 79.
29 Saunders, *Desiring Donne*, p. 184.
30 Jantzen, *Becoming Divine*, p. 243.

which find food for thought in the very 'necrophilic' traditions of art and culture
that she wishes to disrupt. Turning to Kristeva, Jantzen writes of the celebration
of the Eucharist, following Kristeva in describing it as '... a sanitized sacrifice
which ... set[s] clear demarcations and "boundaries to the infinite", and does so in
a context which not merely suppresses the drives but rather give them opportunity
for expression in art, liturgy, ritual – which none the less are once again disciplined
to the service of the symbolic'. She quotes Kristeva that 'Jouissance is thus not
so much forbidden as regulated',[31] claiming that it is 'endlessly recuperated to the
paternal symbolic invested in necrophilia'. And so Jantzen believes that 'religion
can celebrate motherhood, inspire great music and literature, be a patron of the
arts, and in so doing contain and set boundaries to what might otherwise subvert it,
thereby making it safe. Thus the real violence is the violence to the semiotic, and
ultimately to the maternal body and all that is conceptually linked with it'.[32] And
it's here that I part company with Jantzen, for my experience of the Eucharist, and
some of the sublime and powerful music and art of the Christian tradition is not
that it is regulated and safe, but rather stirring and passionate and full of desire, and
more complex in terms of gender than Jantzen would recognize (see her comment,
'[a] philosophy of religion which took the model of flourishing seriously would
necessarily be a political philosophy which confronted social and economic issues
not as marginal philosophical interests but as central to philosophical thought. It
would, in short, be feminist').[33] Saunders thinks that Donne, given his social and
historical context, was profoundly interested in the 'relationship between textuality
and the "facts" of sexual difference' and that he even deliberately exploited the
conditions of textuality in order to challenge some of the misogynistic conceptions
of gender of his time:

> In making this last claim, I am flying in the face of much recent and important
> criticism. Of course, I am not attempting to get all of Donne's works off the
> misogynistic hook, as it were; nor am I unaware of the tendency within critical
> and philosophical thought for masculine perspectives to reproduce themselves
> as 'neutral' or 'ungendered' ... Nor, finally, am I trying to transform Donne into
> a seventeenth-century version of Judith Butler.[34]

But Saunders opens the way to read Donne as someone who played with gender
difference, sexual desire and fantasy, allowing the reader to interpret the poetry
according to their own desires. Saunders' humorous comment about sexual
fantasies can apply to other interpretations that take 'gender' as their base:

---

[31]   Jantzen, *Becoming Divine*, p. 78.
[32]   Jantzen, *Becoming Divine*, p. 198.
[33]   Jantzen, *Becoming Divine*, p. 169.
[34]   Saunders, *Desiring Donne*, p. 125.

Grounding our interpretations of sexual fantasies in notions of gender is not something we can choose not to do – but it might be likened to attempting to hang a picture while standing on a rocking chair.[35]

Death and Dying

Žižek writes:

> Psychoanalysis chances upon the fundamental ontological question: 'Why is there something instead of nothing?' … In a key passage from 'Subversion of the Subject and Dialectic of Desire', [Lacan] answers the question 'What am I?':

> 'I' am in the place from which a voice is heard clamouring 'the universes is a defect in the purity of Non-Being' And not without reason, for by protecting itself this place makes Being itself languish. This place is called *Jouissance*, and it is the absence of this that makes the universe vain.[36]

Why is there something instead of nothing? I suspect Grace would lose patience with this question, and see it as another example of how 'Western civilization, dominated by masculinist structures, has had both a fascination with and a dread of death'.[37] For her, *jouissance* would, I think, come close to *amor mundi* – her reading of Hannah Arendt's 'respect for and fostering of the natality of all human beings and of the world which is our home'.[38] Such respect entails love, obligation and freedom as the subject chooses action for love of the world, and enters the public world and:

> Here we have an altogether more robust sense of what desire can be than is found in traditional philosophy of religion: not a tumultuous passion which can scarcely be controlled, but a free and deliberate dedication to action for love of the world, arising out of an imaginary of natality.[39]

This affirmation of life and flourishing opens up divine horizons in which difference and alterities are honoured and in which 'the aim of the divine incarnation in every woman and man' is furthered.[40]

Which isn't to say that people need never consider death: Jantzen doesn't deny the importance of philosophical and religious reflections on mortality, but insists

---

[35]   Saunders, *Desiring Donne*, p. 137.

[36]   Slavoj Žižek, *The Plague of Fantasies* (London and New York, 1997), pp. 48–9.

[37]   Jantzen, *Becoming Divine*, p. 129.

[38]   Jantzen, *Becoming Divine*, p. 152.

[39]   Jantzen, *Becoming Divine*, p. 154.

[40]   Jantzen, *Becoming Divine*, p. 157.

on the necessity to put these reflections within an imaginary of natality, which is about life *before* death. An over-preoccupation with death merely betrays 'the deep misogyny of Western culture, fear, dread, and fascination with the maternal body, which is however, its human foundation'.[41] Let's return to the passage from 'Death's Duel' with which this chapter began. It's a classic example of what Jantzen means, with its hideous image that confuses a dead foetus with the living child who is still-born from death, *exitus a morte*. Donne locates the very reality of death in the womb, at the source of the life-giving power of the mother: 'being dead we kill her that gave us our first life' – a life of vegetation. You can hear Grace saying that such words are truer that Donne would have realized. He is guilty, along with the rest of the masculinist tradition, of matricide, the fundamental and ongoing matricide that has to be carried out for the Symbolic to be sustained. It is sustained more than anywhere in the church: Jantzen agrees with Mary Daly's insights that birth has been appropriated by the church: 'women suffer childbirth but men have control of the baptism of new birth; women cook actual meals but men preside over the Eucharist; priests wear skirts and lace and frills, and out of their supreme concern for women inculcate in us humility as our first virtue'.[42]

These are words delivered from the pulpit by a man who knew he was going to die soon, to a congregation which included the king, and who were profoundly shocked by his deathly appearance. Donne knew what he was doing; he knew the impact his presence and words would have. It's fair to assume that he deliberately wanted to shock his congregation into a profound sense of their own mortality. Death was there, all around them: it was a reality of life. These were dangerous times; plague and disease were commonplace; infant and maternal mortality a daily occurrence. Religion was dangerous: Donne's own brother Henry died as a young man in Newgate prison in 1593, there because of his association with the Roman Catholic priest Harrington, who was executed for treason the same year. Donne had written, only five or six years before he died, his *Devotions Upon Emergent Occasions* as he recovered from a life-threatening illness – and there too, in the face of death, he talked of birth, addressing Charles again – Prince Charles, to whom the book is dedicated; and remembering that Charles' father King James had supported Donne as he came to be ordained:

> I have had three births; one, naturall, when I came into the world; one supernaturall, when I entred into the Ministery; and now, a preternaturall birth, in returning to Life from this Sicknes. In my second Birth, your Highnesse Royall Father vouchsafed mee his Hand, not onely to sustaine mee in it, but to lead mee to it. In this last Brith, I my selfe am borne a Father: This Child of mine, this Booke, comes into the world, from mee, and with mee. And therefore, I presume (as I did the Father to the Father) to present the Sonne to the Sonne.[43]

---

41   Jantzen, *Becoming Divine*, p. 141.

42   Jantzen, *Becoming Divine*, p. 143.

43   Donne, *Devotions Upon Emergent Occasions*, p. 3.

This book of meditations upon death is presented by Donne as the product of a birth, a creative act that is born out of the deathly illness he has suffered. It is probable that Charles would have recalled these words as he listened to the sermon that also talked of birth as an *exitus a morte, in morte and per morte*, as Death's Duel speaks. Donne sees birth as only secondarily into life – into, remember, a life of vegetation. Primarily, birth is birth from, into, and through death. In Christ death was conquered, Donne believed:

> One short sleepe past, wee wake eternally,
> And death shall be no more, death, thou shalt die.[44]

Given the ever-presence of death in the midst of life, I do not believe that it is surprising that there was such a preoccupation with it and such a desire to find a way through the enormity of grief and pain that profound loss entailed. The desire to find that there was something, not nothing, was an impulse that was real to Donne. He desired to be re-begot, not of absence, darknesse, death; things which are not but rather in Christ to a life that was more real than the present precarious existence. It was an over-riding question; how to counter the nothingness of death. And one way was to bring to birth new books, or poems, or writing: the urge to create was an expression of defiance against death, for Donne, a note of *jouissance*.

Saunders writes that after Lacan, 'desire is not really "something" at all. Instead, it is the ever present nothing that all our demands, ambitions, wishes, and fantasies are designed to conceal',[45] and he argues that Donne anticipates 'the ways in which Lacan's most advanced and sophisticated conceptions of desire as structured by and oriented toward a representational blank or absence are anticipated by Donne in some of his more complex theorizations of love'.[46] More than this, I would argue; for Saunders does not examine at all Donne's religious and holy works. Yes, Donne finds in creative production an assertion, a stand against the nothingness of life in his poetry, but in his religious work he goes to the heart of the nothingness of death, and finds in Christ on the cross the capitulation of death. His art – his poetry, his writing, his friendships – were all natal moments, achieved in the face of death. I find no trouble in saying of Donne that he fulfils Arendt's words:

> The life span of man [sic] running toward death would inevitably carry everything human to ruin and destruction if it were not for the faculty of interrupting it and beginning something new, a faculty which is inherent in action like an ever-present reminder that men, though they must die, are not born in order to die but in order to begin.[47]

---

[44] Donne, *The Poems of John Donne*, p. 297.
[45] Saunders, *Desiring Donne*, p. 171.
[46] Saunders, *Desiring Donne*, p. 173.
[47] Jantzen, *Becoming Divine*, p. 135.

Donne's creative work, like so much art, music and literature within the Christian traditions, can be understood in these terms of natality, of bringing to birth something from nothing. The main difference between Jantzen's use of the term and Donne's is that Donne would claim that it is upon the pattern of the death and resurrection of Christ, and use the language of 'rebirth'.

The Soul and the Body

John Donne, for many years – probably from the 1590s – was the good friend of Magdalen Herbert. To her he dedicated 'La Corona', a cycle of sonnets that rehearse the life, death, resurrection and ascension of Christ. His admiration for her can be heard in the words of the sonnet he wrote linking her name to that of Mary Magdalene, 'Increase their number, Lady, and their fame: To their Devotion, add your Innocence'. He preached at her funeral in 1627, and Izaak Walton says he wept.[48] In that sermon Donne wrote of the relationship between soul and body, indicating, I think, that although it was certainly true that the soul was of prime importance within the scheme of his Christian faith, the resurrection of the body was of real importance too. When Jantzen draws on Adriana Caverero, and quotes her to say: '*True* life is the life of the soul. Bodily life is *mere* life, of an altogether inferior order. What emerges is the persistent "living for death" that constitutes one of the most consistent principles in the philosophical tradition of the West', she agrees that the philosophical tradition has been replete with hostility to the body and determination to master it and the material world of which it is a part.[49] When I read Donne here, I'm not so sure that it is a clear cut case of dualism:

> Shee expected that; dissolution of body, and soule; and rest in both, from the incumbrances, and tentations of this world. But yet, shee is in expectation still; Still a Reversionarie; and a Reversionary upon a long life; The whole world must die, before she come to a possession of the Reversion; which is a Glorified body in the Resurrection. … But when all wee, shall have been mellow'd in the earth, many yeares, or chang'd in the Aire, in the twinkling of an eye, (God knows which) That body upon which you tread now, That body which now, whilst I speake, is mouldring, and crumbling into lesse, and lesse dust, and so hath some motion, though no life, That body, which was the Tabernacle of a holy Soule, and a Temple of the holy Ghost, That body that was eyes to the blinde, and hands, and feet to the lame, whilst it liv'd, and being dead, is so still, by having beene so lively an example … That body at last, shal have her last expectation satisfied, and dwell bodily, with that Righteousnesse, in these new Heavens, and new Earth, for ever, and ever, and ever, and infinite, and super infinite evers. … Beloved, every good Soule is the Spouse of Christ. And this

---

[48]   Walton, *Lives*, p. 267.

[49]   Jantzen, *Becoming Divine*, p. 137, emphasis in the original.

good Soule, being thus laid downe to sleepe in his peace, His left hand under her head, gathering, and composing, and preserving her dust, for future Glory, His right hand embracing her, assuming, and establishing her soule in present Glory, in his name.[50]

As with all affirmations (Stanley Spencer's *The Resurrection, Cookham* comes to mind) of the resurrection of the body – a doctrine that won't seem to disappear from Christian eschatology – we are here, I think, at a refusal of dualism. One way to understand Donne's belief about the body and soul and how they are related intimately is to consider, by way of parallel, how he intermixed the spiritual and erotic in his writing, in often extremely shocking ways. Even here is the suggestion that Lady Danvers' body is now being embraced by Christ as husband – what *is* his right hand doing? The sexual and spiritual, the soul and body mix in Donne's poetry in ways that betray a different understanding to ours. Saunders argues that '[t]he sacred and the secular are so closely entwined as to be inseparable'[51] and draws on Debora Shuger's work to show how Donne used sexual imagery to shape spiritual desire – that we the reader are encouraged to 'take an eroticized devotional pleasure in the text'.[52] It's there in his sonnet 'Batter my heart', where the final lines explicitly use fantasies of captivity and yearning, even of divine rape to shape the relationship between God and the subject. Saunders describes this rightly as a transgressive erotic that applies as much to Donne's divine poems as to his *Songs and Sonets*. 'Show me deare Christ', with its image of the spouse, the Church, lying open to all men is another example. When such transgressive material is read with an appreciation of Donne's wicked sense of humour, the laugh is often on us and our puritan attitudes.

I am suggesting that a too-easy polarization between body and soul might be as much a mistake as finding a rigid division, in Donne's work, between the spiritual and the erotic – or indeed, the common split that's made between Jack Donne and Dr Donne. *Becoming Divine* assumes such a dualism between body and soul within the Christian tradition, and upon that assumption, in part, is build the imaginary of natality, and a sense of the divine as not 'a 'God out there', beyond the realm of human love and action, but rather as within the horizon and constitution of our selves and our world, within and between 'natals'.[53] Jantzen locates divinity in mutuality, bodiliness, diversity and materiality,[54] and indicates that she has no need of a realist concept of God. To become divine is to establish a community in which all flourish, physically and materially. For me the desire is there for this, this kind of becoming divine – but also I desire union with 'God out there' – even

---

[50]   John Donne, *The Sermons of John Donne: Volume X*, George Potter and Evelyn Simpson (eds) (Berkeley, 1962) 8.91.

[51]   Saunders, *Desiring Donne*, p. 36.

[52]   Saunders, *Desiring Donne*, p. 58.

[53]   Jantzen, *Becoming Divine*, p. 153.

[54]   Jantzen, *Becoming Divine*, p. 269.

as I struggle with what that means. I also find myself increasingly valuing the concept of the soul; not as a free-floating entity that escapes the body at death, but as something like the seat within of *jouissance* and creativity; and which cannot but be material, shaping my body and my appearance, even as it also transcends identity and self. Reading John Donne stimulates me – intellectually, spiritually and physically – to become divine, in ways other to that proposed by Jantzen.

Conclusion

I've imagined, as I've been writing, talking this over with Grace, or receiving a response in that careful and distinctive hand-writing. I can sense her frustration at my reluctance to leave the Christian tradition; a realist understanding of God; the centrality I give to Christ, his death and resurrection. Her arguments are persuasive; particularly when it comes to the destruction that humanity has and continues to cause on the created order and our inability to take responsibility for ensuring the survival of this beautiful world. The idea of natality is a wonderful and hopeful ethic that should permeate all our thinking and doing. Yes, we need to have a model of flourishing, whose 'spirituality is holistic, rather than the privatized, subjectivized spirituality so characteristic of contemporary Christianity'.[55] There is much that contemporary Christianity – and the Christianity of John Donne – is guilty of, and an ethical passion to engage politically to create trustworthy communities between peoples and between humanity and the natural world is often sadly and sorely absent. So yes, Grace, I'm with you most of the way, and continue to be challenged and stimulated by *Becoming Divine.*

One of my fantasies as I've been writing is of John Donne and Grace Jantzen sitting down at the feast of heaven, and arguing it all through. It's difficult to imagine! They would find little to talk about, I suspect, with such different passions and desires. To become divine or to become Christ-like? Donne stimulates greater understanding of the nature of desire, with a breadth and depth that has seldom been surpassed, with his eyes fixed, ultimately, on death and dying; Jantzen reminds us of the ethical imperatives of natality, in a continual state of becoming, of being born, of creating new possibilities in a world that too much tends to death. But perhaps they could agree on this, that the creative impulse is primary. In that new moment when something is born, it is then that we know that it is not nothing from which we come and to which we go.

---

[55]   Jantzen, *Becoming Divine*, p. 170.

Chapter 5
'In the Name of Life!'
Psychoanalysis and Grace Jantzen's
Critique of Philosophy

Jeremy Carrette

At the beginning of her proposed multi-volume study, *Death and the Displacement of Beauty*, Grace Jantzen wrote:

> It will be important in a later volume of this project to explore more fully the centrality of the death drive in psychoanalytical theory, one of the master discourses of modernity. What I want to emphasize here is that these psychoanalysts, and writers who follow them, present the death drive and aggressivity as constitutive of 'human nature', whether or not they use that term. In their thinking, to become a subject, to enter the human world of language and the symbolic, is always already to have a structural desire for death.[1]

This intended examination of psychoanalysis in a later volume was crucially important to her entire project, because Jantzen built her critique of Western philosophy from psychoanalysis; and it formed the central part of what she called the 'therapy of philosophy'.[2] Psychoanalysis was one of the central methodological perspectives and the underlying analogy of her critique. In the papers she left after her death, Jantzen's original Routledge proposal for the intended six-volume study mapped out – as she promised in the first published volume – a fifth volume on psychoanalysis; which was to be entitled *The Desire of Psychoanalysis*.[3] There were

---

[1]   Jantzen, G. *Foundations of Violence Volume 1: Death and the Displacement of Beauty* (London, 2004), p. 25.

[2]   Jantzen, *Foundations of Violence*, p. 19.

[3]   I worked on the remaining archive of Grace Jantzen's papers in February 2007 and thank the British Academy and Tina McCrae for supporting me in different ways in this work. Only volume one, *Foundations of Violence* (2004), appeared during Grace Jantzen's life and two posthumous volumes *Violence to Eternity* and *A Place of Springs* are forthcoming (London: Routledge, 2008 and London, Routledge, 2009). There were different versions of her six-volume proposal for Routledge and in some early versions the sections on psychoanalysis formed part of a section for a volume on modernity, rather than a separate volume on psychoanalysis.

three provisionally entitled chapters: Chapter 1, 'The Death Drive and Freud's Fear of Blood'; Chapter 2, 'Aggression and the Bad Breast', presumably on Melanie Klein; and, finally, Chapter 3 'Birth and the Powers of Horror', presumably on Kristeva's work, the beginning of which can be seen in a late essay on Kristeva.[4] There was no evidence of any draft material on these topics and clearly it did not feature in the material she had left for potential posthumous publication.

This essay is my own critical development of Grace Jantzen's own ventures into psychoanalysis, which were left incomplete. It is thus, in one small part, my tribute to her work and that unpublished fifth volume, not least because it was the intellectual point of our original meeting and a theme to which we constantly returned. In this essay, I will seek to carry out a series of close readings of Jantzen's work on psychoanalysis in order to reveal the central argument of her *Death and the Displacement of Beauty* in relation to psychoanalysis. I will seek to show how the gendered preoccupations with the death drive covered an alternative. These excavations are important, not only in outlining the issue for psychoanalytical thought and Jantzen's unpublished volume, but because such an archaeology shows the extent of the links between death, gender and the suppressed dimension of life. My own reconstruction will explore some of the key texts within the psychoanalytical tradition in order to show how the alternative of the life drive can be rescued from the male preoccupations with death. Such an examination of the attitudes towards life and death will entail a disentangling of sexuality and pleasure and the gendered fear of losing control.

Psychoanalysis: Double Readings[5]

It is clear from Jantzen's work that psychoanalysis holds an ambivalent place; it is therapist and patient, liberator and oppressor. Indeed, in her volume of theoretical mappings for a new perspective in the philosophy of religion, *Becoming Divine* (the text I see as the theoretical clearing for her later philosophical thought), she tried 'to show how the psychoanalytical account of the development of subjectivity both subverts traditional philosophy of religion and yet must itself be subverted to make space for women, the urgency of which becomes especially apparent in its linkage of women and death, and the efforts of men to achieve mastery of both'.[6] Up to this point in her work, psychoanalysis had only featured briefly in relation to issues of

---

4   See Jantzen's chapter, 'Death, then, how could I yield to it? Kristeva's mortal visions', in M. Joy, K. O'Grady and J. L. Poxon (eds), *Religion in French Feminist Thought* (London, 2003), pp. 117–30.

5   Grace Jantzen, *Becoming Divine: Towards a Feminist Philosophy of Religion* (Manchester, 1998), p. 61.

6   Jantzen, *Becoming Divine*, p. 33.

reductionism.[7] It only marked the borders of her thinking on mysticism in relation to wider critical studies within feminism, but her knowledge of Freud was significant; a fact testified by her library collection and extensive notations on the texts. The shift from Freud as reductionist and misogynist to that of therapist of Western philosophy almost certainly occurs through her reading of French feminism, as exemplified in her 2003 essay on Kristeva, and its engagement with Lacanian theory; but, as we shall see, the double reading and ambivalence always remain.

Psychoanalysis becomes valuable for Jantzen's work in *Becoming Divine* (1998) and *Foundations of Violence* (2004) because the hypothesis of the unconscious offers a central critique of the Cartesian subject and the language of repression provides a way of analysing Western philosophy and its obsessions and phobias.[8] Indeed, the dynamics of repression, symptom, neurosis and displacement are the ways she reads natality and necrophilia in the Western tradition. *Becoming Divine* takes on the Cartesian subject by enlisting Lacan's model of the divided subject. As Jantzen writes in summary: '[A]ccording to Lacan the subject, far from being an autonomous self, is constituted by a rupture, an internalized otherness. It involves the enactment of the subject/ (m)other division. We are a long way off from Descartes's confidently rational *cogito*'.[9] Jantzen is under no doubt about the radical implications of this position for the philosophy of religion, and Swinburne's philosophy of religion in particular, especially when divine attributes are theorized in terms of a Lacanian subject.[10] This position is underlined in her understanding that 'no topic in the philosophy of religion, traditional or feminist, remains unaffected once we recognise that we are not straightforward, rational, autonomous Cartesian egos, but are embodied, sexuate persons in a web of life, caught up in unconscious desires and fears'.[11] But the need for a double reading becomes apparent for Jantzen after closer critical reading of Lacan. As she writes: 'But if Lacanian theory of the destabilized self has drastic implications for traditional philosophy of religion, it does not leave feminist thought untroubled, either'.[12] Reflecting on Lacan's essay 'God and the Jouissance of the Women', Jantzen reads the phallic order of language

---

[7]   There is one brief reference in *God's World, God's Body* (London, 1984) p. 126, where Freud was mentioned, alongside Feuerbach and Marx, as one of the exponents of reductionism, a position that she believed was not compatible with Christian theology. Jantzen returns to this position in the later *Becoming Divine* when discussing the masters of reductionism, Feuerbach-Freud-Marx, in relation to the issue of projection (Jantzen, *Becoming Divine*, p. 77). There is another brief reference to psychoanalysis in Jantzen's 1995 study, *Power, Gender and Christian Mysticism* (Cambridge, 1995), p. 16, where she pointed to the critical re-evaluations of Freud in such works as Juliet Mitchell's classic text *Feminism and Psychoanalysis* (London, 1974).

[8]   Jantzen, *Becoming Divine*, p. 33ff; Jantzen, *Foundations of Violence*, pp. 4–6.

[9]   Jantzen, *Foundations of Violence*, p. 37.

[10]   Jantzen, *Becoming Divine*, p. 38; 49.

[11]   Jantzen, *Becoming Divine*, p. 42.

[12]   Jantzen, *Becoming Divine*, p. 38.

as 'a position of authority' and, rejecting both Kristeva and Irigaray, as one caught up in the masculinist symbolic.[13] As she argues: 'I want to challenge Lacan's account of the necessary maleness of language and subjectivity'[14]; something that also leads her to seriously question Kristeva.[15]

In a sharp critique of Lacan's engagement with women mystics, for example, she shows how it is not that women do not speak or 'do not/ cannot have language', but that men 'refuse to listen'.[16] In defence of Saint Teresa, against Lacan's 'begging' – 'on knees' – for women to speak about their pleasure, Jantzen eloquently reveals the silenced voices. Referring to Teresa, she pointed out: 'She did, after all, write many books which are easily attainable: if Lacan really wanted to know what she was experiencing, he might at least have taken the trouble to listen to what she herself said about it before saying that she "knew nothing about it"'.[17] Jantzen rightly questions whether Lacan wanted to understand either women or mysticism. It is this resistance to the phallic order of language that enables Jantzen to reflect upon natality and to offer necrophilia as a critical context for understanding male philosophical assumptions. It is also at this point that Jantzen can shift the analysis – 'even within the psychoanalytic structure'.[18] The masculinist position is not obvious or necessary and it is the dynamic of death that provides the opening edge of her critique.[19] According to Jantzen, Lacan, like Freud, links 'the death-drive with the entry into language', highlighting Lacan's insistence that 'death constitutes in the subject the eternalization of his desire'.[20] Death in Lacan and Freud is also linked to female sexuality. Jantzen highlights such associations in Freud's *The Future of Illusion* (1927), where the female is linked to chaos and death.[21]

Strikingly, in both *Becoming Divine* and *Foundations of Violence*, Jantzen notes that the death-drive is 'highly contested'[22] and draws attention to the fact that psychoanalysts 'disagreed among themselves about how' it should be 'understood'.[23] Importantly, Jantzen also recognises how these themes of death and female sexuality are also linked to religion.[24] It is not surprising, therefore, that Jantzen's *Foundations of Violence* includes a preliminary discussion of Freud's *Beyond the Pleasure Principle* (1920); as she both employs the psychoanalytical

---

[13]   Jantzen, *Becoming Divine*, p. 40.

[14]   Jantzen, *Becoming Divine*, p. 51; Hanneke Canters and Grace Jantzen, *Forever Fluid: A Reading of Luce Irigaray's Elemental Passions* (Manchester, 2005), p. 127.

[15]   Jantzen, 'Death, then, how could I yield to it?', p. 118.

[16]   Jantzen, *Becoming Divine*, p. 51.

[17]   Jantzen, *Becoming Divine*, p. 53.

[18]   Jantzen, *Becoming Divine*, p. 51.

[19]   Jantzen, 'Death, then, how could I yield to it?', p. 119.

[20]   Jantzen, *Becoming Divine*, p. 46.

[21]   Jantzen, *Becoming Divine*, p. 44.

[22]   Jantzen, *Becoming Divine*, p. 44.

[23]   Jantzen, *Foundations of Violence*, p. 24.

[24]   Jantzen, *Becoming Divine*, pp. 41, 45.

method and suspends it inside her own critique. The central claim, which would have no doubt been worked out in the proposed volume 5, was that in Freud's account of the death drive 'gender is never far away' and such theory is not 'the only way it could be done'.[25]

Aggression, violence and death have a gendered dimension in Freud, which is continued in Lacan and his feminist exponents. Jantzen is not assuming that death and aggressivity are only male concerns, but rather that they are 'a male preoccupation'.[26] It is here that Jantzen promises an examination of psychoanalysis in 'a later volume'.[27] This sketch of Jantzen's double reading[28] of psychoanalysis constitutes, with a few other brief associations, the unfinished mapping of the gendered nature of psychoanalysis and the need for further analysis. It is an analysis that she herself calls 'post-Freudian' and we are left to speculate as to how she would have developed such an analysis.[29]

If Jantzen seeks to offer the alternative of natality in place of the Western philosophy of necrophilia, we might ask where she would look for the alternative of natality in the psychoanalytical tradition, caught up as it is with death. This takes on added importance because she does not consider necrophilia to be necessary for the structure of psychoanalysis.[30] While she had identified that psychoanalysts after Freud have been ambivalent about the death drive, even as Klein, Lacan and Kristeva maintain such notions of aggression, she had not recovered the alternative voices.[31] In developing her thinking according to one possible trajectory, I will take the theme of Freud's death drive by linking it, first, to a question of gender and then show some of the possible alternative positions hidden in the literature.[32]

Death, Female Sexuality and Religion: Jantzen and Jonte-Pace

When considering how psychoanalysis wrestles with the dynamic of necrophilia, it is impossible to ignore the tensions of the death-drive thesis in Freud's *Beyond the Pleasure Principle* (1920) – the text in which he introduced the concept. The text leaves many unresolved questions, not only about the death drive but about how Freud's formation of the concept results from his inability to articulate or understand female experience. This is evidenced from the fact that Freud formed

---

[25]   Jantzen, *Foundations of Violence*, p. 23; Jantzen, 'Death, then, how could I yield to it?'

[26]   Jantzen, *Foundations of Violence*, p. 16.

[27]   Jantzen, *Foundations of Violence*, p. 25; quoted in full at the beginning of my essay.

[28]   According to Jantzen, this entails a close reading of the text through which one finds ruptures to open alternative readings (Jantzen, *Becoming Divine*, p. 61).

[29]   Jantzen, *Foundations of Violence*, p. 156.

[30]   Jantzen, *Becoming Divine*, p. 51; Jantzen, 'Death, then, how could I yield to it? Kristeva's mortal visions', p. 119.

[31]   Jantzen, *Foundations of Violence*, p. 156.

[32]   Jantzen, *Foundations of Violence*, p. 24.

and shaped his thinking on the death drive from a paper, acknowledged in one of his footnotes, by the Russian female psychoanalyst Sabrina Spielrein. Spielrein's 1912 essay 'Destruction as the Cause of Coming into Being' predates Freud's death drive theory by nine years, but more importantly contains aspects of birth and transformation that Freud did not register or comprehend.[33] Spielrein's paper takes the question of death and birth to the heart of sexual pleasure and the gendered position. It is from this basis that I will thus show, in line with Jantzen, how the death drive can be rejected through a critical reading of gender and sexuality, through an understanding of the life instinct, but we must first understand how death, gender and sexuality are linked together in the work of Freud and how the insights of Spielrein were ignored.

The gendered nature of Freud's texts have been a long concern of feminist theory, going back to such pivotal works as Juliet Mitchell's *Feminism and Psychoanalysis* (1974). However, surprisingly few, as Jonte-Pace confirms, have developed the gendered nature of the death drive and some of the gendered nature of its historical formation.[34] It is, however, in the heart of Freud's death-drive that we can unravel some extraordinary associations of gender in Jantzen's model of natality and necrophilia. This thematic was picked up by Diane Jonte-Pace in her unravelling of Freud's 'counterthesis' to the 'masterplot' of the Oedipus complex, which was a male ordered theory. In Jonte-Pace's 'counterthesis' we find Freud's constellation of a set of issues linking death, women/mothers and the afterlife, including ideas of the 'uncanny' [*unheimliche*] and Jewishness. Jantzen's work registers this 'counterthesis' of gendering death, and I am sure – as we had discussed this – it would have featured in the later volume. For Jonte-Pace the 'counter-thesis' is part of the cultural analytic of misogyny, which strikingly occurs in Freud's writings on religion.[35]

The counter-thesis remains part of Freud's unconscious and 'exists in half-glimpsed images and half-formulated ideas'.[36] It constitutes for Jonte-Pace Freud's 'navel' of the dream interpretation in his *Interpretation of Dreams*.[37] The unknown and 'unfathomable' and 'unplumbable' depth for Freud is registered through the analogy of the maternal link, 'the bodily mark of the passage through the maternal genitals and into the world'.[38] As Jonte-Pace argues:

> It is the site of connection to and separation from the mother that Freud cannot interpret. Freud's turning aside at the 'navel of the dream' is, in a sense, an acknowledgement of the limitations of the heroic paths of figures like Oedipus

---

[33]   S. Spielrein, (1912), 'Destruction as the Cause of Coming into Being', *Journal of Analytical Psychology*, 39 (1994): pp. 155–86.

[34]   Diane Jonte-Pace, *Speaking the Unspeakable: Religion, Misogyny and the Uncanny Mother in Freud's Cultural Texts* (Berkeley, 2000), p. 46.

[35]   Jonte-Pace, *Speaking the Unspeakable*, p. 2.

[36]   Jonte-Pace, *Speaking the Unspeakable*, p. 16.

[37]   Jonte-Pace, *Speaking the Unspeakable*, p. 29.

[38]   Jonte-Pace, *Speaking the Unspeakable*, p. 30.

and Aeneas. As such, it marks a moment at which Freud encounters and retreats from the limits of the Oedipal masterplot.[39]

These themes manifest themselves in Jonte-Pace's account of Freud's essay 'A Religious Experience' in 1928, where Freud responds to an American doctor's concern about the survival of the personality after death. The American doctor explains his crisis of faith and how he doubted his faith at the sight of 'a dead body of a woman'.[40] Freud reads this dead body as an erotic body and the absent God as a hated father. According to Jonte-Pace, Freud dismisses elements outside the Oedipal structure, such as ideas of the dead mother and the afterlife; and themes of matricide. It is this resistance that allows Jonte-Pace to recover such themes in Freud's texts.[41]

Following Pontalis,[42] Jonte-Pace recognises how sex is often substituted for death. The missing element for Jonte-Pace also links to the question of the after life and immortality. Her work recovers this cluster of themes through a close reading of Freud's work, but it is her chapter on death, mothers and the afterlife that overlaps with Jantzen's concerns. Jonte-Pace recovers 'the images of the dead mothers, images of mothers as instructors of death, and images of "uncanny" maternal bodies' in Freud's writings and their links to the afterlife and immortality.[43] These are part of the themes Freud 'initiates but resists', the unspeakable fantasies. They form part of Jantzen's necrophilic architecture of Western thought. The association of mother, death and the afterlife is part of the elision of 'tomb' and 'womb' in the male symbolic.[44] They are, in Freud's understanding, the 'uncanny' aspects of the female body at birth and death.[45] The cultural entanglement that Jonte-Pace and Jantzen recognise is the fear of mothers, female sexuality and misogynist fantasies within Western thought.[46] The text that gathers so many of these themes, and becomes the concern of Jonte-Pace and Jantzen, is Freud's *Beyond the Pleasure Principle*, which as Jonte-Pace notes, begins not with the Oedipal father, but with the 'physiological, biological or cellular "pulsion" toward death'.[47] The death drive for Freud is a drive to return to one's origins, where there were no points of tension and anxiety. Indeed, Freud writes: 'The aim of all life is death'.[48]

---

[39]   Jonte-Pace, *Speaking the Unspeakable*, p. 30.

[40]   Jonte-Pace, *Speaking the Unspeakable*, p. 30.

[41]   Jonte-Pace, *Speaking the Unspeakable*, p. 41.

[42]   Pontalis, J. B., 'On Death-Work in Freud, in the Self, in Culture' in Alan Roland (ed.), *Psychoanalysis, Creativity, and Literature*, trans. Susan Cohen (New York, 1978), p. 86.

[43]   Jonte-Pace, *Speaking the Unspeakable*, p. 46.

[44]   Jonte-Pace, *Speaking the Unspeakable*, p. 68.

[45]   Jantzen, 'Death, then, how could I yield to it?', p. 120.

[46]   Jonte-Pace, *Speaking the Unspeakable*, p. 142.

[47]   Jonte-Pace, *Speaking the Unspeakable*, pp. 48–9.

[48]   Freud, S., (1920), *Beyond the Pleasure Principle in On Metapsychology* (London: Penguin Freud Library Volume 2), [1984]1991, p. 311.

Both Jonte-Pace and Jantzen recall the discussion of the child's game alternating 'fort' (gone) and 'da' (here) as the child throws the cotton reel attached and retrieved by the cotton. According to Freud, this was the fantasy of controlling the absent and dead mother.[49] Jantzen's picks up what she calls the 'gendered necrophilia' of such an interpretation in Lacan's rendering of Freud's text as entering into language, through which the mother is controlled. As Lacan writes, 'Thus the symbol manifests itself first of all as the murder of the thing and this death constitutes in the subject the eternalization of desire'.[50] The critique of Freud and Lacan in reading the 'counterthesis' and the 'gendered necrophilia' respectively is evident, but what is perhaps required is to take this analysis one stage further inside the gendered politic of psychoanalysis. Jantzen's work goes beyond the 'analytic and the 'critical' paradigms that Jonte-Pace discusses in feminist psychoanalytical theory[51] and, after questioning the death drive as a defining feature of human nature, offers as an attempt to open her alternative position.[52]

We can follow Jantzen in questioning death as a central psychical drive of life by returning to Freud's assumed group of instincts of death as a gendered position. In response to Einstein's question to Freud, in their published correspondence in 1933, Freud articulates his theory:

> [W]e have come to suppose that this instinct is at work in every living creature and is striving to bring it to ruin and to reduce life to its original condition of inanimate matter. Thus it quite seriously deserves to be called a death instinct, while erotic instincts represent the effort to live. This would serve as a biological justification for all the ugly and dangerous impulses against which we are struggling. It must be admitted that they stand nearer to Nature than does our resistance to them for which an explanation also needs to be found ... there is no use in trying to get rid of men's aggressive inclinations.[53]

Freud makes death the central aim of life, even in the battle with the life or erotic drive, something he inherits from Schopenhauer.[54] The central force of Jantzen's project is to show how this was an inaccurate and selective gendered choice and that there was an alternative.

---

[49]   Jonte-Pace, *Speaking the Unspeakable*, p. 49.

[50]   Lacan, J. *Écrits* (London: [1966] 1977) p. 104, quoted in Jantzen, *Becoming Divine*, p. 36.

[51]   Jonte-Pace, *Speaking the Unspeakable*, p. 7.

[52]   Jantzen, *Foundations of Violence*, pp. 22ff.

[53]   Sigmund Freud, 1933 'Why War?' [Einstein and Freud] in *Civilization, Society and Religion*, The Penguin Freud Library, Volume 12, (London, [1984]1991) pp. 357–8.

[54]   Freud, *Beyond the Pleasure Principle*, p. 322.

Gendering Birth and Death: Sigmund Freud and Sabina Spielrein

Freud in the *Beyond the Pleasure Principle* sets up a battle of instincts between self-preservation and self-destruction. These instincts are then awkwardly linked to the sexual instinct and the ego-instinct, but then Freud notes that his work has 'drawn far-reaching conclusions from the hypothesis that all living substance is bound to die from internal causes'.[55] He then offers, in the final sections, a reflection on immortality, a move Jonte-Pace believes to 'undercut his own argument'.[56] But Freud's examination of biological material only becomes an excursion; it 'interrupts' as Jonte-Pace states, rather then replaces the death drive thesis. It is, however, worth noting how this excursion brings forward a different dimension into the debate and some irresolvable tensions. In discussing various pieces of contemporary research and the work of Weissman,[57] Freud notes the idea of the germ-cell and the immortality of the single cell organism. He then follows Hartmann[58] in noting that death is the 'termination of individual development', but notes the 'immortality' in the 'transmission' of the 'young off-spring'. In the end Freud sees no value in trying to separate out natural death from protozoa and reasserts his death-drive against wider biological ideas. In turn he also rejects the general energy drive of Jung's libidinal theory.[59] Freud's style of engaging alternate positions and dismissing them reveals his way of resolving tensions and his own internal confusions – what, according to Jonte-Pace, he cannot say. He starts from the assumption of the life and death instinct in reading human life, as a way of controlling the phenomenon, but such control reflects a selection and a restriction, which we might contend are gendered in nature.

This can be seen in the way he becomes entangled, at the end of *Beyond the Pleasure Principle*, with the question of sadism and masochism as dimensions of the death drive and how he attempts to resolve the paradoxes of these positions – it is a blurring of categories that he does not want to maintain. He explores how the erotic and aggressive instinct can be interwoven.[60] The aggressive instinct is seen to be at the service of the sexual instinct in sadism. Freud had extended the concepts of sadism and masochism from Krafft-Ebing to infantile sexuality and derivative forms of behaviour.[61]

---

[55]   Freud, *Beyond the Pleasure Principle*, pp. 316–17.

[56]   Jonte-Pace, *Speaking the Unspeakable*, p. 50, notes, following Ernst Jones, that this was added after completing the 'bulk of the manuscript'.

[57]   A. Weissman, *Über die Dauer des Lebens* (1882, Jena); A. Weissman, *Über Leben und Tod* (1884, Jena); and A. Weissman, *Das Keimplasma* (1892, Jena) are noted by Freud in *Beyond the Pleasure Principle*, pp. 318, 319, 330.

[58]   Hartmann, M. Tod und Fortpflanzung (1906, Munich) in Freud *Beyond the Pleasure Principle*, p. 319.

[59]   Freud, *Beyond the Pleasure Principle*, p. 326.

[60]   Freud, *Beyond the Pleasure Principle*, p. 327.

[61]   J. Laplanche and J. B. Pontalis, *The Language of Psychoanalysis* (London, 1988), p. 244.

With the concept of the death drive he speculates that there might be a 'primary masochism', which is the death drive turned upon oneself, especially when fused with the libido. Its primacy rests on the fact it was not directed to an external object beforehand. Freud is trapped in a net of his own obsessional neurosis – his desire for control and order. At the point the concepts are straining, Freud concedes that he is in a position that leaves him to speculate that he is giving a 'mystical impression'[62] (a confusing impression), but the assertion of 'clinical observation' reinstates his position and consideration of masochism and sadism. Freud entangles himself in complications he cannot resolve and merely ends in reasserting his position.[63] The theoretical tensions are ended by Freud asserting death as a desire for an end of tensions. As Freud remarks:

> The dominating tendency of mental life, and perhaps of nervous life in general, is the effort to reduce, to keep constant or remove internal tension due to stimuli (the *Nirvana principle*, to borrow a term from Barbara Low) – tendency which finds expression in the pleasure principle; and our recognition of that fact is one of our strongest reasons for believing in the existence of death instincts.[64]

In the process of discussing sadism and masochism, he offers a brief footnote to Sabrina Spielrein's 1912 essay, which he concedes had anticipated his speculations and which was also *'unfortunately not entirely clear to me'*.[65] Jantzen's notes how Lacan did not listen or read women's experience and it would seem that Freud does not quite understand Sabrina's gendered insight about 'destruction' and the paradoxical nature of sadism and masochism. The wider politics of Spielrein's relationship with Freud and Jung,[66] and the attribution of some of the death drive theory to her work often hide some of the detailed theoretical concerns, which reveal important issues about gender and sexuality. In Spielrein's essay we have a clear example of a gendered reconfiguration of the death drive, a central questioning of its naturalization and Freud's inability to understand. Spielrein's 1912 paper is worth recalling in some detail because it illustrates a hermeneutic of natality that remained suppressed in Freud's death-drive hypothesis. It contains the first alternative of the life instinct that Freud's gendered position suppressed. More importantly, her gendered alternative is never examined and lost in Freud's theoretical confusions about her work.

---

[62]   Freud, *Beyond the Pleasure Principle*, p. 328.

[63]   Freud, *Beyond the Pleasure Principle*, pp. 328ff.

[64]   Freud, *Beyond the Pleasure Principle*, p. 329.

[65]   Freud, *Beyond the Pleasure Principle*, p. 328: n. 1. [Emphasis added].

[66]   See A. Carotenuto, *A Secret Symmetry: Sabina Spielrein, Between Jung and Freud* (New York, 1984). See also John Kerr, *A Most Dangerous Method: The Story of Jung, Freud and Sabina Spielrein* (New York, 1993).

Spielrein's Transformation Towards Natality

Sprielrein's essay begins with the question of why the 'most powerful [sexual] drive, the reproductive instinct, harbours negative feelings in addition to the inherently anticipated positive feelings'. She examines biological aspects of the relation between 'destruction' and how 'new life originates', giving the example of the May fly in lower organisms, and noting the 'destructive-reconstructive' events of fertilization during intercourse.[67] She then extends this to the psychological dimensions and supports Freud when she writes: 'I believe that Freud is correct when he accepts striving for pleasure and suppression of displeasure as the bases of all psychic productions'.[68] But she then notes that our entire life is not within the ego and it here that a more complex picture unfolds in the divided subject.

Spielrein is able to enter the very 'paradoxes' Freud resists.[69] This enables her to establish a different order of value – the openings towards natality rather than necrophilia. However, Spielrein makes the picture more complex by holding the paradoxes; by refusing the binary death-life inside the divided subject. She holds a model of the self as both individual and collective and also multiple. 'In our depths, there is something that, as paradoxical as it may sound, wills self-injury while the ego counter acts it with pleasure'.[70] She rejects, before Lacan, the individual ego and talks of being not individual but a 'dividual'.[71] As she writes: 'The depth of our psyche knows no "I", but only its summation, the "We"... At the same time, the urgent recognition develops: "I am alienated from myself." Thoughts become depersonalized and "affect" the patients since they come from depths outside the ego, from depths that already have transformed the "I" into a "we" or, perhaps, a "they"'.[72] In her Jungian framework she acknowledges not only the collective, rather than the personal drives, but also a key drive for *transformation*. The difference between Freud's death drive and Spielrein's work is based on this dimension. Where Freud reads the death drive at the point of desire to eliminate tension she reads birth and new life. Spielrein's position is clear: 'Close to our desire to maintain our present condition, there lies a desire for transformation'.[73] Spielrein is not rejecting a destructive aspect of personality and a death instinct, but rather showing that this instinct is NOT primary or essential. For Spielrein, like Jantzen, it is an 'imbalance' in drives.[74] As she writes:

---

[67] Spielrein, 'Destruction as the Cause of Coming into Being', pp. 156–7.

[68] Spielrein, 'Destruction as the Cause of Coming into Being', p. 159.

[69] Spielrein, 'Destruction as the Cause of Coming into Being', pp. 157, 160.

[70] Spielrein, 'Destruction as the Cause of Coming into Being', p. 160.

[71] Spielrein, 'Destruction as the Cause of Coming into Being', p. 160.

[72] Spielrein, 'Destruction as the Cause of Coming into Being', pp. 160, 162.

[73] Spielrein, 'Destruction as the Cause of Coming into Being', p. 163.

[74] Spielrein, 'Destruction as the Cause of Coming into Being', p. 173. Jantzen's thinking avoids setting up the 'binaries' (mortality/natality; destruction/creativity) by holding to the concern with an 'imbalance of attention' (Jantzen, *Foundations of Violence*, p. 6).

This idea readily explains why we overlook the death instinct with the sexual instinct. In normal circumstance, images of coming into being predominate somewhat. Yet destruction is implied because coming into being is the result of destruction.[75]

For Spielrein, 'to thrust an imbalance of destructive images exclusively' is to misread experience.[76] The central drive is for life, but life that always requires change. Self-preservation is a '"dynamic" drive that strives for change, the "resurrection" of the individual in a new form'.[77] Freud cannot acknowledge this aspect of Spielrein; it may even constitute the feature he does not understand. Death and destruction are always about 'a drive for coming into being'.[78] As Spielrein sums up her theory: 'No change can take place without destruction of the former condition'.[79] This is not an essential death-drive, it is rather a dynamic of change and transformation of life and constant new births. She relates this – in a Jungian style – to myths and historical examples, playing with Freud's idea of lying in coffin as symbolic of the womb, the Christian idea of resurrection and ancient mythological ideas of burial as impregnation. Her greatest voice comes through Nietzsche's Zarathustra, with the procreative idea of 'overcoming' in love and knowledge.[80] This reading of an experience as change and transformation rather than death relates directly to Jantzen's alternative reading in her critique of Kristeva. It is the very aspect Freud cannot register. As Jantzen writes: 'We must indeed all separate from our mothers and our mother-substitutes; but the individuation that takes place need not be the death of the relationship but may be its transformation into a different phase. There is loss, but there is also gain. We do not die in this individuation; and we do not kill our mothers. To characterise individuation as death and matricide is, I suggest, already to accept and to re-inscribe the fixation with death and gendered violence which saturates the Western symbolic'.[81] Spielrein is the forgotten voice that shows the life side of death and it is a position that shows there is an alternative within psychoanalytical theory.

Jouissance and Gender: Lacan's Phallic Assumptions

The central difference between Freud and Spielrein is that the death drive is not the return to the point of origin and annihilation, but that of becoming. Freud reads only half of Spielrein's idea and seems unable to even to understand the regeneration of

---

[75]   Spielrein, 'Destruction as the Cause of Coming into Being', p. 173.

[76]   Spielrein, 'Destruction as the Cause of Coming into Being', p. 173.

[77]   Spielrein, 'Destruction as the Cause of Coming into Being', p. 174.

[78]   Spielrein, 'Destruction as the Cause of Coming into Being', p. 184.

[79]   Spielrein, 'Destruction as the Cause of Coming into Being', p. 174.

[80]   Spielrein, 'Destruction as the Cause of Coming into Being', pp. 166, 167, 170.

[81]   Jantzen, 'Death, then, how could I yield to it? Kristeva's mortal visions', p. 119.

birth. Freud reads the 'desire to maintain our condition', but Spielrein holds to the 'desire for transformation'.[82] The question remains as to how far this is a gendered difference between the two. It is, however, something seen at the biological and psychological ground of experiencing in Spielrein's text, particularly when she goes on to explore the idea of 'blending' and 'merging' in transformation.[83] The gendered dimension of the loss of self is key to the hermeneutic of either natality or necrophilia. As Spielrein writes: 'There are examples of neurotics who state explicitly that they are anxious in the face of sexual intercourse because a piece of the individual is lost during ejaculation'.[84] The experience of orgasm, as Jantzen makes clear, is biological and gendered.[85] Jantzen, like Spielrein, is aware of the striking relation between death and male orgasm.[86]

> Love is like death for a man. As long as he retains his semen he remains hard, vital, full of the energy of desire; but when he ejaculates he loses his liquid force and is depleted and limp. And it is the woman and her liquidity – the moisture of her gaze, her soft sexual allure – that draws this from him. But there is a gender difference in the fluidity of sex.[87]

As Jantzen's notes later in her work, the male orgasm is often linked to death.[88] This gendered dimension of sexual experience can be seen, not least, in Lacan and the 'petit morte' (the little death) of the phallic jouissance. The gendered nature of jouissance relates to the lost of self in orgasm and the biological differences in the sexed organism. It raises questions about the philosophical coherence of self. To some extent the idea of jouissance lies behind Jantzen's suggestion that it will be a 'great day' when philosophy of religion is linked to 'desire' and not 'belief'.[89] It is the opening of theology to its loss of control before the big Other, which is different to Lacan's understanding of the phallic jouissance. The phallic jouissance is the controlled pleasure of the organ and not related to the big Other, which cannot be controlled. The phallic jouissance is control over another person, or over oneself, by making oneself and the other into an object. In Seminar 20 Lacan appears to claim that women fail to understand their own jouissance and sees their jouissance as Other, or non-phallic. He claims that women psychoanalysts have not spoken of this jouissance, presumably because they are caught inside the phallic position. He also assumes that, because the female jouissance is Other, 'woman has more of a

---

82   Spielrein, 'Destruction as the Cause of Coming into Being', p. 163.

83   Spielrein, 'Destruction as the Cause of Coming into Being', pp. 163–4.

84   Spielrein, 'Destruction as the Cause of Coming into Being', p. 163.

85   Jantzen, *Becoming Divine*, p. 48; Jantzen, *Foundations of Violence*, pp. 83, 182.

86   Jantzen, *Foundations of Violence*, pp. 83, 182.

87   Jantzen, *Foundations of Violence*, p. 83.

88   Jantzen, *Foundations of Violence*, p. 182.

89   Jantzen, *Becoming Divine*, p. 87.

relationship to God'.[90] However, as Jantzen has indicated, Lacan is rather ignoring such voices, which are there to be read. Indeed, Jantzen, following Bowie's study, makes the amusing comment that Lacan's orgasm is 'Jacques-elation'.[91] While Lacanian analysts suppress talk of the feminine jouissance there have been some French Lacanian theorists that have re-examined the concept.[92]

Jouissance and Cécile Chavel's Life Drive

The French Lacanian theorist Cécile Chavel,[93] for example, critically reads Lacan's jouissance in terms of two positions biologically grounded, but not limited to any specific biological sex. They are metaphors for different psychical positions. The phallic jouissance is the 'possessing' and 'controlling' of pleasure (which corresponds to the individual life drive of survival in men and women). The feminine jouissance is the feeling of 'being-taken' or being possessed by the big Other, that is by something bigger than oneself and which one does not control. This corresponds for Chavel to a specific drive, the collective life drive in the individual, which is the drive for the survival of the human species within every person. She argues Freud and Lacan confuse this with the death drive because the collective life drive can cause an individual death in a desire for progression. This collective life drive is what she calls the 'A drive' ['la pulsion A'], where 'A' is 'autre/amour/altérité', which is the drive towards plenitude.

> La jouissance féminine est, selon Lacan, la jouissance non-phallique, celle qui est au-delà de l'ordre phallique, et qui est illimitée. Nous ajouterons que c'est donc la jouissance d'être possédé(e) par le grand Autre, recevoir l'Autre en soi, de s'abandonner à la sensation de l'illimité, se fondre dans l'absolu, s'ouvrir dans une sorte de hors-temps, dans l'éternité.[94]

---

[90]   Jacques Lacan [1975] *On Feminine Sexuality: the Limits of Love and Knowledge* [Encore: Seminar XX] New York, Norton & Co.1999, pp. 71, 75.

[91]   Jantzen, *Becoming Divine*, p. 48.

[92]   I have attended Lacanian conferences in Paris where male Lacanian psychoanalysts have shouted down papers on female jouissance and erased sections on female empowerment. Even within liberal minded psychoanalytical circles patriarchal and misogynist oppression is very much in evidence, entrenched by blind and dogmatic allegiance to Lacan's work.

[93]   Cécile Chavel, 'La Jouissance Féminine', unpublished conference paper at the University of Kent, *The Flesh and the Text*, 3 November, 2006. See also Chavel, *Métapsychologie de l'acte théâtral, étude clinique sur la jouissance de l'acteur en scène avec son public*, Doctorat de Psychopathologie Fondamentale et Psychanalyse à l'Université Paris VII Denis Diderot, June 2002.

[94]   Chavel, 'Jouissance Feminine'.

[The female jouissance is, according Lacan, the non-phallic jouissance, the one that is beyond the phallic order, and which is illimited. We will add that it is thus the jouissance of being possessed by the big Other, receiving the Other in oneself, to abandon oneself to the sensation of the illimited, to melt into the absolute, to open oneself beyond time, in eternity.]

In this re-reading of Lacan's idea she rejects Freud's death drive and sees it rather as a pathology of obsessional neurosis, which is a fear of being taken by that which is Other. The fear of being taken by a force bigger than oneself results in a fascination with one's own death, because the individual phallic pleasure is going to end and this is placed above the collective life, which goes on beyond the individual; such that those who are afraid of giving themselves up to love are afraid of losing themselves to death.

More in conjunction with Jung than Lacan, she argues that the integration of *both* these positions within the individual allows a movement of healthy engagement with life, which moves constantly and freely between taking control and giving up control. It is the place where women and men can be *taken* in psychical and physical abandonment to pleasure and creativity. The giving up of control is not in itself a death, but as Spielrein argues a transformation. The self 'blends' and 'merges'. These positions are often more akin to the gendered position of women, who constantly sacrifice themselves for the other, giving themselves over, but in Chavel's model men and women can both assume the phallic or female jouissance as modes of being in the world or engaging in the world. She argues that an individual needs both simultaneously to achieve a jouissance of 'being', which is the conjunction of phallic and non-phallic jouissance at the same time. This requires an overlapping of individual and collective drives. The balance of life is to go for something bigger then oneself and yet staying oneself in the same movement, which again relates to Spielrein's transformation. The collective drive – the A drive – the drive to go beyond the limits of the individual self is the drive of creation. When one of the drives is blocked there is a pathology, which is destruction. The important challenge to Freud and Lacan from Chavel's work is that there is no innate death drive, but rather different imbalances between individual and collective life drives.

Freud's difficulty, and indeed the problem of male mastery, self-control and domination that Jantzen identifies at the foundation of Western culture, is that death becomes the attempt to control, because it marks a limit.[95] But male control is limited to the ego position of the individual life through a preoccupation with death. What Spielrein and Chavel show, in different ways, is that such destruction is always part of a larger process. The control of life by death is always an illusion, because the life process constantly returns outside the individual ego event. We are taken by life, rather than ordered by death. Allowing something to move through us is often associated with the gendered position of female life, because of the force of

---

[95]   Jantzen, *Foundations of Violence*, pp. 91, 178, 208.

the birth process that moves through the female body. But the male body also holds the same out of control position with the flaccid penis and its leaking fluids and disturbing irregularity. As I have discussed elsewhere in a paper on Foucault, monks and masturbation, the ontological consistency of the male position is the attempt to control the will of anatomy. This control is either to stop erections and pleasure in the pre-modern texts of John Cassian or to control erections in the condition of modernity, as an act of virility and the fear of impotence in the capitalist market – the fear of not being able to take and be powerful.[96] Indeed, in the academic sphere, Jantzen's delightful critique of Paul Helm's idea of 'incontinence', as rationality not in control, is precisely the male fear of losing control.[97] Thinking with the body in mind, Paul Helm's 'incontinence' can be seen as his fear of impotence, his fear of not being erect and powerful as a thinker in control of his subject, which results in a denial of the relation between body and mind.

Spielrein, Jantzen and Chavel show us the differing dynamics of natality and birth in psychoanalysis. The battle within psychoanalysis is always to overcome the female jouissance and the life drive; the pleasure of being taken by something, again and again, 'encore', as Lacan calls his famous Seminar 20. The life drive does not end with the individual's death it continues in the procreative act and the enrichment of relationship; in so far as the life drive is bigger than any of us, we are taken by it. The male orgasm is the fear of losing that position of control because it demands a giving over, a being taken, it feels like death rather than transforming life because life is registered in terms of control, mastery and domination, life is read in terms of death. When the loss of self is read in terms of Spielrein's 'becoming' of life, ejaculation becomes life and connection, because the seed is given away, abandoned to the other. Losing one's self in the other, and the mother, is the life process. We are always in the other and constructed through the other. This challenge to psychoanalytical theory returns us to the central problem of psychoanalytical thought, the tension between biophilia and necrophilia, which moves us beyond the gendered specificity of these drives and to the work of Erich Fromm.

Biophilia and Necrophilia: Erich Fromm

In a key footnote in Jantzen's *Becoming Divine*, she mentions that she was not the first to use the terms necrophilia to discuss Western culture.[98] She notes that the psychoanalyst Erich Fromm had used the term; indeed, he had contrasted necrophilia with biophilia, the love of life. Jantzen refers to Fromm's 1964 text

---

[96]   Jeremy Carrette, 'Foucault, Monks and Masturbation' in Tom Baldwin, James Fowler and Shane Weller (eds) *The Flesh in the Text: Body, Flesh and Text in French Literature* (Oxford, 2007).

[97]   Jantzen, *Becoming Divine*, p. 85.

[98]   Jantzen, *Becoming Divine*, p. 131, n. 1.

The Heart of Man and his 1973 text *The Anatomy of Human Destructiveness*.[99] It is in these texts that we see how Fromm moves beyond Freud's death drive by giving a moral superiority to the life drive. In the early part of her project, Jantzen never follows up the footnoted links to Fromm's texts, although one imagines her proposed study of psychoanalytical study would not be able to avoid it. Fromm's distinction between necrophilia and biophilia is like Jantzen's distinction between natality and necrophilia, except in so far that Fromm remained gender blind in his formulation of such concepts. Fromm describes the position of necrophilia as follows:

> The necrophilous person is driven by the desire to transform the organic into the inorganic, to approach life mechanically, as if all living persons were things. All living processes, feelings, and thoughts are transformed into things. Memory, rather than experience; having, rather than being, is what counts. The necrophilous person can relate to an object – a flower or a person – only if he possesses it; hence a threat to his possession is a threat to himself; if he loses possession he loses contact with the world. He loves control, and in the act of controlling he kills life. He is deeply afraid of life, because it is disorderly and uncontrollable by its very nature.[100]

Here we see the overlapping of the themes of death, control and life being taken as markers of female and phallic experience, as seen in Chavel's work. According to Fromm, the death instinct 'separates' and 'disintegrates', while the Eros or life instinct 'has the function of binding, integrating, and uniting organisms'.[101] Fromm is keen to show that Freud introduces the death-drive 'hesitantly and tentatively' and that many do not accept the hypothesis.[102] While acknowledging the two positions of death and life, he does not, like Jantzen, see the death drive as normal. He argues instead that the 'primary and most fundamental tendency' is the life drive. As he argues: 'The death instinct represents *psychopathology* and not, as in Freud's view, a part of *normal biology*'.[103] In his later work, *The Crisis of Psychoanalysis* (1970), Fromm explicitly states that psychoanalysis 'must part from Freud who, in the second part of his life, believed that the craving for death and destruction is as fundamental and ineradicable a part of man's the striving for life'.[104]

Fromm also relates the concept of necrophilia to Freud's idea of anal character, which seeks to control and order.[105] Jantzen, perhaps, restricts Fromm's analysis by seeing it 'largely' as related to individual character, but Fromm's work always

---

[99] Eric Fromm [1964] *The Heart of Man: Its Genius for Good and Evil* (New York, 1980) and Fromm [1973] *The Anatomy of Human Destructiveness* (London, 1977).

[100] Fromm, *The Heart of Man*, p. 41.

[101] Fromm, *The Heart of Man*, p. 49.

[102] Fromm, *The Heart of Man*, p. 49.

[103] Fromm, *The Heart of Man*, p. 50.

[104] Eric Fromm, *The Crisis of Psychoanalysis* (London, 1970), p. 212.

[105] Fromm, *The Heart of Man*, p. 53.

locates the individual within the social and relates the concepts of necrophilia and biophilia to the social and the question of war.[106] He thus links necrophilia to the capitalist structure of society and to the 'control' and 'prediction' of bureaucratic and mechanistic society.[107] He sees the contemporary fascination with death as part of the way humans are reduced to objects in such a world.

Briefly then, intellectualization, quantification, abstractification, bureaucratization, and reification – the very characteristics of modern industrial society, when applied to people rather than to things, are not the principles of life but those of mechanics. People living in such a system become indifferent to life and even attracted to death.[108]

The drive for control of life results in death. Fromm and Jantzen are not far from each other at this point, both use psychoanalytical theory with critical awareness. At the end of his *Crisis of Psychoanalysis*, Fromm argues that psychoanalysis 'deals with the issues of critical awareness, the uncovering of the deadly illusions and rationalizations that paralyse the power to act'.[109] Jantzen uses psychoanalysis in this critical manner to reveal the dynamics of natality and necrophilia in Western philosophy. Her choice to use psychoanalysis to read philosophy is grounded on her critical recognition of its potential insight for life. In this sense, she finds a reading that supports Fromm's view that the 'most central issue to which psychoanalysis can make a contribution is the question of the attitude towards life itself'.[110]

Conclusion: 'In the Name of Life!'

Jantzen in her 'double reading' of psychoanalysis reflects the profound issues of choice. She realised that these were 'alternatives' and that necrophilia was a 'pathological perversion' of the life drive.[111] Fromm argued that psychoanalysis could enable people to 'spot death lovers' and that is precisely how Jantzen engages with psychoanalysis and even reads psychoanalysis itself, because she realised that some forms of psychoanalysis were caught in the same problem of necrophilia. Jantzen and Fromm, along with Spielrein and Chavel, share a biophilia – a delight in natality and beauty – and they attempt to employ the critical hermeneutic of psychoanalysis to read such movements.

Fromm argued that the critical task was to examine all aspects of life and thought in terms of their 'necrophilious and biophilious elements'. No matter what the language, whether it was man, women, peace, God or any other ideology, all

---

[106]   Fromm, *The Heart of Man*, pp. 55ff. For a discussion of the relation between the individual and social in Fromm's work see J. Carrette, *Religion and Critical Psychology: Religious Experience in the Knowledge Economy* (London, 2007).

[107]   Fromm, *The Heart of Man*, p. 57.

[108]   Fromm, *The Heart of Man*, p. 59.

[109]   Fromm, *The Crisis of Psychoanalysis*, p. 212.

[110]   Fromm, *The Crisis of Psychoanalysis*, p. 212.

[111]   Jantzen, *Foundations of Violence*, p. 213.

remain ambiguous unless they are accompanied by a word with which to begin and to end: 'In the Name of Life!'. It is in the name of life that Jantzen offered her psychoanalytical model of philosophy, the attempt to heal the broken world, through a gendered awareness of the terms of its engagement. It was in the name of life that Jantzen worked and offered us a way to re-imagine our thinking. Natality does not deny death, but recognises life beyond the individual death. Perhaps, it is not identification and differentiation, but assimilation that joins us in the collective life drive that is beyond us all.

To think in the name of life is to be taken-over not by the death drive of our egos (by what which belongs to me or someone else), but by forever allowing us to be taken-over by life itself. The importance and enormity of Jantzen's task can be seen in her *Foundations of Violence* when she notes how Plato's *Phaedo* associates philosophy with death: 'True philosophers make dying their profession'.[112] In the light of such a foundational perversion within Western culture, Jantzen's 'therapy of philosophy' is to bring the subject to back to life.

---

[112]   Jantzen, *Foundations of Violence*, p. 170.

PART TWO
'In the Name of Life'

Chapter 6
'Choose Life!' Quaker Metaphor and Modernity

Pam Lunn, Betty Hagglund, Edwina Newman and Ben Pink Dandelion

Introduction

In 2003, Grace Jantzen presented the George Richardson Lecture, the annual international lecture in Quaker studies, entitled 'Choose Life! Early Quaker women and violence in modernity', which was published in *Quaker Studies*.[1] It was part of her ongoing work on the preoccupation of modernity with death and violence.[2] In the lecture she argued that Margaret Fell[3] and most other early Quaker women encouraged a choice of life over a preoccupation with death, whilst most male Friends (as Quakers are also called) maintained the violent imagery of the Lamb's War, the spiritual warfare that would usher in the kingdom. Whilst both men and women developed what became the Quaker 'peace testimony' (the witness against war and outward violence), the language used by male and female Friends differed in their description of the inward spiritual life and its consequences and mission. Thus, Grace argued that these women Friends were choosing a language counter to modernity, whilst the male apocalyptic was indeed counter-cultural but still within the frame of modernity. The Quaker women's emphasis on 'Life' was at odds with modernity's emphasis on death and violence. It led to an alternative mode within the Quaker communities in terms of gender relations and the spiritual equality of the sexes, which extended to the whole range of social testimony and witness.[4]

This thesis in itself raises many questions and requires further research. Sally Bruyneel Padgett's work on Margaret Fell's eschatology[5] does not support

---

[1]   Grace Jantzen, 'Choose Life! Early Quaker Women and violence in modernity' *Quaker Studies*, 9 (2003): pp. 137–55.

[2]   Including Grace Jantzen, *Foundations of Violence* (London, 2004).

[3]   Margaret Fell (1614–1702) was a gentry convert to Quakerism in June 1652. She became one of the key leaders of the movement and carried out an extensive correspondence with Quakers everywhere, including many she had never met. Her pastoral skills were matched by her theological and administrative ones. Her husband, Judge Thomas Fell, never became a Quaker but helped protect the movement.

[4]   Jantzen, 'Choose Life!'

[5]   Sally Bruyneel Padgett, 'The Eschatology of Margaret Fell' (PhD thesis, University of Durham, 2003).

Grace's thesis that Margaret Fell had a distinctive approach. Grace was herself clear that not all women Friends fitted her characterisation, and we can point, for instance, to the apocalyptic invectives of Dorothy White (another seventeenth-century English Quaker from the South of England) as a good counter example.[6] However, Catie Gill's recent book on seventeenth-century Quaker women's collective authorship argues that female expression was distinctive in style within the Quaker movement and was particularly characterised by prophecy in the 1650s, and personal testimony in the 1680s.[7] Christine Trevett[8] has shown that English and Welsh women's prophetic writings were particularly silenced by the actions of Second Day's Morning Meeting[9] after 1672; and Phyllis Mack suggests that women Friends placed themselves in a limited and subordinated role in this later period, while at the same time creating a self-affirming literary style that was 'recognizably and consistently female'.[10] By the late 1700s English Quakers were not using the Lamb's War imagery and their testimony against outward fighting had become part of normative Quakerism. Nikki Coffey Tousley's work[11] clearly shows how this second generation of Quakers marginalised the eschatological vision or omitted it altogether from their accounts. Their spiritual epistemology seemed less secure and they no longer placed their personal salvation at the heart of a global eschatological picture.

In this paper, we take Grace's basic thesis, that a female 'Choose Life!' imagery may be set against a male 'Lamb's War' metaphor, and apply it to four sets of Quaker data in other geographic and temporal locations, to explore the extent to which the arguments she sets out can usefully illuminate the nature of Quakerism. We look at the works of Alexander Jaffray and Lilias Skene, seventeenth-century Aberdeen Friends, to explore whether a Scottish location makes a difference to the gendered division identified by Grace in relation to English Friends, and identify a public/private dichotomy in writing styles. Next, we extend the study into the late-eighteenth and early-nineteenth centuries, and focus on Hannah Kilham, whose links with early Methodism, and position as an unusual and late convert to Quakerism, highlight the problem of trying to disentangle a specifically Quaker

---

[6]   Pink Dandelion, *The Liturgies of Quakerism* (Aldershot, 2005), p. 42.

[7]   Catie Gill, *Women in the Seventeenth-Century Quaker Community: A Literary Study of Political Identities, 1650–1700* (Aldershot, 2005), p. 2.

[8]   Christine Trevett, '"Not Fit to be Printed": the Welsh, the women and the Second Day's Morning Meeting,' *Journal of the Friends Historical Society*, 59 (2001): pp. 115–44.

[9]   Second Day Morning Meeting was a publications committee set up in 1672. Only works passed by the committee could be published in the name of Quakers. 'Second Day' referred to the fact it met on a Monday, second day in Quaker parlance, where days and months were numbered rather than named to avoid the use of pagan nomenclature.

[10]   Phyllis Mack, *Visionary Women: Gender and Prophecy in Seventeenth Century England* (Berkeley, 1992), p. 311.

[11]   Nikki Coffey Tousley, 'The Experience of Regeneration and Erosion of Certainty in Second-Generation Quakers: no place for doubt?', *Quaker Studies*, 13 (2008): pp. 6–88.

outlook from a wider historical context. Third, we explore the public discourse amongst early-twentieth-century British Friends concerning the militant phase of the campaign for women's suffrage. We conclude that in this period, while a gendered discourse may be identified, it does not map neatly onto actual men and women. Finally, we chart the nature of twentieth-century liberal British Quakerism, using the changes in framing the historic Quaker opposition to war as a case study. We analyse the language of the 1995 British Quaker book of discipline[12] to explore how far it can be argued that the whole Yearly Meeting[13] is now 'choosing Life' rather than images of victory or destruction. What does the dominant narrative say about the nature of the Yearly Meeting in terms of how gendered its theology is and how it sits within modernity?

This four-fold approach highlights the complexity of the history of Quaker discourse, as well as the continually shifting cultural and social contexts in which Quakers necessarily found themselves embedded. It also brings to the fore how useful an analytical tool Grace has given us and not only in situations where we come to agree with her conclusions.

Seventeenth-Century Friends in Aberdeen: Gendered Divisions?

Looking at texts by English Quakers written between 1649 and 1700, Grace Jantzen found distinct differences in the writings of men and women. The development of Quakerism in Scotland followed a similar but not identical path to that of English Quakerism and therefore forms a good test case for seeing whether Grace's argument holds true for other geographical and temporal locations. An examination of memoirs, poems and letters by Aberdeen Friends underlines the difficulty of separating an individual's written style from their wider and personal contexts; it also demonstrates the need to consider the intended audience as part of the analysis. In order to test Grace's hypothesis, we look first at the writings of a male Friend, to see if the 'Choose Life' imagery, identified by Grace as particularly likely to be found in women's texts, is present; and, conversely, if the Lamb's War imagery, linked by Grace to texts by men, is equally present; we then look for similar features in a set of texts by a contemporaneous woman Friend.

Alexander Jaffray, one of the first Aberdeen converts, was born in 1614 into a wealthy merchant's family. He became a prominent Covenanter[14] and supporter

---

[12]   The 'book of discipline' is an authoritative book of extracts, revised every generation or so, which seeks to convey the current thinking of the Quakers. In Britain, the first book was published in 1783, the latest in 1995.

[13]   The 'Yearly Meeting' is the name given to the Quaker organisation, in this case, in Britain.

[14]   A Scottish Presbyterian who supported either of two agreements, the National Covenant of 1638 or the Solemn League and Covenant of 1643, intended to defend and extend Presbyterianism.

of Cromwell, and represented Aberdeen in parliament between 1644 and 1650. He gradually moved from Presbyterianism to an Independent church position, organising a separatist church in 1652. From 1661 he found himself increasingly drawn to Quakers, although he did not become a Quaker until the visit of the English Quaker William Dewsbury in 1662.[15]

Jaffray wrote a memoir of his life, covering the period from 1614 to 1661. Although the memoir ends before his conversion, the final chapters explore his responses to Quaker ideas. He writes of an indwelling Christ, manifested in but separate from outward creation and spiritual practices:

> He is to be seen in his works of creation, in his works of providence, and by the judgments that he executes and in the Scriptures there is much of him to be seen and learned by a diligent perusal of them; but *no life* is to be found [merely] by what may be learned from *any* or *all* of *these*. ... My life, then, being *only* to be found in Christ, and no where else, in prayer, preaching, nor Scriptures;– where is he to be found? Though Christ may be said to be, and truly is, *every where*, and every where to be found; yet not to the particular end for which he is sought, namely, for mortifying and subduing sin,–*but as enthroned in the heart*.[16]

His emphasis is repeatedly on light and life, further metaphors of inwardness, and on passive receiving rather than active striving:

> First, to mind the light, as it *begins* to appear and dawn in the conscience; for accordingly as this is done, the day dawns, and the day-star (that is, Christ himself) arises; first, as the bright and morning Star, Rev. xxii. 16, whereby, 'the Day-spring from on high' visits such as 'sit in darkness', Luke, i, 78, 79; and at last, 'the Sun of righteousness' itself arises, Mal. iv. 2, and abides with them. Secondly, The next thing to that of minding the light, is, to wait and stand still from self-willing and acting ... the way then to receive the light, and strength by and from it, is, to stand still, in a sober frame of spirit. .. And thus it is, that the Lord communicates strength; *not all at once*, but *by degrees*, as the light is attended to and patiently waited for; *not by willing and running,* but *by sitting still*. ... Thus, may I see and behold him, so as even to say or do *nothing* without him, and – may it not be added – by 'beholding as in a glass the glory of the Lord', be 'changed into the same image, from glory to glory, even as by the Spirit of the Lord'. 'Now the Lord is that Spirit; and where the Spirit of the Lord is, there is liberty'.[17]

---

[15]   G. DesBrisay, 'Jaffray, Alexander (1614–1673)', *Oxford Dictionary of National Bibliography* (Oxford, 2000 [http://www.oforddnb.com/view/article/14582, accessed June 2007]. A. Jaffray, *Diary of Alexander Jaffray* (London, 1833).

[16]   Jaffray, *Diary*, pp. 162–3 [original italics].

[17]   2 Cor. 3. 18, 17. Jaffray, *Diary*, pp. 150–51, 174 [original italics].

Jaffray's language and imagery in his private writings about his spiritual life, therefore, conform to the 'Choose Life' model, associated by Grace with women's writings.

We find, however, a different picture if we look at those of Jaffray's writings which are addressed to the persecutors outside the movement. Here we find fierce and oppositional statements, warning them of the doom to come if they do not stop their attacks on Quakers:

> O fear, fear to be found any more in that guiltiness, which (if persisted in) may make you to be shut out for ever: And let none so look on themselves, as to suppose they are past this hazard, if so be they yet continue, neglecting, opposing, and persecuting, or approving of them who persecute, the growing light of this day, as its come and coming forth with power and great glory.[18]

> Let therefore the dread and terror of the Lord seize upon all, especially the professing people of this Generation ... dreadful is the judgment that is to be met with by such.[19]

> Dear Friends, as yee love your peace and safety beware of this, for it borders too near that guiltiness that will not be forgiven.[20]

This belief that God would avenge his people, the Quakers, and destroy their enemies in the same way that he had destroyed the enemies of the Old Testament Israelites is, as suggested above, common to both male- and female-authored open letters by Aberdeen Quakers of this period. Lilias Skene, for example, a woman Friend from a similar religious and socio-economic background to Jaffray, warned the magistrates and inhabitants of Aberdeen that the Lord would 'rise up against Babylon ... a destroying Wind' and that the 'Hills and Mountains will not cover you' from the coming wrath of God since 'assuredly the Lord will not hold you guiltless'.[21] Unlike Jaffray, Skene also used imagery connected with battle and warfare in her private writings, when writing about the persecution of Quakers (Jaffray's diary ends before the persecutions began). In a poem written in 1677, she wrote that the Lord:

---

[18] A. Jaffray, 'A Word of Exhortation' in George Keith, *Help in the Time of Need from the God of Help. To the People of the (so-called) Church of Scotland, especially the once more zealous and professing, who have so shamefully degenerated and declined from that which their Fathers, the Primitive Protestants attained unto* (Aberdeen, 1665), p. 1.

[19] Jaffray, 'A Word of Exhortation', p. 4.

[20] Jaffray, 'A Word of Exhortation', p. 5.

[21] L. Skene, 'A Warning to the Magistrates and Inhabitants of Aberdeen, writ the 31st Day of the First Month 1677' in J. Besse, *A Collection of the Sufferings of the People called Quakers* (London, ([1667] 1753), pp. 521–3.

for his spiritual warfare hath trained bands
And their provision keeps in his own hands
A house of Magazine well furnished where
For every soldier he hath weapons there
For some a battle axe, a sword a bow
As he hath service, weapons he'll bestow
With some he'll bend the bow with others fill it
By some he'll wound the beast, by others kill it

and called on Quakers to join in the Lamb's War:

Come all ye mighty men bring forth your shield
Yee valiant ones appear now in the field
All ye expect in war gird on your thigh
Your swords, so as in readiness ye be
Yea breast plate buckler, helmet & a shield
That none unharnished[22] may go to the field.
...
The Lord will bath his sword in Edoms blood
And vengeance recompense on all her brood
Who have engaged in this holy war.
And followers of the Lamb accounted are.[23]

It is not until the persecutions cease that language towards non-Quakers becomes more temperate among Aberdeen Quakers, and at that time both men's and women's public writings change in similar ways.[24]

The writings of Alexander Jaffray and Lilias Skene demonstrate the need to consider intended audience and subject matter when analysing early Quaker writings using Grace's model. Both male and female writers may use life-affirming language and imagery when writing private or semi-private texts or when writing to others within the Society of Friends. The same writers may use images and language of guilt, blame, war and destruction, however, when writing to or about those they see as enemies of the fledgling movement.

---

[22] The *Scottish National Dictionary* (1974) gives 'unharnish' as the Scottish form of English 'unharness'.

[23] L. Skene, (1665–1696), 'Lillias Skene's Poems 1665–96', transcribed by W. Walker, c. 1850, University of Aberdeen library, Special Collections, MS. 2774, pp. 25–6.

[24] This may reflect a response to the cessation of persecution; it may equally be the result of the passage of time, with the writings of the second generation of Aberdeen Friends coming to the fore.

Hannah Kilham and Quaker Women of the Late-Eighteenth and Early-Nineteenth Centuries

So far we have looked at Grace's hypothesis only in the context of 'early' Quakerism, the enthusiastic manifestations of the movement in the later-seventeenth century. But how well does it help inform our understanding of later periods, especially those marked by the dramatic social and economic change of the Industrial Revolution, and by the rise of the Evangelical movement? From the eighteenth century, Quakers tried to hold aloof from wider society, and tended to form a close-knit community bound by ties of kinship as well as belief. A centralised, largely male control of the Society had been established, but as well as continuing opportunities for Quaker women to minister, there were also separate women's meetings which gave Quakers a level of gender equality that was unknown in other denominations. A thriving manuscript culture existed among Quaker women, and women oversaw the education of Quaker girls very carefully, reading with them and encouraging them in the 'nuances and ways of reading Quaker language and spirit'.[25] There were, therefore, networks by which a feminised Quaker theology could be sustained.

However, there are problems in trying to extend Grace's hypothesis into the different contexts of later periods, not least in identifying what might be regarded as specifically or exclusively Quaker. The Society was never entirely isolated from wider social influences, and in the course of notable campaigns from the later-eighteenth century, for the abolition of slavery and for penal reform, it became more involved in ecumenical and political activity. Recent scholarship has shown that the insularity of members of the Society has almost certainly been exaggerated and that it is surprisingly difficult to define a typical Quaker in the period.[26] Moreover, published Quaker literature of the period was rather different from that of the seventeenth century: there was no new prophetic or exhortatory work being published, and edited journals and memoirs had come to predominate. Printed testimonies showed how God was seen to be working in individual lives, and served as useful exemplars to other Quakers. Those outside the Society could buy and read these works, but their purpose was not primarily evangelical as early Quakers' public writings had been. Women no longer had the public voice that they had claimed in the earlier period, and male dominated publishing networks determined which of their writings were worthy of a wider readership.

For a variety of reasons, then, it is difficult to establish the extent to which a distinctively feminised Quaker literary style might be said to have persisted. This section of our paper explores some of the developments of this period by focussing

---

[25] M. L. Tartar, 'Reading a Quaker's Book: Elizabeth Ashbridge's testimony of Quaker literary theory', *Quaker Studies*, 9 (2005): pp. 176–90, p. 186.

[26] S. Dixon, 'The Life and Times of Peter Briggins', *Quaker Studies*, 10 (2006): pp. 185–202; J. Jennings, *Gender, Religion and Radicalism in the Long Eighteenth Century* (Aldershot, 2006).

on the *Memoir* of one individual, Hannah Kilham. At first glance Kilham might appear to be representative of Quaker women of the period, and she was certainly an inspirational figure for Quakers at the time and subsequently, but a brief biography shows up some difficulties of definition here. Hannah (née Spurr), was born in 1774 of Anglican parents but, after hearing John Wesley preach, she became a Methodist. When the Methodist preacher, Alexander Kilham, broke away from the Wesleyans and formed his own connection, she joined his congregation and eventually married him. Five years after his death in December 1798, Hannah joined the Religious Society of Friends.[27] From her early life she proved herself very adept at challenging social symbolism and gender stereotypes. Her passionate interest in languages at school was considered improper for a girl; her attraction to Methodism at this time would also have had the power to shock. The very act of leaving the Kilhamite Connection after her husband's death was seen as an affront to the respect and obedience due to his memory. Her life thereafter, as one of active mission in Britain and Africa, was not unique but was still highly unusual for the time, as was her decision to support her family by working in the schools she established.[28] Quaker influence in all this can be seen only as marginal at best.

Hannah moved between an increasingly influential, mainstream Evangelicalism and the comparatively enclosed world of Quakers, so it is instructive to trace the development of her perceptions, and to explore these in relation to Grace's 'Choose Life!' metaphor. After going through a fairly typical Evangelical conversion experience, she was watched over assiduously by the members of her Methodist band meeting. The focus of Evangelicals was Christ's atoning sacrifice on the cross, and their imagery was soaked in the blood of the Lamb. For Hannah, her new-found faith was clearly a struggle. She wrote that she was 'too much given to a kind of lightness' and had not yet 'got the better of my natural disposition'.[29] Her husband-to-be wrote to her of the need to 'look for crosses daily'; 'it is our duty to endure hardships as good soldiers of Christ'.[30] Throughout her life, Hannah had cause to remind herself that 'her natural inclination' needed to be 'crucified'.[31]

---

[27]   According to E. A. Rose 'Alexander Kilham' in D. M. Lewis (ed.) *The Blackwell Dictionary of Evangelical Biography 1730–1860*, vol. II (Oxford,1995) p. 644), Hannah was 'a former Quaker who returned to the Society of Friends after his [Alexander's] death'. However this information is not repeated in biographical accounts of Hannah herself, and given that her parents were Anglican, it seems unlikely that she would have omitted to mention in her Journal a connection with Quakers before her move to Methodism.

[28]   C. Fyfe, 'Killham, Hannah (1774–1832)' *Oxford Dictionary of National Biography*, (Oxford, 2004) [http://www.ofxorddnb.com/view/article/15526, accessed 22 November 2005].

[29]   Kilham, *Memoir of the late Hannah Kilham; chiefly compiled of her Journal* (London, 1837) p. 18.

[30]   Kilham, *Memoir of the late Hannah Kilham*, p. 36, p. 50.

[31]   Kilham, *Memoir of the late Hannah Kilham*, p. 7, p. 370.

There can have been few more driven missionaries than she, and yet she baulked at excessive self-sacrifice, and hinted that it was a notably male attribute.[32]

So there is a distinct strand in the imagery of the *Memoir* which derived from her experience of Evangelicalism, but there was another strand too, which she was never able or willing to suppress, and which eventually led her to find a spiritual home among Quakers. In the face of personal loss, she seemed always able to find God in the here and now. On the death of her husband, she wrote not in terms of the rewards of an afterlife, but of the 'blessings which yet remain', a feeling perhaps occasioned by her pregnancy at the time. At the end of 1799, a few months before attending her first Quaker meeting, she wrote:

> I found in my own spirit a degree of sincerity and love, and it was a conviction more evident, more striking to the mind, than what is brought through reasoning, which convinced me that truth and love had their source in God. ... I loved Him first because He had given me life; and I felt my existence delightful.[33]

The imagery she used was frequently that of colour, light and life. 'Life' was a word she used often, and seemed to mean it in the sense of a divine immanence. 'Oh! That the members of this establishment may be brought to dwell under the feeling of life', she wrote of one school in Sierra Leone, the 'solid feeling which acknowledges the controlling sense of the presence of the Most High'.[34] This was clearly a deeply sustaining force in her daily existence. On the other hand, when she spent time in the company of Evangelicals, as she tended to do, for example, when engaged on missionary work for Africa, she was much more likely to revert to the imagery of the battle to usher in God's kingdom. On returning to London from Africa in 1825, for instance, and obviously in a state of considerable inner turmoil, she described how a meeting with 'Dr S.' 'brought powerfully before me the great sacrifice by which comfort is brought to the Lord's people, and through which the warfare must be accomplished'.[35] Such imagery appeared to owe more to the crucicentric Methodism she had espoused in her youth than to ideas of the Lamb's War, and, unlike seventeenth-century Quakers, she was silent on the dire consequences that might befall those who failed to heed the call.

Hannah was familiar with the writings of John Woolman,[36] and echoed his words in warning against seeking after the world's wealth, urging the need to nurture all

---

32 Kilham, *Memoir of the late Hannah Kilham*, p. 276.

33 Kilham, *Memoir of the late Hannah Kilham*, p. 66.

34 Kilham, *Memoir of the late Hannah Kilham*, p. 251.

35 Kilham, *Memoir of the late Hannah Kilham*, pp. 256–66.

36 John Woolman (1720–1772) was a Quaker from New Jersey, USA. He is best known for his campaigning against slavery, but this extended into what would now be termed ecological concerns, focussing attention, for example, on the environmental damage caused by the dyeing industry.

creation and 'be stewards of our heavenly father's bounty'.[37] Here we see the scope for an ecological approach to life, rather than one of domination and exploitation, as Grace mentioned in her lecture. However, there was a strong paternalistic streak in her approach and she saw her role as that of a shepherd managing a flock. She was entirely sincere in her motives for working for social justice and doing what she could for 'for the present best'.[38] But that was bound up with essentially millennial Evangelical notions of conversion and missionary activity, and a belief in *progress*, developing what she saw as God-given opportunities. To help the poor, something that she argued might once have been 'renounced as visionary and impractical', was now respectable. It need not be considered 'time lost even to the pursuit of business' and would 'afford the most general stimulus to trade at large'.[39]

Her emphasis on progress became more pronounced once she was in Africa where she shared the assumptions of many European missionaries that the region was simply part of the 'heathen lands' where 'much darkness dwells'.[40] She appeared to regard the very anxiety that had called her and other missionaries to work in Africa as evidence that Africans were in need of knowing about the redemption Christ had won for them in order to be saved. Africans were therefore 'susceptible of improvement' but still 'very remote from a state of civilisation'.[41]

So, in the example of Hannah Kilham at least, it cannot be argued that Quaker women were acting within a belief system that was counter cultural. Her example alerts us to considerable methodological difficulties in trying to extend Grace's hypothesis. Hannah Kilham was a Quaker woman, but she was neither born nor brought up a Quaker, did not appear to have the kind of female Quaker networks that were important in maintaining particular values, and was very open to the influence of the wider Evangelical Movement at a time when many in the Society were just beginning to change their theological perspective. Her writings do not present a consistent picture, shifts occurring in relation to the company and context in which she found herself. She certainly played an important role in furthering the cause of gender equality. Her emphasis on life did at times challenge much of a prevailing religious imagery of death and spiritual warfare, and it was her creative and life affirming spirituality that seems to have attracted her to Quakers. But her long-term participation in the endeavours of the Evangelical movement prevented these insights from flourishing into any sort of alternative cultural ethos within the communities in which she worked.

However there is much in Grace's hypothesis that points us to identify a distinctive spirituality and literary style that *is* clearly reflected in Hannah Kilham even if it is not always consistently expressed. Moreover Grace's 2003 lecture encourages us to consider the ways in which Quakers choose to construct their own narratives. It is perhaps significant that in the current book of discipline

---

[37]   Kilham, *Memoir of the late Hannah Kilham*, p. 126.
[38]   Kilham, *Memoir of the late Hannah Kilham*, p. 126.
[39]   Kilham, *Memoir of the late Hannah Kilham*, pp. 126–7.
[40]   Kilham, *Memoir of the late Hannah Kilham*, p. 183.
[41]   Kilham, *Memoir of the late Hannah Kilham*, p. 178, p. 184.

(analysed in more detail below), Quakers choose to remember Hannah Kilham in the following lines, written on one of her sea voyages: 'It is "life" only that can lead to life, and no forms are availing without it. Seek the life in all things, and cherish it by all authorized means'.[42]

Politicised Debate about Gender in the Public Domain

Turning now to the very early years of the twentieth century, we take as a case study the involvement of Quakers in the militant phase of the women's suffrage movement in Britain, 1906–1914.[43] This episode is of particular interest since the women's suffrage campaign as a whole spurred a public debate about the nature of gender differences, and the militant campaign added to this a wide-ranging discussion of gender and violence. Among British Quakers, both men and women participated in public debate about women's suffrage *per se* and about militant tactics. There were both men and women on each side of the debate.

Comment did not appear in Quaker publications in the immediate aftermath of the formation by the Pankhursts of the Women's Social and Political Union (WSPU) in 1906, but in 1907 a male correspondent wrote:

> We should be very sorry that it should appear that our sympathy in this important question needed stimulating by these violent measures, for we have never understood how anyone brought up in Quaker traditions could be other than a supporter of women's suffrage; but we recognise that the heroic self-sacrifice of some of those women who have gone to prison for the cause they have so much at heart must be an increased stimulus to all who believe their cause to be just.[44]

And in 1908 Sarah Tanner, a well-known Quaker woman, had an article published in *The Friends' Quarterly Examiner*:

> If we believe in the equality of men and women in spiritual things, we can hardly deny their equality before human law, because the greater includes the less. In these days when controversy is raging we do well to remember that the movement began with calm philosophic reasoning, and that it stands based on logic and the principles of justice and truth.[45]

---

[42] Kilham, *Memoir of the late Hannah Kilham*, p. 386. *Quaker Faith and Practice: the book of Christian discipline in the Yearly Meeting of the Religious Society of Friends (Quakers) in Britain* (London, 1995), n. 21, 26

[43] For a full historical discussion see Pam Lunn, '"Have You Lost Your Opportunity?": British Quakers and the militant phase of the women's suffrage campaign, 1906–1914', *Quaker Studies*, 2 (1997): 30–56.

[44] *The Friend*, 16 (1907), p. 73.

[45] S. Tanner, 'Women's Suffrage', *The Friend's Quarterly Examiner*, 42 (1908), p. 401.

In both these extracts we see an assumption that the idea of 'equality' should be automatically accepted among Quakers; and in both, a clear contrast between the 'violence' or 'controversy' attendant upon the campaign at large, and the presumed 'heart' of the matter – justice and truth. Interestingly, it is the man who uses the term 'heroic' for the women who were, by then, going to prison for their cause.

As the militant campaign progressed, the debate became sharper, and the concerns about the violence greater. A man wrote:

> The unruly and violent conduct of these women appears unfortunately to find so large an amount of feminine support, and to be so seldom unreservedly condemned by those who strictly confine their own action within constitutional lines, that I regard these distressing occurrences as sufficiently symptomatic of a wide-spread lack of mental balance, to form a serious factor in the question.[46]

And a woman:

> The great spiritual power behind the Suffrage movement is not the desire for the vote as an *asset* or a *right*, but the intense earnest longing of thousands of women for a share in the responsibility of framing the national laws, by which they, with men, are governed, and some of which at present are so hopelessly unjust to women. Friends in the past have been in the front of many a moral fight, but there is an apathy, and even intolerance on the part of many men Friends regarding the present demands of women, which is very difficult to understand. [original emphasis][47]

So here we start to see some contrast between a man's anxiety about the 'violence', and the failure he perceives in others to condemn it; and the woman's restating of the principles of the whole campaign. This letter was the first instance of direct comment about gendered attitudes to this issue within the Religious Society of Friends.

As well as correspondence and articles in the journals, there were pamphlets published, to be distributed at public meetings. A substantial (23 pages) tract was written by Gulielma Crosfield (who subsequently became president of the Friends' League for Women's Suffrage) entitled *Friends and the Women's Movement*. It is closely argued, with the author opposing all violent methods, on the grounds that if: 'women have anything to give to our generation, it is because we claim a higher plane of service than of force'.[48]

Throughout the debate among Quakers, it was the issue of the militants' violence that took up far more space than the underlying question of women's

---

[46]   *The Friend*, 18 (1909), p. 260.

[47]   *The Friend*, 50 (1910), p. 210.

[48]   Gulielma Crosfield, *Friend's and the Women's Movement* (London, 1911), p. 15.

suffrage. In 1913 and 1914 there was pained correspondence from both men and women, deploring the violence. Isabella Sharp, for instance, wrote:

> Many members of our Society have been looking in vain in our periodicals for a protest from our leading Women Suffragists against the wild actions of the militant party in destroying property and endangering human life. Are we to conjecture from this silence that many of our friends are more in sympathy with the militant law-breakers than we had hoped was the case? ... Many of us who would gladly have joined in reasonable methods of agitation, are now so scandalised with the action of the militant party, as to be ready to forgo the desired privilege rather than appear even to countenance such action.[49]

An alternative way of thinking about the violence was proposed in a letter from Lucy Gardner:

> It is very inconvenient to have our letters destroyed and to feel a sense of insecurity with regard to our property; it is distressing to read of women who are rightly and suitably punished for making war upon our material possessions, having so little sense of the justice of their punishment that they prefer to starve rather than submit. But what if, in some sense, they are right? What if they see more deeply into the heart of things than those of us who are content to give – not ourselves – but what we can spare easily from our normal life? What if they are the prophets and have a vision of a world redeemed by suffering and selflessness that we have not?[50]

Here we have women holding two opposing views, and the second has more in common with those men who wrote of the campaign in terms of heroism and self-sacrifice. What Lucy Gardner adds here is a strong religious overtone in her choice of language, especially in the last sentence, thus implicitly laying claim to spiritual authority for the campaign.

In the following year the concern about violence was still uppermost. A man wrote:

> I understand that members of our Society support the propaganda of the Suffragettes by purse and person. They march in their processions; they attend their meetings; they do not deny having sent them money. One lady Friend, a most charming young married woman, assured me that she had not the courage to break windows herself, but honoured and envied those who did. It is evident to me that the Pankhursts and not Millicent Fawcett are the true and trusted leaders of the movement to which the Society of Friends has now. been in a way committed. The example of their leaders, though fortunately not imitated to the

---

[49] Isabella Sharp, *The Friend*, 53 (1913), p. 158.
[50] Lucy Gardner, *The Friend*, 53 (1913), p. 573.

full, has, if I may say so, measurably tinctured the behaviour of their followers. I doubt if the Woman's Question will regain a fair hearing until all symptoms of the feverish and lawless methods prevalent today have died down, and respectable women have ceased to palliate crime, whilst professing to deprecate it.[51]

There is here an echo of a 1909 male correspondent who wrote of 'lack of mental balance', as well as a tone of condescending superiority.

Shortly after this, a male correspondent[52] asserted that there was a Friend suspected of arson, and deplored hearing militancy condemned purely on tactical, rather than moral, grounds. In the same issue a Quaker militant finally declared herself: Ethel Impey wrote to explain her position, that constitutional methods had been exhausted and she, like other militants, now felt compelled by conscience to act: 'We do not support the militant party for amusement nor out of contrariness, but because conscience bids us, and it is a most serious thing to find one's judgement at variance with many of those one most esteems'.[53]

The claiming of 'conscience' has been a powerful and resonant theme among Quakers since the earliest days, so the use of this word at this stage of the debate sends a powerful spiritual signal, in contrast with the constrained legalism of some other contributions. A week later a slightly shocked man responded:

> One is already too sadly aware of the increasing spirit of violence and lawlessness, which is characteristic of the present time, but one was not prepared to have it openly defended by a woman 'Friend' in your last week's issue. How is it possible to reconcile [the advices to Friends] with the acts of militancy, which are being conducted almost daily – to the injury and loss of many innocent people? If our Society owes a duty at all at the present juncture, rather than raise 'its united voice' against the sufferings of women now in prison for their own acts, and who have the remedy for forcible feeding in their own hands, should it not record its solemn protest against their commission of such crimes, and express its sympathy with the innocent victims?[54]

After this date there was no further significant correspondence on the suffrage question. Internal procedural matters (about women's place in the governance of the Society of Friends) became prominent and then, with the outbreak of war, suffrage campaigning was suspended and many Quakers (women and men) turned their attention to war relief work.

So, from this representative selection of extracts, can we draw any clear distinction between the style of discourse of the men and the women? It seems to us that the distinction is more between those broadly supportive of women's

---

[51]   *The Friend*, 54 (1914), p. 115.

[52]   *The Friend*, 54 (1914), p. 206.

[53]   Ethel Impey, *The Friend*, 54 (1914), p. 207.

[54]   *The Friend*, 54 (1914), p. 222.

suffrage, both men and women, who viewed militant tactics in the broader context of a just and necessary outcome; and those who were neutral or opposed in relation to the outcome, both men and women, who straightforwardly deplored militancy and were condescending about women in general.[55] The difference is not so much between discourses of life and death, as between energy and passion for justice and equality,[56] over against constraint, legalism and support for the *status quo*. There is, of course an argument that these latter characteristics may be mapped, respectively, onto the larger categories of natality and necrophilia. Grace Jantzen, in her article with which this paper is in dialogue, hints at this. She writes: 'It is my contention that modernity takes its shape from the choices that were made [in the seventeenth century]: choices to construe the divine as other-worldly, to rank people ... into hierarchies of domination and exploitation'.[57]

Those Quakers who were passionate about the cause of women's suffrage – and who wrote of it in terms of heroism, justice, truth, self-sacrifice, prophecy, and redemptive suffering – were both laying claim to and actively creating an immanent, engaged spirituality; they were locating the divine in the mess and conflict of real-world politics. Overall, there were more Quaker women than men who embodied this position, but the men were not absent. A gendered trope does not map exactly on to actual men and women.

British Liberal Quakerism: Choosing Life

Moving now to the present day: British Quakerism in the twenty-first century is technically described as 'Liberal'. Its fundamental values and perspectives are rooted in a Quaker version of Liberal Christianity, an attempt at a rational form of faith developed at the end of the nineteenth century. This was a Quakerism enjoying full citizenship for the first time after 1870[58] and seeing itself as part of a robust non-conformity that was a participant in civil and world affairs. It was this kind of Quakerism which debated the suffragette issues in the terms we have just explored.

Liberal Quakerism was set up at the end of the nineteenth century on four guiding principles. These both tied Quakerism back to its distinctive seventeenth-century heritage and also symbolised a sense of moving into a new century. The

---

[55]   There were Quaker women, as well as men who believed that it was inappropriate for women, due to their weaker nature, to vote and be involved in public decisions.

[56]   Lack of space prevents a full discussion of this point – there was considerable concern among the upper-class Quaker women suffragists about the plight of poor women; the suffrage campaign was, in their view, about justice in relation to social class and economic status, as well as gender.

[57]   Grace Jantzen, 'Choose Life!', p. 153.

[58]   Non-conformists could enter the professions and Universities of their choice after this date without compromising their faith.

first principle was that spiritual experience was considered to be primary in terms of religious authority. This was a traditional Quaker position but one that had been threatened by Evangelical influences in the nineteenth century. Unlike seventeenth-century Friends, Liberal twentieth-century Quakers did not claim that Scripture would necessarily confirm revelation. Experience was deemed sufficient. The second principle was that faith needed to be relevant to the age. These Quakers wanted to be 'of their time' and able to adapt, rather then being constrained by anachronistic practices such as the earlier traditions of wearing only 'plain' clothes and using 'plain speech' (for example, the numbering of days referred to earlier). The third principle was that Quakers needed to be open to theological innovation. The fourth, linked to this, was that more of God was known in each age, the doctrine of 'progressivism', which set up a temporal authority to revelation. Quakers in a decade's time would necessarily be better informed than those of a decade past.

Taken together, these principles offered a Quakerism which outwardly appeared similar to the original (the style of worship was not altered, for example), and yet was radically innovative in the freedoms it afforded for Friends to abandon tradition altogether in the name of fresh revelation or 'new Light'. The rational underpinning of Liberal Quakerism gradually created resistance to explicit corporate theology, and theology increasingly became an exercise in individual interpretation.

British Friends freed themselves from the theological constraint of any text or tradition, and increasingly through the twentieth century, they used the Bible for devotional purposes rather than as a book of authority. Their main textual authority was and is the 'book of discipline'. First published in 1783, and revised every generation or so, this is a book of extracts chosen to nurture Quaker faith and guide the individual Quaker in their daily life. Until the twentieth century, committees selected the extracts and produced a prescriptive book. In the twentieth century, in line with the changed culture of the movement, the process, and hence the content, became democratised. British Friends, then corporately named 'London Yearly Meeting',[59] replaced the section on 'Christian Doctrine' with 'Illustrative Spiritual Experiences of Friends' in their 1921 revision of the book. As early as 1930, the question was aired as to whether a Quaker needed to be a Christian. Quakers were allowing themselves to become a diverse religious group for the first time. When it came to producing a version of the book of discipline in the late twentieth century, a large committee, explicitly diverse in its theology, spent nine years requesting and selecting extracts, and consulting on the final selection. The book was adopted in 1994 and published in 1995 as *Quaker Faith and Practice*. The book of discipline always has reflected Quaker orthodoxy,[60] by indicating both its 'centre of gravity' and the extent of its 'circumference'; but the 1995 book gives us a perspective on British Quakerism generated by a greater proportion of Quakers than previous editions. Given the

---

[59]   London Yearly Meeting was renamed as Britain Yearly Meeting in 1995.

[60]   Pink Dandelion, *A Sociological Analysis of the Theology of Quakers: The Silent Revolution* (Lampeter, 1996), p. 19.

increasing diversity within the Yearly Meeting and the emphasis on spiritual experience, it is not surprising that this book is longer than previous editions. Additionally, it is descriptive rather than prescriptive.

Quaker attitudes to war and outward violence, as represented in the book of discipline, provide a useful touchstone to explore Grace's model against modern British Quakerism. Jung Jiseok, building on the unpublished work of Elaine Bishop, has carefully articulated four key shifts in the way Quakers reinvented their historic opposition to war in the early part of the twentieth century. First, they renamed their 'testimony against war'[61] as 'the peace testimony'. Second, the basis of the testimony moved from being purely Christian to being Christian *and* non-Christian *and* non-religious. Thirdly, it moved from being part of a prescriptive Quakerism to one option with a permissive Quakerism. Fourthly, the focus shifted from being 'against' war to being 'for peace', from a narrow focus to a broad and diffuse field of involvement.[62] To explore twentieth-century British Quakerism in relation to 'Choose Life!' theology, we take these four shifts in war/peace testimony and link them to an analysis of the 1995 book of discipline.

Part of Grace's argument was that even within an ostensibly pacifist group, the language of warfare (such as the Lamb's War), tied the Quakers who used it to a modernist mindset rooted in violence and the death of beauty. The renaming of the testimony against war in the twentieth century connotes, then, a shift away from such preoccupations towards a more positive and life-giving approach. 'War' appears far less often than 'peace' in the 1995 book of discipline and when it does appear, it has a wholly negative connotation. This absence of 'war imagery' is connected with the shift to theological pluralism within British Quakerism. Quaker Christianity has been replaced by a broader range of theological interpretations. Specifically Christian ideas such as the 'Lamb's War' do not appear in *Quaker Faith and Practice*. They have not been selected because they no longer resonate with the sensibility of the majority of British Friends.

At the same time, the historic opposition to what is 'outward' has relaxed – for early Quakers the 'world' was a pejorative term which referred to anything 'not-Quaker'. As Creasey[63] and Bauman[64] have shown, a central part of early Quaker theology was that the Light of Christ operated inwardly and that communion, and the experience of the unfolding Second Coming, was interior. The outward was 'worldly' and apostate, and the place of authenticity was inward. This influenced the Quaker approach to liturgy and the sacraments as well as to speech and silence.

---

[61] 'Testimony', in Quaker parlance, refers to a tradition of collective witness.

[62] J. Jisoek, *Han Sokhon's Pacifism and the Reunification of Korea: a Quaker Theology of Peace* (Lampeter, 2006), p. 32.

[63] M. A. Creasey, '"Inward" and "Outward": a study in early Quaker language', Supplement No. 30. *Journal of the Friends' Historical Society* (1962): pp. 1–24.

[64] R. Bauman, *Let Your Words be Few: Symbolism of Speaking and Silence Amongst Seventeenth Century Quakers* (Cambridge, 1983).

The location of the workings of Divine agency in the 'inward parts' (after Jeremiah 31.31–34[65]) was common to all early Friends.

Part of the declaration of testimony against war to Charles II, made in 1661 on behalf of the Quaker movement, clearly makes the distinction between the outward and the inward, and is retained in the 1995 selection:

> Our principle is, and our practices have always been, to seek peace, and ensue it, and to follow after righteousness and the knowledge of God, seeking the good and welfare, and doing that which tends to the peace of all. All bloody principles and practices we do utterly deny, with all outward wars, and strife, and fightings with outward weapons, for any end, or under any pretence whatsoever, and this is our testimony to the whole world. That spirit of Christ by which we are guided is not changeable, so as once to command us from a thing as evil, and again to move unto it; and we do certainly know, and so testify to the world, that the spirit of Christ which leads us into all Truth will never move us to fight and war against any man with outward weapons, neither for the kingdom of Christ, nor for the kingdoms of this world.[66]

The following 1908 extract, written by Quaker doctor Hilda Clark, also connects the 'outward' with the 'worldly' but – in the spirit of the new liberal theology becoming dominant in British Quakerism at the time – is less critical of the material world and seeks to work with it: 'Justice is of the Spirit, not of the outside world – but our understanding is so wrapped up in outward things that we can only grow spiritually by applying spiritual things to material ones – therefore we must be just though Nature is not'.[67] An 1987 extract, also written by a woman, also speaks of balancing inward and outward:

> The duty of the Society of Friends is to be the voice of the oppressed but [also] to be conscious that we ourselves are part of that oppression. Uncomfortably we stand with one foot in the kingdom of this world and with the other in the Eternal Kingdom. Seldom can we keep the inward and outward working of love in balance, let alone the consciousness of living both in time and in eternity, in timelessness. Let us not be beguiled into thinking that political action is all that is asked of us, nor that our personal relationship with God excuses us from actively confronting the evil in this world. The political and social struggles must be waged, but a person is more and needs more than politics, else we are in danger of gaining the whole world but losing our souls.[68]

---

65   These verses speak of the new covenant being written on people's hearts.
66   *Quaker Faith and Practice* (London, 1995), 24.04.
67   *Quaker Faith and Practice* (London, 1995), 26.07.
68   *Quaker Faith and Practice* (London, 1995), 23.04.

Thus, 'outward' is no longer linked either to the wholly apostate or the wholly transcendent. Inward and inner are still the motifs of spiritual authenticity, but the outward is a context within which the faithful work, rather than being seen as something to be conquered or destroyed. The testimony *for peace*, in terms of Quaker opposition to war, is open to individual interpretation as well as rejection. It is no longer prescribed although it still symbolises a counter-cultural Quakerism, reinvigorated by a century of passionate opposition to war.

The term 'victory' is used in four extracts, three of them written before 1920. Similar to the use of the term 'victory', the term 'won' is used in its military sense only in historical passages, such as this from 1900:

> the staunchness of early Friends and others to their conscientious convictions in the seventeenth century won the battle of religious freedom for England. We covet a like faithful witness against war from Christians today.[69]

These historical passages are still 'alive' for British Friends because they transmit values and create a Quaker identity, whilst not binding present day Quakerism. Indeed, the shift of focus from 'war' to 'peace' has broadened the interpretation of the testimony, not just in relation to the meaning of a refusal to fight, but also in relation to the meaning of 'peace' itself. 'Peace' has been extended beyond the opposition to war to accommodate a wide variety of 'Choose Life!' positions, including vegetarianism, anti-sexism, anti-racism, concern for the environment, fair-trade and anti-capitalism. While this allows some Quakers to pick and choose the consequences of their Quaker life, it is nevertheless a powerful system of mutual reinforcement and value transmission. In terms of Grace's analysis, these can all be seen as present day modes of the overturning of social symbolism and the desire to reclaim the world for God (or 'God') in the here and now, with an emphasis on Life and the potential for 'newness and creative change'.

In summary, there is a total lack of imagery in *Quaker Faith and Practice* relating to spiritual warfare or spiritual victory over and against an apostate world. Rather, present day British Friends, of both sexes, inhabit the 'Choose Life!' theology attributed by Grace Jantzen to the founding mothers of Quakerism. In Liberal Quakerism's selective reinterpretation of its founding heritage, it has privileged the experiential, the centrality of love and grace, and a social gospel of equality and justice. Theology is plural and marginal. God is perceived as immanent and/or unknowable. In reinterpreting the testimony *against* war to a wider testimony *for* peace, these Quakers have in place a mechanism which both affirms and accommodates numerous aspects of a 'Choose Life!' theology.

---

[69]   *Quaker Faith and Practice* (London, 1995), 24.07.

Conclusion

Ultimately, we argue that Grace's analysis of the very first Quaker writings along gendered lines does not necessarily carry over into other geographical and temporal settings. In the 1670s, we find Alexander Jaffray using 'Choose Life' language for his private writings and Lilias Skene writing to Friends' persecutors with a message of guilt and destruction. By the early nineteenth century, the writings of female Quaker convert Hannah Kilham do not fit into Grace's counter-cultural template. Kilham's work, like the earlier public writings of Jaffray and Skene, tends to conform to the dominant dualistic cultural model, which Grace ascribed only to Quaker men in seventeenth-century England. It also alerts us to the need to consider how different theological discourses came to influence Quakers. The categories of the public debate amongst Friends over women's suffrage at the start of the twentieth century cannot simply be mapped on gendered lines. In these ways, we find a less straightforward division of gender and theological language as we move from the seventeenth century, as explored by Grace, to the early twentieth century. However, in the late twentieth century, we find British Friends, in their most authoritative text, immersed, across the gender binary, in the language of natality and life.

Considering the examples used by Grace in her analysis, this current stance follows the witness and writings of the early women Friends more than those of the early men. This may imply a feminising of modern British Quakerism and its expression. It certainly is counter-cultural and, purely within the dichotomy of 'Life' versus 'death and violence' which Grace set up, places British Quakerism as counter-modern. The movement's preoccupation is not at all with death and violence, exploitation and domination, but is concerned with respecting the integrity of all creation, and working for the realisation of that ideal in wider society. Bryan Wilson labelled twentieth-century British Quakers a 'perfectionist' sect, in that their salvific goal, insofar as any remains, is to change the consciences of those around them.[70] These Quakers have opted to focus on the early Friends' metaphors of 'Love' and 'the Light in their consciences',[71] rather than those of 'the Lamb's War'. They have, as the title of Grace's lecture puts it, 'Chosen Life!'

---

[70]   B. R. Wilson, *Religious Sects* (London, 1970).

[71]   R. Moore, *The Light in their Consciences* (University Park, 2000).

Chapter 7

Searching a Feminine Mystical Way for the Twenty-First Century

Ursula King

Introduction: Grace Jantzen and Julian of Norwich

Julian of Norwich (1342–c.1423) is one of the great Christian mystics of the Middle Ages. She represents an inspiring example of a compassionate spiritual teacher and friend for many contemporaries, as she was for Grace Jantzen who wrote an early, well-known book about her[1] but also frequently referred to Julian's ideas in her later writings.

This is not the place to retell Julian's story or rather, the little known for certain, when she lived the simple life of a recluse in her cell at Norwich. She is best known by the writings she left, the *Showings* or *Revelations of Divine Love*, the first book written by a woman in English and a classic in mystical theology. It is said to contain one of the clearest yet most complex records of the life of a contemplative, mystical soul. Many have commented on Julian's visions, her mystical experiences, contemplation, prayer and theology, as Jantzen does in her own book, and I can add little to this at present.

It would be a rewarding task to trace in detail how Grace Jantzen's ideas about Julian developed and what she saw in her as most significant for us today. Such a task, which should be undertaken sometime, requires a close reading of Jantzen's own work, accompanied by critical reflection and creative commentary. Unfortunately I do not have the necessary time to do this now, so that when I was invited to contribute an essay to this commemorative volume, I suggested instead my Julian Lecture, given at the Julian shrine in Norwich in May 2007. A revised version of this lecture follows below,[2] but I begin with a few comments on Grace Jantzen and Julian of Norwich.

Jantzen was much attracted to Julian's writing and her shrine in Norwich where she returned more than once, appreciating the welcome, friendship and guidance

---

[1]   Grace M. Jantzen, *Julian of Norwich: Mystic and Theologian* (London, 1987) reprinted with a new Introduction in 2000.

[2]   For the original text see Ursula King, 'Inspired by Julian – Seeking a feminine mystical way for the 21st Century', The 27th Julian Lecture, The Julian Centre, Norwich, 2007 (used here with permission).

she found there. In the Preface to the first edition of her Julian book (1987) Jantzen stated the reasons for writing this work:

> The first is that, as a Christian philosopher, it is important to me to learn to receive the love of God, to pray, and to love God and my neighbour. Julian of Norwich is a model for this: she provides both example and instruction. As I became more aware of her teaching, it seemed important to me to try to make more widely known her insights into human personhood and its healing in rootedness in God, her depth of prayer, and her delight in God. I have tried to be true to her own meanings, but if I have read her writings from a late twentieth-century perspective it is because, both in the hours I spent in her anchorhold and when I returned to everyday activity, her words ring true in our own context, and it is this truth above all which I should like to share.[3]

Jantzen describes her book as 'an effort to integrate the findings of scholarship with the interests of contemporary spirituality',[4] but reading it twenty years after its first publication can prove a little disappointing since it does not engage with contemporary debates on spirituality nor does it integrate the important feminist and constructive thinking that Jantzen developed in her later works.

When the Julian book was republished in 2000, Jantzen added a thoughtful Introduction that opens with the challenging question 'What does it mean to be an anchoress in postmodernity?'[5] without, however, changing the main text. One can only speculate on the reasons why the main body of the book itself did not include her more developed critical perspectives on mysticism, but it is not my task to pursue this intriguing question here in depth.

Writing a new Introduction more than ten years after the first publication of the Julian book, Jantzen openly admits her 'embarrassments' about the book as it stands, given the material and discursive conditions of postmodernity. Had she written it later, at the time of the new Introduction, it would have been a different book, but she felt that it was better to let the text remain in its original form than tinker with it here or there.[6] However, she selects several themes and comments on them from a more nuanced postmodern perspective in the Introduction. This commentary reflects the rich unfolding of Jantzen's own ideas – her creative thinking otherwise – since her original writing of the Julian book. Without wishing to summarise this thought-provoking Introduction, which can be read as an independent essay,[7] I want to draw special attention to its first mentioned, and perhaps foremost, theme

---

[3]   See Jantzen, *Julian of Norwich*, p. ix.

[4]   Jantzen, *Julian of Norwich*, p. ix.

[5]   Jantzen, *Julian of Norwich* (2nd edition, 2000), p. vii.

[6]   See Jantzen, *Julian of Norwich* (2nd edition, 2000), pp. xiv, viii.

[7]   Jantzen acknowledges in a note that the Introduction grew out of a lecture commemorating the 900th anniversary of Norwich Cathedral, printed in a pamphlet distributed from the Julian shrine in Norwich; see Jantzen, *Julian of Norwich*, p. xxiii, n. 1.

which concerns Julian's frequent use of the vocabulary of 'desire' which is also the central topic of the Norwich Cathedral lecture on which this Introduction is based.[8] Jantzen is deeply struck by Julian's speech on desire, especially by its contrast to the 'displaced desire' of modernity with its 'devouring and controlling attitudes', a desire 'that has not recognized what it is really about and therefore projects itself destructively on to other things and people'.[9] Julian's desire is quite different; it is reduplicated in that it is a longing to long for God, a desire to be given desire which is reciprocated by what Julian sees as God's longing for her. That is why Jantzen speaks in a later essay[10] of Julian's position as 'a reconfiguration of desire' when she describes human longing for God as a response to divine longing: 'Human desire for God is a reciprocation and mimesis of divine desire'.[11]

Jantzen is deeply committed to the life- and energy-transmitting elements of Julian's message, which she sees as closely connected to her own thinking on natality and human flourishing. Julian does not encourage a privatised spirituality but calls everyone to engagement. Who will then be a postmodern anchoress? Jantzen answers her own question by suggesting 'part-time' anchoresses and anchorites, 'those whose lives and duties are so focused as to make times and spaces for withdrawal from routine and willingness to stand at an angle to the contemporary symbolic in openness to the divine.'[12]

I will say no more about Jantzen nor comment at length about particular passages of Julian's own book, but inspired by Julian I want to ask: Can there be a feminine mystical way for the twenty-first century? In searching for an answer to this question, three different strands of reflection come together: 1. making connections between mysticism and feminism; 2. exploring a *via feminina* for contemporary women and men; 3.the great significance of love and wisdom for a feminine mystical way.

---

[8]   See Grace M. Jantzen, 'Julian of Norwich: Desire and the Divine', Norwich Cathedral, 23 July 1996 where she discusses Julian, Hadewijch of Antwerp and Hildegard of Bingen. I learnt through a personal contact that the lecture was read out by Sheila Lipjohn (Norwich Cathedral Library holds a tape recording of this lecture) since Grace was too ill at the time to give it herself.

[9]   Jantzen, *Julian of Norwich*, p. xi.

[10]   Grace M. Jantzen 'A Reconfiguration of Desire: Reading Medieval Mystics in Postmodernity', *Women's Philosophy Review*, 29 (2002): pp. 23–45. This essay provides a beautiful elaboration of the themes found in the new Introduction of Jantzen's Julian book published in 2000 and of her Norwich Cathedral lecture of 1996.

[11]   Jantzen, 'A Reconfiguration of Desire: Reading Medieval Mystics in Postmodernity', p. 29.

[12]   Jantzen, *Julian of Norwich*, p. xxiii.

Making Connections between Mysticism and Feminism

Mysticism is difficult, if not impossible, to define. Many attempts have been made to understand this extraordinary religious phenomenon and its relationship to the larger context of religion. Although human reason remains ultimately unable to penetrate the mystery at the heart of mysticism, mystical experiences cannot be entirely opaque to reason and explanation either as philosophers of religion, including Grace Jantzen, have discussed at length.[13] The human spirit longs to reach out to something greater, more exalted and transcendent, to meet with and be transformed by the divine Spirit in the midst of life.

Mystics of many ages and faiths communities bear supreme witness to the heights and depths of mystical experience. These mystics speak with many voices; they use a wealth of metaphors and images, and have left us a bewildering range of narratives about their inner life and vision. Because of the great variety of mystical experiences it seems misleading to speak of mysticism in the singular. There are obviously so many mysticisms, and numerous explanations have been offered by both mystics and scholars to account for what mysticism is all about. In the opinion of some authors there exists hardly a more beleaguered category than 'mysticism' in the current academic study of religion',[14] and there exists a profusion of writings to prove this. At one level the term 'mysticism' seems rather artificial and undifferentiated; it seems more a word created by people studying, comparing or talking about particular experiences which individual mystics themselves do not define as such. Mystics always speak about particular experiences, a particular faith or practice, a particular way or path, rather than about mysticism in general. Thus being a mystic is very different from trying to understand what mysticism is, since it is about some of the most intimate and transformative spiritual experiences known to humankind.

Almost thirty years ago I gave a lecture on 'Mysticism and Feminism *or* Why Look at Women Mystics?'[15] at a time when this was a relatively unheard of topic. Some of my listeners on that occasion strongly objected that mystical experience was beyond any feminist concerns. How can contemporary feminism as a social and political movement, but also a radical change in consciousness, be related to the age-old spiritual quest for liberation, freedom, enlightenment and transcendence?

---

[13]   See Grace Jantzen, 'Could there be a Mystical Core to Religion?' *Religious Studies*, 26 (1990): pp. 59–71 and especially her book *Power, Gender and Christian Mysticism* (Cambridge, 1995).

[14]   See Leigh Eric Schmidt, 'The Making of Modern "Mysticism"', *Journal of the American Academy of Religion*, 71/2 (2003): pp. 273–302, for a helpful review of contemporary debates on the study of mysticism. Since my text is based on a lecture to a wider public rather than an academic audience, I have not gone into the postmodern deconstructions of 'mysticism' and 'mystical experience' among academic writers.

[15]   Ursula King, 'Mysticism and Feminism: Why Look at Women Mystics?' in M. A. Rees (ed.), *Teresa de Jesus and her World* (Leeds, 1981), pp. 7–17.

Even with the more advanced, inclusive gender thinking of today, many people are unwilling to see that there is a deep connection between mysticism and feminism, beyond the obvious one that there have been many women mystics.

The literature on mysticism is vast and so is that on feminism. But comparatively few feminist theologians have written on mysticism, at least in comparison with all the other topics they have explored. Moreover, the leading authors on mysticism are still predominantly male and rarely use feminist insights or gender perspectives in their discussions of the subject. This has largely been left to a few women writers.

To most people who are not themselves mystics, mystical experience is only accessible through reading mystical literature, including Julian's work. Such literature is found worldwide across different faiths and also outside them in a wide range of secular texts, consisting of the poetry and literature of many languages. When we examine their descriptions of spiritual experiences cross-culturally, certain common traits emerge. Central to them seems the insistence on a fundamental unity or oneness that transcends all the diversity, fragmentation and superficiality of daily life. Thus mysticism has often been defined as a fundamentally unitive experience. In Christianity and other theistic religions this is understood as the deepest love and communion with God, whereas non-theistic religions conceive of it as a deeply contemplative approach to Ultimate Reality. Union, contemplation, love and bliss all feature in the description of mystical experiences.

Some people consider mysticism primarily as an *historical* phenomenon – something that mainly happened to religious people in the past, but is now largely irrelevant to contemporary scientific and rationalistic ways of thinking. People of faith can never share such a narrow, exclusive approach but are convinced that mysticism is also an important *contemporary* phenomenon. Not only can mysticism be seen as the experiential matrix of religion, but it is also at the heart of spirituality, whether this is pursued inside or outside religious institutions. Mystical spirituality seems especially important for the transformation of religious awareness and spiritual practice in the contemporary global world.

It comes as something of a surprise to realise that the *comparative study* of mysticism – as distinct from the existence of mystics of many faiths – dates only from the beginning of the twentieth century, whether one thinks of William James's famous *Varieties of Religious Experience* from 1902 or Evelyn Underhill's equally famous study on *Mysticism: The Nature and Development of Spiritual Consciousness* of 1911. Many other authors and titles could be listed here. The rediscovery of the life and work of many women mystics of the past occurred also mainly during the twentieth century. This recovery has by no means been the exclusive achievement of women, yet it is striking how many women scholars have made important contributions to the modern study of mysticism.

Contemporary historical, theological and comparative studies on mysticism still pay relatively scant attention to wider gender issues. Nor do they always give sufficient space to women mystics. However, this does now happen more frequently since the works of many women mystics in Christianity, Islam,

Hinduism and other religions have been discovered or rediscovered since the last century. Many women scholars have done significant work on the historical, textual and descriptive study of mysticism, without necessarily being attentive to gender issues either. To mention some names besides Evelyn Underhill, there are Margaret Smith, Grace Warrack, Geraldine Hodgson, Phyllis Hodgson, Hope Emily Allen, Emily Herman, Hilda Graef, Annemarie Schimmel, and more recently Grace Jantzen. These and others have written extensively on mysticism, and sometimes on specific women mystics.

The relationship between mysticism and feminism is ambivalent and rather difficult to unpack. From a critical feminist perspective, many questions can be asked. What have been women's own religious experiences in the past as distinct from those of men? How far have women articulated their experiences differently? Have they used different metaphors, concepts and images of their own? To what extent are their accounts more personal and autobiographical? How do they claim authority for their words, and what writing strategies do they adopt to be accepted by their contemporaries?

The mystical writings of women were often not acknowledged in the official historiographies of religious institutions, nor did they contribute to the systematic articulations of faith created in theological and philosophical schools of learning. Thus many works by women mystics have long remained invisible and marginalized, as is true of Julian of Norwich's important *Showings.*

Much has been written on medieval women mystics, yet relatively few writers combine the insights of the mystical tradition with the critical insights of contemporary feminism. Although 'women of spirit' of earlier ages have sometimes been called 'proto-feminists', many aspects of their life and thinking relate very little to ours. Medieval women mystics were certainly not feminists in any contemporary sense. Their work therefore has to be approached with caution. Much of its remains imprisoned in the patriarchal framework of past hierarchical structures and thinking. This is as true of Julian as it is of Hildegard of Bingen and other women mystics, but Grace Jantzen has shown with remarkable insight and perception how medieval Christian mystics can be read 'otherwise' from a perspective of modernity and postmodernity.[16]

Every religion knows of female saints and mystics – extraordinary women who have provided much spiritual counsel, guidance and largely non-institutionalised spiritual leadership, just as Julian did from her cell in Norwich. It comes as no surprise that such 'women of spirit', women who possessed spiritual power or what Eleanor McLaughlin has called 'power out of holiness',[17] greatly appeal to

---

[16]   See Jantzen, *Julian of Norwich* (second edn, 2000): Introduction, and especially her *Power, Gender and Christian Mysticism* (Cambridge, 1995).

[17]   Eleanor McLaughlin, 'Women, Power and the Pursuit of Holiness' in R. Ruether and E. McLaughlin (eds) *Women of Spirit: female leadership in the Jewish and Christian traditions* (New York 1979), pp. 100–130. I have discussed this and the relationship between mysticism and feminism at greater length in my book *Women and Spirituality;*

people today who are seeking spiritual guidance and inspiration. Religious women of medieval and early modern times provide strong role models in terms of female identity, autonomous agency and inner strength in face of much social and religious opposition. The comparative study of the writings of female and male mystics from a perspective of gender differences is only in its infancy, but it raises searching questions, not least for contemporary religious practice and the development of an appropriate, viable spirituality for both genders in our globalised society.

A surprising development worldwide is the growing realisation of the global spiritual heritage of women across different religions and cultures. So many spiritual 'foremothers', female saints, mystics and female religious communities are being discovered today. Yet a comparative historical enquiry provides plenty of evidence that most religions have validated women's lives primarily in terms of domestic observances and family duties. Religions have been less inclined to encourage women's search for religious experience and enlightenment, or to follow exceptional paths of spiritual devotion and perfection. Imprisoned by the daily tasks and recurrent demands of immediacy that the maintenance and nurture of personal and community life have always required, women have been so much equated with *immanence* that the realms of *transcendence* have remained largely out of their reach, forbidden to their desire.

In spite of the existence of what the German theologian Elisabeth Gössmann calls 'women's counter-tradition' to official Christianity,[18] pursuing the life of the spirit always remained an exceptional path open mainly to individual women from an advantaged social background. We therefore have to ask how far women have really had access to a spiritual space of their own? How far were they really encouraged to pursue, or were ever admitted to the pursuit of, similar spiritual ideals and disciplines than men or, even more important from our perspective, how far did (a few) women possess the necessary freedom to develop their own spirituality? How far could women provide spiritual advice and leadership for both women and men?

It is only in our postmodern era that women *as a group*, and not simply as individuals, have been able to respond in greater numbers to the invitation, challenge and gift of *transcendence*. That raises questions about modern women mystics and the possibility of developing a feminine mystical way in the twenty-first century.

Voices of Protest and Promise (London and Basingstoke, 1993). See Chap. 4, 'Voices of Spiritual Power'.

[18]   Elisabeth Gössmann, 'The Image of God and the Human Being in Women's Counter-Tradition' in Deborah F. Sawyer and Diane M. Collier, *Is There a Future for Feminist Theology* (Sheffield, 1999), pp. 26–56.

Exploring a *via feminina* for Contemporary Women and Men

It is not my task here to review the critical feminist literature on women mystics or on the feminine in Christian mysticism, but I want to refer briefly to a few helpful titles. Grace Jantzen's book *Power, Gender and Christian Mysticism* (1995) is of great importance and has attracted much attention, but its full discussion would require another paper. Equally important is Barbara Newman's excellent analysis,[19] which examines the feminine motifs and the theology of the feminine in Hildegard of Bingen. An earlier, pioneering feminist study on Teresa of Avila and the Western mystical tradition is Deirdre Green's work,[20] still worth reading, especially for its concluding reflections on 'Teresa and the Issue of Women's Spirituality'. Far more theoretically nuanced, but quite difficult, is Amy Hollywood's more recent study.[21] This draws on the psychological theories of Luce Irigaray and Jacques Lacan in its discussion of medieval mystics, and of mysticism and gender. Amy Hollywood also highlights the distinction between affective or erotic forms of mysticism, usually associated with women, and the more speculative, intellectual forms of mysticism, usually associated with men. Another way of saying this is to align *apophatic* mysticism and negative theology with male intellectual speculations whereas *kataphatic* forms of mysticism, associated with imagery, symbolism and affirmative forms of theology, are more frequently linked with women mystics.

I have been particularly inspired by the approach of another American writer, Beverly J. Lanzetta, who has published a daring, innovative book entitled *Radical Wisdom: A Feminist Mystical Theology*,[22] and another study, *Emerging Heart: Global Spirituality and the Sacred.*[23] In seeking a feminine mystical way for the twenty-first century, it is worth listening to Lanzetta's ideas, some of which I want to share here.

Beverly Lanzetta is convinced of the importance of gender implications for the spiritual life. She invites us to a re-reading of mystical theology from a feminist angle in order to discover new spiritual lineages and revelatory traditions. Just as Sara Maitland argued over twenty years ago that we need women map makers of the interior country,[24] so Lanzetta too speaks of women standing on the borders of a new country as mapmakers of uncharted spiritual territory. She asks: 'What metaphors, symbols, images of God do women see, unite with, and reveal if they

---

[19] Barbara Newman, *Sister of Wisdom: St. Hildegard's Theology of the Feminine* (Berkeley, 1997).

[20] Deidre Green, *Gold in the Crucible* (Shaftesbury, 1989).

[21] Amy Hollywood, *Sensible Ecstasy* (Chicago, 2002).

[22] Beverley J. Lanzetta, *Radical Wisdom: a feminist mystical theology* (Minneapolis, 2005).

[23] Beverley J. Lanzetta, *Emerging Heart: global spirituality and the sacred* (Minneapolis, 2007).

[24] See Sara Maitland, *A Map of the New Country: Women and Christianity* (London, 1983).

travel by the way of the feminine? What wisdom can be gleaned from medieval women mystics on the geography of the soul?'[25] She deliberately speaks of the *via feminina*, a feminine way not restricted to women but open to both women and men, although it expresses itself differently in females than in males. She means by this feminine way a quality of religious consciousness and a mystical path that treads new ground. Thus she redefines the spiritual journey from the perspective of women, but not in an exclusive sense. Instead of seeking union with God through either the *via positiva* or the *via negativa*, she sees the *via feminina*, the feminine mystical way, as a 'third way', unveiling to us 'the feminine heart of divinity and the spiritual equality of women'.[26] She presents the *via feminina* as a 'radical mysticism' which seeks new forms of expression and engagement, while recognizing at the same time that some features of traditional mysticism reveal themselves as products of patriarchy. These have to be dismantled and replaced by something new for the present world.

It would be intriguing to guess what Grace Jantzen's reactions to Lanzetta's work might be. She writes in her Introduction to the Julian book:

> Perhaps central in importance is that when women find a voice we should find our own, *women's*, voice, not simply appropriate a masculine subjectivity or speak in a male tongue; and that we should do so without falling back into essentialism or some prescribed idea of 'real women'. Indeed, what is important is not to find simply woman's voice, but the voices of all the varieties of women, old women and young, women of colour and white women, lesbian women and heterosexual women and celibate women. Luce Irigaray … places great stress on women having 'a God according to our gender': I have developed this at length in *Becoming Divine*.[27] What is important to note here is that such a God is just what Julian portrays in her moving account of Mother Jesus.[28]

But Jantzen also comments that Julian does not consider any other aspects of womanhood than mothering and repeats many gender stereotypes. Although she speaks of 'God our Mother', she always uses exclusively male pronouns for God, a usage which Jantzen followed in her Julian book, but which she 'would not do so now'.[29]

Beverly Lanzetta's feminist mystical theology develops from this perspective of 'now' with the full awareness that much of past mystical thinking requires

---

[25] Lanzetta, *Radical Wisdom*, p. 8.

[26] Lanzetta, *Radical Wisdom*, p. 13.

[27] See Grace M. Jantzen, *Becoming Divine: Towards a Feminist Philosophy of Religion* (Manchester, 1998), which contains several references to Julian of Norwich. The title of the Norwich Cathedral 1996 lecture is listed in the Bibliography of this book as Jantzen, 1996, *Desire and the Divine*, Bungay, Norfolk: All Hallows Convent.

[28] Jantzen, *Julian of Norwich* (London, 2000), p. xiii.

[29] Jantzen, *Julian of Norwich*, p. xiv.

deconstruction. She writes: 'If mysticism traces the journey to freedom, then women cannot achieve their full spiritual potential without confronting the injustice and violence within which the terms *female-feminine-woman* have been inscribed throughout recorded history'.[30] She addresses the historical subservience of women in theological and spiritual circles, and critiques the still-prevalent prohibition against women in the highest spheres of spiritual authority and the still-rampant oppression of women in religious institutions.[31] However, beyond this critique or the 'un-saying' of 'woman' as traditionally understood – 'deconstructing and un-saying all that falsely defines "woman" and "feminine"'[32] – and the elimination of all forms of oppression, the *via feminina* moves on as a path of spiritual liberation. This includes a dynamic relationship between embodiment and transcendence. It pays particular attention to the multiple wisdom of body, psyche and soul in order to name and heal what diminishes or violates women. Its most distinguishing feature is that as a spiritual path this new 'feminine way'

> does not transcend differences – whether of gender, culture, race, or sex – but enters into them directly to experience a deeper unity capable of transforming the underlying causes of soul suffering. … [It] is vigilant about the ways in which the categories that name and define the spiritual life – redemption, salvation, soul, self, God, virtue – as well as the processes or stages of mystical ascent – purgation, dark night, union – repeat subtle forms of gender, racial, or social violence.[33]

Lanzetta's reflections emerge out of her experience as a spiritual director as well as her role as a scholar. The depth and richness of her work invite numerous re-readings, much critical reflection and engaging debate. If I understand Lanzetta correctly, she seeks to dismantle 'the great lie about the feminine'[34] in her trenchant critique of some of the oppressive aspects of traditional mysticism and spirituality. This is especially so when she speaks with much sensitivity and wisdom about women's spiritual oppression and wounding, and their great need for healing. She understands so intimately what it means 'to experience the wound of being female in this world'.[35] By way of critique it must be mentioned, however, that Lanzetta unfortunately ignores the central issues of power and authority, so carefully analysed in Jantzen's book *Power, Gender and Christian Mysticism*.

On the constructive side, Lanzetta suggests a wholesome, integral, embodied and undivided spirituality that is desirable, helpful and healing for both women and men. She characterizes the feminine mystical way (*via feminina*) as 'a socially-

---

30   Lanzetta, *Radical Wisdom*, p. 16.
31   Lanzetta, *Radical Wisdom*, p. 18.
32   Lanzetta, *Radical Wisdom*, p. 24.
33   Lanzetta, *Radical Wisdom*, p. 22.
34   Lanzetta, *Radical Wisdom*, p. 17.
35   Lanzetta, *Radical Wisdom*, p. 135.

engaged and bodily contemplative practice' that will assist 'in the expansion and refinement of a spirituality that is truly representative of our global, changing, and plural world'.[36]

It is particularly exciting to see how in charting the *via feminina* as a partly new way, Lanzetta draws support from the experiences of medieval women mystics, especially Julian of Norwich and Teresa of Avila. Both are presented as 'cartographers of the soul' and 'sisters in spirit' who stand out through their wise and mature guidance. Both women share spiritual lives and theologies that resonate remarkably with each other. Both travelled from female subordination to dignity and freedom:

> As marginalized females in predominately-male-dominated cultures, it was through their contemplative experiences and prayerful dialogues with God that they worked out their personal wounding and social concerns. In their struggles toward spiritual equality they mapped out an inner feminism – the territory of the soul by which mysticism becomes the site of women's empowerment and dignity.[37]

Lanzetta describes Julian's mystical experience as 'graphic and raw', especially when Julian contemplates the thirsting face and crucified body of Jesus on the cross. She recognizes Julian's distinctive theology of the feminine, 'in which the meaning of sin and suffering is transformed and her worth as a woman is affirmed. Conceptualizing this journey through the image of the motherhood of God, Julian works out her equality and dignity of personhood, and the sinlessness of her fellow Christians'.[38] Lanzetta affirms our need for a feminine Divine, our longing to experience God as mother, as Julian does so movingly when she speaks about God and Jesus as our mother and praises God's all-embracing motherly love for the whole of creation again and again.

Much more could be said on all of these, but I want to move on in order to reflect on the place of love and wisdom that figure so centrally in Julian's visions and are so much needed for healing our deep spiritual wounds today. They form a distinctive part of a feminine mystical way that can help to renew contemporary spirituality.

Love, Wisdom and the Feminine Mystical Way

Counsellors, pastors, even some politicians, and many ordinary people are all well aware of the great spiritual hunger that reveals itself in so many contemporary phenomena. What can be done to bring about more justice, harmony, peace and happiness in a world so deeply torn apart, where so many people suffer great material, emotional and spiritual deprivation?

---

[36] Lanzetta, *Radical Wisdom*, p. 24.
[37] Lanzetta, *Radical Wisdom*, p. 83.
[38] Lanzetta, *Radical Wisdom*, p. 84.

Countless individuals, groups of activists and institutions wrestle with these questions. Numerous suggestions and plans have been developed; some religious thinkers have proposed a global ethic, others speak of the need for global meditation, but also global action, to change the world together for the better. Beverly Lanzetta comes up with the excellent idea of recognizing distinctive *spiritual rights* that build upon international human rights. This brings a new perspective to global suffering, including women's suffering, since spiritual rights ask us 'to see each other and all creation from a divine perspective', with God's eyes, so to speak. She writes:

> Because the highest calling of the person is to have fullness of being, spiritual rights address what prevents or violates this pursuit.
>
> As the common element in all human cultures and traditions, the spiritual dimension of life is intertwined with and underlies all other rights…It recognizes that spirituality is life itself; thus, a life of dignity is inconceivable without spiritual integrity and freedom.
>
> Derived from 'a belief that recognizes within other people the presence of the divine through which a person attains full humanity,' spiritual rights place the expressly spiritual as a recognized right interdependent with and interrelated to civil and political rights, and economic and social rights.[39]

I find the notion of 'spiritual rights' a very helpful one, although it needs further elaboration. The inclusion of spiritual rights into the vocabulary of rights enables us to think about human dignity from a different perspective. It also reminds us that mental and spiritual violence as well as physical violence can destroy not only the body, but also the human spirit. In Lanzetta's words, spiritual rights are 'attentive to a certain quality of consciousness and a certain depth of heart that heal and transform. An indivisible relationship exists between the attainment of planetary responsibility and the necessity for spiritual practices, prayer, and meditative solitude'.[40]

The distinctiveness of spiritual rights leads Lanzetta to an 'ethic of ultimate concern', an embodied engagement that moves out of contemplation into action in the human sphere and into love for the world. She calls this a 'mystical ethic' which she describes as 'in essence, a mothering one; it embraces the world as a mother's body surrounds and nurtures life within her womb. Metaphors of pregnancy and birth help convey how each day we bear – lay our bodies down for – the spiritual renewal of life.'[41]

---

[39]   Lanzetta, *Radical Wisdom*, p. 183.
[40]   Lanzetta, *Radical Wisdom*, p. 184.
[41]   Lanzetta, *Radical Wisdom*, p. 201.

As human beings we are not only responsible for attention to our own selfhood, or for what happens to our family, friends and neighbours. As a morally and spiritually evolving species we also carry a common responsibility for the human family around the globe. For this we need to learn to nurture much more the qualities of love and wisdom than we have done hitherto by being attentive to spiritual energy resources as well as material ones.

In reflecting on the nature of a mystical ethic, Lanzetta draws partly on Julian who, she writes, 'enshrines this mystical love for the world in her reflection on the motherhood of Jesus. ... By associating the qualities of unconditional love and mercy with the mother figure, Julian conveys a more embodied, physical sense of the healing of sins and the unity of creation.'[42]

For Julian, 'love was our Lord's meaning'. All her revelations are summed up in these terse words of the last chapter of the Long Text of her *Showings*:

> What, do you wish to know your Lord's meaning in this thing? Know it well, love was his meaning. Who reveals it to you? Love. What did he reveal to you? Love. Why does he reveal it to you? For love. Remain in this, and you will know more of the same.

She also says that God revealed this 'because he wants to have it better known than it is'.[43] Thus we have to learn to recognize God's love in our lives and respond to it by accepting ourselves and loving others. It also means that we have much work to do to transform ourselves and our material culture that is so 'blinded to the unseen'.[44]

To quote a more recent Christian mystic, according to Pierre Teilhard de Chardin the day will come when humanity, after harnessing the energies of space, winds, water, and gravity, will harness the energies of love for God – and on that day humans, for the second time, will have discovered fire![45] Like Julian, Teilhard affirms that without the all-transforming power of love and the zest for life, human development at an individual and social level cannot be sustained.

It is remarkable how many similar ideas about the spiritual energy resources of love and wisdom are emerging among different individuals and groups around the globe. Contemporary thought in the sciences and arts, in religion and psychology, in psychotherapy and counselling, in human development and social thinking, provide many examples of this convergence of similarly conceived ideals for the human community. It is not only mystics, theologians or novelists who wrestle with love. Today whole research groups and projects are devoted to this topic. They are trying to find out what difference personal and altruistic love can make

---

[42]   Lanzetta, *Radical Wisdom*, p. 202.

[43]   See Julian of Norwich, *Showings* (trans. Edmund Colledge and James Walsh), Classics of Western Spirituality (London, 1978), p. 342.

[44]   Lanzetta, *Radical Wisdom*, p. 173.

[45]   See Pierre Teilhard de Chardin, *Toward the Future* (London, 1975), p. 87.

to the life of human beings in terms of health, happiness, joy and contentment. The theme of love also reverberates throughout Grace Jantzen's work where it resonates in her discussions of natality, desire, plenitude and flourishing as Morny Joy's essay in this volume shows.

A striking instance of some powerful parallel, but entirely independent, thinking about the transformative power of love is found in the writings of Pierre Teilhard de Chardin (1881–1955) and in the magisterial study on *The Ways and Power of Love* by Russian-American sociologist, Pitirim A. Sorokin (1889–1968),[46] founding professor of sociology at Harvard University. Both consider altruistic love as the highest human energy resource for the transformation of human society. Both also agree that humans at present know less about 'love energy' than about the different forms of physical energy such as light, heat and electricity. The transformative energies of love must be studied in all their different dimensions, whether cosmic, physical, biological, psychological, social, religious, or ethical. Sorokin speaks of love as one of the highest energies known to human being. Like Teilhard, he thinks that the production and distribution of love has until now been given little systematic thought in practically all societies. This shows an astounding lack of organized effort on the part of humanity – or one might say, a lack of spiritual focus and depth – and this lack now threatens humanity's very future. Throughout history, the family has been one of the most efficient agencies in producing altruistic love, and so have small religious communities, saints and mystics, but altruistic love must now be extended beyond these small groups to 'the human "world market"' according to Sorokin.[47] He paints a bold picture of the transformative power of love and the systematic possibility of developing, accumulating, and storing its energy for the benefit of individuals and communities. The great geniuses, heroes, or apostles of love throughout history, including the mystics, are like 'great power stations producing love for generations of human beings'.[48] But their example alone is not enough. What is needed now is an increase of love production by ordinary people and groups, in fact, by the whole culture, so that 'love, radiated by culture and by social institutions, would form a permanent atmosphere that would pervade all human beings from the cradle to the grave'.[49]

Is this merely a utopian dream or is it possible to work for such change? For this to happen, a global *spiritual awakening* has to occur. This requires *spiritual education* at all levels, not only for children and young people but as an integral part of life-long adult learning. Only then can we achieve what I call *spiritual*

---

[46]   Pitirim A. Sorokin, *The Ways and Power of Love. Types, Factors, and Techniques of Moral Transformation* (Philadelphia and London, [1954] 2002) A more detailed discussion of this convergence of thought is found in my article 'Love – A Higher Form of Human Energy in the Work of Teilhard de Chardin and Sorokin', *Zygon: Journal of Religion and Science*, 39/1 (2004): pp. 77–102.

[47]   Sorokin, *The Ways of Power and Love*, p. 39.

[48]   Sorokin, *The Ways of Power and Love*, p. 40.

[49]   Sorokin, *The Ways of Power and Love*, p. 45.

literacy, a literacy that goes beyond learning to read and write, beyond emotional and ethical literacy, to a much deeper dimension of insight and wisdom that grows from the heart, and fosters compassion and love.

The figure of wisdom – *sapientia* or *sophia* – has played a central role in the theologies of the feminine in different historical periods. This is true of medieval times where Hildegard of Bingen has been called 'sister of wisdom'[50] and Julian has been described as 'wisdom's daughter'.[51] Julian herself says that 'God all wisdom is our loving Mother'.[52] There has been a modern revival of sapiential theology, from the Romantics to Eastern Orthodox thinkers like Soloviev, Bulgakov or Florensky, but also in Teilhard de Chardin, with his poem on 'The Eternal Feminine'. Over the centuries, both men and women have been attracted to such theologies of the feminine. In Barbara Newman's view, 'these systems of thought cannot be explained solely by women's alleged need to identify with powerful feminine symbols, or by men's purported need to project these symbols as images of desire. Such motives may indeed be operative in the cases of individual writers, St. Hildegard included.'[53]

Thus symbols of the feminine, of the figure of Wisdom, and indeed of a feminine Divine, may be addressing the psychological needs of both women and men. Yet explanations of how they came about and what may be the meaning of these symbols for people's lives today vary enormously, from psycholinguistic theories to social and political explanations, and to a variety of philosophical and theological perspectives. Wisdom as *Sophia* plays an important role in feminist spirituality and theology. Yet it is not only Wisdom as female representation of the Divine, but women's own wisdom which has found new recognition today.

The American ecological thinker Thomas Berry describes the wisdom of women as one of four essential resources for contemporary cultural and spiritual renewal. He sees 'the great work' of building a viable future for people and planet as a human project that belongs to both women and men. However, it demands the transformation of all our institutions, from global politics, governance, education and financial arrangements to all aspects of culture, including religion. Berry thinks that humankind will not be able to achieve this radical transformation if we do not draw on all available resources. Most important among these are four kinds of wisdom: that of indigenous peoples, the wisdom of women, that of the classical philosophical and religious traditions of the world, and the new wisdom of science, still in its beginning phase, but advancing with amazing speed and success. The wisdom of women is very ancient, but it is now reasserting itself in new forms, transforming Western and other civilizations. Berry says: 'The wisdom of women

---

[50]   See Newman, *Sister of Wisdom*, especially Chap. 7 where she discusses sapiential theologies, feminism and the future.

[51]   Joan Nuth, *Wisdom's Daughter: The Theology of Julian of Norwich* (New York, 1991).

[52]   Julian of Norwich, *Showings*, p. 293.

[53]   Newman, *Sister of Wisdom*, p. 266.

is to join the knowing of the body to that of mind, to join soul to spirit, intuition to reasoning, feeling consciousness to intellectual analysis, intimacy to detachment, subjective presence to objective distance.'[54] This can be read as a description of some of the qualities associated with a feminine mystical way that is now open to both women and men and is prefigured in the lives of earlier women mystics.

The American Dominican, Father Richard Woods, has explored the similarity between the experiences of medieval and modern women mystics, perceiving their liberating, even revolutionary, force and prophetic function. He also recognizes with much discernment:

> that women today are accomplishing what women in the Middle Ages sought to achieve in their own time – they are redefining the sense of God as a supportive presence not only favourable toward women (as well as men), but as a spirit of liberation from the fear, disdain, prejudice, stereotypes, and active discrimination that has characterised men's attitudes towards women throughout much of the modern era and in many, perhaps most areas of the world ... with regard to their position in the Christian church in particular, women are protesting against their disenfranchisement as children to one God, co-heirs with Christ, full members of the Body of Christ, and adult citizens of the Reign of God, the heavenly City. They are doing so not only by pressing for full incorporation into ministry, but, as happened with Augustinian canonesses, Hildegard, the Cistercian nuns, the beguines, and even Julian of Norwich, establishing havens or sanctuaries where they are free to express their spirituality and ... to mature personally and collectively ....
>
> Emancipation and liberation are not themselves the goal of mystical experience. And yet, paradoxically, it is for that reason that it attains them.[55]

Julian's work is now attracting ever more attention and advanced scholarship. The most recent study I have read is by a Dutch woman, Petra Galama, on 'The Theology and Mystagogy of Julian of Norwich's *Showing of Love*', entitled *Behold How I Love You*.[56] Her analysis of Julian's *Showings* wants to contribute 'to the recognition of the theological and spiritual strength of women who speak and write about God'.[57] She argues persuasively that Julian's deep probing of her visionary experience of God's love and compassion can be a source of

---

[54]   Thomas Berry, *The Great Work: Our Way Into the Future* (New York, 1999), p. 180.

[55]   Richard Woods, OP., *Mediaeval and Modern Women Mystics: The Evidential Character of Religious Experience* (Lampeter: Religious Experience Research Centre. 2nd Series Occasional Paper 7), 19–20.

[56]   Petronella Hedwig Herman Maria Galama, 'Behold How I Love You. The Theology and Mystagogy of Julian of Norwich's Showing of Love' (PhD thesis, University of Bristol, 2005).

[57]   Petronella Galama, 'Behold How I Love You', p. 3.

renewal for contemporary theology. Furthermore, it has significant implications for the contemporary practice of spiritual direction and can help to advance the development of spirituality.

Conclusion

Theologians like Karl Rahner and William Johnston only see a future for Christianity, the church, or even religion, if mysticism and mystical spirituality will take the lead in people's lives. As Beverly Lanzetta writes in her latest book: '… it is the mystical quest that underlies and informs global spirituality today'.[58] The contribution of women mystics, and the further emergence of a feminine mystical way that embraces the powers of love and wisdom, are indispensable for this.

It is not all that long ago that the great contemporary interest in Julian's *Showing of Love*[59] first took off. In earlier centuries, Walter Hilton, Richard Rolle and the *Cloud of Unknowing* were much better known than Julian of Norwich. It was those men who were then considered as the typical 'English mystics', whereas now it is Julian of Norwich who seems to be the best known of all the English medieval mystics. May be we are moving into the age of the feminine in two different senses.

First, in spite of the ongoing oppression and violence towards women, and continuing gender disparity, we have to recognise that women in the West, but increasingly also globally, have achieved much material advancement in the social, economic, legal and educational sphere. But it is also part of women's calling to gain full equality and authority in the spiritual sphere by developing a new '*spiritual literacy*', whereby women define religion and spirituality for themselves rather than being passively defined by them. This is now happening in all religions, although the pace of change may differ widely. But this radical shift among women and religion is so little generally known that it has been described as a 'silent revolution' going on around the world.

Second, given the global rise in women's general and spiritual literacy, it is not surprising that women are developing new approaches to spirituality which combine the insights of faith and feminism. That includes various attempts to develop a more inclusive feminine mystical way, a new 'radical wisdom' that embraces an embodied and actively engaged contemplation nurtured by a mystical ethic 'enfolded in love', as suggested by Beverly Lanzetta and others, and permeating Julian's visions and writings.

---

[58]   See Beverly Lanzetta, *Emerging Heart. Global Spirituality and the Sacred* (Minneapolis, 2007), Chap. 3; Woods, *Mediaeval and Modern Women Mystics*, 19–20.

[59]   This is the title chosen for the textual edition and translation edited by Anna Maria Reynolds and Julia Bolton Holloway. (Florence, Sismel, 2001).

Spiritual work is demanding, not light work whose benefits can be gained without effort. To lead women and men of today to spiritual awakening, to a deeper awareness, to a new spiritual consciousness and actively engaged spiritual practice, is the great calling of our time. It demands many spiritual resources. It requires great integrity, deep honesty and truthfulness, and a passionate commitment to the life of the Spirit, to become 'attuned to the rivers of longing that flow between the divine and human heart'.[60]

Julian's vision of love, especially of God's all embracing motherly love, are a great inspiration for this task. Anchored in a passionate and compassionate spirituality, Julian can inspire people to seek a new feminine mystical way that, through love and wisdom, can help to heal the wounds of our world – an urgent and demanding task that, I think, also guided Grace Jantzen's heart in her affirmation of natality and human flourishing, even though envisioned in a very different time and context from that of Julian.

---

[60]   Lanzetta, *Radical Wisdom*, p. 87.

Chapter 8

On Jantzen and Theology: a Conversation with William Desmond

Clare Greer

The philosophy of religion traditionally investigates religion in general using reason and logic as its authorities, whereas theology traditionally appeals to apologetics, scripture and tradition. My interest in this essay is to explore what from a theological perspective would appear to be difficulties underlying the philosophical model of transcendence upon which Grace Jantzen's theory of divinity is based.

The discipline of theology requires a theory of relationship between the divine and human, since if the two are either completely the same or infinitely qualitatively different then there could be no relationship between them, which amounts in practice to atheism. I wish to use the work of William Desmond[1] to point out some difficulties that Jantzen's philosophy of religion poses for theology. I argue that the metaphysical claims that Jantzen is making do not establish relationship between divine (T^3) and human but are measurable in terms of what William Desmond calls T^1 and T^2.

William Desmond outlines three kinds of transcendence: T^1, T^2, and T^3. T^1 refers to other-being; 'the transcendence of external beings as other in nature: their transcendence is in their not being the product of our thinking, or doing'.[2] The very existence of things and beings that are outside our selves and not caused by our selves is the first form of transcendence. T^2 refers to 'the transcendence of *self-being* such as we meet especially in the self-surpassing power of the human being. The meaning of possibility here can be defined immanently rather than just determined externally'.[3] Human beings are inherently self-surpassing and this self-surpassing is immanent, finite, creative, and not dependent upon outside help: examples of this kind of transcendence are the self-surpassing of scientific progress, or the child's development into adulthood. T^3 refers to 'transcendence itself', God, or transcendence as other, which is not just an 'exterior transcendence' or an 'interior' transcendence but a 'superior' transcendence, a '"real" possibilizing power', original, completely other, and infinite.[4]

---

[1]   William Desmond, *Hegel's God* (Aldershot and Burlington, 2003); William Desmond, *God and The Between* (Malden, Oxford and Victoria, 2008).

[2]   Desmond, *Hegel's God*, p. 3.

[3]   Desmond, *Hegel's God*, p. 3.

[4]   Desmond, *Hegel's God*, pp. 3–4.

For Desmond, to speak of the 'between' or 'metaxu' is to speak of an ontological 'primal ethos' or 'given milieu of being' which is 'in excess of our determinations' or 'overdetermined'.[5] Although we participate in the given ethos, we are only aware of it through secondary ethē; determinate, ordered senses of being which we construct ourselves to make sense of the given, and which 'function as enablers and censors' in terms of the question of God.[6] To find new ways to God we need to 'be awoken from this sleep of the second ethos', to glimpse the first ethos.[7]

Desmond outlines four ways of being in the second ethos which represent different ways of relating to the primal ethos: the 'univocal way' 'stresses sameness to the diminution or underplaying of differences'.[8] The 'equivocal way' 'reaffirms the importance of difference(s) … but sometimes to the neglect or shortchanging of more lasting constancies'.[9] The 'dialectical way' 'is a mediation of the univocal and equivocal, and tries to do justice to the dynamic interplay of sameness and otherness … [but] one finds a tendency to privilege a more ultimate identity as inclusive of identity and difference' and 'the danger is a higher speculative univocity'.[10] The 'metaxological way' 'stands in openness to the overdeterminacy, even as it recurs to the interplay of sameness and difference'.[11]

Each of the ways communicates 'in immanence' a sign of that which exceeds immanence (T³). Desmond calls these signs 'hyperboles of being'.[12] The 'idiocy of being' emphasises 'the sheer "that it is" of given finite being', stunning us into mindfulness such that 'our thinking can become porous to what exceeds finite determination'.[13] The 'aesthetics of happening', emphasises astonishment before 'the beauty and sublimity of finitude that communicates an otherness exceeding all finitization'.[14] The 'erotics of selving', emphasises the 'infinitely self-surpassing' nature of our being, which means that 'we point and are pointed to a measure exceeding finite measure' that is more than our 'self-overcoming'. The 'agapeics of community' 'intimates a surplus generosity' in which the 'absolved porosity of the *passio essendi*' 'ethically lives itself as a *compassio essendi*' in which something that exceeds the ethical 'incarnates the holy'.[15]

Desmond's work provides a systematic map of the senses of being, in terms of which may be articulated hyperbolic 'indirections'[16] towards God (T³). This

---

[5]   Desmond, *God and the Between*, p. 3.

[6]   Desmond, *God and the Between*, p. 2.

[7]   Desmond, *God and the Between*, p. 3.

[8]   Desmond, *God and the Between*, p. 9.

[9]   Desmond, *God and the Between*, p. 9.

[10] Desmond, *God and the Between*, pp. 9–10.

[11] Desmond, *God and the Between*, p. 10.

[12] Desmond, *God and the Between*, p. 4.

[13] Desmond, *God and the Between*, p. 11.

[14] Desmond, *God and the Between*, p. 11.

[15] Desmond, *God and the Between*, p. 12.

[16] Desmond, *God and the Between*, p. 122.

allows me to investigate Jantzen's work in terms of the three transcendences T¹, T² and T³. Using Desmond's categories, I examine what senses of being are evident in Jantzen's work along with their strengths and weaknesses and the types of transcendence that they imply. Then I evaluate the status of her engagement with T³. Desmond's senses of being and hyperboles of being are inter-connected, and so each can be discerned in her work to some extent, although her work has most in common with the dialectical way and the erotics of selving.

For Jantzen, to speak of a 'between' in terms of the divine-human relationship is to speak not of a primal ethos but of a human construction, whether in a realist or non-realist framework. She argues that divinity as traditionally conceived has been a mirror of the male self, a Feuerbachian argument in which the between is characterised by the projection and gradual divination of human characteristics. Jantzen's appropriation of what could be called a projected 'between' is in the interests of moving towards a more adequate reflection of humanity in the divine, by 'becoming divine' by which she means creating a 'worthy divine horizon' rather than one that is distorted by multiple exclusions, and her project in *Becoming Divine* is to outline the content of this projection.[17]

So how does her work map on to the univocal and equivocal ways, or the idiocy of being and aesthetic astonishment before 'other-being'? She writes that:

> Rather than taking the creedal as fundamental, as traditional philosophy of religion does, a feminist symbolic [of divinity] whose source and criteria are found in women's lives starts from the ethical, indeed from acting for love of the world ... *not ethical as derived from the ontological, but ethical as response to the Other*' (emphasis mine).[18]

Whilst Desmond uses the 'four senses of being' as mediators of our accession to the 'between', or the 'elemental ontological resource' from which we can approach God and the good,[19] Jantzen strongly criticises the use of ontology as a basis for morality. According to Jantzen, the debate on ontology is about 'whether morality has an ontological foundation: whether what is "good" is derivable from what "is"', specifically God as the primary ontological foundation.[20] Jantzen cites Levinas's argument that if ontology is primary then knowledge is knowledge of beings, and beings must be subordinated to concepts to be understood. This means that 'knowledge is an activity which *appropriates* and *grasps* the otherness of the known'[21] (quoting Levinas) which 'effectively subordinates ethics to ontology'

---

[17]   Grace Jantzen, *Becoming Divine: Towards a Feminist Philosophy of Religion* (Manchester, 1998), pp. 89–92.

[18]   Jantzen, *Becoming Divine*, p. 236.

[19]   Desmond, *God and the Between*, p. 4.

[20]   Jantzen, *Becoming Divine*, p. 232.

[21]   Jantzen, *Becoming Divine*, p. 233.

and means that 'ethics itself is founded in violence – that is, in the unethical'.[22] Jantzen agrees that 'if knowledge is the apprehension or appropriation of being to myself, then knowledge is like digestion, making what is taken in a part of me. Everything then becomes part of "the same"'.[23] She argues that religion should be above all ethical, but 'not ethical as derived from the ontological': 'only in terms of an ethical response to actual humans is religion admissible'.[24] God is not defined as an ontological being; the divine is only defined in and through human relationships.[25]

Yet Jantzen concedes that Levinas's project is 'fraught with ambivalence'.[26] She criticises his emphasis on the threat of the other, the possibility of killing the other, and the menace of the other which 'forbids us to kill',[27] arguing that Levinas assumes a sovereign subject which takes responsibility for the other upon itself: this may 'come dangerously near an inverted bid for omnipotence'.[28] Jantzen's solution is to retain Levinas's rejection of ontology but to emphasise that as characterised by 'natality' – a 'fundamental human condition' which defines us as '[rooted] in the physical and material'[29] – all people are inter-dependent[30] and share moral responsibility for life: no one is sovereign.[31] This is intended to emphasise the harmonious plurality of others in a shared world.

But is this really sufficient? In terms of Desmond's four ways the problem is cast in a different light. According to Desmond, the problem of the 'same' is associated with the first sense of being or the 'univocal way': 'When we encounter the astonishing diversity of happenings ... our search for intelligibility looks for ... sameness in the muchness of multiplicity'.[32] Modernity is an attempt to make intelligible the utter plenitude of ontological givenness, a hyperbolic state which Desmond calls the very 'idiocy' of being itself. However the weakness of the univocal way is that the tendency to determine reality schematically results in the 'conquering of wonder'.[33] The mechanisation of the world goes hand in hand with a religious dualism that insists on preserving God's transcendence,[34] and this results in a 'culture of [human] autonomy' that is tempted to absolutise itself: with the

---

[22]   Jantzen, *Becoming Divine*, p. 233.

[23]   Jantzen, *Becoming Divine*, p. 233.

[24]   Jantzen, *Becoming Divine*, p. 236.

[25]   Jantzen, *Becoming Divine*, p. 253.

[26]   Jantzen, *Becoming Divine*, p. 238.

[27]   Jantzen, *Becoming Divine*, p. 238.

[28]   Jantzen, *Becoming Divine*, p. 244.

[29]   Jantzen, *Becoming Divine*, pp. 144–5.

[30]   Jantzen, *Becoming Divine*, p. 243.

[31]   Jantzen, *Becoming Divine*, p. 245.

[32]   Desmond, *God and the Between*, p. 49.

[33]   Desmond, *God and the Between*, p. 50.

[34]   Desmond, *God and the Between*, p. 62.

loss of the sense of 'sacred power' in things we begin to show '*aggression against creation*' as other-being is either subsumed under the same, or else repressed.[35]

Like Jantzen, Desmond argues that it is an awakening to other-being that shatters our illusion of omnipotence and so the univocal way recedes as the equivocal way breaks through in a new awareness of other-being. He writes that 'the *inescapability of manyness*',[36] '[breaks] our fixation on sameness', and '[awakens] what is non objectifiable, both in ourselves and in nature as other',[37] and he calls this the 'aesthetics of happening'. Like Jantzen, Desmond recognises that the confrontation with other-being can be destructive: he writes that we suffer from an 'ontological insecurity in the unmastered impermanence of being',[38] a fear of death or attack in which 'a posture of dualistic opposition to other-being justifies itself, just by the other's ambiguity – it will destroy me, therefore I disarm by attack first'.[39] Evil's equivocity takes three forms; overwhelming 'destructive power'; 'ourselves as divided within ourselves against ourselves', in which we internalise evil and 'feel ourselves stained' by it,[40] and '*God's otherness*' which manifests itself as uncertainty over the apparent capriciousness of God. Equivocity turns us 'back on ourselves' and we decide that '[henceforth] we will rely on ourselves alone',[41] which can lead to the will to power and the '*negation of being-other*'.[42]

However Desmond's critique of equivocity reveals problems in Jantzen's solution to the equivalences of Levinasian equivocity. By continuing to prioritise ethics over ontology, she has overlooked the 'vulnerability of ... finitude',[43] and in defining divinity only through human relations, or first transcendence (T¹),[44] she risks the 'ontological danger' 'that we [will] idolize ourselves and think it our destiny to create the world anew in our image'.[45] This would be a return to the devaluation of being. Desmond's ontological approach attempts to restrain the dominating *conatus essendi* (endeavour to be), by cultivating mindfulness of the *passio essendi* (patience of being) – 'our porosity to the divine ... as having received our being rather than as having determined it for ourselves'.[46]

Furthermore Levinas's argument that theology's ontological focus on being is a drive to 'totality' inadequate to being does not do justice to Desmond's hyperboles

---

[35] Desmond, *God and the Between*, p. 63.

[36] Desmond, *God and the Between*, p. 52 (emphasis in the original).

[37] Desmond, *God and the Between*, p. 74.

[38] Desmond, *God and the Between*, p. 78.

[39] Desmond, *God and the Between*, p. 79.

[40] Desmond, *God and the Between*, p. 80.

[41] Desmond, God *and the Between*, p. 83.

[42] Desmond, *God and the Between*, p. 83.

[43] Desmond, *God and the Between*, p. 21.

[44] Jantzen, *Becoming Divine*, p. 250.

[45] Desmond, *God and the Between*, p. 22.

[46] Desmond, *God and the Between*, p. 21.

of being,[47] which focus on participation in a givenness that is a happening of the good in an attempt to re-evaluate being (ontology) as given to be. While Jantzen's use of transcendence as other-being (T¹) risks the 'idolatry of autonomy' in finitude,[48] Desmond seeks to avoid this problem by clarifying the relationship between T¹ and T³ which exceeds it.

So how does Jantzen's work map on to the dialectical way and the erotics of selving? She writes that:

> Divinity in the face of natals is a horizon of becoming, a process of divinity ever new.[49]

And that:

> Although pantheism has been feared as the abyss in which all things would be a 'variant of the same', I shall show that the exact opposite is the case: A pantheist symbolic opens the way to difference, to the Other, to alterities of every sort.[50]

Desmond's 'dialectical way' is the interplay of the univocal and equivocal, in which they are surpassed in 'mindfulness of ... togetherness'[51] such that 'what stands in opposition also stands in relation'.[52] Modern 'pan(en)theism' – a locution which he uses to indicate the 'God of the *whole*'[53] – exemplifies the dialectical way. As the 'whole' or 'all in all'[54] the divine mediates 'equivocal manyness', meaning that while there is 'no simple univocal "either/or" between immanence and transcendence', a 'certain view of immanence is privileged over against dualistic transcendence'.[55] Desmond defines pan(en)theism in terms of the 'erotics of selving' in which the 'self-surpassing of the divine ... creates itself in creating the world – the world as the embodiment of the divine is the immanent other that allows this erotic self-surpassing of the divine to be an embracing self-mediation of the whole with itself'.[56] The dialectical way is characterised by the transcendence of self-being (T²), rather than 'robust otherness' (T³), and it carries the risk of another 'idolatry of autonomy' by making an 'absolutely inclusive whole', or a '"higher" univocity'.[57]

---

[47]   Desmond, *God and the Between*, p. 242.

[48]   Desmond, *God and the Between*, p. 42.

[49]   Jantzen, *Becoming Divine*, p. 254.

[50]   Jantzen, *Becoming Divine*, p. 265.

[51]   Desmond, *God and the Between*, p. 92.

[52]   Desmond, *God and the Between*, p. 91.

[53]   Desmond, *God and the Between*, p. 226, n. 1.

[54]   Desmond, *God and the Between*, p. 225.

[55]   Desmond, *God and the Between*, p. 225.

[56]   Desmond, *God and the Between*, p. 226.

[57]   Desmond, *God and the Between*, pp. 92–3.

However let us examine Jantzen's position more closely: Jantzen finds valuable resources for the feminist symbolic in 'process thought'; the idea that 'God, like everything else, is in process, involved in change'[58] (first quotation). She argues that 'their insistence on embodiment and ecology'[59] and on 'growth and change [as] characteristic of the divine' coheres well with 'natality', a term which she borrows from Hannah Arendt and develops into a philosophical position in which 'the emergence of *this* life [birth] and *this* world' are treated with the same seriousness as death and 'the striving for other worlds'.[60] As the condition of possibility and potentiality rooted 'in the physical and material',[61] natality affirms the dignity of each life, 'interconnection in the web of life',[62] and 'love of the world'.[63] For Jantzen, we are the mediators, and in the 'through us' of the transcendent (T^2), our irreducibility, we are 'bringing the god to life',[64] which resonates with the dialectical way. She finds further resources for the symbolic in panentheist and pantheist conceptions of the God-world relationship[65] (second quotation), particularly Whitehead and Hartshorne's proposal that 'God is inseparable from the world' understood in the 'strong' sense that 'the world could be said to be the "embodiment" of God' 'not ... extraneous to God'.[66] The sense that God is a self-mediating whole also resonates with the dialectical way.[67]

However Jantzen's work issues a serious ethical challenge to Desmond. She attempts to do philosophy of religion in a way that takes note of 'actual suffering and how it comes about, who are the victims and who are the perpetrators'; philosophy that is aware of its own implication in power and dominance.[68] Failure to take responsibility for such power becomes collusion in injustice. However she goes further, arguing that the traditional split between spirit and matter is a pattern used to justify oppressive hierarchies; spirit and matter, male and female, in a pattern of 'expulsion of alterities' in which the second term is, using a quotation from Elizabeth Grosz, a 'negation or denial'.[69] For Jantzen, the idea, borrowed from process thought, that God is part of and 'suffers with and through the suffering of the world' is the only ethically acceptable conception of God: 'Pantheism rejects

---

58   Jantzen, *Becoming Divine*, p. 255.

59   Jantzen, *Becoming Divine*, p. 258.

60   Jantzen, *Becoming Divine*, p. 2.

61   Jantzen, *Becoming Divine*, p. 145.

62   Jantzen, *Becoming Divine*, p. 151.

63   Jantzen, *Becoming Divine*, p. 152.

64   Jantzen, *Becoming Divine*, p. 272.

65   Jantzen, *Becoming Divine*, p. 258.

66   Jantzen, *Becoming Divine*, p. 258.

67   Jantzen, *Becoming Divine*, p. 256.

68   Jantzen, *Becoming Divine*, p. 263.

69   Jantzen, *Becoming Divine*, p. 267.

the split between spirit and matter, light and darkness, and the rest; it thereby rejects the hierarchies based on these splits'.[70]

Like Jantzen, Desmond criticises the type of transcendence in which a voluntaristic 'God is removed beyond the world' 'in a metaphorics of the machine [world] and its maker' that is 'a *reduction* of nature to powers indifferently subpersonal';[71] he writes that the pan(en)theist approach is 'a rebound from this devoid nature'.[72] However he also identifies two problems in the way that that pantheism is making this move: the first problem is that of the one and the many; how we hold together 'the multiplicity of things' with 'a One that runs through all'.[73] The second problem is 'why being or beings at all?'.[74]

Jantzen considers the one and the many to be an ethical problem, and she attempts to resolve it within the terms of a pantheist approach; her goal is to preserve 'recognition and respect for alterities [rather than] than collapsing [them] into polarities' in which the other is repressed.[75] In order to resist making a hierarchy of transcendences while retaining the sense that divinity is a 'beyond', Jantzen must conceptually maintain two separate 'differences'; the difference within or between beings, and the difference between beings and God. She compares the 'divine/world relationship' with the relationship of a person to her or his (gendered) body';[76] reiterating the conclusions of her early work, that '[if] human embodiment does not reduce personal significance to physiology, neither would the postulate that God's body is the universe mean that God is finally describable in exclusively physical terms'.[77] There is a sense in which the earth, like a human body is irreducible to physicality, and in which 'transcendence is compatible with divine embodiment',[78] a model that undermines patterns of hierarchical polarity in which the human other is negated or repressed, and therefore promotes the non-destructive co-existence of difference between beings.

She also tries to resolve within a pantheist framework the problem of 'why being or beings at all': The traditional doctrine of creation *ex nihilo* is resistant to the 'God of the whole', because if the divine is seen as either 'once' coming to be, or else 'never' coming to be at all, then this 'never' 'retreats beyond our conceptual mastery',[79] in other words 'if the absolute One is the self-compacted whole' then how did the one come to be?[80] There must be something outside the whole, or prior

---

[70]   Jantzen, *Becoming Divine*, p. 267.

[71]   Desmond, *God and the Between*, p. 227.

[72]   Desmond, *God and the Between*, p. 229.

[73]   Desmond, *God and the Between*, p. 231.

[74]   Desmond, *God and the Between*, p. 231.

[75]   Jantzen, *Becoming Divine*, p. 266.

[76]   Jantzen, *Becoming Divine*, p. 267.

[77]   Grace Jantzen, *God's World, God's Body*, (London, 1984), p. 127.

[78]   Jantzen, *God's World, God's Body*, p. 127.

[79]   Desmond, *God and the Between*, p. 54.

[80]   Cf. Jantzen, *God's World, God's Body*, p. 131.

to it.[81] However Jantzen argues that being content to live and 'flourish' within the limits of finitude is an ethical imperative, and that the traditional preoccupation with immortality, infinity and 'other worlds' is the 'rejection of limits' equates to a destructive quest for 'mastery'.[82] Using a pantheist argument, therefore, she maintains that the universe is the embodiment of God; that it has always existed and God *shaped* it rather than creating it *ex nihilo*, meaning that although the universe has an 'eternal' and 'absolute dependence' on God, it has no temporal beginning.[83] For Jantzen, accepting the limits of the temporal whole is necessary; even if that is to concede that what is outside it is unthinkable.

Desmond's criticism of pan(en)theism or the God of the whole, is that when the whole is prioritized over the infinite then '[there] can be no other God left remaining to remind us of the sin of hubris'.[84] He argues that the 'rupture of the human and God' is particularly evident in the 'projective theory of religion' – a 'dialectical self-mediation in and through an other that is no other finally'.[85] He writes that '[we] have dialectically reconstructed ourselves as the false double of God. In truth this is a return to the equivocal, a return dissembled and dissembling, hence a return to evil, though it announces itself as the final liberation of human creativity'.[86] For Desmond, the revaluation of the world depends on the possibility of T³; of 'a God beyond the [temporal] whole'[87] that is the origin of the *passio essendi*, an ontological "yes" to the primal origin or 'between', which restricts the *conatus essendi* and its tendency to dominate. There is 'no argument for the ... ontological "yes"; it is a happening'.[88] In respect of Jantzen's ethical concerns, however, the question finally amounts to whether the ethical good is best served by regarding divinity as hyperbolic (T³) or holistic (T²):

The crux of the disagreement between Jantzen and Desmond is the status of third transcendence (T³). Desmond develops his ideas about T³ in his 'metaxological way', and there are indications of Jantzen's position regarding transcendence as other throughout her work. In concluding the arguments of *Becoming Divine*, she writes that:

> It is indeed true that if the divine is to serve as the horizon of our becoming, then the divine must be transcendent, ever beyond present actuality, and certainly not reducible to the set of physical particularities of the material universe ... But

[81]   Desmond, *God and the Between*, p. 55.

[82]   Jantzen, *God's World, God's Body*, pp. 154–5.

[83]   Jantzen, *God's World, God's Body*, p. 132.

[84]   Desmond, *God and the Between*, p. 115.

[85]   Desmond, *God and the Between*, p. 115, n. 16.

[86]   Desmond, *God and the Between*, p. 115.

[87]   Desmond, *God and the Between*, p. 54.

[88]   Desmond, *God and the Between*, p. 35.

from this it does not follow that the divine must be a separate entity, an 'other' being, somewhere else.[89]

Desmond's metaxological way is an attempt, he writes, 'to think the divine "more" by calling on a metaphysical mindfulness finessed for the surpluses of being manifest in the immanent while',[90] an attempt to become aware of third transcendence or T³ that takes 'care not to compromise divine transcendence as it is intimated in the surpluses of immanent being'.[91]

Jantzen, unlike Desmond, does not seek closure on the debate between realism and non-realism in thought about the divine. She argues that 'there is every reason to suspend the question of truth in the interests of allowing more scope to the creative imagination, and seeing to what extent a feminist projection of a female divine might help shift the ground of what has too often been a highly oppressive concept of God'.[92] According to Jantzen, realists 'regularly address gender-concerns in staunchly pro-feminist ways' while 'an anti-realist position is no guarantee of a shift in the masculinist symbolic',[93] so she is 'prepared to allow that such openness could occur within either an antirealist or a (chastened) realist position'.[94]

By producing a philosophy of religion that is not necessarily realist, the question with which Jantzen's work most challenges Desmond is the question of whether religion and the divine are necessary to human flourishing at all. Of her own work she asks, '[would] it not be more honest just to admit that what we have here is an abandonment of theism, a thinly disguised secularism?'[95] For Jantzen it is a matter of producing a strategic response to the 'dualistic and hierarchical Western symbolic, which Western secularism largely leaves in place'.[96] Secularism is not a ready answer. Her strategy is to interrupt the symbolism of traditional religion so that any divine that is projected can more inclusively represent 'the perfection of [diverse human] subjectivity' rather than just the subjectivity of traditionally dominant groups (whites, males, the wealthy, the able-bodied and heterosexuals).

For Desmond, conversely, transcendence as other is importantly real, and porosity to transcendence as other is part of a journey through godlessness that is the path to goodness. For Desmond the divine is so elemental and the question of the divine is 'innate', that there can be no question of projection.[97] Atheism is a 'crime against nature';[98] an ontological problem, in which being is separated

---

[89] Jantzen, *Becoming Divine*, p. 271.
[90] Desmond, *God and the Between*, p. 117.
[91] Desmond, *God and the Between*, p. 116.
[92] Jantzen, *Becoming Divine*, p. 192.
[93] Jantzen, *Becoming Divine*, p. 191.
[94] Jantzen, *Becoming Divine*, p. 192.
[95] Jantzen, *Becoming Divine*, p. 248.
[96] Jantzen, *Becoming Divine*, p. 275.
[97] Desmond, *God and the Between*, p. 18.
[98] Desmond, *God and the Between*, p. 18.

from the good,[99] which is innate only to the *passio essendi* and derived from the source. For Desmond godlessness leads humans to make ourselves gods, while for Jantzen it is the hierarchies of traditional transcendence. Yet Desmond's God is not the hierarchical masculine God of modernity, and its traditional attributes are secondary to a sense of over-determinate being, which communicates something that is a complex 'hyperbolic "more"',[100] a 'hyperbolic goodness'.[101] It is a 'metaxological' alternative to the extremes of secularism and absolute transcendence, which begins to address the metaphysical hierarchy that Jantzen so strongly condemns. Nonetheless it lacks Jantzen's strong ethical insistence that efforts to preserve the uniqueness and transcendence of a divine being should take second place to addressing the concrete issues in *this* world.

So how does Jantzen use of first and second transcendence (T^1 and T^2) to promote her ethical goal? In her discussion of Levinas, she develops what could be called first transcendence (T^1) in association with the theory of natality. According to Jantzen, Levinas's prioritisation of the ethical in the face of the other (T^1) suggests a new way of looking at desire, in which it is not about self-realisation or the search for fulfilment (which 'would only be the return of the self to itself'), but is 'reshaped by the face of the Other ... beyond myself', and in this, writes Jantzen, 'it bears the trace of the divine'. [102] In terms of Jantzen's feminist symbolic the interaction with other-being creates 'a gap for a deliberate appeal to desire in the development of the feminist projection of the divine, welcoming the imagination while accountable to the material and discursive conditions of women's lives'.[103] Transcendence 'must be in accordance with the deepest of human desires',[104] and Jantzen's work is a paradigmatic example of the ethical power of first transcendence.

Jantzen also uses second transcendence (T^2), to promote her ethical goal. This may seem paradoxical: her aim is to promote flourishing and 'human autonomy',[105] however the traditional critique of pantheism, also levelled against Spinoza, is that in it 'everything [is] swallowed up in an undifferentiated wholeness' like an 'abyss' which would be detrimental to freedom and individuality.[106] Jantzen's answer to this criticism is to ask 'whose freedom exactly is at stake?' She suggests that the traditional understanding of freedom associated it strongly with 'rational autonomy', but that rationality is often defined sharply against physicality. According to Jantzen, where freedom depends on a same being defined against an

---

[99]   Desmond, *God and the Between*, p. 20.
[100] Desmond, *God and the Between*, p. 287.
[101] Desmond, *God and the Between*, p. 340.
[102] Jantzen, *Becoming Divine*, p. 251.
[103] Jantzen, *Becoming Divine*, p. 251.
[104] Jantzen, *Becoming Divine*, p. 251.
[105] Jantzen, *Becoming Divine*, p. 272.
[106] Jantzen, *Becoming Divine*, p. 273.

other, then the motivation is suspect.[107] Jantzen's pantheism makes such definitions impossible and takes the risk that rather than being absorbed into the other in a larger univocity or sameness, that it will promote a new sort of equality at the level of the symbolic between the powerful and those who would otherwise be excluded and repressed as 'others'.

In conclusion, Jantzen's work contains aspects of first and second transcendence (T^1 and T^2), which each promote her ethical goal in a way that is profound. Her work does not leave room for a sort of 'superior transcendence' as is found in the work of William Desmond. The question of the relationship between divine and human is for Jantzen a projected middle, to 'become divine' is not to change one's ontological state; it is a metaphor which alludes to the historical and cultural promotion of white, male, heterosexual characteristics as the highest human values, and the way that they have been gradually 'become divine' in the construction of the traditional 'God' and his attributes. Jantzen wants to harness a similar process of divinisation, but to project a more inclusive version of human subjectivity; multi-racial, female, gay and lesbian, and this she calls 'becoming divine'. It is to project a 'divine horizon' of values that all people can look to and see themselves included.

Desmond's work provides a systematic map of types of transcendence and ways to God, Jantzen's work on Levinas and ethics is an encounter with the equivocity of other-being, and her use of pan(en)theist thought takes a dialectical path, in which God mediates Godself in the world and is not separate from the world. Desmond's own theory of God, or the metaxological way, does not fit into the dualistic model of traditional Christianity that Jantzen so profoundly criticises. His approach is ontological but it figures God as an excess or hyperbole of being, rather than a voluntarist God which is absolutely other and controls the world by divine command. The debate between Jantzen and Desmond centres on the question of whether ontology is a good foundation for ethics. Jantzen radically prefers ethics over ontology, and Desmond's work highlights important weaknesses in this approach; it risks the 'idolatry of autonomy' and the inflation of finitude, a problem which Desmond attempts to address in his own work by using third transcendence as a restriction on the finite. However Jantzen is prepared to take this risk on the grounds that the inherent limits on finitude and the limit of the self, who as a natal living among other natals is inherently interdependent and therefore limited by this human condition.

Jantzen's challenge to theologians is not necessarily to renounce realism, it is to be aware that the plenitude of being is more than the traditional divine attributes, and that, even if the divine is shown, as Desmond argues, by the 'hyperboles of being', divinity should reflect the diversity of that being more fully.

---

[107]   Jantzen, *Becoming Divine*, p. 273.

Chapter 9
Life, Death and Discernment: Ignatian Perspectives

Kate Stogdon

Introduction

Grace Jantzen put her energy firmly into outlining a this-worldly imaginary where women could recognize themselves as subjects of their own life, and to the interrogation of the foundations supporting the 'violent, death-obsessed symbolic of the west'.[1] This was no small project and one that has been lamentably cut short. This essay takes its cue from Grace's unearthing of gendered trajectories of desire both in the passionate writings of the medieval women mystics[2] and in the repression of desire within 'creedal discourses'.[3] Rather than re-inscribe notions of desire as premised on lack Grace sought to identify its role in the creation of flourishing and fullness of life. Through a consideration of the schooling in desire found in the 'Spiritual Exercises' of Ignatius of Loyola (1491–1556) I will argue that Ignatian discernment displays the potential to disrupt as well as reinforce a death-dealing imaginary through its criteria of choosing life in the face of death (Deut 30. 15,19; John 10.10). This is illustrated by reading in the spirit of and yet against the grain of the 'Exercises'. By gendering the sexless Ignatian subject and noting the destabilizing role played by desire within the process of discernment I leave the reader with a question: 'what difference does it make to pay attention to *who* is the 'one' who discerns and about *what* and *how* do they go about it?'

The Ignatian Way

When Ignatius wrote his 'Spiritual Exercises', compiled over some twenty years, he produced both a very personal and yet public text. As founder of the Society of Jesus Ignatius embodied the spirit of the Catholic response to the Protestant Reformation and yet his handbook for spiritual directors encouraged a most

---

[1] Grace Jantzen, *Foundations of Violence, Volume 1: Death and the Displacement of Beauty* (London and New York, 2004), p. 4.

[2] Grace Jantzen, *Power, Gender and Christian Mysticism* (Cambridge, 1995).

[3] Grace Jantzen, *Becoming Divine: Towards a Feminist Philosophy of Religion* (Manchester, 1998), p. 77.

profound immediacy with God through the life of prayer.[4] The 'Exercises' have formed the basis of the Ignatian tradition of discernment, which continues to be both studied and practised in the twenty-first century.[5] The directory of 1599 emphasises that Ignatius' instructions on the spiritual life were inspired 'not so much from books as from the anointing of the Holy Spirit and his own inward experience and practice'.[6] By reflecting on his own spiritual growth and accompanying others in the life of prayer Ignatius formulated an ordered yet flexible process which facilitated an ongoing conversion to the will of God. Structured into four 'weeks' of prayer the 'Exercises' are premised on the teleological vision that 'all human life and all human action' find their 'ultimate meaning' within the wholeness of God's creation. Within this framework human desires are understood to find their true fulfilment through their alignment with God's overarching purpose for all creation. The ideal human response to this divine creative force is one of loving obedience to God's call by means of 'total spiritual freedom'.[7] Such disinterested freedom is attained through a nuanced attention to the interplay of desire and grace as the exercitant (the one who makes the 'Exercises') prays for the gifts necessary to live out their personal vocation. The 'first principle and foundation' and the 'contemplation to attain the love of God' act as containers of the dynamic movement of the 'Exercises' through their expression of gift and response to be found through participation in the ongoing creative love of God.[8]

It is important to notice the lengthy process engaged in by Ignatius as he refined his thinking in relation to the practice of giving the 'Exercises'.[9] Philip Endean has pointed out that his rules for discernment of the will of God did not 'drop out of heaven ready-made' and Ignatius did not claim that they were 'true of all people at all times and in every place'. The rules then are 'rough, provisional generalizations, grounded on the possession of a skill, on a growing familiarity with the ways of God's action in human hearts'. They are not 'the last word' but ways of working with 'spiritual growth', in such a way that the person who prays risks 'expansion ... transformation' through encounter with the 'divine fullness'. Endean underlines that Ignatius' encounter with God was a 'generative' one, so

---

[4] David Lonsdale, *Eyes to See, Ears to Hear: An Introduction to Ignatian Spirituality* (London, [1990] 2000).

[5] David L. Fleming, *Like the Lightening: The Dynamics of Ignatian Exercises* (St Louis, MO, 2004).

[6] Martine E. Palmer, *On Giving the Spiritual Exercises: The Early Jesuit Manuscript Directories and the Official Directory of 1559* (St Lois, MO, 1996), p. 290.

[7] Marian Cowan and John Carroll Futrell, *Companions To Grace: A Handbook for the Directors of the Spiritual Exercises of Saint Ignatius of Loyola* (Saint Lois, MO, 2000), pp. 6–7.

[8] Ignatius of Loyola (Louis J. Puhl (trans.) *The Spiritual Exercises of St Ignatius, based on studies in the language of the autograph* (Chicago, 1951), [# 23, 230–7].

[9] The paragraphs of the 'Spiritual Exercises' are denoted in the text in square brackets for example [#186].

that 'patterns of meaning' necessarily change over time.[10] New contexts then invite fresh interpretations.

The Ignatian Path to Holiness: a Privatising, Genderless Interpretation of Spirituality?

Central to Grace's hermeneutical task was her deconstruction of the categories of mysticism and spirituality, laying bare the gendered and socially constructed natures of spiritual traditions within Christianity. In her analysis of medieval women mystics she argued that they 'pushed back boundaries' and demanded reconsideration of the 'categories by which they were defined'; thereby contributing to changes in the 'structures of power and gender' which delimited them.[11] Her illustration of the ways in which such women were unavoidably restricted by their religious context and yet wrested meaning from it has helped to inform my analysis of the 'Exercises'. Grace was wary about whether modern constructions of spirituality were adequate to the task of social and political critique, noting the tendency towards the privatisation of religious experience. She singled out for comment *God of Surprises*[12] (the popular and influential work on Ignatian spirituality) because of what she saw as its overemphasis on 'personal psychological well-being'.[13] Such a stress on personal happiness at the expense of social concern, she argued, served to sedate people, reinforce 'structures of injustice' and domesticate spirituality.[14] Whilst her criticism is based on a somewhat reductionist account of Hughes' work, it raises the issue of popular spirituality by sound-bite and the resulting blunting of prophetic content. Commentators on the 'Exercises' in fact insist on the vital link between personal and social action within the dynamic. So Michael Ivens[15] argues that although the 'Exercises' provide a conversion tool and a school of prayer their principal purpose has always been to form apostles.[16] This apostolic commitment continues to critique privatising tendencies at work within the religious culture in which the 'Exercises' are practised.[17] Nevertheless, Grace's

---

[10]   Philip Endean, 'Discerning Behind the Rules', *Way Supplement* (Spring 1989): pp. 45–7.

[11]   Jantzen, *Power, Gender and Christian Mysticism*, p. 16.

[12]   Gerard W. Hughes, *God of Surprises* (London, 1985).

[13]   Jantzen, *Power, Gender and Christian Mysticism*, p. 19.

[14]   Jantzen, *Power, Gender and Christian Mysticism*, p. 19.

[15]   Michael Ivens, 'Ignatius Loyola', in C. Jones, G. Wainwright and E. Yarnold (eds) *The Study of Spirituality* (London, 1986), pp. 357–62.

[16]   Michael Ivens, *Understanding the Spiritual Exercises* (Leominster, 1988).

[17]   For contemporary Ignatian expressions see the work of the Woodstock Theological Center (US) http://woodstock.georgetown.edu/index.html#About and the Heythrop Institute of Religion, Ethics and Public Life (UK) http://www.heythrop.ac.uk/index.php/content/view/418/387/.

challenge remains an important one. By her insistence on the social construction of mysticism she sought to keep a Foucauldian interrogation of vested interests at the forefront of debates.[18]

This investigation of the co-option of the spiritual life, its meaning and its effects has been continued by Carrette and King[19] in their exposition on the 'silent takeover of "the religious" by contemporary capitalist ideologies' utilizing discourses of 'spirituality'. It is this emphasis on the 'individual', they contend, which has made possible emerging 'consumerist and capitalist spiritualities' which have now infiltrated so many aspects of social life. Such ideologies subsume the 'ethical and religious' within an 'overriding economic agenda' and 'promote accommodation' rather than 'challenge' to the social, economic and social institutions within societies.[20] However, the 'contested site' of religion in its capacity to evoke both 'positive and negative images' is also a potent possibility for re-imagination. Looking more closely at what consumerist ideologies seek to silence makes it possible to articulate concerns about 'community ... social justice' as a 'counter discourse'.[21]

As well as her attentiveness to the dangers of the privatisation of mysticism Grace insisted on the vital role played by gender in constructions of the divine and the interpretation of spiritual experiences. Her ethic of natality emphasises the sources of flourishing that enable women to disrupt the masculinist symbolic and to re-imagine a divine horizon which enables them to be subjects as women.[22] When addressing the gendered impact of the 'Spiritual Exercises' on women and men Grace's method of disrupting the cultural dynamic through 'double reading' provides a helpful tool.[23] Indebted to Derrida and Irigaray this way of 'thinking differently' looks for possible ruptures in the text, which can open up the possibility of a different interpretation of accepted readings.[24] When considering the text of the 'Exercises' it can be very beguiling to read Ignatius' language about 'the one who is to go through the Exercises' (the exercitant) [for example #5] and 'the one who is giving the Exercises' (the director) [as in #6] as if they were somehow disembodied, sexless beings, transcending their particular historical time and context. It is significant then to make explicit who are the persons engaged in practices of discernment and to take into account the ways in which their desires have interacted with the rules of the tradition, embedded within their particular

---

[18]   Jantzen, *Power, Gender and Christian Mysticism*, pp. 18–25.

[19]   Jeremy Carrette and Richard King, *Selling Spirituality: The Silent Takeover of Religion* (London, 2005), p. 2.

[20]   Carrette and King, *Selling Spirituality*, pp. 4–5.

[21]   Carrette and King, *Selling Spirituality*, pp. 70–72.

[22]   Jantzen, *Becoming Divine*, p. 12.

[23]   Jantzen, *Becoming Divine*, p. 61.

[24]   Jantzen, *Becoming Divine*, p. 73.

social location.[25] Attending to desires which interrupt gendered understandings of what it means to be women and men in relation to the divine is a way of reading 'against the grain' of the 'Spiritual Exercises'. In this way I can reveal the ways in which their practitioners while remaining faithful to the Ignatian spirit can generate novel ways of what it means to be the desiring subject.

Obedient/Disobedient Gendered Subjects: the 'Exercises' and Women

While Ignatius and the early directories of the society presumed that it would be highly unusual for women to be given the complete 'Exercises', generally limiting their prayer to the exercises of the 'First Week' as 'sufficient',[26] this was not always the case. Ignatius emphasised that the full 'Exercises' should be given 'only to very capable subjects', assumptions about class and gender necessarily informing his understanding of their suitability.[27] However, practice of giving the 'Exercises' by the early generations of Jesuits resulted in a broadening of understanding. Although as Palmer notes, Nadal[28] judged that laywomen should generally be restricted to the 'first week' he gave a qualified assent to nuns' capability to go further: 'Nuns may be given more that this, but judiciously and without the elections'.[29] The Directory of 1599 gave more scope, acknowledging that women 'occasionally ask to make the Exercises'. While generally advising that annotation 18 be followed (limited adaptation) there was a recognition that 'there may be cases of women who possess such good judgment and capacity for spiritual things, and sufficient leisure at home, that they can make all or most of the Exercises in full form. There is nothing to prevent this.' The Society tried to limit such exposure to those women whose state in life afforded the conditions to experience the full 'Exercises' and urged 'prudence'. At the same time, they conceded that the dynamic of the 'Exercises' was suitable for persons of both sexes.[30] Despite such reservations about the capacity of certain sorts of persons to truly benefit from the riches of the complete 'Exercises' the principle of adaptation meant that the dynamic of the text was transmitted through successive generations.

Such developments however were fraught with difficulties as those who sought to establish Ignatian retreats for women discovered, as for example Mme Catherine de Francheville in the seventeenth century and Thérèse Couderc in the

---

[25] Mary McClintock Fulkerson, *Changing the Subject: Women's Discourses and Feminist Theology* (Minneapolis, 1984).

[26] Palmer, *On Giving the Spiritual Exercises*, p. 25.

[27] Palmer, *On Giving the Spiritual Exercises*, p. 24.

[28] Palmer, *On Giving the Spiritual Exercises*, p. 39.

[29] Palmer, *On Giving the Spiritual Exercises*, p. 39.

[30] Palmer, *On Giving the Spiritual Exercises*, p. 37.

nineteenth century.[31] Furthermore, those women who drew on the 'Exercises' to inspire prophetic actions met considerable opposition. This is illustrated most strikingly by the experience of Mary Ward in her attempts to create a new form of uncloistered religious life for women in the early seventeenth century, modelled on the Jesuits.[32] Ward drew on Ignatian discernment to confirm her call to 'take of the same of the society' although her vision failed during her lifetime. Derided as 'Jesuitresses' and called the 'galloping girls' Ward and her companions refused the restrictions of the cloistered life and distinctive habit in order to live their perceived apostolic charism. Ward relied on the method of the 'Exercises' to support her and was insistent that they should form the novices in her institute. It was this process of discernment that she trusted rather than any one spiritual director, having no consistent person to fulfil this role.[33] Seventeenth century attempts to expand the ways in which women participated in the 'Exercises' were unsuccessful. Subsequently however, the fragmented religious and political landscape of nineteenth century France afforded opportunities for women to both undergo and direct the full 'Spiritual Exercises', trained and supervised by the Society of Jesus.[34] By the end of this century such occasions were again curtailed and it was only after the renewal of the Second Vatican Council in the 1960s that women were able to act as directors of the complete 'Exercises'.

Influenced by the advent of feminist theological critiques in the latter part of the twentieth century there has been some attempt to address the issue of gender and its impact on the practice of Ignatian spirituality.[35] As women have participated more widely in the ministry of spiritual direction and accompaniment, there has been a concern to evaluate women's experience and contribution.[36] More recently, a notable commentary and rereading of the 'Spiritual Exercises' from a feminist perspective is to be found in *The Spiritual Exercises Reclaimed*.[37] These authors highlight the gendered assumptions at work in the text and utilize feminist hermeneutics to revision it for contemporary presentation. Through an emphasis

---

[31]   Katherine M. Stogdon, 'The Risk of Surrender: Se Livrer in the Life of Thérèse Couderc (1805–1885)' (PhD Thesis, University of Manchester, 2004), p. 149.

[32]   Ellen A. Macek, '"Ghostly Fathers" and their "Virtuous Daghyters": The Role of Spiritual Direction in the Loves of Three Early Modern English Women', *The Catholic Historical Review*, 90/2 (2004): pp. 213–35.

[33]   Laurence Lux-Sterritt, *Redefining Female Religious Life: French Ursulines and English Ladies in Seventeenth-Century Catholicism* (Aldershot, 2005).

[34]   Stogden, 'The Risk of Surrender', pp. 141–83.

[35]   Regina Bechtle, 'Reclaiming the Truth of Women's Lives', *Way*, 28 (1988): 50–59; Diana Collier, 'Gender Issues', *Way* (Supplement) 64 (1990): 29–36; Kathleen Fischer, *Women at the Well: Feminist Perspectives on Spiritual Direction* (New York, 1988).

[36]   Mary Sharon Riley, 'Women and Contemplation', *Way* (Supplement) 82 (1995): pp. 35–43.

[37]   Katherine Dyckman, Mary Garvin and Elizabeth Liebert, *The Spiritual Exercises Reclaimed: Uncovering Liberating Possibilities for Women* (New York, 2001).

on the distinctiveness of the exercitant's relationship with God [#15] and the principle of adaptability [# 4, 18, 19] to be found in Ignatius' thinking they draw out the expansive potential of Ignatian spirituality. These authors[38] illustrate both the difficulties arising from androcentric understandings within the text and yet the 'surprisingly liberating possibilities for contemporary women' also at work.[39] Crucially, they remind the reader that the 'Exercises have formed countless women and men in a way of holiness'. Employing both *obedient* and *disobedient* readings of the 'Exercises' illustrates how they can act as both a source of restriction and liberation for their gendered subjects.[40] Ignatian Spirituality as a two-edged sword (spirituality that regulates … reinforces *and* transgresses … interrupts).

The 'Exercises' then have played a paradoxical role in the negotiation of gendered relationships with the divine. The Ignatian tradition may be interpreted as a force that strengthens a necrophilic symbolic imaginary, with particularly damaging results for women. Yet, there can be surprises. The 'Exercises' are not merely a theoretical instrument for the ordering of the self to the will of God, but are based on the exercitant's relationship with God through Christ. The material for discernment consists of the multi-layered and contradictory impulses and desires of each individual. These human desirings are brought into play with 'named graces', which contain the dynamism of the Christian path of discipleship,[41] through the very regulation of desires according to the principle of 'indifference' innovative patterns of spirituality may form. It is by examining the contexts and consequences of discernments that new perspectives on the will of God may be articulated in any age. The 'Exercises' can hold this function of rupture precisely because of their dynamic of interior conversion. As a tool for the disciplining of desires they both restrict (creating docile subjects of the Christian life) and liberate those who practise them (affording the opportunity for apostleship). I am informed here by Foucault's[42] later thinking on the 'technologies of the self'. Persons undergoing the 'Exercises' are both *formed* by notions of desire, freedom, and choice contained within them and are able to perform 'practices of liberty' through their living out of them in different contexts. This affords the opportunity for natal suggestions that run contrary to a necrophilic imaginary. This can happen through that 'ecstatic transcendence of the self,'[43] the undoing of the humanistic self that negatively but powerfully issues in a new birthing. At root discernment is about making choices. In the making of real choices a whole array of desires are let loose which prove crucial to the end results of the process. The Exercises provide a

---

[38]   Dyckman et. al., *The Spiritual Exercises Reclaimed.*

[39]   Dyckman et. al., *The Spiritual Exercises Reclaimed*, p. 3.

[40]   Dyckman et. al., *The Spiritual Exercises Reclaimed*, p. 15.

[41]   Lavinia Byrne, 'Asking for the Grace', *Way* (Supplement) 28 (1989): pp. 29–31.

[42]   Michel Foucault, *The Uses of Pleasure: The History of Sexuality Volume 2* (R. Hurley, trans), (Harmondsworth, 1985).

[43]   James. W. Bernauer, 'Michel Foucault's Ecstatic Thinking', in J. Bernauer and D. Rasmussen (eds) *The Final Foucault* (London, [1987] 1988), p. 70.

schooling in desire and whether those desires are successfully controlled or prove to be transgressive, their existence bears witness to the constitutive elements of an ethic of natality which take shape in relation to the context in which they are at work. What better example than the way Mary Ward trusted that her desire to 'take of the same' of the Society of Jesus was a God-given desire, which subsequently issued in a new path of apostolic vocations for women?

Re-Reading in Service of New Life: Ongoing Discernment of Desires

Grace stressed the centrality of desire within religion, not just as the 'dangerous other of rationality' but as providing 'an opening for thinking differently', which could lead to creative possibilities.[44] Conscious that a feminist trajectory of desire needs to offer criteria for discernment she used the thinking of Hannah Arendt on 'natality' as a creative suggestion to theorize the implications of the 'condition of human possibility' that is found in birth. This 'faculty of beginning' described by Arendt as the 'foundation of freedom' is necessarily, Grace points out, 'material' and 'embodied'. Therefore her feminist imaginary of natality has to be rooted 'in the physical and material'.[45] Is Grace's unequivocal commitment to the fostering of desires at odds with the dynamic of the 'Spiritual Exercises' premised it would seem on their control and restraint? Or does the strategy of reading against the grain of the text reveal the presence of a pregnant space within the process of Ignatian desiring which offers the possibility of creative beginnings?

Ruling Desires

Ignatius describes the objective of the 'Exercises' as 'the conquest of self and the regulation of one's life, in such a way that no decision is made under the influence of any inordinate attachment' [#21]. This language does not immediately inspire thoughts of newness forming in the heart of the individual. Words such as 'conquest' and 'regulation' bring to mind Foucauldian ideas of the 'self-policing' and 'self-regulation' of desiring subjects.[46] To what end however, are human desires to be governed? This is spelt out in the 'principle' where Ignatius declares that 'man is created to praise, reverence and serve God our Lord, and by this means to save his soul'. All of creation is understood to play a role in helping persons to attain this end for which they have been created. The central tenet of this 'consideration' is the description of a radical freedom that is 'indifferent' to all 'created things' (for example, health or sickness, long life or short, riches or poverty), which

---

44   Jantzen, *Becoming Divine*, p. 88.

45   Jantzen, *Becoming Divine*, p. 145.

46   Michel Foucault, *The Will to Knowledge: The History of Sexuality* (R. Hurley, trans.) (Harmondsworth, 1978), pp. 19–21.

results in a radical relativisation of all. What has been called the 'plumb line' of the 'Exercises' is found in the phrase 'Our one desire and choice should be what is more conducive to the end for which we are created', emphasising the unique vocation of the individual in Christ (#23).[47] The 'negative purpose' of the 'Exercises', Ganss[48] argues, is 'to overcome oneself' and to remove obstacles to 'spiritual progress'. Yet, this path of negation prepares for a deepening union with the purposes of God. The principle of 'indifference' facilitates the deferment of choices, keeping the person 'undecided', 'impartial', about the way forward.[49]

Aschenbrenner underlines the open ended potential encapsulated in the 'principle':

> As a being created by God, you are involved in a relationship with the Creator that gleams with a moment-by-moment immediacy. Creation is not some fatalistic scenario, within which you rudely awaken, nor your own act of self-determination, nor an ancient act that long ago began the process of being. No, creation has the immediacy of constant present tense.[50]

The exercitant is invited to participate in an ongoing creative divine outpouring of love. The focus is not on a masculinist striving for power. The 'paramount concern' of the 'principle' according to Aschenbrenner 'is God's magnanimous, creative love, not your struggling to forge the steel of your will into the mould of indifference'. The gift of spiritual freedom is acquired not through 'wrestling' the self into the 'requisite position' but of opening oneself to 'God's intimately immediate, glorious love'. This movement of openness towards God enables an ongoing conversion to seeing ourselves in relation to the rest of creation and therefore moves us away from an individual focus on self-interest.[51] The desire which is elicited through the 'principle' counters the language of self-control, evoking an endlessly recreative action in which human beings participate not as masters but as co-creators of an ecstatic outpouring of love.

I Ask for What I Desire

The process of attaining the spiritual freedom described in the 'principle' is through the dynamic use of the *id quod volo* where the exercitant asks 'God our

---

[47]   George A. Aschenbrenner, *Stretched for Greater Glory: What to Expect From the Spiritual Exercises* (Chicago, 2004), p. 43.

[48]   Ignatius of Loyola, *The Spiritual Exercises of Saint Ignatius: A Translation and Commentary* (trans. George E. Ganss) (St Louis MO, 1992).

[49]   George E. Ganss, *The Spiritual Exercises of Saint Ignatius* (St Louis, 1992), pp. 146–51.

[50]   Aschenbrenner, *Stretched for Greater Glory*, pp. 38–9.

[51]   Aschenbrenner, *Stretched for Greater Glory*, pp. 40–48.

Lord for what I want and desire'. Can we really take this at face value? What are the implications of this permission to name what is really desired? Troublingly it would seem Ignatius stresses that 'the petition made in this prelude must be according to the subject matter'. Byrne[52] points to the ambivalent position occupied by the exercitant praying for what they desire when what they are to desire is at the same time specified.[53] In the first exercise of the 'first week' they ask 'for shame and confusion' [#48]. The graces begged from God then change in keeping with the movement of the 'Exercises'. These prayers of desire are all grounded in the continuous use of the 'preparatory' prayer [#46] reiterating the essence of the 'principle'. Ignatius presumes that the exercitants' desires develop and interact with the graces that are suggested by him. The 'Exercises' structure this attuning according to the pattern of the Christian paschal mystery. However, what that looks like varies considerably. The 'subjects of desire' Foucault argues exercise 'practices of liberty' even as they conform to canonical prescriptions.[54] The Ignatian principle of flexibility offers a variety of ways of praying the 'Exercises' while still being faithful to their spirit.

In this way the discourse of the 'Exercises' generates the formulation of creative possibilities, which can contradict the conventions of the particular social location in which they are practised. The rupturing of social, religious norms is made possible by the interaction of gendered, embodied desires and the divine creative purpose appealed to in the 'principle'. It is fruitful then to pay attention to what I will call a *pause* (in practice) between the articulation of 'what I want and desire' .... and the specified grace given by Ignatius. What happens during the necessary interval between the articulation of desires and the reception of graces? When it is taken into account that those desires are always gendered and socially located and that the relationship between the exercitant and God is experienced in the here and now, the transformation of desires into graces necessarily has to be an embodied process. In her thought-provoking account of the interplay of power shared by exercitant, director and God during the course of the 'Exercises', Byrne[55] argues that the dynamic uncovers distortions of human power and reveals what divine empowerment looks like. In paragraph 237 then (the culmination of the 'Exercises' in the last point of the 'contemplatio') human power is situated within the power of God where 'my limited power comes from the supreme and infinite power above, and so too, justice, goodness, mercy etc'. Yet this does not need to result in a passive exercise of subjectivity:

> Ultimate power lies with God and is contextualized by God's other attributes ... all of which God desires to share. But I too am powerful, even though my

---

52 Byrne, 'Asking for the Grace'.
53 The graces: # 46, 55, 65, 91, 104, 139, 147, 152, 180, 193, 203, 221, 233.
54 Michel Foucault, *The Uses of Pleasure* (London, 1985), pp. 5, 25.
55 Byrne, 'Asking for the Grace'.

power is limited. By the end of the retreat therefore, the retreatant is invited to experience the glory of knowing that she or he is empowered by God.[56]

The exercitant's desires provide the crucial material which makes such empowerment possible. Byrne points out that Ignatius covers 'the full range of human feelings' in his specified graces.[57] In the *pause* the exercitant allows *whatever* presents itself to become part of the discernment process. This can be exhilarating and frightening for both exercitant and director alike. William Barry speaks about the difficulty of harmonizing one's desire to the 'one action of God' when persons live 'in a world of conflicting desires, of conflicting groups, of conflicting claims'.[58] In learning the skill of attunement the exercitant needs to struggle, he says, with 'two seemingly incompatible attitudes: to trust myself and my reactions and to recognize how easily I can delude myself'.[59] This double message has the potential to confuse the one who discerns and arouses just suspicion in feminist hermeneutics. Yet as Grace noted there is a need for the evaluation of desires and some criteria for judging them.[60]

Philip Sheldrake[61] emphasises that the *id quod volo* provides a vital starting point for the 'unfolding' of the deepest and most passionate human longings and engagements. The often 'confusing mass' of 'insistent wants, needs and longings' can obscure the 'Great Desire' at work beneath them.[62] 'Discernment' he argues is 'a journey through desires – a process whereby we move from a multitude of desires, or from surface desires, to our deepest desire which, as it were, *contains* all that is true and vital about ourselves'.[63] The seeker looks for the 'point of intersection' between their 'deepest desires' and 'God's desiring' at work within them. By discovering 'the thread' that links these myriad of desires together the 'deep desire' becomes visible.[64] 'Indifference' then for Sheldrake is about 'reaching out towards our deepest desire, which is to be what we were created for', recognizing that in the end it is 'God who alone puts proper order into our desires'.[65]

Ignatius accentuates the sacred space in which divine grace is communicated to the exercitant and seeks to keep this place within the dynamic of the 'Exercises' as free and unencumbered as possible. The director is warned not to over-explain the points of the exercises because if exercitants are able to discover insights for

---

[56] Byrne, 'Asking for the Grace', p. 30.

[57] Byrne, 'Asking for the Grace', p. 31.

[58] William Barry, 'Towards a Theology of Discernment', *Way* (Supplement) 64 (1989): pp. 129–40.

[59] Barry, 'Towards a Theology of Discernment', p. 136.

[60] Jantzen, *Becoming Divine*, p. 87.

[61] Philip Sheldrake, *Befriending Our Desires* (London, 2001).

[62] Sheldrake, *Befriending Our Desires*, p. 29.

[63] Sheldrake, *Befriending Our Desires*, p. 34.

[64] Sheldrake, *Befriending Our Desires*, pp. 64–5.

[65] Sheldrake, *Befriending Our Desires*, p. 113.

themselves it 'produces greater spiritual relish and fruit' [#2]. Even more strikingly this idea of non-interference is carried to lengths that could smack of illuminism and which Ignatius carefully balances by his 'rules for thinking with the church' [# 352–70]. Spiritual freedom however is also enjoined on the director, recognizing this power-laden position:

> While one is engaged in the Spiritual Exercises, it is more suitable and much better that the Creator and Lord in person communicate Himself to the devout soul in quest of the divine will, that He inflame it with His love and praise, and dispose it for the way in which it could better serve God in the future. Therefore, the director of the Exercises, as a balance at equilibrium, without leaning to one side or the other, should permit the Creator to deal directly with the creature, and the creature directly with his Creator and Lord [#15].

The Ignatian emphasis on the sacredness of the relationship between the individual and God provides an opening through which the person's desires and the desirings of God at work within them can co-create a future only half-imagined. How does one evaluate, however, if these desirings are truly 'of God'? Ignatius tackles this through the 'rules for discernment of spirits'.

On the Side of Life or Death?

Aschenbrenner emphasises that the discernment of spirits 'is not something you do to and for yourself. It does not leave you placid, untouched or unmoved; rather it sets loose a swarm of spontaneous inner spirits'.[66] The rules help the exercitant to interpret and respond to a variety of spiritual movements. The issue of hermeneutics then is crucial. Ignatius gives guidance on how to discriminate between interior movements to see which are from God (in order to co-operate with them) and which are not (to act against them). Central to the rules are the definitions of 'spiritual consolation' and 'spiritual desolation'. *Consolation* Ignatius describes as 'when an interior movement is aroused in the soul, by which it is inflamed with love of its Creator and Lord' [# 316]. There is an attraction towards God that is known by an inner 'peace and quiet in its Creator and Lord' (not to be confused with emotional feelings of peace which may be unrelated to relationship with God). The experience is multifaceted. Toner differentiates between firstly, 'the consolation in the proper or exclusive meaning (affective feelings such as peace or gladness)', secondly 'the causes or sources, subjective and objective of consolation', and thirdly 'the consequences of consolation' (the effect on how the exercitant perceives, remembers, responds).[67] This results from

---

[66] Aschenbrenner, *Stretched for Greater Glory*, p. 161.

[67] Jules A. Toner, *A Commentary On St Ignatius' Rules for the Discernment of Spirits* (St Louis, 1982), p. 86.

the complexity of 'feelings, acts and consequences' having a divine origin and encourages the exercitant to move towards God.[68] *Desolation* is the 'contrary' of consolation, displaying the same components, namely 'desolation proper' (affective feelings), the 'sources' that have given rise to the feelings and the 'consequences' on the person's 'acts' and 'decisions'.[69] Ignatius uses words like 'turmoil of spirit' 'restlessness', 'temptations' linked to a feeling of sadness and separation from God [# 317]. Consolation and desolation then should not be reduced to affective feelings as underlined by Dyckman, et. al. 'Rather, consolation is the affective reverberation of the work of the Holy Spirit that draws toward God, and desolation is the affective reverberation of the anti-spiritual that pulls in the opposite direction.'[70]

In his rules for the 1st week [# 313–27] Ignatius analyzes these spiritual movements of consolation and desolation, questioning their causes and noting their consequences. His guidance on appropriate responses seek to strengthen those desires which have their source in God and to resist disordered impulses that lead to a lessening of trust and faith in God. During the 2nd week rules [# 328–36] his thinking becomes more nuanced reflecting the spiritual growth that happens during the course of this week. As the person becomes more skilled in noticing the working of what Ignatius names the 'evil spirit' the movements of the spirits become less easy to read. Spiritual experiences of consolation can be commandeered by the anti-spiritual in order to subvert an originally good intention, changing it little by little. Ignatius illustrates how 'consolation' may be utilized by what he sees as 'evil forces' in order to turn the person who discerns towards a deceptive appearance of good (as seen in his description of the 'angel of light' [# 332]). Since Ignatius has identified two sorts of spiritual consolation during this time (which can feel the same but have contrary purposes) he stresses the need to look at the entire course of such movements, in order to identify and review the process of the distortion of desires [# 333–4]. He pays particular attention to the disposition of the exercitant noting that when they are 'progressing' towards God the action of the 'good spirit' is 'delicate, gentle, delightful. It may be compared to a drop of water penetrating a sponge'. In contrast the 'evil spirit' is 'violent, noisy, and disturbing, and may be compared to a drop of water falling upon a stone' [# 335]. Ignatius even alerts the one who discerns to the danger of the afterglow noting the need for differentiation of 'the actual time of the consolation from the period which follows it' where various 'resolutions' and 'plans' may be made that again may undermine the original consolation [# 336]. The subtleties of distinguishing the marks and qualities of each spirit and the consequences of allowing each free reign enable the exercitant to identify what may draw them deeper into relationship with God or impede this. Such attention to what can seem like details in fact enables the exercitant to discern the will of God in and through

---

68 Dyckman, et. al., *The Spiritual Exercises Reclaimed*, p. 254.

69 Toner, *A Commentary on St Ignatius' Rules*, p. 123.

70 Dyckman et. al., *The Spiritual Exercises Reclaimed*, p. 254.

turbulent and confusing situations and provides one tool alongside more rational ways of coming to decisions in a time of 'tranquillity' [# 176].[71]

Despite the rational language utilized by Toner to analyse the discernment of spirits Ignatius is clear that he expects the exercitant to be 'affected' by spiritual experiences and inner movements [#6]. This is an embodied robust process which calls for a careful consideration of the elements at work within both exercitant and director. It bears closer analysis in the light of Carrette and King's[72] colonization theory of spirituality. What I wish to emphasize here is the creative role given to desires within Ignatian discernment, which can reveal death-dealing dynamics and life-affirming new trajectories.

Conclusion

While it has been the case that Ignatian spirituality can serve to reinforce a patriarchal mindset I have illustrated how women's relationship with the 'Exercises' has not always reinforced their gendered position within the Church and at times has resulted in the expansion of ideas and practices about their roles. It has been my contention that this transgressive potential is located within the dynamic of the 'Exercises' themselves in their emphasis on desire, in conversation with the Ignatian rules. However, it can be noted that Ignatian subjects are routinely deprived of the potential expansiveness of their desires when they are theorized as disembodied, private, sexless individuals, thereby reinforcing their appropriation of the expected graces of the status quo. This, I would stress, is not in the spirit of Ignatius himself who invites persons to make their own the graces of the 'Exercises'. Dyckman, et. al.[73] have begun to describe the embodied, provocative, prophetic spirituality that can result when questions of gender are made explicit.

At the centre of the 'Exercises' is the challenge of transformation afforded by entering into relationship with God made incarnate in Jesus the Christ who continues to form people through the power of the Holy Spirit. The beginning and the ending of the 'Exercises' ('principle' and 'contemplatio') invites the exercitant to commit themselves again and again to a living, incarnate God who is to be found 'in all things' [# 235]. Human persons find their freedom in recognizing both their finitude *and* their capacity to participate in divine creativity. The reshaping of desires, transformed in the power of the Spirit, leads to the Ignatian 'more', the excess that bears witness to the presence of the divine.[74] A gendered Ignatian spirituality could become an ally in shifting the imaginary from a masculinist invocation of the 'good old God' critiqued by Grace towards her suggestions of

---

[71]   David Lonsdale, *Listening to the Music of the Spirit: The Art of Discernment* (Notre Dame, 1993).

[72]   Carrette and King, *Selling Spirituality*.

[73]   Dyckman et. al., *The Spritual Exercises Reclaimed*.

[74]   Jantzen, *Becoming Divine*, p. 251.

natality. This is precisely because of its capacity to enlarge the imagination of the embodied subject while at the same time rooting that subjectivity in specific contexts. It needs to be asked however, what happens when women and men trust their desires as God-given even when they run contrary to the current thinking of the Church? Do such desires count? Do the objective Ignatian 'rules for thinking with the church' make the fruits of certain discernments invalid? The rich panoply of discernments evoked through the Ignatian way could lay the foundations of paths not yet conceived. Toner stresses the limits of discernment.[75] Yet Mary Ward is an example of a woman whose acts of faith beyond the limits of social convention helped to contribute to a new flowering: that of female apostolic religious life. Her gender both limited what was possible at that time and yet contributed to the future horizon of possibility for the Ignatian desiring subject. Present-day discernments are alive with opportunities yet to be realized.

---

[75] Jules J. Toner, *Discerning God's Will: Ignatius of Loyola's Teaching on Christian Decision Making* (St Louis, 1991), pp. 45–69.

PART THREE
'Choose Life!'

Chapter 10
The Metaphysics of the Body

Graham Ward

> [To] be no part of any body, is to be nothing. ... At most, the greatest persons, are but wrens, and excrescences; men of wit and delightfull conversation, but as moales for ornament, except they be incorporated into the body of the world, that they contribute something to the sustentation of the world.[1]

Introduction

In this essay, I intend to make some moves towards the construction of a metaphysics of the body. I embark upon such a venture rejecting the dualism of physical and metaphysical, materiality and spirituality, nature and culture. What I mean by metaphysical with respect to the body is the system of values pertaining to embodiment *through which* embodiment is viewed, shaped and performed. These are moral values like goodness, social values like justice, aesthetic values like beauty and claims to truth or the way things are. There is no materiality as such, then; materiality is always imbricated in conceptual evaluations. That does not mean that there is no difference between matter and thought, only that they cannot be separated in any enquiry into either. As Judith Butler pointed out a number of years ago now 'matter *matters*'.[2] How matter *matters* is related to how it is made to speak, how it speaks and what it speaks. Recently, we have been reminded that '[b]odies only speak if and when they are made heavy with meaning'.[3] To be made 'heavy with meaning' concerns the events in which the body presents itself, announces itself, and performs its meaningfulness. This is a series of operations that enact a metaphysics. While one would have to admit that the dualism of matter and thought announces (rather than enacts) a metaphysics, it does so by creating a false clinical space

---

[1] John Donne as quoted in John Stubbs, *Donne: The Reformed Soul* (Harmondsworth, [2002] 2007), p. 229.

[2] Judith Butler, *Bodies that Matter: On the Discursive Limits of 'Sex'* (New York, 1993), pp. 27–56.

[3] Annemarie Mol, *The Body Multiple: Ontology in Medical Practice* (Durham, NJ, 2002), p. 10. Mol's work is fascinating for the way in which she tries to overcome the notion of the 'body' as a single object; in fact, for raising the question of what an object is as such.

in which materiality can appear as itself, shorn of any values, naked under the clinician's objective gaze. The body becomes an object and its nakedness announces a metaphysics of the unveiled real. This is how things are: the God's eye view. The creation of such a falsehood constitutes a bad rather than a good metaphysics. Ironically, the philosophical implications of this falsehood provide the foundations for a purely empirical view of any material object that deems itself anti-metaphysical! A good metaphysics, on the other hand, is one that avoids such falsehood-creating reductions; acknowledges the co-implication of meaning and matter; and recognises that this co-implication is not epiphenomenal or a contamination of one by the other, but rather points to the necessary cohabitation of the material and the metaphysical.

Why does it seem absolutely critical that we move towards constructing a good metaphysics of the body; and bodies made 'heavy with meaning'? Because of a cultural devaluation of the body that is shockingly ironic given the attention to fitness and diets. It is a devaluation that parallels the plethora of material goods that flood our high streets and the attention to branding which idealistically elevates the name above any material content. But let Bret Easton Ellis's novel *American Psycho* open up this contemporary phenomenon for us.

This is not a novel for the squeamish, but to my mind it is a parable of the reductions brought about by rapacious free-market capitalism. Bateman, Ellis's protagonist, is a high earning young executive living in New York with a perfectly toned body. He is film-star handsome. He moves among a similar kind; people with what Brett calls 'hardbodies', clothed from socks to tie in designer-wear, continually on the look out for new, expensive and exclusive restaurants; people who look so alike and are so accustomed to using others they are frequently fail to identify each other. Bateman is also a sadistic killer who carves up and sometimes eats his victims with little show of emotion. 'In my locker at Xclusive lie three vaginas I recently sliced out of various women I attacked in the past week. Two of them are washed off, one isn't. There's a barrette clipped to one of them, a blue ribbon from Hermès tied round my favourite.'[4]

The book was written in the 90s and it points to a fascination with embodiment that has emerged with postmodernity and continues up to the present day with the public exhibition of dead bodies in a plastic coating.[5] We might call this 'the return of the flesh', using the Pauline understanding of *sarx*: human beings reduced to their sheer physicality.[6] But *American Psycho* is a testimony to the hell of such a

---

[4]   Bret Easton Ellis, *American Psycho* (London, 1991), p. 370.

[5]   See the highly controversial exhibition *Bodies* recently put on at Earls Court. The programme notes announce: 'A collection of 22 life-sized, whole human bodies are on display in *Bodies: The Exhibition*, accompanied by 260 assorted organs and body parts. Stripped of their skin and plastinated in various poses, the exhibits are intended to show the science of human biology up close and personal'.

[6]   More recently, Giorgio Agamben has examined this reduction in terms of 'bare life' and views the creation of 'bare life' as endemic to contemporary political living. See *Homo*

reduction – in fact Dante's *Inferno* echoes throughout the text, along with ads for *Les Miserables*. Bateman is the dark side of our fascination with the body. What concerns me amidst this bourgeois cultural obsession with fitness, cooking, sex and bodily fluids is its unapologetic materiality; a materiality that in fact cheapens the body. The over-production of the body not only commodifies it, it dehumanizes it. And that's what Ellis's novel plays out. The body is just a billboard for an accumulation of brand names. Beneath it there is nothing; a void. Bateman senses neither he or anyone else is anything: '… where there was nature and earth, life and water, I saw a desert landscape that was unending, resembling some sort of crater, so devoid of reason and light and spirit that the mind could not grasp it. … [T]his was how I lived my life, what I constructed my movement around, how I dealt with the tangible."[7] Action is 'movement' not agency and only constructed; the tangible only an image from a war with Afghanistan, Iraq, Lebanon, Darfur. The bodies are not persons, only screens for the commercialized world of labels. Ellis presents us with the experience of contemporary nominalism.

I want then to 'humanize' the body by arguing the body can only be valued positively when it is viewed metaphysically and made 'heavy with meaning'. Again, in Pauline language, I want to put the *soma* back into the *sarx*; because the danger is not just mass murder in the name of a no-one. The danger is the disintegration of the social into the cultural. Ellis's novel, I would argue, depicts a final stage in atomism and alienation. Beyond the rampant and competitive individualism of *liassez-faire* capitalism lies the marketing of people as products; beyond the reduction to materialism lies the omnipresence of the image and the virtually real. In the past I have employed phenomenological analyses by thinkers like Merleau-Ponty, Michel Henry, Jean-Louis Chrétien and explored the nature of touch. For touch cannot reduce the body to an object seen, to a visible surface, in the way sight can. I have also examined the Eucharist as a site in Christian theology for rethinking embodiment; and rethinking Jesus Christ's body and the ecclesial body in terms of displacement and transcorporeality. But it strikes me that beginning with the human body, even if it belongs to Jesus of Nazareth, only capitulates to the modern moment. It isolates this body as this object to investigate and prevents an understanding of the body as multiple; the body as enacted within a diverse range of scenarios that each of which stages different meanings and values that eludes neat and stable identifications. The body as object, as Giorgio Agamben has observed, 'is the new subject of politics'. And democracy is born precisely as the assertion and presentation of this

> body: *habeas corpus ad subjeciendum*, 'you will have to have a body to show'.
> This new centrality of the 'body' in the sphere of politico-juridical terminology
> thus coincides with the more general process by which *corpus* is given such

Sacer: Sovereignty and Bare Life (trans. Daniel Heller-Roazen), (Stanford, 1998).

[7]   Ellis, *American Psycho*, pp. 374–5.

a privileged position in the philosophy and science of the Baroque age, from Descartes to Newton, from Leibniz to Spinoza.[8]

In this essay therefore I want to begin from another perspective entirely, not with the human body but the more amorphous and fluid body politic.

The Body Politic

Influenced no doubt by Hellenistic part and whole thinking, there is a tendency to understand the word 'body' in the body politic as a metaphor: the physical body is an organized whole made of various interdependent parts and so we extend this understanding of embodiment to a political organization. And so the body, either physically or politically is a homogenous entity. Some commentators view this as Paul's use of the body analogy for the church in *First Letter to the Corinthians*: the body is used properly with respect to the physical and metaphorically with respect to the ecclesial (or political). I will argue here that that is wrong. In fact, Paul uses *soma* to speak of sin (Rom. 6.6), humiliation (Phil. 3.21), dishonour (1 Cor. 15.43) and death (Rom. 7.24) as well. It is these other uses of the word body that can re-orientate our thinking of embodiment and open up a repositioning of our thinking about the human body in terms of the body politic.

In political thought, the body politic has had a long history. How long is still a matter of debate among Biblical scholars and historians of late antiquity, though there are landmarks like John of Salisbury's twelfth-century text *Policraticus* and Christine de Pizan's fifteenth-century *Livre de corps de policie*. Hobbes, of course, famously describes the State as an 'artificial man'. Hobbes, in fact, signals a new development in our understanding of the body and so this is where we will begin. For the medievals recognised an analogical relation between human embodiment and social embodiment; an ontological continuity between personal and political corporeality. This relation was grounded in the ecclesial and sacramental understandings of body, and the doctrine of the incarnation. The perfect form of embedment (of being human) was Jesus Christ and then, following the ascension of Christ into heaven, the Church understood as a kingdom of God being but not yet fully realised; what Augustine termed the *ecclesia peregrinans* on its way to the *civitate Dei*. In *Corpus Mysticum*, Henri de Lubac details the development and complexities of this understanding of the body – although, unfortunately, because his emphasis is upon the development of Eucharistic theology he does not relate it to the body politic.[9] He could well have done: John of Salisbury's *Policratus* and Christina de Pisan's *Book of the Body Politic* could have added a significant other layer to the theological nexus he excavates. But he doesn't. The

---

[8]   Agamben, *Homo Sacer*, pp. 123–4.

[9]   Henri de Lubac, *Corpus Mysticum: l'Eucharistie et l'Église au Moyen Âge* (Paris, 1944).

work of Ernst Kantorowicz on *The King's Two Bodies* charts much more of this story.[10] Nevertheless, Hobbes announces a new distinction between the natural and the artificial; the ontological relation no longer holds, and the 'artificial man' is a human construct, a contracted relation, to reign in the murderous lusts of the natural man. There is no longer a controlling sacramental world order analogically related to a transcendent principle. Corporate living in which, as for Augustine, the private was related to the Latin 'privatio' – a sin because a lack of something substantial to being human – was now a matter of convention. The social, from *socius* – a friend, a relation, an associate, a fellow human being – now divorced from a theological account of grace-bound nature was now subjected to the cultural. As Bruno Latour points out: 'From the myth of the social contract onward, the body politic has always been ... a *problem*, a ghost always in risk of complete dissolution'.[11] There is now no political body as an attestable fact. There is only an image and a series of actions which point to the event of that body, that make manifest a body. But it is not substantial and therefore only open to analysis in tracing the points at which it acts, politically.

Communities were on their way to being imaginary – in Benedict Anderson's understanding of that process[12] – voluntary associations in which certain cultural vehicles (a map, a museum, a national newspaper) create the means for reinforcing a collectivity and homogeneity that advances in communications makes possible.

My question is: what happens to the body – political and personal – when communities become imaginary and the body as a specific focus in a designated locality begins to disappear? Recently Hardt and Negri expose a suggestive genealogy in the move from the body of the nation state to what they term the contemporary Empire. 'The traditional army thus forms an organic fighting body, with generals for its head, lieutenants for its midsection, and the common soldier and sailors for its limbs', they write.[13] But in the move towards Empire there is a 'command shift from a centralized model to a distributed network model'.[14] They proceed to examine what this shift entails for the political body; I want to extend their analysis also to include the personal, physical body. My suggestion is that in this shift towards the motile and the imaginary, bodies become virtual, disposable because dispersed across networks of symbolic exchanges, enmeshed in the march of metaphors (to cite Nietzsche). And this situation, I would argue, is implicated in a bad metaphysics.

How then do we go about examining and therefore producing a good metaphysics of the body politic? Of course, we could reconstruct the analogical

---

[10]   Ernst Hartwig Kantorowicz, *The King's Two Bodies: A Study of Mediaeval Political Theology* (Princeton, 1957).

[11]   Bruno Latour, *Reassembling the Social: An Introduction of Actor-Network Theory* (Oxford, 2005), p. 162.

[12]   Benedict Anderson, *Imagined Communities* (London, 1991).

[13]   Michael Hardt and Antonio Negri, *Multitude* (New York, 2004), p. 56.

[14]   Hardt and Negri, *Multitude*, p. 5.

world-view; re-imagining bodies from a certain catholic theological perspective. And in *Cities of God* this is what I was attempting to do. But I want this time to examine the metaphysics of the State – the State conceived, after Hobbes, Locke and Hegel, as the body politic. For the State is a metaphysical entity. Fascism recognises this. John Maynard Keynes, writing in 1915 about Germany, could speak of 'a sort of idealism'. The nation will grow into a 'closed unity',[15] a monad in which all parts constitute a whole. The fascist state as a collectivist state demands the commitment, even sacrifice, of its members for the good of the Fatherland. There is something ultimately Spinozistic about this – there are no individuals only modifications of the transcendent One. The body figures forth this oneness, this 'closed unity'. For Spinoza that one body is God's: his is the ultimate monotheism; the dissolution of all difference. With the fascist state the polity of the radical immanence of Spinoza's metaphysics is made plain, only monotheism has become an imperial *Volksgemeinschaft* – the State as a religion.

But let us not suppose that liberal democracy avoids the metaphysics of the State. Though in theory, political liberalism has required the minimalisation of the State for the maximisation of individual freedom, in practice the minimalisation of the State has merely meant concealing the State's intervention in civil society. In fact, from Jürgen Habermas[16] through to post-democratic thinkers like Colin Crouch,[17] political thinkers have pointed to the way the rise of the neo-liberal state from the mid-seventies onwards has increasingly eroded the public sphere and both surveillanced private freedoms and sought to fashion the society it governs. It does not speak of a 'closed unity' but rather of being inclusive of difference, embracing plurality positively. But ultimately, any government has to govern; has to command a sovereign obedience. The State in liberal democracy only hides its transcendent sovereignty by working through juridical systems and even, when necessary, declaring states of exception. For both Thatcher and Reagan and certainly for the two Bushes, the neo-liberal State went hand in glove with fostering national allegiance: a religion of the State.

It is thinkers of the liberal democratic state who tend to view the body with respect to the political as a metaphor. While fascists like Mussolini accepted, like Hobbes, that political corporatism was the body macro made up of the bodies micro. But whereas the metaphysics of Mussolini's and Hitler's understanding of corporatism were wrapped in the pseudo-scientism of natural law, *Blut und Boden*, Hobbes's corporatism was linked to mechanics, as we saw. Again, the seeming lack of such a correlation between the political and physical body in the liberal democratic state might well be related to the hidden sovereignty in such a polity. That is, liberal democracy likes to portray itself as a political organism without a head; or with a head who is only *primus inter pares* and accountable to his or

---

[15]   Quoted in F. A. Hayek, *The Road to Serfdom* (London, 2001), pp. 188–9.

[16]   Jürgen Habermas, *The Structural Transformation of the Public Sphere: An Inquiry into a Category of Bourgeois Society* (trans. Thomas Burger) (Cambridge, 1989).

[17]   Colin Crouch, *Post-Democracy* (Cambridge, 2004).

her cabinet, party and the electorate. The head can be removed – impeached, for example, or voted out next time. But there is a headship; hung parliaments and coalition governments are always weak parliaments and weak governments. And the stronger the leadership given by such a head, the more realised is a complete political vision for the State. This headship is frequently, it seems to me, expressed in terms of spearheading the nation's destiny: a nation's messianic mission. F. A. Hayek, in his famous and highly influential 1944 book against socialism, *The Road to Serfdom*, at one point quotes the English political historian, Paul Lensch who wrote in a book published in 1918, about German socialism fulfilling 'her historic mission of revolutionising the world'.[18] The rhetoric is there in Lenin, as it was in Hitler and Mussolini: not just that certain nations have to be the political and economic *avant garde* idea of nationhood, but this is their destiny. But how frequently have we heard this same rhetoric in more recent years in the speeches of leading liberal democratic leaders? Since the 1980s decisionist leadership is a major style of neo-liberal politics. I like to call this the return of the king.

Let me take this argument one step further before focussing more explicitly on the metaphysics of the body. To return to Hobbes: the physiology and fluid mechanics of the body was just beginning to emerge when Hobbes was writing and one of the key figures in that emergence was Hobbes's Oxford friend, Richard Harvey. The mechanical body was then both a political and a physiological phenomenon at the same time. A similar correlation held between eugenics and an understanding of the State in fascism. The physical body or the way in which embodiment is understood and fashioned is then directly related to the body politic. I don't want to say one is the cause of the other. As I pointed out above, the distributed networks composing the new political 'body' of Hardt and Negri's Empire must affect our conceptions of physical embodiment; the cultural and social forces that produce both discursive knowledges are very complex (and something I wish to analyse in the future). But while the Third Reich was being constructed, while its mythology was being cultivated, films were made that presented models of the Aryan body and its healthy physical development. The Fatherland was to be composed as sturdy, energetic, well-formed blonde and blue-eyed men and women. Foucault would call this bio-power; a key aspect in modern methods of governmentality. And bio-power is just as strong in liberal democracies as the enforced bans of smoking in public places and the suggestion in Britain those patients who do not follow their doctor's instructions and persist in bad habits – over-eating, for example – may be refused treatment by the same doctors in the future, demonstrate. But rather than bio-power, I prefer the term used by Althusser – which Foucault adapted to his own end: state apparatuses.[19] The body politic works out its ideology through various state-informed practices acting through various state-related institutions – schools, universities, religious

---

[18]   Hayek, *The Road to Serfdom*, p. 179.

[19]   Louis Althusser, *Lenin and Philosophy and Other Essays* (trans. Ben Brewster) (New York, 2001).

bodies supportive of state policy, the army, the police force, the courts amongst others. These apparatuses not only promote certain values and views of the bodies political and physical, they shape them through specific disciplines imbued with specific values (usually said to be moral values). By this means the metaphysics of one kind of body produce the metaphysics of another, and *visa versa*.

I hope it has now become evident why I thought it important to sketch the cultural appearance of the body in *American Psycho* as the trigger for this present examination.

Hegel's Metaphysics of the Body Politic

It is time now to examine more closely these metaphysics, bearing in mind what I said earlier; the rejection of the dualism that pitches the materiality of the body against its spirituality, matter against thought. Hegel also rejected this dualism (though not the nature/culture distinction): the actual is the rational: the concept and its existence are two aspects of the same thing. Philosophical enquiry, either with regard to individual human bodies or the state itself seeks to discern 'in the semblance of the temporal and transient the substance which is immanent and the eternal which is present'.[20] The word 'eternal' points to Hegel's conviction that the metaphysics of the body implies a theology of the body. We will develop this later. For now it is important to understand that Hegel begins his treatise on the body politic with an analysis of human embodiment, leading eventually, in the closing section of the book with a study of international law and the world-spirit.

> The concept and its existence [*Existenz*] are two aspects [of the same thing], separate and united, like soul and body. The body is the same life as the soul, and yet the two can be said to lie outside one another. A soul without a body would not be a living thing, and vice versa. The existence [*Dasein*] of the concept is its body, just as the latter obeys the soul which produces it.[21]

To some extent this could have come straight from Aristotle's *de Anima*, but what Hegel does explicitly is develop the logic of existence (body), concept (soul), and their interrelationship into an account of the content and form of the state and the operation of reason that governs both of them: 'For *form* in its most concrete significance is reason as conceptual cognition, and *content* is reason as the substantial essence of both ethical and natural actuality'.[22] For Hegel, then, the political body can only be understood in terms of thinking *about* and a *reasoning*

---

[20]   G. W. F. Hegel, *Elements of the Philosophy of Right* (trans. H. B. Nisbet) (Cambridge, 1991), p. 20.

[21]   Hegel, *Elements of the Philosophy of Right*, p. 25.

[22]   Hegel, *Elements of the Philosophy of Right*, p. 22.

concerning the body.[23] The body politic is for Hegel, as we argued in the opening of this examination, inseparable from 'concepts of truth and the laws of ethics'.[24] The state is a metaphysical entity because it is an 'inherently rational entity',[25] that is, its form and content, its soul and body, participate in the great dialectical reasoning of *Geist* as its moves towards the actualization of the Absolute.

> The states, nations [*Völker*], and the individuals involved in this business of the world spirit emerge with their own *particular and determinate principle*, which has its interpretations and actuality in their *constitution* and throughout the whole *extent* of their *condition*. In their consciousness of this actuality and in their preoccupation with its interests, they are at the same time the unconscious instruments and organs of that inner activity in which the shapes which they themselves assume pass away, while the spirit in and for itself prepares and works its way towards the transition to its next and higher stage.[26]

A nation, composed of individuals in families, particular estates organised into corporations, and a governing class of professional civil servants, becomes a state. A group of individualised states, freely consenting to an international law code and under the sovereignty not of any single ruler but governed by the dialectic of the 'universal spirit, the spirit of the world',[27] give way to the final state which is the actualization of that universal spirit. In terms of feeling and the ethical life this final state is the embodiment of faith, love, and hope. This is the point where the metaphysics of body become inseparable from a theology of the body. For the final embodiment of faith, love and hope, a triad, Hegel takes from *First Letter to the Corinthians* (13.13) is the Christian kingdom of God; Christianity being the highest expression of the spiritual and the rational: 'heaven down to earth in this world, to the ordinary secularity of actuality and representational thought'.[28] This is the end of history, though not the end of time.

Francis Fukuyama is right then to read Hegel as announcing a final consummation, although Fukuyama emphasizes the key virtue of such a realm is individual freedom, rather than faith, love and hope, expressed in a universal

---

[23] In the *Preface* to *Elements of the Philosophy of Right*, Hegel argues polemically for the role philosophy has to play in understanding the state and the political. He counters contemporary suggestions about the secularity of the state ad the denigration of metaphysics in political science, speaking of the need to establish any thinking about the state in terms of 'universal principles' (p. 18). For such people 'the claims of the concept constitute an embarrassment', but, Hegel adds, this is an embarrassment 'from which they are nevertheless unable to escape' (p. 19).

[24] Hegel, *Elements of the Philosophy of Right*, p. 19.

[25] Hegel, *Elements of the Philosophy of Right*, p. 21.

[26] Hegel, *Elements of the Philosophy of Right*, p. 373.

[27] Hegel, *Elements of the Philosophy of Right*, p. 371.

[28] Hegel, *Elements of the Philosophy of Right*, p. 380.

democratic condition.[29] He misunderstands the nature of freedom for Hegel. Because Hegel would not concur; he is no liberal. The individual as he makes plain in the 'Introduction' to his *Phenomenology of Spirit*, loses his or her identity as such. An individual's freedom is sublated to the freedom of the whole in the actualization of the freedom of the Absolute *Geist*. The only true freedom is the 'free infinite personality'.[30] The state is the end in itself, everything else, every one else, is sacrificed to the logic of the state. This is hardly Fukuyama's apotheosis of free market liberal democracy. In fact, though Hegel's account is evidently communitarian, there is a question over whether it is democratic at all. A whole crowd of commentators have believed he provides the philosophical basis for totalitarianism. This is wrong. Hegel positively endorses constitutional monarchy – 'the achievement of the modern world, in which the substantial Idea has attained infinite form'.[31] This is as far as he goes in his last major work, *Elements of the Philosophy of Right*, but in view of Hegel's theology and the working of the universal spirit beyond the particularities of nationhood, constitutional monarchy would find its consummation in a Messianic rule.

> [T]he usual sense in which the term 'popular sovereignty' has begun to be used in recent times is to denote *the opposite of that sovereignty which exists in the monarch*. In this oppositional sense, popular sovereignty is one of those confused thoughts which are based on a *garbled* notion [*Vorstellung*] of the people. *Without* its monarch and that *articulation* of the whole which is necessarily and immediately associated with monarchy, *the* people are a formless mass. The latter is no longer a state.[32]

The constitutional monarchs of nations must give way, in the final actualization of *Geist*, to the absolute monarch; the realisation of the kingdom of God is the realisation of the rule of Christ whose Spirit was given totally to the world following the death of God on the Cross. We will return to the 'formlessness' of popular sovereignty at the end of this essay, for now it is important to understand that Hegel cannot easily be secularised in the way Fukuyama, after Kojève, makes him. In fact, secularisation is the final achievement of the coming down of heaven to earth, of the labouring of faith, love and hope; only then is the transcendent principle made fully immanent.

In one sense, that Fukuyama reads Hegel badly is not the point. The point here is that Hegel's state as the body politic is a thoroughly metaphysical notion, and those individuals whose wills and desires are sublated to the logic of the state's development participate in a spirituality that refuses the sheer materialism and its consequent irrationalism announced in Ellis's novel. It is because bodies are

---

29 Francis Fukuyama, *The End of History and the Last Man* (Harmondsworth, 1992).
30 G. W. F. Hegel, *Phenomenology of Spirit*, trans. A. V. Miller (Oxford, 1977), p. 20.
31 Hegel, *Elements of the Philosophy of Right*, p. 308.
32 Hegel, *Elements of the Philosophy of Right*, p. 319.

spiritual they are free and must be political. One observes in *American Psycho* there is no political action. In fact, there cannot be when all action and agency is reduced to the anonymity and moral anaesthesis of 'movement' in an infinite Sierra Nevada. 'Hardbodies' are consumers, customers or clients; they are not citizens. Nevertheless, there is a certain symmetry between Bateman's world and Hegel's. For, with Hegel, one has to understand that the language of the infinite, the truth, the eternal, the universal, and the absolute, is defined within the dialectic circles of the immanent. His speculative philosophy is a metaphysics, announcing, in Kantian terms, a transcendental logic, but it has nothing to do with transcendence itself. For Hegel this is a theological point that turns upon a conception of the trinity in its working in the world. Christ on the Cross dissolved the transcendence of God the Father into the immanent operations of the spirit of Christ within the world. Two important corollaries issue from this philosophical theology.

First, there is, then, no alterior standpoint beyond the dialectics of this world. The salvation this effects results from a relation between the mental (*geistliche*) contemplation that goes on within this world, such as the philosopher's speculative logic, and the movement of absolute mind (*Geist*). The relation does not admit alterity, a fundamental and unsublatable difference such as might be possible in the analogical world-view. Instead, there is a univocal relationship between the spiritual (*geistliche*) operations within human beings and the Absolute spirit (*Geist*).

Secondly, the theological dynamic for the dialectic of history is the way of the Cross. The work of the Spirit is a work of negation. The trajectory along which the politics of the state moves towards the ultimate kingdom is constituted by negativity. Hegel analyses this work of negation in terms of the will and desire in determining the particularity of the '*I*'. There are two moments in this particularisation. In the first moment is the 'I's emergence from 'the element of *pure indeterminacy*", from a negative freedom that Hegel describes as 'the freedom of the void, which is raised to the status of an actual shape and passion'.[33] At this point what is posited to the 'I' in its self-contemplation is a representation, an abstraction. But Hegel is not content, in this analysis of the 'I', to restrict himself to psychology. There can be a collective 'I', a corporate personality. Hegel then immediately adds: 'if it turns to actuality, it becomes in the realm of politics or religion the fanaticism of destruction, demolishing the whole existing social order, eliminating all individuals regarded as suspect by a given order, and annihilating any organisation which attempts to rise up anew'.[34] What we glimpse here is Hegel's positive evaluation of the French Revolution as it appears more clearly in his letters: the pure destructiveness and iconoclasm that characterised the Reign of Terror. This is Hegel's account of a negative or apophatic body politics. But the second moment in the determination of the 'I' is not a cataphatic reversal. The actual *positing* of this determinacy and differentiation 'is just as much a *negativity* and cancellation (*Aufheben*) as the first – for it is the cancellation of the first abstract negativity. Just as the particular

---

[33] Hegel, *Elements of the Philosophy of Right*, p. 38.
[34] Hegel, *Elements of the Philosophy of Right*, p. 38.

is in general contained within the universal, so in consequence is this second moment already contained within the first and is merely the *positing* of what the first already is *in itself*'.[35] Indeterminacy is negated to become the determined and the determined then is overreached in a further dialectical sublation, and so on. Speculative philosophy, then, as a political science must 'apprehend the negativity which is immanent within the universal'.[36]

What are the consequences of this radical immanence driven by the universal labouring of negativity, for a metaphysics of the body politic? One first has to observe we are not treating monism in anything like the way it appears in Spinoza – exactly because Hegelian metaphysics is dynamic and differentiation is not epiphenomenal. If the fascist state can be associated with Spinoza's metaphysics, then with Hegel we approach something similar to Lenin's notion of the permanent revolution. The world spirit working in and as the human spirit continually transforms the cultural given. Hegel notes that modern society and its prevailing polity is an outworking of the Reformation and the French Revolution. But as we saw, this modern politics will too give way to what has yet to appear, though it remains concealed in the present as a potential. If there is one overriding polity it is a theocracy, only there is no direct rule by God; the operations of the Absolute are always and only mediations through concrete circumstance. Though Hegel's own representation of the state comes closest to being oligarchic – since the monarch is only a figurehead and the actual governing proceeds through bureaucratic leaders – the content of the state is never fixed. Its essential form is neither liberal democratic, communist, monarchic, fascist or oligarchic; and yet potentially it is all these polities and more. Hegel did not celebrate the French Revolution because it was a move from absolute monarchy to democracy. He celebrated it because 'the human spirit has outgrown like the shoes of a child' the *ancien regime*.[37] While any state has specific content, then, it is continually subject to indeterminacy. There is always a body image, if you like, that gives shape to the body itself, but the image is governed by a prevailing iconoclasm, a political and theological apophaticism. This forestalls idolatry, as in a manner similar to the way the apophatic safeguards the mystery and transcendence of the divine for the mystic theologian. But it is with the mention of 'transcendence' that we have to recall the immanentalism of Hegel's thinking on the body politic. The working of the negative in Hegel is a continual reminder of limitations, of finitude; but it is also, because it is an operation of *Geist*, a continual reminder of the infinite. One might suggest that Hegel has transposed the mystic's cosmological notion of transcendence into an historical one, only history cannot be infinitely open for Hegel – he would then fall victim to his own analysis of the nihilism of the 'bad infinite'. A final state, an end of history, is presupposed. The system has a closure – and Hegel does not view the

---

[35]   Hegel, *Elements of the Philosophy of Right*, p. 39.

[36]   Hegel, *Elements of the Philosophy of Right*, p. 40.

[37]   Hegel, *Elements of the Philosophy of Right*, p. 397.

immanent development and exposition of *Geist* as a circle that endlessly repeats itself: what Nietzsche would call eternal reoccurrence.[38]

As with the mystic's apophasis, Hegel's negativity announces a limited understanding, the lack of a panoptic view. But Hegel is convinced we develop a greater and greater understanding and discernment of the Absolute – that is what thought and rationalisation is concerned with bringing about. The body (political or otherwise) does not understand itself fully, cannot grasp itself as an object. It is on a journey, collectively, through a long crucifixion, to an eternal salvation: a final disenchantment, an ultimate enlightenment which is a grand demystification. The labouring of the negative requires an ascesis, just as it requires a teleology, but does it also require a continual suffering? Is this why war is seen as both inevitable and necessary, for Hegel? Why peace is viewed as stasis as 'people become stuck in their ways'[39] ? Why, in the closing sections of his analysis the descriptor that is foregrounded is 'sacrifice'? In the Gospels the ascesis of the body also demands a health, a glorification, a delight; the eschatology is both futural and present: the kingdom is not just to come, it is already here. I can see how Hegel would concur with this eschatology, but I wonder whether his anthropology (and by extension political science) remains too Lutheran: too orientated to the working of the crucifixion. The passage from Good Friday to Easter Sunday is a developmental and dialectical one. And my question is whether this metaphysics of the body can adequately sustain a metaphysics of the body; whether a sustainable metaphysics requires an exteriority, a threshold of transcendence, a God otherwise than being that is not one with the operations of sublation? Does Hegel need a more adequate doctrine of analogy that would announce a sacramental politics of the body? How would this sacramental understanding of the body (political and otherwise) revise Hegel's thought?

These questions can best be sharpened when comparing Hegel's metaphysics of the body politic with those of St. Paul. Although St. Paul is strictly examining the nature of the church, the corollary of Hegel's argument is that the state is the church.[40]

---

[38]   Walter Kaufman quotes Heinrich Heine as Nietzsche's source for the idea of 'eternal reoccurrence'. Heine sums this idea up in his famous words: 'time is infinite, but the things in time, the concrete bodies are finite. Now, however long a time may pass, according to the eternal laws governing the combinations of this eternal play of repetition, all configurations that have previously existed on this earth must yet meet, attract, repulse, kiss, and corrupt each other again'. Cited in Walter Kaufmann, *Nietzsche; Philosopher, Psychologist, Antichrist* (Princeton, 1959), p. 276.

[39]   Hegel, *Elements of the Philosophy of Right*, p. 362.

[40]   For Hegel's exposition of the relations between Church and State, see *Elements of the Philosophy of Right*, pp. 291–304. His views are based on the premise that 'religion is that moment which integrates the state at the deepest level of the disposition [of the citizens], the state ought even to require all its citizens to belong to such a [religious] community' (p. 295).

St. Paul's Metaphysics of the Body Politic

In recent years there has been much critical attention paid to Paul and the political. This has only partly come from the New Testament critical industry itself – through the work of Richard Horsley,[41] Neil Elliot[42] and Bruno Blumenfeld.[43] It has also come from philosophico-political voices concerned with examining and responding to where we are culturally situated today – through the work of Alain Badiou,[44] Giorgio Agamben[45] and Slavoj Žižek.[46] But there remains an interesting reticence in both the NT cultural historians and interpreters with respect to examining the major model organising Pauline ecclesiology – the body. Blumenfeld recognises 'the critical, foundational role that the body of Jesus plays'.[47] He comes closest to breaking through that reticence when, in his exposition of the political subtext of Paul's *Letter to the Philippians*, he observes Paul's 'wide body-language register' and concludes: 'The *polis* reaches the depths of physicality'.[48] The *ekklesia* is for Blumenfeld the heart of the new political community (the *polis*) Paul is committed to forging. But he adds little to more to these observations, given how critical and foundational the body is, later in his book, in his detailed analysis of the *Letter to the Romans* (one of the four major texts employing the body analogy). We are told again that '[t]he idea of Christ as the body of which the people are members, connects again with the idea of the *polis*', that Paul is abandoning the older '*polis-psuche* similarity' (of Plato and Aristotle) and this 'could have been mediated by the Hellenistic Pythagorean pseudepigrapha, which used both political similes' (for example Pseudo-Archytas).[49] Earlier in the book, Blumenfeld has taken us exhaustively through every one of these political pieces of pseudepigrapha. Where these new analyses of the political Paul, by both NT scholars and cultural theorists, leave us is very unclear. For Badiou, Agamben and Žižek, in quite different ways and with different agendas, Paul is a revolutionary, a leftwing radical *avant le lettre* and able to offer we victims of both modernity and liberal democracy a way forward. To

---

[41]   Richard Horsley (ed.) *Paul and Empire: Religion and Power in Roman Imperial Society* (Harrisburg, 1997) and *Paul and Politics: Ekklesia, Israel, Imperium, Interpretation* (Harrisburg, 2000).

[42]   Neil Elliot, 'Paul and the Politics of Empire' in *Paul and Politics* (2000), pp. 15–39 and *Liberating Paul: The Justice of God and the Politics of the Apostle* (Minneapolis, 2005).

[43]   Bruno Blumenfeld, *The Political Paul: Justice, Democracy and Kingship in a Hellenistic Framework* (Sheffield, 2001).

[44]   Alain Badiou, *St. Paul: The Foundation of Universalism* (trans. Ray Brassier) (Stanford, 2003).

[45]   Giorgio Agamben, *The Time That Remains: A Commentary on the Letter to the Romans* (trans. Patricia Dailey) (Stanford, 2005).

[46]   Slavoj Žižek, *The Puppet and the Dwarf: the Perverse Core of Christianity* (Cambridge, 2003).

[47]   Blumenfeld, *The Political Paul*, p. 383.

[48]   Blumenfeld, *The Political Paul*, pp. 299–300.

[49]   Blumenfeld, *The Political Paul*, p. 383.

Blumenfeld, Paul is a conservative supporter of Roman Imperialism (a precursor to the famous example of Jewish accommodationist policy by Josephus) and a defender of the *Pax Romanum*. For Elliot, Paul is a pragmatic thinker who we should not expect to find having 'a clear, consistent, univocal "pro-Roman" or "anti-Roman" posture'.[50]

To this celebrated collection of critics excavating the political Paul should be added a second group of NT commentators working with *traditionsgeschlichtlich* interests in the Pauline body going back to at least 1919 and Traugott Schmidt's *Der Leib Christi*.[51] From this scholarship, two theologies of the body as a *societas* are evident, the first found paradigmatically in Paul's *First Letter to the Corinthians* and the second found paradigmatically in *Letter to the Ephesians*. The latter has Christ as 'the head of the church, his body' (Eph. 5.23); the former has the Church as an ancephalous body. Critical opinion is divided as to whether these two theologies cohere and much of the argument revolves around whether Paul can be recognised at the author of the *Letter to the Ephesians*. For myself, on the basis of the undoubted Pauline authorship of the *Letter to Philemon* and the *Letter to the Colossians*, and the profound relationship between these two letters and the *Letter to the Ephesians*, I accept *Ephesians* as Pauline and view the two theologies as constituting one coherent line of thought.

> For just as the body is one and has many members, and all the members of the body, though many, are one body [*onta en estin soma*], so it is with Christ [*outos kai o Christos*]. For by [*en*] one Spirit we were all baptised into one body – Jews and Greeks, slaves and free – and were all made to drink of [*en*] one Spirit. For [*kai gar*] the body does not consist of one member but of many. If the foot should say, 'Because I am not a hand, I do not belong to [*estin ek*] the body', that would not make it any less a part of the body. And if the ear should say, 'Because I am not an eye, I do not belong to the body', that would not make it any less part of the body. If the whole body were an eye, where would be the hearing? If the whole body were an ear, where would be the sense of smell? But as it is, God arranged the organs in the body [*etheto ta mele*], each one of them, as he chose. If all were a single organ, where would the body be? As it is, there are many parts, yet one body. The eye cannot say to the hand, 'I have no need of you' nor again the head to the feet, 'I have no need of you'. On the contrary, the parts of the body which seem to be weaker are indispensable, and

---

[50]   Elliot, *Paul and Politics*, p. 13.

[51]   The literature is expansive but a chain of enquiry often goes back to Traugott Schmidt's *Der Leib Christi* (Leipzig, 1919) and continues through Ernst Käsemann, *Leib und Leib Christi* (Tübingen, 1933) to such class studies in English as John A. T. Robinson, *The Body: A study in Pauline Theology* (London, 1952) and Ernst Best, *One Body in Christ* (London, 1955). The most recent studies would include Gosnell L. O. R. Yorke, *The Church as the Body of Christ in the Pauline Corpus* (Lanham, MD, 1991); Dale Martin, *The Corinthian Body* (New Haven, 1995) and Michelle V. Lee, *Paul, the Stoics, and the Body of Christ* (Cambridge, 2006).

those parts of the body which we think less honourable we invest with greater honour, and our unpresentable parts are treated with greater modesty, which our more presentable parts do not require. But God has so composed [*sunekerasen*] the body, giving greater honour to the inferior part, that there may be no discord [*schisma*] in the body, but that the members have the same care for one another. If one member suffers, all suffer together; if one member is honoured, all rejoice together. Now you are the body of Christ and individually members of it [*kai mele ek merous*]. (1 Cor. 12.12–27)

There are several points to observe about this passage: first, its predominantly ontological tenor – the repeated use of *estin* and *onta*. The verb 'to be' is not merely used as a cupola, is the employed emphatically in the sense of 'to participate' as the prepositions '*en*' and '*ek*' emphasise. Hence the translation 'belong to', in this R.S.V. version (the A.V. translates more literally). But the ontology announced here is not one which is concurrent with the natural order: we do not grow into becoming members of this body, we are initiated into it through baptism. By inference, then (and this would be a second point) this body 'which is also Christ' [*outos kai o Christos*] – note the two nominative subjects in that clause – is both related to and yet different from other physical bodies. *Kathaper* is the Greek term introducing a similitude; but the similitude does not have the grammatical logic of simile where the predicate intrinsically and ontologically belongs to the substantive ('as white as snow').[52] *Kathaper* has the grammatical logic of analogy where the properties of two substantives (in this case the human body and the body of Christ) share properties but in a way that neither admits of their being intrinsically related or extrinsically associated. I concur with the New Testament scholar, John A. T. Robinson: 'Paul uses the analogy of the human body to elucidate his teaching that Christians form Christ's body. But the analogy holds because they are in literal fact the risen organism of Christ's person in all its concrete reality ... It is almost impossible to exaggerate the materialism and crudity of Paul's doctrine of the Church as literally now the resurrected *body* of Christ'.[53] As I argued in *Cities of God* the body of Christ becomes the governing body, and the condition for the possibility for a new ordering of the human body. I grant this is a theological rather than a philosophical argument. In the grammar of analogy the attribution of properties proceeds from the primary to the secondary analogate. What I am suggesting here is that the transcendent body of Christ redefines the human body from a more exalted, in fact, glorified position – so that the properties of co-abiding

---

[52]   Lee refers to the famous fable by Dionysius of Halicarnassus (in Ant. Rom., 6.83.2) in which the body is likened to a commonwealth, and Livy, *History of Rome* 2.328–12, where it is likened to the state. (*Paul, the Stoics, and the Body of Christ*, p. 9). But this is very different to the Pauline emphasis that the kingdom of God *is* a body. As she points out, Paul's use is much closer to Stoics like Seneca and Cicero who also both employ the body analogy politically to speak of a universal humanity.

[53]   Robinson, *The Body: A study in Pauline Theology*, p. 51

in Christ's body are communicated to the human body. This does not merely boil down to: I do not naturally as a human body belong to the body of Christ. Though, baptism 'by (*en*) the one Spirit' marks an ontological shift from being in the world to being *en Christo* (a favourite use by Paul of the dative of location).[54] But then neither members nor even Christ is translated out of this world – the use of *en* suggests rather another level of ontological intensity available in this world but not concurrent with it. There is an incorporation effected by baptism and this incorporate does not leave the human body as such unchanged. The character of that change we will pursue below and conclude here that the incorporation is made possible because of the analogical relation.

This incorporation brings about two changes that seem to be antithetical to life in the world. The first change is with respect to social and racial differences: Jews, Greeks, slaves, free are indicators of social tensions and hierarchies. In the *Letter to the Galatians*, Paul will add 'male and female' and characterise the socio-sexual tensions and hierarchies. Each of these positions was embedded within value systems concerning the human body – class notions of embodiment, ethnic notions, sexual notions amongst others. But incorporated *en pneumati* and *en Christo* a new social order is announced. The Christocentric body politic constitutes this order. It is not an order where difference is elided – the body is not one organ but many different functions. This is not then Spinoza's monism. But the differences, functioning as such, live out this polity. Paul does not equate this body with a group of people, not even the church in Corinth. It is a not an object visible in the world. This is not a collection of people so much as a coordination of operations. The body is made manifest in those events in which it is seen to be working. Its only location (which is not a location with either spatial or temporal co-ordinates that can be mapped) is in Christ and the Spirit. There are not necessarily any institutions: no estates, no civil society. Though the institution of the church necessarily presents a visible representation of the notion 'church'. How else would the people learn about the church, its meaning and its values? But there is governance. The governing is an inner composition (*sunekerasen*) effected by God. The word *sunekerasen* is the aorist active of the verb *sugkerannumi*, a highly unusual word for Paul. Although it is found in Plato, the verb does not occur in the LXX at all and is only found twice in the New Testament, here and in Hebrews 4.2. In both cases it means to mix, temper or be united with; though in the passive it can describe very close relationships between people. It is related to the verb *parakolutheo* – 'to follow closely', 'to follow beside' (as in discipleship) – and *sudzeugnumi* – 'to yoke' (again used in the Gospels with respect to discipleship).

---

[54] Baptism functions as a liturgical practice signifying what Paul elsewhere calls 'adoption' (Gal. 4.5) – by nature we are not children of God. This 'adoption' marks a different between teleology (as in Aristotle and Hegel) in which an efficient cause moves final cause, that for which it was created, and eschatology in which there is a shift to another order of being wrought by divine grace.

The tense and voice here with Paul suggests God put together this body at some definite point in the past and that this action continues until now. Commentators seemed to fight shy of this verse, but I would suggest that what Paul is referring to here is the making of the primal human being. For the verse has shifted from the body of Christ to the physical body itself; in the context of Paul's wider theological interests, from the second to the first Adam. The body then, human and divine, does not issue from Bateman's void and is therefore without meaning. It is created by an act of God and pre-eminently significant, 'heavy with meaning'. The politics of incorporation in the body of Christ fashion an understanding of the body as God first created it. Again, to go back to what I said above – the Christic body becomes the model for understanding all embodiment. The act of discipleship, which is the operation of Christic politics, realises these coterminous bodies – the human and the divine.

Let us take this further. Earlier, I mentioned Althusser's notion of state apparatuses that fashion ideologies which we live out, often unconsciously; ideologies that have implicit within them value systems. As I said, Foucault examined such apparatuses in terms of 'technologies', particularly technologies of the self. And Talal Asad in the two of the essays collected in *Genealogies of Religion* examined these technologies in terms of medieval monastic institutions[55] – extending Foucault analyses of confession, for example. But I want to go further, on the basis of this relation exposited by Paul. Of course, the human bodies constituting the ecclesial community at Corinth will be fashioned by specific institutional practices. In fact, Paul will go on later in the letter and in other letters to outline a number of those practices – and Dale Martin, among others, has helped us to see the understanding of the human body with respect to these practices and their context.[56] Martin enables us the see the human body as a cultural product. I want to enable us to glimpse the human body as a product of the Christic polity; the product of a fundamental realignment that goes on in that incorporation into the body of Christ. For no doubt also the Greek, the Jew, the slave and the freeborn will each be fashioned by the dominant practices defining their own cultural situation. The Greek will live out her Greekness, and all that culturally entailed; the Jew will live out his Jewishness, with all that that entailed. The slave will live out his slavery and the freeborn what was then valued and expected on one who is born free. But institutions or state apparatuses aside, when the Greek, the Jew the slave and the freeborn are incorporated into the body of Christ these fashionings are transposed by a further working of the Spirit. Paul's language describes that transposition. For the Greek, the abrupt contrast between the things of the soul (*psuchikos*) and the things of the spirit (*pneumatikos*) in 1 Cor. 2.14 or the phrase 'the mind of flesh' (*tou noos tes sarkos*) in Col. 2.18) is nonsense. For the Jew the phrase 'in the flesh' (*en sarki*) in Rom. 7.5 and 8.9 brings confusion because human beings *are* flesh they are not *in* a domain that is fleshly. The language of freedom

---

[55]   Talal Asad, *Genealogies of Religion: Disciplines and Reasons of Power in Christianity and Islam* (Baltimore, 1993).

[56]   Dale B. Martin, *The Corinthian Body* (New Haven, 1995).

and bondage equally overturns what either of these terms might mean to one born free and another born into slavery. *En Christo*, Greek, Jew, slave, and freeborn become something else. They live out and become produced as hands, feet, eyes, ears, honoured parts, inferior parts, weaker parts and stronger parts within this new body. They become incorporated into other forms of behaviour, other value systems, other conceptions of embodiment and pneumatic movements that fashion their bodies anew – in accordance with the living, that is, operational body of Christ. Hence Paul's elliptical phrase 'the Lord for the body' [*o kurios to somatic*] (1 Cor. 6.13) – where Lord is a political title. The human body is fashioned by the politics of the body of Christ and the position of that body with respect to other cultural corporations that make up 'the world'. What does this signify?

Any possible democratisation in terms of equality – as individual members within one body, ruled over by one Spirit, equally valued before God and so on – does not occur necessarily in terms of social, sexual or racial status. It occurs through the new politics of living in Christ and being governed by a command to love one another. Love in the thirteenth chapter of *First Letter to the Corinthians* constitutes the great erasure of statuses of any kind because it 'bears all things, believes all things, hopes all things, endures all things' (13.7). What being a member of the body of Christ entails, in other words, is a political discipleship that does not readily translate into institutions or even modes of political activity in this world. Of course, this discipleship and the politics it enacts take place in and with respect to this world, but its import lies in the operations of God with respect to salvation understood as becoming truly human, truly embodied. This is important for understanding the apophaticism of the body of Christ. The New Testament scholar, John A. T. Robinson sums up why, commenting on *First Letter to the Corinthians* 13–20: 'It is in their [Christians'] "bodies" (v.15) – as *somata* and not merely "spirit" – that Christians are members of Christ ... so there is no real line between the body of His [Christ's] resurrection and the flesh-bodies of those who are risen with Him'.[57] *Sarx* or mere flesh dies, it is mortal, weak, corruptible and prey to sin. But since there is only one body, *soma*, composed of many bodies, *somata*, and that body is a glorified and resurrected body, *soma* is immortal, eternal. This '[b]ody is not among the things that are seen (*ta blepomena*, that is the *sarx*) and belong to this age only (*proskaira*), but it *aionion* [eternal], belonging to the age to come', Robinson concludes.[58] The human body participating in the risen, eschatological body politic of Christ lives in a transpositional state. It has only liminal identity. It lives physically in this world and equally as physical in the world to come. We can observe this liminal condition in the verbal tenses of Paul's description in *Letter to the Ephesians*: God 'raised us up with him [*sunegeiren* – aorist active] and made us to sit with him [*sunekathisen* – aorist active] in the heavenly place in (*en*) Christ' (Eph. 2.6). The verbs are newly coined by Paul to emphasise our conformity in the one body. Just as, in Paul, there is a continuity

---

[57] Robinson, *The Body: A study in Pauline Theology*, p. 53.

[58] Robinson, *The Body: A study in Pauline Theology*, p. 76.

between the physical and historical body of Jesus the Christ and his resurrected body, so there 'is therefore no ultimate distinction between the individual resurrection and the one resurrection Body'.[59] The cataphatic body, that which is visible (after the Greek *kataphasis* – that which is can be spoken about) is also, in Christ, apophatic (after the Greek *apophasis* – a denial, a negation), that which is beyond the powers of human beings to conceive or think. According to Liddel-Scott, *phasis* is often in Greek associated with *phainomai*, appearance. Hence Paul has to invent a new language in which to sketch his theological conception of this body.[60] For what individual *soma* can say 'I am a hand ... or a foot ... or an eye ... or an ear'? No one can identify their function. And if they cannot identify their function, then their functioning is hidden from them also. Maybe not hidden entirely insofar as they have a sense of vocation, but the events in which they enact the church as a 'foot' or a 'hand' or an 'ear' – those events into which they are identified as the operative body of Christ – are only graspable as acts of faith. Their identity within the body of Christ is worked out in Christian terms of practices of faith, hope and love that go beyond the naming and labelling in this world. While remaining a Greek, a Jew, a male, a female, a slave or a freeborn one is also and more significantly a member of the body of Christ. A body which is 'heavy with meaning' that is not possible to translate. One condition or identity is not necessarily effaced in the other, but it is transformed in ways beyond telling. One discovers one's somatic nature in the tranquillity of recollection; it is not self-evident. It is discovered not discreetly but by continuing to work within the body of Christ, a new polity, with new relationships and new distributions of power that can never find their full realisation in any political system in this world; which therefore resist accommodation with the politics of this world and offer possibilities for an alternative politics. The altar on which Paul asks the Roman Christians to present their bodies as a living sacrifice can never be identified with a particular throne. The body is continually being given, continually moving out and enacted elsewhere, and as such it continually transcends strict identifications that it imposes upon itself or is imposed upon it. The body is never there as such (as if a static object in a freeze-framed still); the body is there only because it moves, it circulates, it acts, it disseminates its knowledges, rejecting, absorbing and adapting itself to new knowledges. It is in this way that it can be deemed apophatic.

It is because *soma* is apophatic that it is for Paul always and only a theological and metaphysical entity. Hence there is a body of sin and a body of death. These are metaphysical conditions of embodiment affecting *sarx*; conditions *sarx* has little or no understanding of, because *sarx* is the secularised, de-mystified body. This is the body that can be viewed as a physical and, politically, artificial machine for Hobbes and a worthless, political nonentity dressed in designer labels that bear no relation to the products they are labelling, for Bateman. *Sarx*, even though it possesses for Paul a psychic nature (the 'fleshly mind' of Col. 2.18), is a materialist

---

[59]   Robinson, *The Body: A study in Pauline Theology*, p. 79.
[60]   Robinson, *The Body: A study in Pauline Theology*, p. 63.

reduction of embodiment; not necessarily bad in itself for it is the purely natural condition for humanity. Though to be human is have a body, not just be flesh. *Sarx* cannot inherit the kingdom of God (1 Cor. 15.50) and it is the body, not the flesh, which is redeemed. The bodies of sin and death are like the body of Christ, realms; but they realms of enslavement. They too are metaphysical and operate transcendentally in this world; but they constitute a bad metaphysics. The good metaphysics is only arrived at through enacting the body in and through the body of Christ, through the politics of discipleship, through the eternal life of the Spirit. This returns us to Hegel.

What is immediately apparent is that the working of the negative in Hegel is quite different from the operation of the living Spirit in Paul. For Hegel, God has given Himself entirely to this world through the death of Jesus Christ on the Cross. Through the work of the 'inwardness of this principle is the … reconciliation and resolution of all opposition'.[61] For Paul, the immanent logics of this world have to bow to the power not of the death of God but the resurrected Christ. There is no reconciliation and resolution of all opposition; those not participating in the body of Christ are sundered from the life of God. Any reconciliation and resolution is on the basis of total commitment to a new covenant between God and human beings. Paul speaks of an end to 'discord [*schisma*] in the body … [when] the members have the same care for one another'.[62] But opposition for Hegel is the dialectical encounter with the other, and resolution is the sublation of that otherness, an incorporation. The body politic, like the human body, is caught up in temporality, desiring and willing an eternal condition of rest beyond representation in the absoluteness of the Idea. There is something Gnostic in this desiring; a yearning to be beyond the materiality of state institutions, religions, and sciences in an unbounded universalism. And yet it is never so simple with Hegel, who to the end affirms the concrete and the actual in what can only be the development of this world into the kingdom of God. The Christian body politic for Paul is already constituted in the risen Christ – it can never be then a development from within this world. Furthermore, in the incorporation into Christ's body otherness and difference remain and are unsublatable. The Greek will continue Greek, the Jew; the hand will not be the eye, the ear will never be the foot. The difference and materiality of *somati* are guaranteed by the one transcendent *soma*. Not being of this world, and yet enabling the world to participate in it, this body can be truly metaphysical in a way that makes possible a post-materialist condition. It enables a true apophasis of the body that guarantees its mystery and its sanctity through a politics of redemption.

---

[61]   Hegel, *Elements of the Philosophy of Right*, p. 380.
[62]   I Cor. 12.25.

Chapter 11

Passion For Life:
Power For Building Justice and Peace

Mary Elizabeth Moore

Grace Jantzen's life is marked by passion, especially passion for life. From her childhood in Canada, wearing clothes made from flour sacks and valuing simple virtues, to the completion of two PhDs, to the study of Julian of Norwich while living in her cell, to the analysis of medieval women's mysticism, to her intellectual probing of natality and necrophilia, Grace Jantzen was powered by a deep passion for life. She loved her partner and close friends and colleagues. She mentored students with supportive, challenging compassion. She expected the best of everyone, including herself, because human life leaves a mark on this world and she wanted people to leave life-giving marks, rather than death-dealing ones.

The theme of this book highlights the challenge of Grace's life, to critique and reshape philosophical and religious thought patterns, thus to contribute to reshaping the social fabric. The purpose of this chapter is to explore the assumption in Grace Jantzen's work that a human passion for life is complexly intertwined with a person's or community's power to build justice and peace. To that end, I explore the life narratives of two women as test cases, focusing on how these women from different contexts weave their passions for life with their power to build justice and peace. I then identify elements in Jantzen's work that point toward *a philosophy of life-bearing*, drawing Jantzen into conversation with process-relational philosophy.

My hope is to underscore the potential of a philosophy grounded in natality. True to Jantzen's analysis, I begin with a warning: to remember how easily the human passion for life can be distorted into a love and fascination with death (necrophilia) or fear of death (necrophobia), which invites people into deeper spirals of violence.[1] The genius of Grace's work is her capacity to be realistic about that danger while boldly asserting an alternative philosophical, religious, and political approach to life.

---

[1]   Grace Jantzen, *Foundations of Violence: Death and the Displacement of Beauty*, Vol. 1 (London, 2004), pp. 5–6.

Portraits of Women

We turn first to portraits of two women, inviting the textures of their lives to inform the theoretical analysis that follows. The method is compatible with Jantzen's work at the intersections of human life with philosophical thought, a method that led her frequently to analyse life narratives in order to formulate and test theoretical constructions.[2] This chapter does not represent a broad sample of women in history, but the engagement with women's lives lessens bias and expands complexity in the theoretical analysis. The particular focus of the portraits is the women's love of life in relation to their yearning to contribute to human and planetary wellbeing.

This project is exploratory and not comparative. Thus, I focus on women for two compelling reasons: to limit the range of variables by attending to a same-gender sample and to give intellectual and political privilege to women's lives in this initial study. In so doing, I make neither essentialist nor comparative claims about gender, whether female, male, transgender, or omnigender. My concern is to engage in gender analysis within larger social-contextual and theological matrices.

Beatrix Potter

In the recent film, 'Miss Potter', and in Linda Lear's biography of Beatrix Potter,[3] we find an intriguing portrait of a woman who shared Grace Jantzen's love of life, as well as her enthusiasm for the natural world, sensual and aesthetic imagination, rationality, and even the Lake District. In the film, we discover a woman who loves life too much to give up her passion for art to a mother who did not comprehend. Yet, she loved people too much to refuse a costly agreement with her parents when she wanted to marry. She agreed to postpone her marriage to satisfy her parents' desire for her not to rush into a marriage that did not satisfy their limited perspectives on social acceptability.

As a child, Beatrix spent many hours in the natural world, often alone and sometimes with her younger brother or father. She thrived on observing natural wonders, especially small creatures, such as rabbits, and gardens and landscapes. She also thrived on imagination, telling her brother stories about the animals as they faded into sleep. According to the movie, Beatrix's stories were quite different from those of her nanny, who described scary fairies hovering outside the window and waiting to come into the nursery and grab any child who dared to get out of bed.

---

[2]   Jantzen sometimes engaged in biographical analysis (see *Julian of Norwich*, London, second edn, 2000). At other times, she studied women's lives as sources for philosophical meta-analysis (see *Power, Gender and Christian Mysticism*, Cambridge, 1995); or to develop or test the adequacy of a philosophical idea (see 'Mysticism and Experience', *Religious Studies*, 25/3 1989): pp. 295–315 and 'Choose Life! Early Quaker Women and Violence in Modernity', *Quaker Studies*, 9/2 (2005): pp. 137–55).

[3]   Linda Lear, *Beatrix Potter: A Life of Nature* (New York, 2007).

Beatrix's stories were full of life, and Nanny's were full of threats to life. This film portrayal of Nurse Ann Mackenzie is amplified by Linda Lear's quoting of Beatrix's journal, in which she recalls 'the tyranny of a cross old nurse'. Beatrix proceeded to describe the nurse's legacy to her as 'a firm belief in witches, fairies and the creed of the terrible John Calvin (the creed rubbed off, but the fairies remained)'.[4]

From such beginnings, Beatrix Potter gained strength to defy her parents' social-climbing values, to follow her own passions, and to seek more just, earth-loving ways of life. Whether insisting on publishing her books at prices that ordinary families could afford, or buying farmland in the Lake District to prevent development, or donating that same land to the National Trust for preservation, she was willing to go beyond the limits of social acceptability for the sake of protecting and caring for life.

Beatrix Potter's passions were a curious blend of Lancashire values, Unitarianism, the aesthetic values of her family, and the fierce independence of a young girl who grew up to trust rationality and the natural world. On both sides of her family, she inherited the values of cotton people and hard workers from the North of England, as she did their Unitarian commitments. Her maternal Grandmother Leech was an influential philanthropist in the Unitarian Church of Stalybridge, donating her family home for the church to use as a school, expanding the school for mill workers during the cotton famine, and establishing kitchens for all mill workers in town.[5] Beatrix's parents continued the Unitarian traditions, though they were not so active in practice as her grandparents. Indeed, as a child, Beatrix missed the colourful celebrations of church festivals and holidays that she saw others enjoy.[6]

Beatrix did glean many Unitarian emphases, such as 'an inner self-reliance, a distinctly pragmatic approach to life, and a tendency towards rebelliousness'.[7] Lear explains:

> From childhood on she exhibited a reticence towards dogma and an aversion to creeds of any sort. The culture of Unitarianism contributed to her compatibility with the 'application of reason' as a method of intellectual inquiry.[8]

Of course, this heritage did not prevent Beatrix from questioning Unitarianism. She wrote in her journal:

> I shall always call myself a Unitarian because of my father and grandmother ..., but for the Unitarians as a Dissenting body, as I have known them in London, I

---

[4] Lear, *Beatrix Potter*, pp. 29–30.
[5] Lear, *Beatrix Potter*, p. 15.
[6] Lear, *Beatrix Potter*, p. 41.
[7] Lear, *Beatrix Potter*, p. 41.
[8] Lear, *Beatrix Potter*, p. 41.

have no respect. Their creed is apt to be a timid, illogical compromise, and their forms of Service, a badly performed imitation of the Church.[9]

We see here a woman whose religious sensibilities were keen, as were her intellectual questions. Both were part of her natality, a combination of observing and delighting in life and sharing that love of life with others.

One further observation pertains to Potter's writing and illustrations. Lear points out that Potter created 'a new form of animal fable: one in which anthropomorphized animals behave always as real animals with true animal instincts and are accurately drawn by a scientific illustrator'.[10] Lear adds that the gap between animals and humans is narrow in Potter's work. In *The Tale of Peter Rabbit*, 'Potter achieves a seamless harmony between animal and human nature'.[11] Similarly, gardens entered her illustrations as part of the stories she tells. Potter was a woman for whom human life is *internally* connected with other parts of the natural world, each indwelling the other. People, rabbits, and gardens are distinctive, but they are intimately related; further, people and rabbits sometimes behave similarly. Potter's passion for life was embodied in a worldview of integrated wholeness and in actions of storytelling, artistic illustration, and ecological preservation that preserve and nourish the whole.

Ayanna Abi-Kyles

I turn now to a second life story, drawn from Emory University's Oral History Project. Women selected for this project have influenced religion and culture within their social contexts. Some are well known; others are known only in their small circle of relationships. Ayanna Abi-Kyles[12] was nominated by students who appreciate her wise counsel in Candler School of Theology, where she serves as Program Associate for Black Church Studies and Women in Theology and Ministry.

Abi-Kyles grew up in Detroit, Michigan, during the 1960s.[13] When we asked how she became involved in the Shrine of the Black Madonna, an Afrocentric religious community, she responded:

A lot of it had to do with my location. I was born and raised in Detroit, Michigan. And in 1954, ... this country was embroiled in very strong racial – I call – racial war. ... Detroit was fuelled by people who had left the South and had

---

[9]   Beatrix Potter, *Journal*.

[10]   Lear, *Beatrix Potter*, p. 153.

[11]   Lear, *Beatrix Potter*, pp. 153–4.

[12]   Ayanna Abi-Kyles, *Interview, Oral History Project*, Candler School of Theology, Atlanta GA (10 November 2004).

[13]   Ayanna, Abi-Kyles, *Interviews, Oral History Project*, Candler School of Theology, Atlanta, GA (15–16 November 2006).

come to the North and worked in the big three, the Detroit automobile factories. And the U.A.W., the United Auto Workers, was very influential in organising poor workers, and particularly black workers, politically. ... Our family was very politically active because everybody in my family worked at Ford Motor Company, Chrysler, or General Motors.

So, that was an awareness for us because, in our family, everyone worked in elections, any election, city, state, and federal election. We all worked the polls. And we were aware how politics influenced our lives. That's one part of how I became involved in the Shrine. There was not one thing, there were many things. Another important part for me was the influence of my father who was a black nationalist.[14]

Abi-Kyles elaborated further on the moment of religious decision for her:

I ended up at the Shrine of the Black Madonna, not because of its theology, but because of its community activism ... I left the A.M.E. Church at 12 years old, when my grandmother told me, 'Now you're twelve. You can either decide if you're going to heaven or hell, and that's your choice. You don't have to go to church, but you're going to go to hell.' So I still chose not to go to church.

I didn't go to church at all until I went to the Shrine of the Black Madonna. And what really influenced me was the work that it was doing in community. I didn't consider the theological position of the Shrine important for me. *There* was a place for ... young black people who were trying to work, to make a difference for black people in the world. That's how I started.

And there's another part of me that was spiritually searching for a home. Because it was, you know, the turbulence of the late sixties and early seventies and I needed a place to find some peace. And I could not find it in the mainstream traditional black churches because of the lack of emphasis on social action. ... My spirit was longing for a space, and so the Shrine best fit that need for me.[15]

These excerpts from Ayanna's life narrative suggest that she had an early consciousness of the relation between her religious passions for life and her commitments to justice.

The particular form of Ayanna's natality, or love of life, was infused with determination to 'make a difference for black people in the world'. Her choice of religious community, and her later critique of the community's lack of attention to justice for women, were tempered by her recognition that necrophilia, or love of death, is a real threat to life. She knew as a child that communities claiming to support life, such as her grandmother's African Methodist Episcopal Church,

---

[14]   Abi-Kyles, *Interview* (2004), pp. 1–2.

[15]   Abi-Kyles, *Interview* (2004), pp. 3–4.

sometimes ignore critical dimensions of life, such as justice for black people. Later Ayanna learned that a community can ardently support one aspect of life while dismissing others. She saw in the Shrine of the Black Madonna an impressive emphasis on racial justice, which sometimes impeded gender justice. In the language of Grace Jantzen, the forces of natality were limited in both religious communities, allowing necrophilia into the fabric of community life, justified by a hierarchy of values in which individual salvation superseded social justice, or racial justice superseded gender justice.

Toward a Philosophy of Life-Bearing

What visions emerge from these stories for a philosophy of natality, or life-bearing? That question can occupy a lifetime, as it did for Grace Jantzen. In this chapter, I sketch an outline, identifying elements vital for fresh philosophical thinking and transformed patterns of life. To that end, I engage in dialogue with Grace Jantzen and the process-relational philosophy of Alfred North Whitehead, both focused on life and aimed toward the flourishing of life. Together with women's narratives, these philosophical traditions illumine the search.

Compassion

The first philosophical element in a philosophy of life-bearing is *compassion, or the experience of feeling and appreciating the textures of life*. This is my term.[16] Grace Janzen describes the phenomenon as embodied sensuality; process thinkers identify it with prehension and the process of concrescence.

Jantzen begins the Preface of *Foundations of Violence* with a personal testimony to the power of compassionate engagement with the senses:

> One of the many pleasures of the Lake District is the luminous green of the grass, setting off the beauty of the trees and fells, the becks and tams, the harsh and gentle landscape. It has been my good fortune to live for the past six years in an ancient cottage in South Lakeland, to wake up daily to the ever-changing beauty of sea and sky, tree and hill, and to walk the fells and valleys letting their beauty soak into my soul. In these years, too, it has been my great privilege to learn to play the cello, and thus to be opened to still another kind of beauty with its multiple demands and rewards.[17]

---

[16]   Mary Elizabeth Moore, 'The Ethics of Institutions: Compassion, Critique, Creativity and Form-Giving' in Theodore Walker, Jr., and Mihály Toth (eds) *Whitheadean Ethics* (Cambridge, 2008).

[17]   Jantzen, *Foundations of Violence*, p. vii.

This is the sensual setting within which Jantzen mourned the turn of the world to increasing violence and where she analysed the Western tradition of necrophilia. She contrasted her world of sensual beauty with the 'jet aircraft screaming overhead', the maimed and killed children of Afghanistan and Iraq, and the plight of young people in Palestinian refugee camps.[18] Jantzen's sensual appreciation of the world continually awakened her to social destruction, which fed her passion for cultural transformation. As she herself said, 'the dissonance between beauty and violence' prompted her final project. In her final years, she became increasingly concerned with the Western love of death, which she saw manifested in destruction and violence, in denial of beauty, and 'in fear and hatred of bodiliness, sensory experience, and sexuality'.[19]

In Jantzen's view, a turn to natality requires people to give attention to bodies and sensual experience. This is fundamental to compassion – to loving life and sharing life with others. Indeed, natality inevitably awakens people to their bodies: 'To be born is to be embodied, enfleshed'.[20] In this view, we cannot separate body and soul, or body and rationality, without existential distortions. To focus on natality is to deny such distortions and develop a larger view of human existence:

> Without denying the possibility of life after death, and certainly without denying that we will die and the importance of taking death seriously, a focus on natality shows the significance of embodiment and of our bodily life here and now. It shows that the flourishing of human beings requires that bodily needs must be met, and therefore that it is wholly misguided to bypass issues of justice and liberation and appropriate distribution of the world's resources in favour of a spirituality focused on salvation of a soul from some other world.[21]

With these words, Jantzen calls attention to the vast range of compassion's gaze; compassion invokes concern for *all* aspects of embodied life. Further, it awakens people to the preciousness and potential of *every* living being. This is the hope of natality and compassion: '[W]ith each new infant, new possibilities are born, new freedom and creativity, the potential that this child will help make the world better'.[22]

A process-relational view of the world resonates with Jantzen's, but it focuses on the microscopic process involved in the world's continual becoming – the births that take place in every microscopic event in every moment of time and every part of the universe. Each emerging occasion prehends, or feels, the movements of God and the inheritance of the world. That inheritance enters into the new event through a process of concrescence, in which the 'many become one and are increased

---

[18] Jantzen, *Foundations of Violence*, p. vii.
[19] Jantzen, *Foundations of Violence*, p. vii.
[20] Jantzen, *Foundations of Violence*, p. 36.
[21] Jantzen, *Foundations of Violence*, p. 37.
[22] Jantzen, *Foundations of Violence*, p. 38.

by one'.[23] The process of prehension and concrescence is, thus, a receptive and creative movement (a 'birth'): an emerging occasion receives the rhythms of the universe and integrates them into a new symphonic moment.

This process can be described as compassion, for every emerging event *feels* Divine movement toward it and simultaneously *feels* the world, thus creating a new moment in the history of the universe, one filled with unique life and power. Being attuned to this complex, wonder-filled process evokes compassion for the vast web of existence. Such compassion, as in Jantzen's view of natality, generates concern and respect for the life and life potential of every being and community of beings. Such compassion might be marked by anger at destruction or sympathy for people and parts of the universe in pain. It will take many forms, but will always be marked by feeling with and for the life of the world.

In our two case studies, we see compassion as fundamental to the two women's lives. For Beatrix Potter, compassion was directed to the animals and plants in her midst, to her intimate relations, and to the lands that she loved. For Ayanna Abi-Kyles, compassion was directed to the freedom of her people, her allies in the struggle for freedom, and later to the freedom of women within her own communities. Both Potter and Abi-Kyles found compassion to be a costly source of power – power to engage in counter-cultural social action and to separate from immediate families and communities on matters of intense concern. We see in Beatrix Potter a pleasurable and renewing compassion that nourished her life, but eventually became a source of determination to make difficult decisions and to distance herself physically and psychologically from those she loved and upon whom she depended. We see Abi-Kyles' compassion sweeping her into the centre of a religious community and social movement, later leading her to the edges of her community as a determined witness for change within the ongoing freedom movement.

These two women embody the life-focused perspectives of Jantzen and process thinkers. Their compassion is bodily and sensual (as in Jantzen's thought), moving and changing (as in process thought), and challenging toward new decisions for new moments in time (as in both). Such compassion is powerful in building justice and peace.

Rationality

A second element of a philosophy of natality is *rationality, or analyzing the beauty, pain and brokenness of the world for the sake of envisioning more life-giving ways of thinking and acting*. This accent emerges naturally from compassion. As people and other creatures *feel* the world, they discern the world's beauty and brokenness, which can motivate them to reconstruct thought and support a habitus of natality.

---

[23]   Alfred North Whitehead, *Process and Reality: An Essay in Cosmology* (New York, 1978), p. 21.

The dominant rationality in much of the world is repetitive and socially destructive. Bold inquiry can lead people to question this rationality and construct radical alternatives, discarding the death-dealing habitus for one that nourishes life.

Building on Pierre Bourdieu, Grace Jantzen focuses on this idea of habitus. She recognises the power of habitus to create a 'common sense world' that people take for granted and rarely question. When a habitus reigns, a whole society foregoes deep questioning and falls into 'the grip of a dominant symbolic system'. The society is then 'shaped by the internalization of that symbolic, without paying attention to it as such or bringing it to scrutiny'.[24] The symbolic itself includes systems of language, thought, and values. It also includes assumptions about the diverse roles and valuations of diverse classes, races, and genders. Even so, a common code persists,[25] which, in Western culture, is marked by a love of death:

> The habitus of Western society is a disposition towards the enactment of death and its concomitants, especially anxiety and a drive to control, to exert mastery over anything perceived as threatening. Natality, creativity and beauty have been displaced, despised or ignored.[26]

Western societies thus carry the enduring influence of necrophilia.

Because this habitus of necrophilia has displaced a habitus of natality, most Western society believes that this thought pattern is natural rather than socially constructed. One dangerous aspect of such naturalised thought patterns is the construction of enemies: '[W]e routinely construct the world linguistically as if it were filled with enemies whom we seek to exterminate'. According to Jantzen, this 'reflects our deathly symbolic and also reinforces it'.[27] Another danger is that the habitus of necrophilia has become so deeply engrained that people deny the possibility of reconstructing it, arguing that it is both natural and inescapable.[28] With the strength of such a habitus, the need for rationality escalates.

One finds similar claims for rationality in process-relational thinking, particularly in Alfred North Whitehead's idea that propositions are lures for feeling. Propositions are ideas or constructs that invite fresh perspectives and possibilities. Whitehead[29] believed, therefore, that it is more important for a proposition to be interesting than true. In his view, propositions contribute to an ongoing process of reflecting upon the world, a process that has no end. Translated into Jantzen's language, the role of propositions is to deconstruct a destructive habitus, thus clearing space to construct another habitus that promotes life's flourishing. In

---

[24]   Jantzen, *Foundations of Violence*, pp. 10, 6–11.

[25]   Jantzen, *Foundations of Violence*, pp. 7–8.

[26]   Jantzen, *Foundations of Violence*, p. 10.

[27]   Jantzen, *Foundations of Violence*, p. 14.

[28]   Jantzen, *Foundations of Violence*, pp. 21–34.

[29]   Whitehead, *Process and Reality*, pp. 259–60.

Whitehead's language, 'The function of reason is to promote the art of life'.[30] For both, reason can potentially contribute to a life-bearing telos.

The practice of reason includes many forms, including Jantzen's playing the cello and Whitehead's adventuring with ideas. For both thinkers, it also includes traditional forms, such as logic. Whitehead[31] understood logic, for example, to be important for the dual purposes of precise investigation and philosophical rumination. Indeed, logic was an important tool for both Jantzen and Whitehead, and the two occasionally used similar approaches to logic. Both, for example, traced and evaluated the logics of Western civilisation, evaluating the adequacies and inadequacies of the Western inheritance. Such historical-analytic investigations have continuing potential to open the world in a new way. Indeed, this is what Whitehead advocated: 'Logic, properly used, does not shackle thought. It gives freedom, and above all, boldness'.[32] Rationality is thereby a way for people to explore the heights and depths and breadth of life. In Whitehead's view, reason breaks open abstractions that prevent people from 'straying across country'[33] with new ideas and combinations of ideas. In Jantzen's more socially conscious view, reason helps people break open the destructive habitus of necrophilia and construct, or reconstruct, a habitus of natality.

The view of rationality offered here is infused with value and emotion. It is a rationality grounded in feeling the world and giving priority to the habitus of natality. One finds such rationality in the lives we have explored in this chapter. Beatrix Potter's Unitarian inheritance encouraged her to learn constantly, to keep an open mind and to think independently of social influences. Ayanna Abi-Kyles' experience of Detroit in the 1950s and 1960s awakened her to complex social analysis and action-reflection, which she later expanded into gendered race analysis and action-reflection in other venues. Both women fine-tuned their rationality over time. They based their developing rationalities on observation and description of present realities, on critique of dominant systems of thought, and on their deepest intuitions and feelings of the world.

I will test these ideas further by relating them with public discourses on human rights and peacemaking, where similar accents appear. For example, one finds a similarly comprehensive approach to rationality in Martha Nussbaum, who insists that shared human values and emotion play an important role in the rationality of legal ethics. She urges ethicists and people responsible for legal and political policy to develop 'a roughly shared conception of what violations are outrageous,

---

30   Alfred North Whitehead, *The Function of Reason* (Boston, 1958).

31   Alfred North Whitehead, *The Aims of Education and Other Essays* (New York, 1929), p. 89.

32   Whitehead, *The Aims of Education*, p. 118.

33   Alfred North Whitehead, *Science and the Modern World* (Cambridge, 1933), p. 197.

what losses give rise to a profound grief, what vulnerable human beings have reason to fear'.[34]

This view also resonates with Marc Gopin, a global activist in the peace movement. Gopin draws emotion and value into his approach to rationality by accenting the role of mourning and ritual in peacemaking. Dialogue is not sufficient in itself; people need space to mourn their painful histories with one another, thus uncovering, respecting, releasing, and transforming the feelings that threaten peace.[35] Another accent is Gopin's effort to discern and build upon 'early warnings of peace'.[36] Both accents – on mourning and on early warnings of peace – are born in realistic analysis of complicated situations and in recognition that reason is suffused with emotions that need to be engaged. Further, both involve active choices for a habitus that can contribute to nourishing life.

Whether attending to the philosophical constructions of Grace Jantzen and Alfred North Whitehead or to the daily lives of women or to the rationality of global activists and theorists, we discover the power of rationality in a philosophy of life-bearing. We are invited into philosophical analysis that nourishes the quality of daily life and guides the formation of political and social policies. When rationality is awake to necrophilia and centred on natality, it has potential to shape personal, communal, and political choices that protect and enhance flourishing.

Creativity and Imagination

A third element of a life-bearing philosophy is *creativity and imagination, or the search for alternative possibilities*. Grace Jantzen accents the imaginary, and process-relational theorists accent the creative movements of the universe. For Jantzen, creativity and imagination are necessary for the transformation of the world. She seeks 'to change the world of post/modernity, and to change the thought patterns which have rigidified into its death-dealing discursive and material structures'.[37] She does not mean change for change's sake; indeed, she bemoans changes that repeat and spread the destructive, death-dealing patterns of Western society. For her, the urgent direction of change 'is to find some way of thinking – and living – otherwise, some path to the healing of the Western psyche so that instead of its death-dealing structures the present may be redeemed and

---

[34]   Martha Nussbaum, *Hiding From Humanity: Disgust, Shame and the Law* (Princeton, 2004), p. 6. See also Martha Nussbaum, *Upheavals of Thought: The Intelligence of Emotions* (Cambridge, 2001).

[35]   Marc Gopin, *Holy War, Holy Peace: How Religion Can Bring Peace to The Middle East* (Oxford, 2002), pp. 204–19; Marc Gopin, *Healing The Heart of Conflict: 8 Crucial Steps To Making Peace With Yourself and Others* (Emmaus, PA, 2004), pp. 33–57.

[36]   Marc Gopin, *Lecture* (Emory University, Atlanta, Georgia, 22 March 2007).

[37]   Jantzen, *Foundations of Violence*, p. 4.

the earth and its peoples may flourish'. Such change takes place by bringing forth 'repressed dimensions of history' and releasing 'the springs of wellbeing'.[38]

For process thinkers, the hope for philosophical thinking and for each moment of life is to contribute to the 'creative advance' of the world.[39] Whitehead sees the principle of creativity as underlying the dynamism of the universe; thus, everything in the universe, whether micro-realities or meta-movements, is imbued with creativity. The creative process is best exemplified by the process of concrescence, earlier described as that process by which all elements of past experience are brought into a new unity in a becoming occasion; the new occasion then becomes an element of experience for future occasions. Whitehead[40] reiterates this process throughout his writing, recognising the creative interplay of past and present with novelty in the ever-becoming processes of this world. He sees this process at subatomic levels and in the sweep of history. He sees it in grand movements of the cosmos and in the immediacy of daily experience. The process of becoming is a beacon of hope, opening endless possibilities for the creative advance of the world. It is not a guarantee of positive, life-bearing advance, but it offers potential and hope.

Both of these accents resonate with John Paul Lederach's idea that moral imagination is necessary for peace-building. As a peace activist and social theorist, he argues, 'Grounded realism and constructive pessimism require a type of imagination capable of transcending violence while engaging the immediate and historical challenges that continue to produce it'.[41] This description reveals the importance of engaging in tough analysis of the world as it is and vivid imagination of what the world can be. We need a space that 'opens up, even invokes, the spirit and belief that creativity is humanly possible'.[42]

The comparison with Lederach is significant because he extends the creativity discourse of Jantzen and process theorists into the matrix of active peace-building. In his lifetime of action-reflection, Lederach has come to see imagination as an aesthetic act that illumines extant realities and points beyond them to what is possible. He sees this process enacted in human lives: '[W]here cycles of violence are overcome, people demonstrate a capacity to envision and give birth to that which already exists, a wider set of interdependent relationships'.[43] For him, creativity is thus a way to attune to raw realities and then imagine the world as it could be: 'Time and again, where in small or large ways the shackles of violence are broken, we find a singular tap root that gives life to the moral imagination: the capacity of individuals and communities to imagine themselves in a web of

---

[38]   Jantzen, *Foundations of Violence*, p. 4.

[39]   Whitehead, *Process and Reality*, pp. 21, 188, 289.

[40]   Alfred North Whitehead, Adve*ntures of Ideas* (New York, 1967), pp. 192–3.

[41]   John Paul Lederach, *The Moral Imagination: The Art and Soul of Building Peace* (Oxford, 2005), pp. 58–9.

[42]   Lederach, *The Moral Imagination*, p. 38.

[43]   Lederach, *The Moral Imagination*, p. 34.

relationship even with their enemies'.[44] Lederach concludes with two persistent accents in peace movements: discerning creative movements in the world and then making choices to build on those movements and imagine a peace-filled world.

The challenge in evoking an imaginary of natality is that it is not a simple rational process, though it includes rationality, as argued above. It is a multi-faceted aesthetic process, which Grace Jantzen understood as deeply as anyone. She explains:

> If the imagination is called into play just to invent a new theory which is presented at a straightforward conceptual level in confrontation with the old one, we cannot hope to make much progress. But, if on the other hand, the imagination is invoked at the stage where we have become conscious of what has been repressed and are actively looking for new symbols, new ways forward, a 'new morning of the world' (Irigaray), then it is an indispensable well-spring, a way that shifts can be brought about in the imaginary and in the symbolic which it subtends.[45]

This quote underscores the range of creativity and imagination, far surpassing a thought experiment. Jantzen underscores the impossibility of merely substituting a theory of necrophilia with a theory of natality. What is needed is 'the reconfiguration of the landscape of our symbolic and our subjectivity'.[46]

Such an approach to creativity and imagination is embodied in complex ways, and the embodiments uncover ever-deeper insights. We have already seen how Beatrix Potter drew upon her imagination to invite others into more intimate relation with the animal world. In the second half of her life, she re-invented her lifestyle, becoming a Lake District farmer and buying and preserving land for the future. As a teenager, Ayanna Abi-Kyles imagined the possibility of making a difference for black people. She later imagined ways of expanding the freedom movement to be more inclusive of women.

Grace Jantzen was herself fascinated with such embodiments, identifying women and men who lived their lives as symbols of hope. She saw how Margaret Fell, often designated as the Mother of Quakerism, invoked tropes of life to communicate with people that life is creative, offering ever-new possibilities. Fell did this by urging people to discern the inner voice of the Spirit. Hope, for Fell, lay in 'returning to the life of God and finding in oneself that welling up of divine life'.[47] Fell thus lived and taught the possibility of creativity as a Divinely-given reality. Fell's life, as that of Potter and Abi-Kyles, are reminders that creativity and imagination are not only central philosophical premises, but are also a way of life.

---

[44]   Lederach, *The Moral Imagination*, p. 34.

[45]   Grace Jantzen, *Becoming Divine: Towards a Feminist Philosophy of Religion* (Bloomington, 1989), p. 98).

[46]   Jantzen, *Becoming Divine*, p. 98.

[47]   Grace Jantzen, 'Choose Life! Early Quaker Women and Violence in Modernity', *Quaker Studies*, 9/2 (2005): pp. 137–55, 144.

Beauty

A fourth element of a life-bearing philosophy is *beauty, or the appreciation and creation of forms that bear beauty and point beyond the harshest realities to alternative futures.* Grace Jantzen makes just such claims for beauty. She argues that beauty can change a society's imaginary: 'Attention to beauty opens a way to redeeming the present, transforming the imaginary from its necrophilic obsessions to a celebration of natality, a celebration that includes the acceptance of death as the end of life but not its goal'.[48] Jantzen does not offer simple cause and effect arguments; she does urge people to cultivate an alternate social imagination that is more conducive to life.

Jantzen's view is compatible with process metaphysics. In a process-relational perspective, all living things do create forms in every moment of existence, and this 'process is inherently kalogenic or beauty creating'.[49] Such beauty is an aesthetic achievement, but it may be, and often is, permeated with tragedy. To name it as beauty is to recognise that human agents (and all creatures) are continually enacting new moments of form, but these are capable of sustaining, reshaping, or destroying life. This view resonates with the peculiarly mixed definitions of beauty in the English language. Although primary definitions have to do with loveliness or excellent quality, other definitions have to do with extreme or egregious examples of something, such as 'that mistake was a *beauty*'.[50] This suggests that beauty is a form that may embody varying degrees of harmony and loveliness. The term thus holds contrasts and tensions, but invites people to enhance that which nourishes life.

In the grounded reality of Ayanna Abi-Kyles' life, the impulse toward beauty led her to work intensely for gender justice within her beloved Shrine of the Black Madonna. It also led her to lessen those efforts when she found herself dwelling on hopelessness (Jantzen's necrophilia). Ayanna appreciated the beauty of women and mourned the diminishment of that beauty by active or indirect oppression within a vibrant institution. She found herself in a cycle of frustration. Because her own vision of beauty was marked by gender justice, she made difficult and practical decisions about where to place her efforts during this time in her life.

Beauty is seen in Ayanna's life narrative as an active concept, a view shared by Grace Jantzen and process-relational philosophers. In aesthetics, we find a similar view in Elaine Scarry,[51] who concerns herself with the ethics of peacemaking. For Scarry, beauty is both generative and powerful: 'Beauty brings copies of itself into

---

[48]   Jantzen, *Foundations of Violence*, p. 42.

[49]   Brian Henning, *The Ethics of Creativity: Beauty, Morality and Nature in a Processive Cosmos* (Pittsburgh, 2005), p. 125.

[50]   Merriam-Webster OnLine, 2007.

[51]   Elaine Scarry, *On Beauty and Being Just* (Princeton, 1999).

being'[52] in a process of 'unceasing begetting'.[53] Beauty thus carries moral weight. It is 'lifesaving', for it 'makes life more vivid, animated, living, worth living'.[54]

This discussion leads back to Whitehead's idea of beauty as harmony and intensity and Jantzen's view of beauty as redemptive and transformative. In these views, beauty is intimately connected with justice and peace, as are compassion, rationality, and imagination. These four approaches to life can form the base for a philosophy of life-bearing. Together, they are agents of natality in a world yearning for life.

---

[52]   Scarry, *On Beauty and Being Just*, p. 3.

[53]   Scarry, *On Beauty*, p. 5.

[54]   Scarry, *On Beauty*, pp. 24–5.

Chapter 12
Natality and *Flourishing* in Contexts of Disability and Impairment

Mary Grey

Introduction: A 'Humble, Earthly Paradise in the *Now*'

This was how a group of Latin American women – preparing for the UN Assembly at Beijing in 1995 – dreamed of Heaven on earth.[1] This was how flourishing was embodied for them. Definitely not a state of affairs endlessly deferred to post-mortem existence. Let me pause to reflect on what is meant by 'flourishing', asking why the concept continues to be so significant in feminist circles and beyond.[2] Grace Jantzen, whose early death is deeply mourned, and whose work is being honoured in this current volume, used the concept – following Hannah Arendt, Luce Irigaray and Adriana Caverero – to create a new symbolic order for the Feminist Philosophy of Religion she was developing.[3] Linguistically, she built on the world evoked by a family of related terms. The English word 'flourish' is from the Latin, *florere*, French *flourir*, with associations of blossoming and beauty being evoked; a German synonym is *blühen*, or *gedeihen*, which is like the English word thrive, used in a technical sense to tell if a baby will live and grow in the quality of loving care provided. A Dutch equivalent is *bloeien*, [to blossom], in de *bloeitjd zijn*, [to

---

[1]   'A Woman's Creed' is cited in the Beijing Preparatory documents, and quoted in Catherine Keller, *Apocalypse now and Then* (Boston, 1996), p. 268. Actually it was composed by Robin Morgan with a group of Latin American women sponsored by a women's Environment and Development organisation.

'Bread. A clean sky. Active peace. A woman's voice singing somewhere, melody drifting like smoke from the cook fires. The army disbanded, the harvest abundant. The wound healed, the child wanted, the prisoner freed, the body's integrity honoured, the lover returned. The labour equal, fair and valued. Delight in the challenge for consensus to solve problems. No hand raised in any gesture but greeting. Secure interiors – of heart, home, land – so firm as to make secure borders irrelevant at last. And everywhere, laughter, care, dancing, contentment. A humble, earthly paradise in the *now.*'

[2]   Mary Grey, *The Outrageous Pursuit of Hope: Prophetic Dreams for the 21st Century* (London, 2000); Mary Grey, 'The Spiritual Journey of Impaired Pilgrims' in Tim Macquiban (ed.) *The Faith of Impaired Pilgrims* (Salisbury, 2006), pp. 20–27; Mary Grey, *To Rwanda and Back: Liberation Theology and Reconciliation* (London, 2007).

[3]   Grace Jantzen, *Becoming Divine: Towards a Feminist Philosophy of Religion* (Bloomington, 1999).

experience a time of blooming], or simply *leven*, [to be fully alive], with similar connotations of well-being and fullness of life.[4] The word is deliberately chosen as a term with ecological roots, body/earth/spirit belonging together in this life-determining process. Flourishing means all that is life-giving for people, earth, and earth creatures together. It evokes Jewish *shalom* and Islamic *salaam*. The Yoruba, a Nigerian people, use the word *alafia*, (like Tanzanian *ubuntu*), meaning the 'fullness of life'.[5] Within this thought-world God can be understood as source of *alafia*, grace, hospitality and compassion. Aristotle's word was ευδαιμονια, *eudaimonia*, which means well-being and happiness in the context of the 'good life' as he defined it – but his usage does not cover all the meanings I want to evoke here.

Visions of Flourishing

What do we mean by fullness of life? The 'Good Life'? How do our visions and dreams express it? Do faith traditions give us clues as to how to imagine the peace and justice of the Reign of God in this violent world?

The Bible of Christianity, Judaism and Islam begins with a mythic story in a garden, Eden, from which humanity was expelled, a tragedy for which a woman, Eve, has frequently been blamed.[6] Unfortunately, this has had the effect that Christianity is still troubled by nostalgia for this lost garden, for return to Eden, seen as a pre-Fall state of affairs, and has constructed a belief system where human destiny is for the next world, for Heaven – a place of bliss far removed from anything that is of the earth. Women became identified more with the earth, flesh, (and sinful flesh at that), and with sexuality, (negatively understood): the other side of the coin is that holiness and sanctity became viewed as belonging to the spirit (soul) not the body, and as being more associated with masculinity than femininity.

But this view is not shared by Judaism, which has a more positive exegesis of this part of the Book of Genesis, one that does not include a Fall. Although even within Judaism women have been considered inferior to and subject to men. In Islam, the subjection of women which still occurs in many Arab States is not ordained by the Koran. Nor are women blamed for the first sin:

> Both the man and the woman listened to the whisper of Satan,
> ate the fruit, repented and were sent out of the garden together.[7]

---

[4]   What follows here is my own development of the concept.

[5]   Mercy A. Oduyoye, *Introducing African Women's Theology* (Sheffield, 2001), pp. 14, 113.

[6]   Jewish exegesis interprets the story differently, more as a picture of how human beings behave. We do sin, disobey, and transgress limits, bring forth children in pain, and till the earth with great struggles.

[7]   Mukti Barton, *Scripture as Empowerment for Liberation and Justice: the Experience of Christina and Muslim Women in Bangladesh* (Bristol, 1999).

Yet, given the tradition of reading our scriptures and sacred texts from within a patriarchal system, where, by and large, women have been the property of men until recent liberation and justice movements across the world, small wonder that in most of our religions the flourishing of women is not a major concern. Hence I began this chapter citing women's own dreams of flourishing. In this text so many dimensions are embodied – true peace, food in plenty, celebration, bodily integrity – all within a context of renewed and restored relation. Something definitely to be celebrated as a this-worldly reality – not endlessly deferred to eternal bliss. Nor should this be dismissed as the dream only of women who are confident of worldly prosperity, or as giving up on the whole dimension of eternity. For many poor communities, as well as for people with severe impairment, this is a crucial issue: where no flourishing is experienced on earth, hope in heaven is all that sustains. Surely the transcendence and eternity of God, Sacred Being and Divine Immanent Presence will take care of eternity, with oceans of mercy and justice; whereas for humanity, care and responsibility for this earth – the only one we have and cherish – and all earth dwellers, human and non-human, is (literally) the burning issue?

This religiously-inspired vision is dependent on the binding, connecting, sustaining of all life through sacred power and energy for well-being and flourishing. Divine spirit, through its sacred energy is the source and resource for this grounded, sustaining hope. 'Flourishing' draws on sacred texts from many faiths and traditions: the prophet Isaiah, in a text problematic for the context of impairment, envisioned the flourishing of earth and people as intertwined:

> The wilderness and the dry land will be glad,
> The desert shall rejoice and blossom;
> Like the crocus it shall blossom abundantly,
> and rejoice with joy and singing ....
> Then the eyes of the blind shall be opened,
> And the ears of the deaf be unstopped;
> then shall the lame leap like a deer,
> and the tongue of the speechless sing for joy,
> For water shall break forth in the wilderness,
> and streams in the desert.
> (Isaiah 35. 1. 5–6).

This text of flourishing has also been imaginatively adapted for the urban situation, bringing hope to the wilderness of the city:

> Let the tenement and the derelict park land be glad,
> Let the slums and ghettos rejoice and burst into comfort and beauty.
> Let them flower with well-kept gardens,
> let music and laughter be heard in the streets. ...
> Then there will be vision for those blinded by despair,
> and the people who long for a friendly voice will hear love songs.

Those *crippled* with poverty will jump up and run into plenty. …
Free at last, God's people will possess the city
and shout out in delight at God's triumph
and their joy will last forever![8]

It is noteworthy, for the context of disability that 'crippled' in this text is used purely as metaphor.

As Jews recall the promise of Shalom, and the vision of plenty on the holy mountain, (Isaiah 24), Muslims also recall a vision of flourishing, calling to mind the kindness of Mohammad to Muslim women:

God hath promised to believers,
Men and women, Gardens
under which rivers flow,
To swell therein,
and beautiful mansions
In Gardens of everlasting bliss.
But the greatest bliss
is the Good pleasure of God.[9]

Before exploring how a symbol system based on flourishing might work in contexts of disability, I ask what use it might be when dealing with traumatised memories of genocide and war, with ongoing violence and injustice as in Palestine, Iraq and the Sudan. Adrienne Rich, a contemporary feminist Jewish American poet, asked exactly this as she tried to cling on to some sense of vision, in the wreck of post-holocaust, post-Hiroshima and post-Chernobyl survival, in a poem called *The Desert as Garden of Paradise*:

What would it mean
to think you are part of a generation
that simply must pass on?
What would it mean to live
in the desert, try to live
a human life, something
to hand on to the children
to take up to the Land?
What would it mean to think

---

[8]   Heather Pencavel, 'An Urban Vision of Isaiah 25', in Geoffrey Duncan (ed.) *Wisdom is Calling: an Anthology of Hope: an Agenda for Change* (Norwich, 1999), pp. 20–21.

[9]   From Surah 9: At-Taubah: 71–2; The Holy Qur'an 461 in Rifat Hassan, 'Muslim Women in Post-Patriarchal Islam' in Paula M. Cooey, William R. Eakin and J. B. McDaniel (eds) *After Patriarchy: Feminist Transformations of the World Religions* (Maryknoll, 1992), pp. 52–3.

you were born in chains and only time,
nothing you can do
could redeem the slavery
you were born into?[10]

This sense of struggling to create meaning out of despair evokes the impasse and traumatised deadlock experienced by survivors in Rwanda, Bosnia and post-conflict situations. It takes a multi-faceted approach to break this deadlock. Visions of flourishing are invoked not only for the sake of ecological well-being, but fully mindful of time and place with its wounded history, with all the specificity of the cultural and historical memories that constitute identity, costly here because it meant life or death. These are memories enshrined in bone and blood, in the sight of skulls arrayed inside churches and museums – as in Rwanda – frayed garments, children's cups and toys, in the silent stories of a landscape, deforested hillsides, abandoned plantations and burnt-down houses. And in the mutilations and disabilities that are the legacy of war. Texts are more than mere words. They are written in stone and wood, glimpsed as fragments of ruined houses, the drawings of children as they crouched in cellars hearing the bombs drop on their city and the crutches and artificial limbs of war's victims.

Building on specific Christian inspiration for flourishing in the promise of Jesus that 'I came so that you may have life in the full', (John 10.10), and in the way that he gave redemption an embodied meaning, the focus on flourishing I found specifically in Rwanda was its relevance for *bringing back the beauty of life* (emphasis in the original).[11] People needed to be fed, welcomed, treated with compassion, clothed and healed: this must be the grounding for flourishing and well-being. Liberation spiritualities the world over call for the re-membering of this, insisting on honesty and truth-telling in the acknowledgement of the lack of honour and integrity given to women's bodies trafficked in the sex trade, to the bodies of the poor forced to sell vital organs so as to be able to eat, and to the traumatised spirits of genocide survivors.

Yet, given the tradition of reading our scriptures and sacred texts from within a patriarchal system, where, by and large, women have been the property of men until recent liberation and justice movements across the world, small wonder that in most of our religions the flourishing of women, and those marginalized through a variety of impairments has not been a major concern.

---

[10]   Adrienne Rich, 'The Desert as Garden of Paradise' in *Poems 1985–1988* (New York, 1988), pp. 29–30.

[11]   Grey, *To Rwanda and Back*.

From the Logic of Salvation to the Economy of the Spirit

But there is a further step that brings into sharp relief problems around disability. Jantzen proposed the symbolic matrix around the notion of flourishing as alternative to the traditional concepts of salvation and redemption, because these seemed to imply removing us from a fully embodied situation, saving us *out of this world*.

Secondly, on the same track, feminist theology has constantly critiqued the apparent love of redemptive violence (associated with the Cross of Christ), through which salvation is to be won. Called by Mary Daly, *necrophilia*, love of death, paradoxically, this *necrophilia* is at the same time *nekrophobia*, fear of death. One does not have to be a cultural analyst to notice how Western society conceals and shuns death; by association, people with disability share in this marginalization because their very presence is a reminder of death. People now die in hospitals or homes for the elderly, rarely in their own homes, surrounded by the extended family. The mourning period in the West is almost non-existent compared with other cultures. Most children have never seen a dead body – except on TV. Much money and scientific research focuses on how to push back the approach of death. But, more serious is the symbolic focus on which this is built. One story is told of a Headmasters' Conference some years ago where each head teacher was asked what was the aim of their school's education. The Headmaster of a famous monastic school replied: 'To prepare the boys for death'. Wherever this story is told, it is done so as to illustrate the moral superiority of this philosophy. What it really illustrates is religion's focus on the transcendent and the after-life. For too long spirituality has been based on *contemptus mundi*, escape from the world, a privileging of the infinite over the finite and not on *amor mundi*, love of the world with full acceptance of the demands of embodied life.

Analysing this as *mortality, mortalité*, the privileging of death as the core of a symbolic order, Jantzen's proposal was a focus on *natalité*, birth, birth-giving or creativity. She suggested that instead of calling ourselves *mortals*, we use the term '*natals*'. This death-based symbolic order, which sanctions a system of interlocking oppressions, (racism, sexism, militarism and so on), termed *a matrix of domination*, is actually based on the unacknowledged foundation of life in birth, of embodied and material dimensions and the body of the mother. Mythic and religious traditions have plenty of examples of the masculine re-appropriation of birth, for example, the Greek legend of the birth of Athena from Zeus's head. Focus on death has not only seemed to encourage military violence, the pressure to give one's life to save the country, (whatever the cause), but has meant symbolising women as responsible for decay and death, at the same time maintaining an indifference to women's own deaths – at least formerly, in the West, and still the case in many cultures.

In her more recent work Jantzen linked the silencing of birth and the displacement of beauty with this.[12] If there were to be a focus on birth, ensuing

---

[12]   Grace Jantzen, *Foundations of Violence* (London 2004), p. 36.

cultural differences would include a focus on *embodiment*, for example: attention would focus on the flourishing of the person in this life holistically. Without denying life after death, the significance of bodily life here and now takes centre-stage. Embodied life is gendered and particular, and lived out in webs of relationship. It also respects limits. Finitude, not infinity is at its heart. Lastly, Jantzen writes, with birth and creativity, hope is born anew, with new possibilities offered with each child.

She cites Arendt's phrase: 'Amo: volo ut sis', [I love you: I want you to be].[13] This means taking responsibility for the flourishing of the child situated in an entire web of relations:

> To act for love of the world is to act in such a way as to try to ensure that newcomers will not be worldless, that their uniqueness is valued, so that they need not lose themselves in 'the masses'.[14]

Acting responsibly in this way in the face of whatever sorrow, deprivation or disaster should befall, is totally different from the traditional response of philosophers of religion which has been to defend the honour and goodness of God in the face of 'evil'.

It should be emphasised that Jantzen is not exclusively focusing on mothers and mothering but has a wider connotation for birth-giving. In fact what she does has scriptural roots, where, for example, Isaiah speaks of the birthing of the new Israel. The people are writhing with birth pangs, unable to deliver, but God brings a new birth from their failure:

> The dead shall live, their bodies shall rise.
> O dwellers in the dust, awake and sing for joy! (Isaiah 26.19)

This new symbolic nexus of symbols of flourishing brings a new spirituality, I argue, namely a more inclusive understanding of the Holy Spirit. Flourishing means the flourishing of all, within the larger earth story. The Holy Spirit, in the root meaning of *pneuma* as life and breath, creates awareness of the woundedness of bodies and spirits inflicted all through history by culturally-sanctioned violence, poverty, caste discrimination, and many forms of sickness and disability. The promise of flourishing language is to take us beyond the level of human rights language, seeking life-giving dimensions of beauty accessible to all.

Violence done to body, spirit and soul is underpinned by language's presumption of violence as norm, on metaphors of God emphasizing power and might, and distorted models of salvation. Naming and uncovering these is the necessary first step towards their eradication, a step that frees the Spirit to cross the boundaries of

---

[13]   Jantzen, *Becoming Divine*, p. 153.
[14]   Jantzen, *Becoming Divine*, p. 153.

human and non-human, of culture, race and ethnicity to bring to birth something nurturing and life-giving.

Flourishing and Disability (1): the Problem

The very word-coupling of flourishing and disability may jar the senses. Until recently charity, compassion and the achievement of an appropriate level of care governed the approach to disability of all kinds. Liberation theologians from diverse contexts, even activists for social justice did not put themes of disability and impairment high on their agenda. Nancy Eiesland's book, *The Disabled God* was a rare exception to this.[15] We are surrounded by a society and Church with assumptions of normality that are exclusive – even if at the same time paying lip-service to Liberation Theology that privileges all categories of the poor, vulnerable and discriminated against.[16] It is far simpler for Liberation Theologians – with a few exceptions[17] – to focus solely on economic categories of poverty in the Southern hemisphere and ignore the colonising tendencies and patronising ways that disability/impairment/chronic pain are regarded in this country. That is, until sickness, pain or disability hits us personally – maybe ourselves, a terminal illness, a child's life threatened, a child born with a range of impairments, the early death of a partner, or simply the ongoing day-to-day task of caring for someone twenty-four hours a day. The truth is that most people try to keep these issues at a distance. And I want to explore the personal, social and structural reasons for doing this.

I first look at the personal reality of disability and chronic pain. Born with a disability/impairment, the chances are, unless you are someone like Diane De Vries,[18] who was born without arms or legs and who simply accepted that was her situation in life and rejected prosthetic limbs as artificial, the chances are, that most people spend their lives trying to achieve the nearest proximity to the standards of normality accepted by society. The boundaries to be confronted are presented by the standards of health care in the country, personal finances, cultural attitudes and the level of legislation achieved as to benefits and access.

With the situation of chronic pain, the reality of pain forms a person's total horizon and restricts the contours of her life. Panic sets in with the realisation that this pain is here to stay and to worsen. There can be occasions of waking up, imagining for a few seconds that the pain has gone, before reality sets in – rather, the shock hits the sufferer, that *this is how it will always be*. Barriers are created

---

[15]   Nancy Eiesland, *The Disabled God: Towards a Liberatory Theology of Disability* (Nashville, 1994).

[16]   An earlier, shorter version of this section is included in Grey, 'The Spiritual Journey of Impaired Pilgrims', pp. 6–12.

[17]   For example Timothy J. Gorringe, *The Education of Desire* (London, 2001), pp. 28–52.

[18]   See Eiesland, *The Disabled God*, pp. 33–40.

between chronic pain sufferers and so-called normal people. People with some impairment or chronic illness are frequently regarded simply as objects of pity, needing only our sympathy and tolerance. Wheelchair users tell us so much about this: access is tolerated, even encouraged, but the experience of being talked-down-to, patronised or even ignored, is frequent. And that is to describe only a few situations – the difficulty is that the range of impairments/illness/types of chronic pain is so vast that some may be excluded. It is also important to be clear that it is impairment/disability that is the focus, rather than ageing/dying processes per se that are an integral to the human condition.

Here my focus is on commonalities more than specific differences. This is because when, recently at Sarum College, Salisbury, the 'journey of impaired pilgrims' was embarked upon,[19] what connected the group assembled (who had travelled with their family and carers from far afield), were shared experiences of marginalization by Church and society alike. People had lost jobs, homes, reputation and self-esteem. And the second element shared was the conviction that here was a spirituality that had much to offer faith community and society.

In society in general, the sense of being on the edge, even being hidden away, invisible, of never being able to match the norm, of clashing with the norm, is always present. My own experience when living in Belgium some years ago, was poignant in this regard. When trying to integrate a group of children with elderly women who had become classed as mentally challenged simply by long incarceration in a mental hospital, I discovered a large house isolated in the Flemish countryside around Brussels. I had a strange intuition that something wrong was going on. I knocked at the door and discovered that it was a home run by religious sisters for blind and mentally impaired children. My group's attempts to bring these children into our homes, trying to include them and give them new experiences, failed, because the sisters could only cope with the children if they were passive, and conformed to a routine of early bed and no excitement. But the children themselves adored the experiences we offered them.

Chronic pain sufferers become boring to so-called normal people because illness is regarded as something that we should recover from. Take the antibiotic, swallow the pill and get better quickly is the norm. And please do not bore us with stories of pain. The analogy with dying is strong. When a loved one dies there is sympathy for perhaps a fortnight, and then society expects us to brace up and get on with life and not to talk about the sorrow one is now living with. There is scant recognition of the need to start rebuilding and recreating a whole world in the contexts of pain, bereavement and loss.

---

[19] Tim MacQuiban (ed.), *The Faith Journey of Impaired Pilgrims* (Salisbury, 2006).

Faith Responses

And what happens on the level of faith? On the level of an individual's faith reaction, the response is often, 'O God, why have you done this to me?' (I did exactly this when I found I had cancer some 17 years ago). As if, first of all, that this illness is God-inflicted and must have a purpose or must be a punishment. So many reactions were of the nature, 'What did you do wrong that you got cancer?' The reaction of course begged the question, 'Why *not* me?' – as well as ignoring the socially shared factors of illness, (for example radiation, polluted environment, viruses in the food chain amongst others).Why should I be spared what millions of women experience? So often the faith stories surrounding illness/impairment are of the ilk: 'How I became a better person by living with this illness/ physical/mental challenge'. God sent this to make me holy. It becomes part of the justification of suffering that it is Divinely ordained to teach us to become holy. The 'no pain, no gain' theology is still widespread, as well as the idealising even ideologising, of suffering, endurance, patience and humility. The biblical model of Job comes to mind – or one interpretation of it.

The crux of the matter comes with the way suffering is associated with redemption – both in this world, in terms of healing, and in the next world as 'another jewel in the crown'. Here there is a further level of suffering in the way that, behind attitudes to healing still lurks the sense that in the Bible sin is associated with illness/mental illness. This is still the case even if Jesus rejected the idea in John's Gospel, Chapter 9, in the story of the man born blind. When approached by the Jews, and asked, 'Who has sinned, this man or his parents?' he replied, 'Neither'. Rather, the meaning lay in the way God's goodness might be revealed through him. Yet the idea not only still lurks but is very strong, that God wants healing *from illness/impairment*. And of course this has relevance for natality and flourishing. How can the impaired person flourish if not healed? The paralytic, the blind man, the deaf man, are all examples of Jesus' successful healing ministry. Isaiah's prophecies are all about the blind seeing, the lame walking, water in the desert, all as sign and foretaste – we suppose – of the coming Messianic Kingdom coming. They do not address the situation of not being healed, or of continually living with impairment and pain. So is flourishing language relevant at all?

An even more serious problem for faith is the way disability is used as a metaphor for weak and imperfect faith. It would be apt to call this the 'I'm blind but now I see' syndrome. How often are sermons based on moral blindness? On being deaf to the voice of the Lord? Being deaf, or hard of hearing to the Gospel message? The last thing a person needs to hear when trying to live with a certain impairment or disability is for this to be used as a metaphor for deficient faith! This is paralleled by the situation in the Church of the experience of impaired people always being ministered to, cared for (albeit inadequately) – and seldom enabled to use their own ministerial gifts.

Flourishing and Disability (2): New Approaches

As is the case with many kinds of injustices, responses and actions need to be on many levels.

Human Rights Approaches

Martha Nussbaum is one example of a philosopher challenging traditional concepts of the human person that have acted as obstacles to the full inclusion of people with disabilities to society.[20] Long known for her challenges to the narrow post-enlightenment rationalism, here she challenges the classical social contract theory, and posits the need for:

> a political psychology, a political theory of the good and account of justification.[21]

Put at its simplest, what is being argued for is a richer notion of the social contract theory, together with notions of basic human dignity and respect and the primacy of care. Care for Nussbaum is tackled in terms of the Indian economist Amartya Sen's 'Capability Approach' to which she adds her own arguments. The basic question to ask, she writes, is:

> not, how much money do people with impairments have. But what are they actually able to do and to be? And then ... what are the obstacles in the way of their ability to function up to the appropriate threshold level?[22]

The list of Capabilities has been published in various places.[23] Here what Nussbaum stresses is the primacy of care:

> Good care for dependents, whether children, elderly, ill or disabled focuses on support for capabilities of life, health, and bodily integrity. It also provides support for stimulation for senses, imagination, and thought. It supports emotional attachments and removes overwhelming fear and anxiety ... good care also supports the capacity of the cared-for for practical reason and choice; it encourages affiliations of many other sorts, including social and political affiliations where appropriate.[24]

---

[20]   Martha Nussbaum, *Frontiers of Justice: Disability, Nationality, Species Membership* (Cambridge, Mass. 2006), pp. 96–203.

[21]   Nussbaum, *Frontiers of Justice*, pp. 152–4.

[22]   Nussbaum, *Frontiers of Justice*, p. 168.

[23]   Martha Nussbaum and Jonathan Glovers (eds), *Women, Culture and Development: A Study of Human Capabilities* (New York, 1995); Martha Nussbaum, *Women and Development* (Cambridge, 2000).

[24]   Nussbaum, *Frontiers of Justice*, p. 168.

For the last three decades there has been a considerable movement in the human rights area. There is Disability Discrimination Legislation in many but not all countries. Access to public buildings has greatly improved, facilities for the loop in Church – it is undeniable that there have been great changes. Churches are becoming more sensitised. But access is but one area. The advantage of listening to Nussbaum and Sen's Capability approach is that we move from the area of basic human rights towards something akin to Jantzen's flourishing. Secondly, we can begin to challenge and dismantle underlying structures and norms for human identity.

Challenging Models of Normality

As was hinted already by Nussbaum's querying of the model of the idealising of the 'man of reason', I suggest, first, that the contemporary model of normality is a social construction that currently props up the culture generated by global capitalism, even if the latter is inclined to privilege 'mindless spending', rather than the traditional model of rationality. The prevailing view of 'normality' has not emerged out of the blue but is the product of a long historical process of conquest. There is a link here with European attitudes to conquered peoples, perhaps even a relic of imperialism and colonialism, recalling that colonised peoples used to be classed as degenerates, as sub-human. Sharon Betcher suggests that colonialism created a psychosocial map of 'zones of degeneracy'. The stigma of debility is associated with social spaces like slums.[25] I think of the people rendered disabled by the trafficking in human organs in poor countries.

Secondly, Western capitalism nurtures the vision of the perfect body, kept in shape by constant diet of fashion, workouts, special foods and of course expensive clothes. Whoever does not fit the norm must be marginalized. In the USA 2/3 of people with disability or impairment are unemployed – a staggering figure.

But, thirdly, faith structures play their part in keeping this model in place. I think of the way notions of 'wholeness' govern the healing ministry: all prayers are focused on a restoration of wholeness. Is this not a 'wholeness' based on the ideal perfect body held up as the norm? Disability haunts and prevents the achieving of this norm, which is considered as a human right. It is therefore to be shunned.

Lastly, the prevailing model of Jesus is as healer, miracle-worker, and that of the Spirit is that of rescuing and repairing us from our broken bodies. In other words repudiating the human condition. As Sharon Betcher wrote:

> The metaphor of disablement has been used to establish over against it the physics of spirit as a terrestrially transcendent power.[26]

---

[25]   Sharon Betcher, 'Monstrosities, Miracles and Mission: the Politics of Disablement', in Catherine Keller, Michael Nausner and Myra Rivera (eds), *Postcolonial Theologies: Divinity and Empire* (St Louis, Missouri, 2004), pp. 77–99.

[26]   Sharon Betcher, 'Monstrosities, Miracles and Mission', p. 84.

But, what is the situation of those whom Jesus did and does not heal?

Challenging and Reimaging Models of Healing and Wholeness

First, we need to re-read the Gospel with a different lens: yes, Jesus as healer has been selected by many as the preferred model. The Jewish writer Geza Vermes describes Jesus as the prototype of the Galilean faith-healer.[27] But there is another way to read the Gospels. When reading texts, the senses become eliminated. Words are before us, but in their written form we cannot hear voices, touch or smell people. Jesus heard the cries of people in pain. *It is their pain and their voices that have vanished from the text.* And this would not have been true of the earlier, oral versions. Jesus must have only healed a fraction of the people who came near him. The stories of the pain-filled lives of countless others, people who were not healed, have simply vanished from text and history. A good example of reading Scripture anew with this lens is *This Abled Body*.[28] The writers speak of their amazement at having written out of their consciousness the many references to disability. Here the reader is presented with disabled children engaging in dialogue in reaction to scriptural texts.

I reflect further on the story of the paralytic (Matthew 9.1–8). As a child I could never understand why Jesus seems to reluctant to cure him physically. I always wanted to ignore the interchange about forgiveness of sins and wished Jesus to get on with what – to me, naively, – was really important. Why was the forgiveness of sins more important than the healing? *What could the man have possibly done anyway, in his impaired state?* Now, in a contemporary context of impairment, I would worry how to get a wheelchair near enough to Jesus. There is a mystery here as there is in Jesus' encounter with all sick/people with impairment. He shows compassion. He engages with the situation – but he seems to stress that *being in right relation with God* is the crucial point, more important than physical healing.

Third, and most crucial is the need to incorporate notions of vulnerability and dependency within multiple models of what it means to be human and multiple models of flourishing. All human beings are vulnerable. With pain, disability and impairment this vulnerability is very obvious, glaringly obvious. In the face of that I want to place the biblical truth in a central place, that: 'We are created in the image of God', called, chosen and loved. Whatever bodily shape we are in. What others in their folly may shun and marginalise, God loves.

Finally, disability, impairment makes us dependent. But independence is in any case a myth. 'We all lead interdependent and subsidised lives' wrote Michaela Moser[29] in a work seeking an alternative economy enabling poor women to enjoy

---

[27]   Geza Vermes, *The Changing Faces of Jesus* (London, 2000).

[28]   Hector Avalos, Sarah J. Melcher and Jeremy Schipper (eds) *This Abled Body: Rethinking Disabilities and Biblical Studies* (Atlanta, 2007).

[29]   Micheala Moser, *A Good Life for All! Feminist Ethical Reflections on Women Poverty and the Possibilities of Creating a Change* (Lampeter, 2008), pp. 150–51.

the meaning of flourishing. Money underpins this myth of independence: if people are rich they seem to be able to buy their way to the so-called good life, a life of flourishing. But in the life of connectedness in the web of life, the real truth is that interdependence is the bedrock enabling well-being for all.

Conclusion: A Spirituality of Liberation in the context of Impairment.

First, I return to the creed: a humble, earthly paradise in the *now* was emphasised. Possibilities for joy, beauty, love and celebration are sought by all human beings, whatever their limitations. Impaired people experience limitations in a very severe way and manifest humanity's dependent needs for supportive community in sharp relief.

Secondly, this is a liberation spirituality, so resistance and the struggle for justice and human rights will always be central. But struggle does not have the last word: some of the qualities inherent in such a spirituality have been teased out in the recent thesis of Peter Cole,[30] who emphasises dimensions like 'being stripped' of identity and purpose; of wrestling, waiting and being attentive, of interdependence and of subversive healing. This means searching for healing in the context of brokenness and impairment. Vulnerability also shines out of this spirituality – the vulnerability inherent in humanity and often concealed, but more importantly, the vulnerability of God incarnate in the whole of creation.

But is this 'natality' in Jantzen's sense? A recent study 'Being Ill and Being me',[31] charts the narratives of eight people with multiple sclerosis, using categories of 'self', 'body' and 'time'. What happened when severe deterioration set in was that it was no longer possible to live life under the old terms, as horizons became more restricted. Illusions of ever being well again vanished:

> ... All I wanted to be was *well enough*.[32] *(my italics)*

Another writes of the effects of seeing the world in narrowly bounded spaces:

> ... You experience nature in a different way, not a landscape but a square foot
> of lawn, a titmouse of a wren in the garden are individually received. Pleasure is
> being able to stand up, to move your fingers as you wish, or to read and talk.[33]

---

[30]   Peter Cole, 'The Spirituality of Disability', unpublished MA thesis (Sarum College, 2007).

[31]   Judith Monks and Ronald Frankenberg, 'Being Ill and Being Me: Self, Body and Time in Multiple Sclerosis Narratives', in Benedicte Ingstad and Susan Reynolds Whyte (eds) *Disability and Culture* (Berkeley, 1995), pp. 107–34.

[32]   Monks and Frankenberg, 'Being Ill and Being Me', p. 122.

[33]   Monks and Frankenberg, 'Being Ill and Being Me', p. 123.

This writer admits that living her life in a lower gear still means room for 'seeing much beauty'. Another speaks of 'plenty of life, plenty of hope'. I think what we are being given here is a crucial gift, mindful of the need neither to generalise, nor to romanticise, not to remove authentic voice from anyone. Spiritualities of disability light the way for every human being. We are shown how, in the most extreme experiences of suffering and limitation, we may not be 'saved', or 'healed' in the traditional understanding – that Jantzen wanted to replace. Yet, impaired pilgrims live and grow in whatever way possible. In so doing the wider community – church and society – is given a pedagogy as to how to cope with diminishment, loss of identity and position.

I have a small image of a wild duck given to me by a group of women in the Grail Centre, in The Netherlands. At that point in time all members of the group were recovering from some form of cancer – a period when I was supported also by Grace Jantzen herself. The duck was reminiscent of Ibsen's play, *The Wild Duck.* In the play it is quite a complex symbol and crucial to the plot. But in the context of our reflection, what was important was that the wild duck had been wounded (shot) and driven to the bottom of the lake, but it surfaced and carried on. Or it was dragged up by the dog. For me it is an image of impaired humanity – a glimpse of our shared condition. Even if we sink to the lowest level of our existence; even if we are struggling with the mud and the reeds, if only we can hang onto our determination to keep diving back to the surface and keep living to the fullness of which we are capable, whatever our condition. That is becoming, growing, even flourishing as we reflect God's image. We can look forward to 'all tears being wiped away' in the fullness of time. But even now, as strength and power diminish, we can keep moving towards the light.

Chapter 13

The Postnatural as Anti-Human?
Resurrection, Natality and Creatureliness

Peter Manley Scott

That he not busy being born is busy dying. (Bob Dylan)

Introduction

'Ideological power', writes John B. Thompson,[1] 'is a matter of making a meaning stick'. The two terms – perhaps unfamiliar – in my title are an attempt to unstick a meaning. That is, this essay is concerned to challenge a view of non-human nature as that which we have tried to dominate through the second half of the twentieth century and this nature is now taking its revenge. On this view, whether through climate chaos and pollution, the interruption of hydrological cycles or population growth, nature is returning with a vengeance. And we must find some way – whether by challenging cherished notions of progress[2] or adopting high tech solutions to honour Gaia[3] or developing increasingly sophisticated forms of environmental management[4] – to adapt to the constraints that nature imposes. In what follows, I want to acknowledge ecological distress but also to offer different meanings of nature as a way of moving outside this fearful narrative of the domination of nature/return of nature.

If ideological power makes a meaning stick, from where does this power come? The short answer is: ideology lives out of social contradictions. The social contradiction that I have in mind here is the one identified as the second contradiction of capitalism by US Marxist economist James O'Connor. This second contradiction is to be found between the economic practices of production and the conditions of this production. O'Connor argues that there are three conditions of production in this second contradiction: physical conditions; the working conditions of workers themselves; and general social conditions in which workers

[1]   John B. Thompson, *Studies in the Theory of Ideology* (Cambridge, 1984), p. 132.

[2]   John Gray, *Straw Dogs: Thought on Human and Other Animals* (London, 2002).

[3]   James Lovelock, *The Revenge of Gaia: Why the Earth is Fighting Back – and How We Can Still Save Humanity* (London, 2007).

[4]   Albert Weale, Geoffrey Pridham and Michelle Cini et. al., *Environmental Governance in Europe* (Oxford, 2003).

live. These conditions are broadly ecological: physical conditions refer us to the sustainability of ecosystems; working conditions range widely and focus on the physical and mental well-being of workers; social conditions refer to conditions in and through which labour power is reproduced: housing, education and transport, amongst others.[5]

The meaning of nature that I want to unstick – of the attempted domination of nature and its return – knows little of this second contradiction. It advances by way of an asocial meaning of nature. That is, this dominant meaning of nature is concerned little with how nature is produced through economic, social and cultural processes. If this forgetfulness of the production of nature is the social location of the narrative of the asocial domination of nature/return of nature, a Jantzian question seems pertinent: whose interests does such a narrative serve?

This question first occurred to me as I attended a Bob Dylan concert in Sheffield, England in April 2007. Nearly as remarkable as the concert itself was the age range of the audience, extending to those in their mid 60s and older, mostly men. Doing the maths, I calculated that it was quite possible to have seen Dylan in concert in the UK during his celebrated 1966 'electric' tour, backed by the band that was to become The Band, *and* catch Dylan in Sheffield in 2007 during the Modern Times part of his Never-ending Tour. To be 25 in 1966 would make you only 66 or 67 now. And, aged 25 in 1966, you could also have followed Dylan's pre-1966 acoustic folk/'protest song' period.[6]

Why tell this anecdote about a Dylan concert? For this reason: was not part of the argument of the 60s a struggle over meanings of nature, human and non-human? Consider only that Dylan sang at Martin Luther King's 'I have a dream' rally in Washington (28 August 1963), and some of his songs – 'Blowin' in the wind' (1963), 'The times they are a' changing' (1964), 'Like a rolling stone' (1965) – made a contribution to that struggle over civil rights and wider cultural change. Central to this change were questions about lifestyle and human sexuality. Here, of course, different meanings of nature are clearly evident and in contest: for human sexuality is where human nature opens out onto nature more broadly, as natural law theory has always known. Or, as human geographer Noel Castree puts this matter,[7] 'nature' has companion or 'collateral' concepts, including 'race' and 'sex'. To discuss human sexuality is to raise the matter of nature: what is constitutive of the human, what is 'natural' to the human, and whether what is natural to the human has wider resonances in the realm of non-human animals. What is being struggled over here – at least in part – is meanings of nature.[8]

---

[5]   James O'Connor, *Natural Causes* (New York: 1988), pp. 160–61.

[6]   For an interesting account by a theologian of how Dylan's status has been persistently misunderstood by 'progressives', see Stephen H. Webb, *Dylan Redeemed: From Highway 61 to Saved* (London, 2006).

[7]   Noel Castree, *Nature* (London and New York, 2005).

[8]   'Old lady judges watch people in pairs/limited in sex they dare/to push fake morals, insult and stare/while money doesn't talk, it swears/obscenity, who really cares?/propaganda,

That we have been arguing over meanings of nature through the last 40 years seems to be confirmed if we also note that the 60s cry for freedom, for emancipation from oppressive constructions of the natural, was already accompanied by environmental laments: Rachel Carson's *Silent Spring* was published in 1962; Joseph Sittler, that great US Lutheran theologian, was giving public lectures on the cosmic Christ amidst environmental stresses in the early 60s.[9] It is not that we have oppressed nature, and now nature breaks out once more to take its revenge; that the recent Western or North Atlantic effort to be free has crashed into the necessities of nature. It is rather that different concepts and meanings of nature are always accompanying us. We are still in the middle of an argument over the meanings of nature and we ought to be alert to efforts to make a meaning stick.

To advance my critique, I begin with a discussion of the postnatural before proceeding to consider the concept of the anti-human. Thereafter, I explore the notion of natality as a link between the postnatural and the anti-human. And, finally, I return to the matter of the organisation and disorganisation of creatureliness. The terms of my title may therefore be understood as an attempt to unstick a meaning by means of theological critique and to offer different meanings of nature through the development of an anti-human theological anthropology.

The Postnatural and the Human

To begin, I note, with Grace Jantzen, the current imperative for ecological thinking: that is, an important theme for religious engagement is the matter of human – non-human interdependence. Indeed, engagement and interdependence are related: as Jantzen[10] puts it, '[T]he mind-body dualism and the male-female dualism generate an ecological crisis of technological proportion as the technological dominance of nature proceeds; and in the background is the theological rationalization of a cosmic dualism between a God of ultimate value and a material universe of no intrinsic worth'. In other words, religious engagement is frustrated by this background belief that downplays the interdependencies of creatureliness. Or, in H. Paul Santmire's formulation,[11] this is the spiritual and anti-ecological metaphor of ascent in Christianity. Having said that, I doubt that the matter is one of a 'cosmic dualism' as that would require the view that God is an agent of the cosmos which Christianity, in its major traditions, denies. In turn, I see no need

---

all is phoney', Bob Dylan, 'It's all right, Ma (I'm only bleeding)' (1967).

[9]   See Joseph Sittler, *Evocations of Grace: Writings on Ecology, Theology and Ethics* (Grand Rapids, 2000).

[10]   Grace Jantzen, 'Healing our Brokenness: The Spirit and Creation', in Mary Heather MacKinnon and Moni McIntyre (eds) *Readings in Ecology and Feminist Theology* (Kansas City, 1995), pp. 284–98.

[11]   Paul H. Santmire, *The Travail of Nature: The Ambiguous Ecological Promise of Christianity* (Philadelphia, 1985), pp. 16–29.

to abandon theism for pantheism as, arguably, Grace Jantzen does.[12] Such a move
– an ideological reflex – merely mimics the claim that the story from the Fordist
period to our present situation at the beginning of the twenty-first century is one of
the attempted mastery of nature, and its return. What is required is a rather different
concept of nature, and my purpose in this chapter is to explore this by reference to
the anti-human. Indeed, it may be the case not that pantheism needs to be preferred
to theism but rather that theism needs rescuing from distortions of itself.

I note with her, second, that Christianity has been conceptually under-resourced
– in her view, fatally so? – And I try to repair this weakness by reference to her
development of the notion of natality, theologically interpreted. In other words, I
consider whether the construal of humanity in Christianity might be understood
in less hierarchical and gendered ways than heretofore for, as she notes, this
hierarchical and oppressively gendered anthropology may not be the 'only possible
Christian understanding of personhood ....'[13]

Is it then possible to identify the human in a different way? Throughout this
essay, I shall be using the phrase, 'postnatural humanity'. This phrase identifies
a default position that I shall be arguing for: of humanity in nature and nature in
humanity. In my view, the doctrine of creation points to this default position. In
this way, I seek to differentiate my position from 'natural humanity' and 'unnatural
humanity'.[14] What do I mean by this? There is a tendency in ecological discourses to
interpret ourselves in opposition to nature (unnatural) or in relation to the non-human
(natural). Elsewhere I have dubbed these approaches personalism and naturalism.
I define personalism as the attempt to understand 'humanity as other than nature';
and naturalism as stressing 'the place of humanity in nature'.[15] Postnatural humanity
– my preferred term – is an attempt to free anthropology from these strategies of
personalism and naturalism and argue that humanity is in nature and that nature is
both for and exceeds humanity. Humanity is always post*natural*: following after
non-human nature; and *post*natural: transcending non-human nature.[16]

---

[12]   In 'Feminism and Pantheism', *The Monist*, vol. 80 No. 2, 1997: Jantzen argues in
favour of pantheism on philosophically pragmatic grounds: that such an affirmation calls
into question the West's dominant religious imaginary based on 'dualism'. However, by
her own report, she struggles to indicate why her anti-dualist position should be called
pantheism. Nonetheless, and importantly for my argument, she affirms if 'that which is
divine precisely *is* the world and its ceaselessly shifting bodies and signifiers, then it is
this that must be celebrated as of ultimate value' (282), and calls this position pantheist.
Whether this is an adequate account of pantheism is, in my judgement, open to question.
Interestingly, she is emphatic in her refusal of pan*en*theism (see n. 28).

[13]   Jantzen, 'Healing our Brokenness', p. 286.

[14]   In Scott, *A Political Theology of Nature* (Cambridge, 2003), I offered 'un/natural
humanity' as my preferred term. I am now revising this terminology, offering 'postnatural'
in place of 'un/natural', and understanding 'unnatural' as part of the personalist position.

[15]   Scott, *A Political Theology of Nature* (Cambridge, 2003), pp. 32–8.

[16]   This paragraph from Scott, 2007: 112.

Stressing the 'post' in '*post*natural' indicates that the human is mixed up with nature; the separation of humanity and nature cannot be maintained. Emphasising the 'natural' in post*natural* indicates that nature has not disappeared; nature still exceeds and encompasses the human. I go further: theologically, we must speak of the haveability of nature yet not in ways that separate the human from nature nor in ways that suggest that the human can 'master' the non-human. Nature is haveable and yet elusive. Although there is no pure nature for us to have – nature is always a constituted nature – yet nature cannot be contained and 'mastered' by us. This nature is haveable yet beyond our control.[17]

The postnatural is a critical term: it seeks to indicate the limits of our knowledge and action. By it I join with Louis Dupré in his historical interpretation that nature is a pre-modern and modern – indeed, anti-theological – invention; nature emerges in modernity as graceless, as somehow disassociated from the purposes of God.[18] And I join Bruno Latour in his affirmation of amodernity. For Latour, modernity separates nature and society, and seeks to maintain the boundary between them in a work of ontological policing. The effort is remarkable yet unpersuasive, for we have always been hybrid beings.[19]

Thus we are postnatural: that is to say, we may neither escape from nature nor are we obliged to conform to it. We are mixed entities, participating in a wider environment of attachments (including non-human animals) by way of our machines. This postnatural order is neither given nor can it be overcome.[20]

All very well, you may say, but does not Christianity privilege the human? Have not the creation narratives in the three opening chapters of Genesis been read in such fashion? After all, is it not the human only who bears the image of God? And is not Isaiah Berlin[21] correct in his depiction of the basic images of biblical Judaism?

> Let us look at another example – a parallel culture, that of the Bible, that of the Jews at a comparable period. You will find a totally different model dominating, a totally different set of ideas, which would have been unintelligible to the Greeks. The notion from which both Judaism and Christianity to a large degree sprang is the notion of family life, the relations of father and son, perhaps the relations of members of a tribe to one another. Such fundamental relationships – in terms of which nature and life are to be explained – as the love of children for their father, the brotherhood of man, forgiveness, commands issued by a superior to an inferior, the sense of duty, transgression, sin and therefore the

---

[17] This paragraph, and the next two, from Peter Scott, 'The End of Nature and the Last Human? Thinking Theologically about Nature in a Posthuman Condition', in David Albertson and Cabell King (eds) *Without Nature* (Fordham, 2009).

[18] See Scott, *A Political Theology of Nature*, p. 11.

[19] Peter Scott, 'We have never been gods: transcendence, contingence and the affirmation of hybridity', *Ecotheology*, 9/2 (2004): p. 200.

[20] Scott, 'We have never been gods', pp. 213–16

[21] Isaiah Berlin, *The Roots of Romanticism* (London, 2000), p. 3.

need to atone for it – this whole complex of qualities, in terms of which the whole of the universe is to be explained by those who created the Bible, and by those who were to a large extent influenced by it, would have been totally unintelligible to the Greeks.

Is not Berlin's presentation of the commitments of the biblical 'world view' the conclusive rebuttal to those who claim that Christianity might be anti-human?

The Anti-Human – What is That?

To try to answer this question, I want to explore the relation between natality and the anti-human. I am arguing for the view that postnatural humanity is anti-human humanity. And natality is my bridge between the postnatural and the anti-human.

On natality, Jantzen[22] writes: 'Birth is the basis of every person's existence, which by that very fact is always already material, embodied, gendered, and connected with other human beings and connected with other human beings and with human history'. And, later: 'Natality is a fundamental human condition'.[23] An obvious and welcome implication here is that through being born we are connected with others and with the wider environment into which we are born. 'An imaginary of natality … therefore recognizes our rootedness in the physical and material.'[24] And Jantzen now draws the compelling implication: 'Another result of focusing on natality rather than death is the recognition that our interconnection in the web of life includes not only other people but also animals and ultimately the whole physical world'.[25] In affirming this conclusion, I want to ask: what is the content of this recognition?

In other words, if we participate in this web of life, conditioned by natality, how is the recognition of this wider interconnection to be understood? Here it is useful to note that there is a restriction to the concept of natality: to those who are born. Plainly, this works well for human selves – and for animals, if somewhat differently. However, the 'physical world' is not born in any obvious sense, and many entities in that world are not born either. In other words, there are phenomena, both organic and inorganic, that it is not easy to understand what their being born means. In what sense is a forest or a lake born, or a mountain? Put differently, reference to natality needs to be augmented as the matter of being born does not identify all life, inorganic as well as organic.

---

[22]   Grace Jantzen, *Becoming Divine: Towards a Feminist Philosophy of Religion* (Manchester, 1988), p. 141.

[23]   Jantzen, *Becoming Divine*, p. 145.

[24]   Jantzen, *Becoming Divine*, p. 145.

[25]   Jantzen, *Becoming Divine*, p. 151.

Hannah Arendt, from whose work this theme of natality comes, proposes another condition to assist here. That condition is 'the earth'.[26] The question at this point is: what is the relation between the conditioning that is natality with the conditioning that is the earth? What is the relationship between being born and being naturally or ecologically situated? It is here that the notion of the anti-human is important.

So what do I mean by the anti-human? By the anti-human, I mean roughly this: as a theological concept, the anti-human is a contribution to re-thinking the situation and status of the human: that theology is not quite as humanocentric as might at first be thought. Indeed, the notion of natality is helpful in elaborating this notion of the anti-human, which requires the human to understand itself as a co-participant with the non-human and as the representative of the non-human.

Elaborating a little, I propose that the anti-human has three theological meanings. First, it honours the stress on a 'web of life' and the interconnections between things. 'Web' is not my favourite way of understanding this; I prefer more social metaphors. For present purposes, however, what is important is that some account is given of human – non-human relations and interactions. This is the sense of the postnatural as the nature that cannot be escaped, so to speak, of nature as that which embraces the human.

Such an affirmation of the anti-human connects directly and explicitly with Jantzen's criticism of anthropocentrism, including its gendered aspects. A type of de-centring takes place here in which the assumed superiority of the human over the animals and the assumed superiority of the male over the female is called into question. The anti-human undercuts *that* account of the human. In such an undercutting, the striving for freedom by the human takes place with attachments: the attachments of animals and machines. In other words, the struggle for human emancipation does not mean striving to free the human from animals and machines.

The anti-human also incorporates a stress on social structures and processes in the production of nature and the production of nature's meanings. It thereby continues the stress on the de-centering of the human and, moreover, builds upon the earlier discussion of the source of ideological power in the second contradiction of capitalism. That is, the anti-human relocates the human in the institutional and social processes of the production of nature. This, then, is the affirmation of the mass, the collective and the personal and its location in production processes. Further, the anti-human questions the impersonality of the individual: if the individual is constructed as consumer and so becomes through a likeness with all other consumers, identical and so interchangeable,[27] the anti-human stresses the collective, the attachments of machines and animals and the recovery of the truly personal and the properly individual. To sloganize: without the anti-human, no individuality!

Second, it remains the case that, as Jantzen points out, human beings are political agents acting in the plurality of political action. Through such political

---

[26]   See Hannah Arendt, *The Human Condition* (Chicago and London, 1958/1998), p. 11.

[27]   Alain Badiou, *Metapolitics* (London, 2006), p. xxviii.

action, this sense of the embrace of nature cannot be forgotten. The question is: how should this embrace and situatedness be understood politically? Here, I have recourse to the language of representation: that the human must, as part of its anti-humanness, represent the non-human. This is an anti-human stance in that the human is here charged with the difficult task of exploring the agencies and interests of the non-human and giving these some sort of voice, even on occasion to the detriment of the human interest, narrowly interpreted. We might call this an anti-human assembly.

Bruno Latour[28] (1993) discusses some of this in his recommendation of a 'Parliament of Things'. For Latour, modern politics is riven by two anxieties. The first is whether the claim of scientists to speak of nature is convincing or whether scientists deceive themselves in this and thereby deceive the rest of us as well. The second anxiety is whether the Hobbesian ruler speaks on behalf of all citizens entering into the social contract or whether this sovereign may be pursuing their own interest. For modern politics to work, Latour argues, we must have confidence in both translations. If the first fails, nature is lost; if the second fails, we are returned to the pre-contractual warfare of the 'state of nature'. Modern politics constructed in this fashion should be abandoned, Latour argues, in favour of a more hybrid model in which humans play the role of mediators. There are many natures and many mediators; and the sovereign may have its own mediators also who must also represent a society that comprises machines and other objects as well as humans. In summary: 'Natures are present, but with their representatives, scientists who speak in their name. Societies are present, but with the objects that have been serving as their ballast from time immemorial'.[29]

We might say that the practice of a fuller democracy is required: an anti-human assembly. It will be a democracy, we should add, in which the public sphere will be constituted by arguments over hybrid networks and not simply by the integrity of formal processes of negotiation between elected representatives. At this point, I see no reason why the representation of natures should be restricted to scientists. In the context of some ecological concerns – anthropogenic climate change, genetically modified crops – it is not clear to me that the representation of natures should only be performed by scientists. Do not island dwellers and organic farmers have interests in, and therefore may be representatives of, a relevant nature? Furthermore, some understanding will have to be arrived at concerning how it is that the human represents the non-human in a way that insists that the obligation to speak for natures cannot be rescinded just at the point when short-term human interests clash with the interests of nature(s). Moreover, the practice of a fuller democracy may have to proceed more slowly than democratic deliberation does at present if the full measure of the consequences of a decision is to be taken. These commitments enjoy a basis in divine action, as I have tried to argue elsewhere.[30]

---

[28] Bruno Latour, *We Have Never Been Modern* (New York, 1993), pp. 142–5.

[29] Latour, *We Have Never Been Modern*, p. 144.

[30] See Peter Scott, 'The End of Nature and the Last Human?'

Third, the human bears witness, in some prophetic mode, to a different understanding of the relations between the human and the non-human predicated upon neither the separation of the human from its attachments nor immersion by the human in some nature. Instead, as has already been intimated through the discussion of Latour, I am aiming for an understanding that is more dynamic, interactive, and peaceable. Elsewhere, I have written of such anti-human praxis as a form of rioting action.[31] Such an affirmation of the riot is founded upon the emphasis on the human as mass, as collective and develops the emphasis that I share with Latour on hybrid, mediating action.

Furthermore, I identified this rioting action as resourced by the actions of the Spirit.[32] I reprise this position here. As resourced by the actions of the Spirit such action is political *and* ecological. That is, the life of God is always consistent. The Spirit thereby consistently 'extends' and renders concrete the incarnate Word. The resurrection of the incarnate Word indicates that natural relations are included in this resurrection in that the resurrection of Christ's body includes the natural contingencies (birth, genetic inheritance, growth, maturation, unconscious) of this body. The Spirit works in and through these natural contingencies. Yet the Spirit is not constrained by these contingencies as if the eschatological agency of the Spirit must conform to the world. Such conformity must be refused. Instead, the insurgency of the Spirit is directed towards the reconstruction of livelihoods, understood comprehensively, and works through natural and human freedoms.

This, then, is the theological anti-human: a de-centering of the human, to be sure, but also a political charge laid upon the human, as a natal, to be a representative for natals with less power and for those natural entities that are not natals. And, finally, actively to bear witness to an eschaton of the creature. This seemingly paradoxical convergence of the anti-human on human responsibility is hardly novel: as Tony Davies[33] points out, 'antihumanisms … generally serve openly humanist ends of intellectual clarity and emancipation, articulated around a recognisable ethic of human capacity and need'. Nor will it have escaped notice that this account of the anti-human is three-fold. Indeed, I should confess at this point that this threefold anthropology corresponds to God's action in creating a world, to God's action in atoning or liberating work that re-constitutes this world, and to God's action in eschatological transformation of this world. This threefold anthropology is a trinitarian anthropology.

A moment ago, I mentioned de-centering. By that I meant that the anti-human invites us to see humanity as the summary of creation but not as its pinnacle. The human is always ecologically placed or situated: neither at the centre nor at the boundary but partially constituted by, and always supported by, broader natural dynamics towards life. As Latour puts this matter, 'Reveal [the human's] work of

---

[31]   Peter Scott, 'Anarchy in the UK? Political authority and the rioting of God', *Ecotheology*, 11/1 (2006): pp. 32–56.

[32]   See Scott, 'Anarchy in the UK?' pp. 48–50.

[33]   Tony Davies, *Humanism* (London and New York, 1997), p. 35.

mediation, and it will take on human form. Conceal it again, and we shall have to talk about inhumanity, even if it is draping itself in the Bill of Rights'.[34] This is not rendering the human as animal or mechanism nor the rendering of the animal or mechanism as human. However, it is the effort to see the human as suspended in, distributed through, and transcending such animal-human-mechanical networks or patterns of agency. It is not to assimilate the human to the animal or to the machine. Rather, it is the effort to re-identify the human in and through its networks – just as God is re-identified through God's incarnation in Jesus of Nazareth. Loss/ rediscovery are here contrasted with death/end. The loss of the human is here the rediscovery of the human. This is not the same as the death of the human; the death of the human is simply the end of the human. From the perspective of the anti-human, the distribution of the human among objects in networks is the recovery of the collective and truly individual human.

Obviously, this requires an interpretation of incarnation. As Jantzen rightly notes: 'Yet all this emphasis on mortality and mortification obviously sat rather uneasily with other Christian doctrines like those of incarnation and resurrection'.[35] Incarnation and resurrection are better understood in relation to natality and flourishing. At this point, I want to affirm that the incarnation is anti-human for the sake of humanity. In other words, the incarnation assumes and organises more than the human. That is, 'more than the human' describes, first, the participatory placedness of the human in the agencies of the non-human; second, the attempt by the human to represent such agencies; and, third, the rioting praxis of renewing such participation. In the next section, I explore a concept of resurrection that supports my reading of incarnation.

The Reconditioning of Natality: the Unconditioned and the Conditioned

What interpretation of incarnation is being proposed here? Just as the occlusion of the human by its attachments reveals its humanness, so God's immersion in the incarnate Jesus reveals the Godness of God (as Creator and Spirit). The incarnate God is God incognito or demobbed yet God remains Lord.

In my view, such an account of incarnation is resourced out of the transcendence of the resurrection, which is the renewal of human, social action (and so the continuation of natality). For the transcendence of resurrection supports new or fresh action, and as such relates such new action most fully to the condition of natality. Thus natality conditions sociality, and the resurrection renews sociality and thereby affirms natality. The renewal of sociality in the resurrection pluralizes action, and thereby refers to the condition of such plural action in natality.[36] Yet this action of plurality is not to be identified as a narrow human action, but as

---

[34]   Latour, *We Have Never Been Modern*, p. 137.

[35]   Jantzen, *Becoming Divine*, p. 138.

[36]   I think that Arendt, *The Human Condition*, p. 9, is making this argument.

the plurality of action of natural as well as social agencies. Thus the resurrection invokes natality and the earth. This resurrection is the affirmation of natality. If there has been too much reference in theology to crucifixion and mortality, as Jantzen implicitly argues, then attention to resurrection, privileges natality instead.

However, at this point we encounter a difficulty. Arendt writes of natality as a condition of the human.[37] Yet the transcendence of resurrection does not recommend the view that resurrection is itself a condition. I prefer to say that resurrection, as a divine act, is unconditioned, and therefore is best understood by reference to the *creatio ex nihilo* tradition of theological thinking on creation's relation to the Creator. The claim that resurrection is unconditioned serves as the basis of the claim that resurrection is the re-establishment of the condition of natality. For one condition cannot re-establish another. One condition may condition another – and frequently does, we may accept. For example, the condition of the earth, to borrow Arendt's term once more, may condition the condition of natality. But the earth cannot re-establish natality or function as its true basis. The conditions of human living affect one another but do not re-constitute each other. The resurrection cannot therefore be a condition in this sense. For a condition to be re-established, we need that which is not a condition. Precisely this is what is provided by the attested resurrection of Jesus Christ.

If it is not a condition, what then is the resurrection? What is important to note here is that the resurrection, as an eschatological event, is not otherworldly, in the pejorative sense. It is the renewal of sociality and the re-conditioning of natality. As such, it enjoys the same quality as *creatio ex nihilo*, and must therefore be understood as divinely transcendent. In a beautiful sentence, Jantzen[38] writes: 'The divine, then, will not be a "God out there", beyond the realm of human love and action, but rather the divine as the horizon and constitution of our selves and our world, within and between "natals"'. Likewise, the transcendence of the resurrection and the reconditioning of natality that I am recommending do not propose a 'god out there'. On this view, the account of divine transcendence traditionally maintained in Christian theology is the affirmation of creatureliness, and the basis of creaturely renewal.

The concept of the incarnation being proposed here thereby identifies a dynamic of divine action in which loss leads to recovery and in which 'more than the human' is assumed. The incarnation is neither the affirmation of materiality *simpliciter* nor the identification of a stripped-down human as the bearer of *imago dei*. The incarnation does not provide us with an image that assumes matter in the abstract nor does it propose the human form alone as theomorphic. Instead, incarnation identifies the divine action in which the freedom of God is disclosed by way of natural contingencies and the comprehensive character of creatureliness – its ecological situatedness – is disclosed *post mortem Christi*. Analogously, the human is disclosed in and through its attachments, and human emancipations

---

[37]   Arendt, *The Human Condition*, pp. 8–11.
[38]   Jantzen, *Becoming Divine*, p. 153.

require specific entanglements with objects rather than freedom from them. We are, I think, close to the position that maintains that 'a human person, in respect of his or her humanity, just *is* the node of a set of relations, a location in a community',[39] yet the 'community' I am presenting is peopled by 'more than the human'. In my bolder argument, all collectives find their image in the incarnate Son who assumes 'more than the human' in a redistribution of divine and natural-human agencies. In redistributive loss is the recovery of collective.

Epilogue

So far I have argued that the sort of creatureliness that we are presented with is a sort of anti-human organisation. I have sought to show how a notion of the anti-human dwells in the notion of the postnatural. This notion of the anti-human is founded in the continuation of sociality that is the resurrection of Jesus Christ. In my view, such an account of the anti-human is available in the theological trinitarianism that I am proposing.

A theological temptation at this point is to construe this too conservatively, to propose too orderly an organisation of creatureliness. Back in 1980, I well recall leading groups of tourists to a Greek Orthodox Church at Dafni, outside Athens. On its vaulted ceiling, it has the most wonderful depiction of *Christos Pantacrator* dating from AD1090–1100: an order that functions as a sort of non-dynamic cosmic sheltering sky under which action and responsibility are not central.

An image with greater theological integrity would be one that stretches the human across its attachments. By stretching, I mean an extension of our moral sympathies to re-examine the moral considerability of the non-human and to temper the human struggle for recognition by opposition to the non-human. And it would need to be an image located in a social contradiction that resists appeals to natural order and proposes the redistribution of agency through multiple collectives. It is not enough to proceed from *amor mundi* to *imago mundi*. While it is true that our loving informs our vocation as imaging the world/earth, yet the earth is too general an image. Not least, we are also in the image of animals and machines. We are *imago bestiae et ferae*[40] and *imago artis* as well as *imago mundi* and *imago dei*.

Although I do not have an image to offer, it is the argument of this essay that the postnatural human – a trinitarian anthropology – might make a contribution to this search for an image that is not orderly, that proposes the unruly organisation of postnatural creatureliness. If it is true that this anti-human anthropology might

---

[39]   Robert Jenson, 'Anima Ecclesiastica', in R. Kendell Soulen and Linda Woodhead (eds), *God and Human Dignity*, (Grand Rapids, 2006), pp. 59–71, p. 59.

[40]   Interestingly, in that it would refer to being in the image of living beings, *imago animalis* would not be an appropriate term here. That 'animal' has come to be associated with the non-human is an interesting development. I thank Alison Sharrock for this point and her suggestions regarding Latin terms.

be a reliable guide at this point, perhaps we might conclude – despite today's changeable weather patterns attributed to climate chaos – that the 1967 Dylan was right after all: 'You don't need a weatherman to tell which way the wind blows'.

Chapter 14

The Implications of a Politics of Natality for Transnational Feminist Advocacy: Transforming the Human Rights Moral Imaginary

Nanci Hogan

Grace's intellectual influence on my thinking has been profound. In her I found an intellectual mentor par excellence and it is no exaggeration for me to say that her work has not only influenced, but has shaped, and will continue to shape the rest of my life's work both as an academic and as a political activist. Although I had studied for three years under Grace's tutelage as a part-time M.A. student in the Centre for Religion, Gender and Culture in the Religions and Theology Department of the University of Manchester, I was only one year into my PhD course under her supervision when she died. Her death was a profound personal loss for me and it is my hope that my ongoing development of implications of her work for feminist ethics and for international politics will serve as a fitting tribute to the intellectual legacy she has bequeathed me.

Grace knew that her work had implications for political philosophy and she encouraged me to develop her work further from my own educational background and hands-on experience in international politics. Although I did not discover it until after her death, she was an activist in her own right and had served as a Commissioner for the Royal Canadian Commission on New Reproductive Technologies from 1992–1993 and was herself active in campaigns around reproductive rights.[1] The Commission was tasked with exploring the ethical implications of the new reproductive technologies that were becoming available and with making recommendations as to what policies and safeguards should be applied to these technologies.[2] One of Grace's primary roles on this Commission was to serve as an ethicist.

---

[1]   Royal Canadian Commission on New Reproductive Technologies (RCCONRT), *Proceed with Care: The New Reproductive Technologies and the Ethic of Care* with Patricia Baird, chair of the Commission, and three other commissioners. Two volumes, with fifteen volumes of attached research (Government of Canada, Ottawa, 1993).

[2]   RCCONRT, *Proceed with Care*.

While I was working on my M.A. dissertation under her supervision on the implications of a praxis of a politics of natality for the eradication of female genital mutilation (FGM) as a practice harmful to women, she mentioned to me that it was the challenges posed by the religious and cultural context for this practice to a universal human rights approach that inspired some of her thinking in *Becoming Divine*. She was keenly interested in my development of this work and prior to her death we had discussed co-publishing a book on this topic.

Grace's work has inspired me to first to develop the contours of a politics of natality and then to begin exploring what the implications this politics would for resolving the social justice issues, particularly those involving gender-specific issues that concern transnational feminist activists. What interests me most about Grace's work is the potential that it has for not only diagnosing and providing imaginative and creative suggestions for transforming the western moral imaginary, but also for diagnosing and transforming moral imaginaries across religions and cultures in ways that are more characteristic of a politics of natality grounded in an ethic of flourishing. I am convinced that Grace's work creates much needed space in political discourses and action in transnational feminist activist networks (TNAs) that would better allow for the flourishing of all human beings regardless of ethnicity, race, class, religion or gender.

Grace's work diagnosed some of the flaws in the Western moral imaginary. In this essay I will briefly explore specifically how the narratives informing transnational feminist activist projects reflect some of these weaknesses in Grace has uncovered in one particular form of Western liberal thinking, the human rights discourse. I will also investigate how this discourse shuts down any exploration of difference which, if examined, might yield transformative insights that are characteristic of natality and flourishing as Grace defines them. Then, I will use the rest of this essay to further develop a research methodology that builds on Grace's feminist epistemological approach in *Becoming Divine*. I believe that the theoretical lens afforded by a politics of natality will yield fruitful insights across many cultures and religions that might help transform the human rights discourse into one that is more characteristic of natality and flourishing.

Definitions: the Moral Imaginary and Natality

Before I continue, it is necessary to provide a few definitions. First of all it is important to define how Grace defines the terms 'habitus' and 'moral imaginary' in her work. The moral imaginary, a term first developed and used by Pierre Bordieu is 'the space – literal and figurative – from which moral thinking is done', and which 'frames what we can think in relation to moral attitudes and behaviour'.[3] It includes the norms, assumptions and prejudices, and prejudgements which give

---

[3]   Grace Jantzen, 'Flourishing: Towards an Ethics of Natality', *Feminist Theory*, 2 (2001): pp. 219–32.

content to our dispositions to act and think and 'determine what is actually morally thinkable'.[4] Grace equates the imaginary with Bordieu's notion of the 'cultural unconsciousness' which she defines as 'those images, symbols, metaphors, and representations which help construct various forms of subjectivity, and which we employ in all our thinking usually without being conscious of doing so'.[5] This moral imaginary forms one aspect of the *habitus*, 'the common sense world', or 'the disposition' from and by which choices are made, 'a spontaneity without consciousness or will' which generates 'reasonable' or 'common sense behaviour that is neither mechanical nor unpredictable'.[6] In the moral imaginary that forms the habitus, certain subjects are given epistemological and ontological privilege over others as being the ones who count as subjects and as the ones who determine what constitutes all forms of knowledge including what is considered to be moral and ethical.[7]

In what follows, I do not mean to conflate the Western moral imaginary with human rights discourse. Rather, the human rights discourse is one of many possible expressions of the Western moral imaginary. However, it is a powerful one and one that is used to justify and mobilize transnational advocacy and development projects in order to address injustices, oppressions, and inequalities.

One of the unique contributions of Grace's work is her insistence on taking Hannah Arendt's position that birth, not life, should be the central category of political and philosophical thought seriously.[8] By this she does not mean essentializing the attributes of motherhood or a woman's point of view as being more facilitative of peace. Nor does she intend to privilege it as being superior to a man's point of view, construed by some as being more warlike and violent. Rather, all people are born and they are born of mothers. According to Grace, valuing birth meant valuing women, nature, the maternal, embodiedness, not just valuing thought and reason.

As Grace developed the concept from the work of Hannah Arendt, therefore, natality provides the basis for a feminist critique of the moral imaginary because she observed that birth, a uniquely female capacity, is suppressed in Western philosophical thinking on two levels. First she argued that Western philosophers make death, not birth, the measure of the authenticity of human being and the central category of Western philosophy. She based these insights on the post-structural feminist thought of Luce Irigaray and Julia Kristeva, who insisted that both subjectivity and society are each built on the unacknowledged foundation of

---

    [4]   Jantzen, 'Flourishing: Towards an Ethic of Natality', pp. 222–3.

    [5]   Grace Jantzen, 'Necrophilia and Natality: What Does it Mean to be Religious?' *Scottish Journal of Religious Studies*, 80 (1997): pp. 101–21.

    [6]   Jantzen, 'Flourishing: Towards an Ethic of Natality', p. 223.

    [7]   Jantzen, 'Flourishing: Towards an Ethic of Natality', pp. 222–3.

    [8]   Grace Jantzen, *Becoming Divine: Towards a Feminist Philosophy of Religion* (Manchester, 1998), p. 144.

women's bodies.[9] Secondly, she made the case that men have appropriated birth as their own as a birth into singular, autonomous, disembodied thought, reason, and a life of the mind rather than a life of material, embodied, human beings born into a web of relationships.

From this she also develops aspects of a human anthropology of natality which is markedly different from a human anthropology grounded in a preoccupation with death. I will explore this later. For now though, I will examine how the current human rights discourse mobilized by transnational feminist activists is characteristic of this western moral imaginary of death. Although well-meaning, this narrative is one of sameness that perpetuates further ethical violence on those it is meant to 'rescue.'

Transnational Feminist Activism and the Western Moral Imaginary

Transnational feminist advocates are individuals that are brought together by a central core of principled ideals. They share a common discourse; they believe that individuals can make a difference, and they use information in order to employ sophisticated political strategies for social justice as they define it which heavily relies on the use of symbolism to advance their political causes. They deal with ideas and values and there is a sense of moral right and wrong and they consciously use moral leverage to achieve their goals.[10] According to research, the most successful TNAs are those who address those issues that are labelled as being 'transcendent', such as either those involving bodily harm or those involving legal equality of opportunity.[11] By transcendent is meant those issues that can be addressed universally irrespective of religious, gender, cultural or national boundaries. Campaigns work within a specific human rights framework and do not challenge the metaphysical assumptions that underpin this framework.

'Women's rights as human rights', specifically in the case of feminist activism as a universal moral discourse transcending cultural, national and religious borders, was first made possible by the formulation and the adoption of the UN Declaration for Human Rights (1948). Subsequent UN conferences and UN-sponsored events including the UN Decade for Women from 1975–1985, the subsequent four world conferences on women culminating in 1995 with the Beijing Women's Conference, and various other UN conferences in the 1990s ranging from Rio to the Vienna Conference on Human Rights, has contributed to the development of women's human rights as human rights as the moral or normative framework for transnational

---

[9]   Jantzen, *Becoming Divine*.

[10]   M. Sikkink, *Activists Beyond Borders: Advocacy Networks in International Politics* (New York: Ithaca, 1998), p. 19.

[11]   L. Chappell, 'Contesting Women's Rights: The Influence of Religious forces at the United Nations', *Australian Political Studies Association Conference* (Adelaide, 2004), p. 8.

feminist activists and TNAs.[12] New women's human rights instruments, like the Convention on the Elimination of all Forms of Discrimination Against Women (CEDAW) were signed and ratified by most member UN states. Women's rights as human rights have come to form the ethical basis for transnational feminist advocacy on behalf of women oppressed around the world irrespective of their nationality, race, location, class or religion on a range of issues including issues involving violence against women, the environment and development.

It has been my own experience, however, that most transnational feminist activists tend to be wary of religion. This is born out in the literature as well, where religion is dismissed as 'irrational' or as irredeemably patriarchal. Louise Chappell documents how religious discourse is played out practically in transnational women's advocacy around the issue of women's reproductive health rights. She documents how conservative religious forces, including the Holy See, right-wing American evangelicals and delegates representing conservative Muslim states, who form a conservative counter transnational advocacy network and movement, mobilize certain religious doctrines and notions of female subjectivity to support their stance on women's sexual and reproductive health.[13] They use religious arguments to deprive women's own rights over their own bodies and their own sexual rights and frame women as wives and mothers that belong solely in heterosexual family units.[14]

I saw this first hand at the Beijing +10 meeting where the conservative Bush administration aligned with the Holy See, conservative Catholic delegates from certain South American states, and various conservative Muslim states, held up the reaffirmation of the Beijing Platform for Action for the first week of the 2005 UN Commission on the Status of Women because of disagreements around what constituted a woman's access to sexual and reproductive health. Conversation was polarized between the more 'progressive feminist' 'us' versus the 'backward, conservative' 'them' which inhibited constructive dialogue on other important issues such as increasing the number of women in positions of nationally elected leadership roles around the world.

The most sympathetic feminist human rights normative approach to religion is exemplified by the writings of Martha Nussbaum, a liberal feminist ethicist, philosopher and activist, who does try to account for religion in modern ethical life. Nussbaum does not challenge the boundaries of the discourse of religion in Western modernity. She notes that in the modern liberal state religion is a matter of private and personal preference and is separate from the political sphere. In fact, it is subordinate to the State and where religion conflicts with the values enshrined in the State, she argues that it is the State's responsibility to regulate

---

[12]   Charlotte Bunch, Peggy Antrobus, Samantha Frost and Niamh Reilly, 'International Networking for Women's Human Rights', in Michael Edwards and John Gaventa (eds), *Global Citizen Action* (Colorado Springs, 2001), (np).

[13]   Chappell, 'Contesting Women's Rights', p. 15.

[14]   Chappell, 'Contesting Women's Rights', p. 32.

religion. She writes, 'any religion that diverges too far from the shared moral understanding that is embodied in the core of the political conception does not deserve the honorific name of religion'.[15] Here religion is an aspect of civil life which should be regulated by the State and in instances where one's individual human rights to practise one's religion according to one's conscience contradicts women's individual human rights to bodily integrity (as in the case of Female Genital Mutilation), women's individual human rights serve as the trump card.[16]

Furthermore, although Nussbaum states that it is 'generally difficult to determine to what extent the religions in a nation reflect influences from other aspects of the culture and to what extend they influence culture', she does not examine how the norms inherent in the liberal imaginary about what constitutes the secular state and women's individual human rights might have been initially shaped and might now be sustained or challenged by certain religious discourses at the epistemological and ontological level.[17]

An ethics and politics of natality, which recognizes natality rather than mortality as the philosophical starting point, hinges on Grace's suggestions for transforming the current religious discourse which shapes and sustains the Western moral imaginary. She argued that the current Western moral imaginary is shaped by discourses of 'Christendom'.

Unlike Nussbaum, Grace argued that religious discourses shape and influence the ontologies and epistemologies behind any society's given moral imaginary. She insisted that the discourse of religion is one of many (others being law, science and economics) that actually shapes the imaginary and resulting symbolic of Western civilization.[18] Since religion is one of the ways in which we construct human reality, as 'a grand myth or set of myths that we live by (where myth does not have "truth" as its opposite)',[19] then how we restructure that myth in ways that foster human dignity is of ultimate value. Because religion informs who we value and how we live, then religion can no longer be relegated to the private sphere.[20] This opens up the possibility that religion, since it inevitably does influence and shape the imaginary of a culture, can and must play a transformative role if movement towards social justice is to occur.

---

[15]   Martha C. Nussbaum, *Women and Human Development: The Capabilities Approach* (Cambridge, 2000).

[16]   Martha C. Nussbaum, *Sex and Social Justice* (Oxford and New York, 1999).

[17]   Nussbaum, *Sex and Social Justice*, p. 86.

[18]   Jantzen, *Becoming Divine*, p. 161.

[19]   Jantzen, *Becoming Divine*, p. 161.

[20]   Jantzen, *Becoming Divine*, p. 258.

Transnational Feminist Activism is Characterized by Dualism

Grace also critiques the Western moral imaginary for its inherent dualism which meant that doesn't allow for the emergence of plural subjectivities. She argued that the discourse of religion, or Christendom, has both shaped and sustained this dualism in which hierarchies of value exist. These dualistic terms include limit/unlimited, odd/even, one/plurality, right/left, male/female, resting/moving, straight/curved, light/darkness, good/bad, square/oblong where the first word in the pair was considered to masculine, good, and orderly and the second word in the pair was feminine, bad and chaotic.[21] The first terms came to be associated with mind/spirit and the second terms in the pairs were associated with body and matter. The less desirable qualities of the two in each were denigrated and the first term was what was elevated as normative for human subjects.

This dualism can also be seen in the human rights narrative around which many transnational feminist activists mobilize. All too often, the narratives used by transnational feminists, both in their advocacy and fieldwork, are characterised by binaries of either 'cultural relativism' or a laissez-faire approach to potentially harmful and oppressive practices which serves to reify monolithic static and conservative versions of 'traditional cultures', or liberal 'moral outrage' in which Western 'enlightened' versions of emancipation are held up as being universal and morally superior to 'primitive' traditional culture.[22] Both of these binaries are reductionist and often ignore, or are unable to fully explore and uncover, the specific historical, social, religious, economic and national context in which the plural subjects of their explicitly emancipatory projects live and breathe.

For example Christine Walley explores the Western feminists' advocacy on behalf of the eradication of female genital cutting (FGC) in places like West Africa.[23] She criticizes representations of FGC, referred to pejoratively as female mutilation, by Alice Walker (in *Warrior Marks*) and Fran Hoskens (*The Hoskens Report*) for being guilty of neo-imperialistic 'moral outrage' where the its practitioners are seen as barbaric, primitive and cruel. For instance, in an textual analysis of the film by Alice Walker, *Warrior Marks*, Micere Mugo, an African

---

[21]   Jantzen, *Becoming Divine*, p. 267.

[22]   C. Walley, '"Searching For Voices": Feminism, anthropology and the Global Debate over Female Genital Mutilation' in S. M. James and C. C. Robertson (eds) *Genital Cutting and Transnational Sisterhood: Disputing U.S. Polemics* (Chicago, 2002), (np); Amy Farrell and Patrice Farrell and McDermott, 'Claiming Afghan Women: The Challenge of Human Rights Discourse for Transnational Feminism', in Wendy Hesford and Wendy Kozol (eds), *Just Advocacy? Women's Rights, Transnational Feminism, and the Politics of Representation* (New Brunswick, New Jersey, 2005); M. Raimondo, 'Intensifications: Representing Gender and Sexuality at the UN General Assembly Special Session on HIV/AIDS' (np) in Wendy S. Hesford and Wendy Kozol (eds) *Women's Human Rights, Transnational Feminisms and the Politics of Representation* (New Brunswick NJ., 2005).

[23]   Walley, 'Searching for voices'.

literary and cultural scholar, maintains that Walker portrays the African women as 'victims' who are to 'be pitied and patronized, instead of being cherished, nurtured and invested with faith as human subjects, potentially capable of understanding and changing the conditions that dehumanize them'.[24] Elsewhere, another Western woman portrays African women as 'prisoners of ritual'.[25]

Specifically in relationship to previous Western approaches to FGC, Walley states that 'much of the Western-oriented literature by Euro-Americans that opposes female genital operations invokes a series of binary oppositions'.[26] These include first world/third world, modernity/tradition, science/superstition, civilized/ barbarous, freedom/torture and repression, women as actors/women as oppressed, medical knowledge/ignorance and disease, where the first term of the binary is desirable and referring to the wisdom of the first world and the second term of the binary refers to and marginalizes the Other, the Third World.

These binaries are suspiciously similar to Grace's list of binaries found in the Western cultural imaginary of death.[27] It would seem these binaries have found their way into international politics and development praxis with respect to FGC and, probably, into other issues as well. They obscure the complex religious and cultural reasons why women practise various forms of FGC in their cultures that go beyond the simple explanation of 'patriarchy' or the commoditization of women as objects existing under hegemonic and hierarchical male domination rather than as natals capable of forging their own subjectivities. Failure to address these reasons by simply legislating against FGC at the international level as a violation of women's human rights allows these practices to continue because they do not consider religious and cultural motivations for them or how there might be other cultural and religious voices in the culture who do not uphold these practices. As I will explore later, it is by actually starting with the experiences of these women and those trying to eradicate the practice on the ground in their specific cultural, religious, and national contexts, which might provide insights in how to transform the moral imaginary in a way that is less oppositional.

Transnational Feminist Activists Deploy the Metaphor of Salvation in their Narratives

The final diagnosis I am going to explore that Grace made about the Western moral imaginary is that it is dominated by the metaphor of salvation rather than a

---

[24]   S. James, 'Reflections Around Female Genital Cutting', in Robertson, S. (ed.) *Genital Cutting and Transnational Sisterhood: Disputing U.S. Polemics* (Chicago, 2002), (np).

[25]   H. Lightfoot-Klein, *Prisoners of Ritual: An Odyssey Into Female Genital Circumcision in Africa* (New York and London, 1989).

[26]   Walley, 'Searching for Voices', pp. 37–8.

[27]   Jantzen, *Becoming Divine*, pp. 267–8.

metaphor of flourishing. She notes how these metaphors, when privileged, promote and sustain different human anthropologies.

In the religious imaginary of Christendom which has shaped, sustained and in turn been shaped by the Western imaginary and habitus, Grace argued that the theological doctrine of salvation had been privileged over that of human flourishing. In this metaphor, salvation denotes dependence: it implies that there needs to be a 'heroic' saviour from the outside who can come and rescue people from their oppression.[28] She noted that the resulting human anthropology that this metaphor privileges is one where people need to be rescued, life is problematic, people are dependent and they cannot help themselves.[29] Her basic premise is the idea that whether or not people are viewed as inherently capable and resilient or as inherently sinful and incapable and in need of rescue, has powerful consequences for what approach to take in researching what injustices in various communities and then how best to address them.

This metaphor of salvation and the human anthropology of dependence which characterizes the Western moral imaginary can be seen in all the previous examples of transnational feminist advocacy. The objects of transnational activism are 'victims' in need of rescue. They are not recognized as having agency and their identity is reduced to their terms of oppression rather than recognizing their agency and resiliency. Those involved in writing critically on specific human rights efforts have also documented this victim versus rescuer narrative locked into the human rights discourse which obscures any political space to uncover insights on the ground where the supposed 'victims' are actually flourishing, not just in spite of their oppression or in resistance to it, but outside of it.[30]

In one particular essay, Amy Farrell and Patrice McDermott criticize the advocacy work of an American transnational feminist advocacy group, the Feminist Majority on behalf of RAWA, an indigenous Afghan women's NGO that was formed in the late 1980s before the Soviet invasion of Afghanistan. The essay highlights the fraught relationship between the two organization over whose voice on behalf of all Afghan women is more authentic. They concluded that 'transnational feminist coalitions based on a human rights bipolar construction of the local and global engage groups like RAWA solely in terms of their specific experience as the powerless'.[31] They note that the human rights discourse only allowed RAWA the agency to be seen to collect testimonies and stories of victimhood although they did a lot of grassroots literacy work with Afghan women in Afghanistan and did not allow them the publicly acknowledged agency to resolve these issues themselves without outside intervention. Instead the Feminist Majority wrote in a 2002 *Ms* Magazine article about their work in Afghanistan

---

[28]   Jantzen, *Becoming Divine*, p. 160.

[29]   Jantzen, *Becoming Divine*, p. 161.

[30]   Wendy S. Hesford, and Wendy Kozol (eds) *Just Advocacy? Women's Human Rights, Transnational Feminisms and the Politics of Representations* (New Brunswick, NJ, 2005).

[31]   Farrell and Farrell and McDermott, 'Claiming Afghan Women', p. 41.

and about their important role in as influencing US foreign policy post 9/11 and presented themselves as representing an all-inclusive feminism. This offended RAWA because Feminist Majority did not acknowledge its work or agency on the ground in helping providing education for Afghan women in spite of the Taliban's sanctions against educating women and girls.

Furthermore, the voice of the Feminist Majority was co-opted by the Bush Administration as a rationale for war, that is one of the reasons the US government justified its invasion of Afghanistan was to liberate its women from Taliban oppression.[32] They concluded that 'the very representation of non-Western women "in need" constructs and reinforces a narrative in which all that is Islamic/Muslim/non-Western is painted as "uncivilized" and "barbaric", the women are seen as "victims", and Westerners, as providing a "civilizing" effect'.[33]

The victim/rescuer narrative obscures aspects of oppression and victimhood of the 'rescuers' and ignores the strengths and capabilities of those they deem in need of rescue. The only agency it seemed that was granted to RAWA was to collect testimonies and stories of abuse since it was the stories of victimhood which were going to garner an international response. The Feminist Majority's human rights narrative totally ignored the role of RAWA within Afghanistan itself. Furthermore this human rights narrative continues to obscure how RAWA's own authority and agency to speak for all Afghan women within Afghanistan has been fractured, now that the U.S.-backed Karzai government has formed a Ministry of Women's Affairs and a U.S. State Department sponsored U.S.-Afghan Women's Council. The authors also note how the rescuer versus victim narrative also prevented the Feminist Majority from addressing pressing issues of gender equality within the United States such as the abuse of women prisoners and the problems women face in the military, and what they term as the 'murkier' issues such as the plastic surgery and diet industries in which U.S. women 'freely participate'.[34]

Grace's intervention into the moral imaginary here is to privilege a metaphor of flourishing which she says is more compatible with natality. This metaphor of flourishing is consistent with and supports a human anthropology of flourishing consistent with the ontological implications of natality.

Grace bases her conception of human flourishing on the Latin word, *florere*, when applied to human beings, 'denotes abundance, overflowing with vigour and energy and productiveness, prosperity, success and good health'.[35] Flourishing, grounded in an ethic of natality, views human life as a positive state full of possibilities and potential and its anthropology is one of people, embodied, gendered, and interconnected in a web of relationships, who have considerable inner resources and an inner impetus of natural energy and who are overflowing with vigour.[36]

[32]   Farrell and Farrell and McDermott, 'Claiming Afghan Women', pp. 48–9.

[33]   Farrell and McDermott, 'Claiming Afghan Women', p. 51.

[34]   Farrell and McDermott, 'Claiming Afghan Women', p. 50.

[35]   Jantzen, *Becoming Divine*, p. 160.

[36]   Jantzen, *Becoming Divine*, p. 160.

From this it can be inferred that an aspect of flourishing, rooted in an anthropology of natality, is one in which human beings are inherently resourceful and resilient. They are capable of doing new things. They are not, therefore, perpetual victims in need of constant rescuing. In this sense, flourishing places a premium on an ethics and politics grounded in performance and action.

Another aspect of the human anthropology of natality is that human beings are creative. They are capable of not just doing violence and harm, but they are capable of doing new and surprising things; they are capable of transcending the present circumstances and overcoming violence and oppression. They are creative, but this creativity is not creating something out of nothing, but is made possible by their very material existence and bodiliness.[37] In support of this aspect of natality Grace referred Arendt's last book, *The Life of the Mind*, 'This very capacity for beginning in *natality*, and by no means in creativity (in making something out of nothing, rather than out of material embodiment), not in a gift but in the fact human beings, new men, again and again appear in the world by virtue of birth.[38] Therefore, change is possible.

Research Implications of Interventions into the Discourse of Religion

Grace's project, the development of insights from oppressed religious women working in communities in order to transform the religious discourse or symbolic that contributes to the moral imaginary, had a much narrower focus than mine. I am interested in more than just those living and working in religious communities and my project involves working cross-culturally beyond the Western moral imaginary to which she has limited herself. However, I think her approach provides critical epistemological insights which will guide the development of the framework for this methodology in a manner that is more consistent with epistemological implications of a politics of natality. I will unpack this below.

Grace's epistemology of natality contains several aspects which I will explore here for their methodological implications. These epistemological considerations would indicate the desirability of doing field research and provide my rationale for choosing the particular research participants; individuals of differing genders, religions, ethnicities, and class, who are working in some capacity for transnational feminist NGOs working on a particular issue, such as female genital mutilation.

The first aspect of epistemology in the service of politics of natality that is important in designing a research methodology is the idea of the 'beloved community'. Jantzen puts this forth as the place where new insights and new creativity will be brought to birth.[39] She writes:

---

[37]   Jantzen, *Becoming Divine*, pp. 143–5.

[38]   Hannah Arendt, *The Human Condition* (Chicago, [1958] 1991) Second Edition, p. 84.

[39]   Jantzen, *Becoming Divine*, p. 218.

It is from the creative rage and grief and joy of such a 'beloved community' working together for justice that insight comes into a new religious symbolic, indeed into becoming divine .... Love, joy, attentiveness to the web of life, worship of beauty and interdependence; these are the sources of creative power for justice and flourishing and these are divine.[40]

From this it is possible to see that an essential attribute of these epistemological communities is that they are places from which individuals are actively working together for justice, or social change. The partial perspectives are birthed from the members' direct engagement with what they perceive as injustice and out of direct participation in trying to bring about social change. These communities are made up of active, engaged natals who are dissatisfied with the status quo. In the case of transnational feminist activism, this methodology could be deployed to interview individuals who are working on behalf of a wide range of nongovernmental organizations that are involved in a wide range of projects, whether through human rights advocacy or grass roots development projects aimed at resolving or transforming situations of oppression

Secondly, similar to other feminist epistemologies, a politics of natality is concerned with starting its theorizing from the point of experience. As Grace notes, however, the nature of experience is not 'raw' or analyzable devoid of context. Rather, it contains the discursive and material conditions in which people exist, or how they themselves actually interpret it within the social and economic frameworks into which they are born.[41] In this approach, knowledge is not seen as abstract, objective and universally true in all contexts, but it is viewed as situated, contextual, and nuanced depending on the knowledge bearer's own location in a particular society.

In developing this methodology I have taken up Grace's suggestion that experience be viewed a resource for the development of a feminist religious symbolic, rather than as forming the empirical basis for truth claims.[42] This is an important distinction as the purpose of this research methodology will not be to look for 'truth' per se, but it will involve exploring experience for what kinds of resources it provides for transforming the moral imaginary to be one that is more in keeping with flourishing and natality. The question will become not so much whether insights gained from experience are 'true' but to investigate to what extent certain experiences serve to contribute to the development of 'a symbolic that celebrates natality, makes for flourishing, promotes action for the love of the world, as contrasted with a symbolic, which shuts down on flourishing for some or all people or for the earth. Is it the flourishing of some at the expense of the others?'[43] Although Grace uses the word 'symbolic' here rather than the term moral

---

40   Jantzen, *Becoming Divine*, p. 218.

41   Jantzen, *Becoming Divine*, p. 127.

42   Jantzen, *Becoming Divine*, p. 102.

43   Jantzen, *Becoming Divine*, p. 212.

imaginary, it still holds. The moral imaginary is shaped by the symbolic. I will use terms interchangeably when speaking about the proposed research methodology I am developing from her epistemology.

The third aspect of the epistemological implications of a politics of natality for this particular feminist methodology is will also need to reflect the modified approach to feminist standpoint theory that Grace developed. Specifically, she sought to avoid the essentialist versus relativist argument provoked in response to the work of standpoint feminist theorists like Sandra Harding, Nancy Harstock, and Donna Haraway whilst mobilizing some of their insights for her project.[44] Whereas some standpoint feminists have argued that it is possible for one unique feminist marginal position to represent all the perspectives of women in a society, others take the more relativist view that there are multiple perspectives and since there is no agreed way to adjudicate between their truth-claims, these perspectives are relative. In order to avoid these binaries, Grace argued that the value of insights gleaned from standpoint feminism should not be viewed as truth claims, but rather they could be creative, diverse ways of freeing the imagination that would serve to generate alternative myths, and symbols which would disturb 'the masculinist dominant symbolic'.[45]

One of the epistemological insights that Jantzen emphasizes from her reading of Harstock, is that the oppressed occupy a privileged epistemological standpoint from the margins of society from which, by virtue of active struggle in the face of this oppression, they are able to develop knowledge that critiques the ideology of their oppressors.[46] This insight from experience in the margins does not come automatically simply because a person occupies a marginalized space, but it comes out of active struggle and resistance against the dominant group who reflect the dominant ideology. By privileged, I do not mean to say that these insights are superior to the dominant ideology as some early standpoint feminist theorists would. Instead I take the position articulated by Laura Weldon who has reflected on ways in which standpoint feminist theory does provide for a more inclusive research methodology whether or not one is feminist. Weldon writes, 'Viewing social relations from the position of the oppressed does not just add another set of experiences to existing accounts; it forces revision of the dominant accounts, since it reveals them as partial and limited'.[47] She notes that these partial perspectives from the margins are also valuable because they reveal social phenomenon that the more powerful cannot see, and I would argue, even if they could see them, they might not actually be able to hear them or interpret them.[48]

---

[44]   Jantzen, *Becoming Divine*, pp. 212–18.

[45]   Jantzen, *Becoming Divine*, p. 127.

[46]   Jantzen, *Becoming Divine*, p. 215.

[47]   S. Weldon, 'Inclusion and Understanding: a collective methodology for feminist international relations', in. B. Ackerly, Stern, Maria and Jacqui True (eds) *Feminist Methodologies for International Relations* (Cambridge, 2006), pp. 62–88, p. 65.

[48]   Weldon, 'Inclusion and Understanding', p. 65.

This research methodology insists, therefore, on uncovering a wide range of partial perspectives from a wide variety of subject positions which have been attained both through active conscious resistance and struggle as well as through active flourishing from the margins. In the case of transnational feminist activists and feminist development workers it would be critical to explore the insights of those actively engaged in the projects of both indigenous and international NGOS. In the case of Afghanistan, exploring the particular creative insights gained from the partial perspectives of the various women that are members of the Feminist Majority and the partial perspectives of indigenous Afghan NGOs like RAWA, the governmental organization, the Afghan government Ministry of Women's Affairs and the quasi-governmental Afghan Women's Council which is sponsored by the U.S. State Department.

To uncover these insights it would be important to interview individuals who are not part of the social elites but to interview those who are active at the grass roots level who represent both dominant and marginalized subject positions within these societies. This means listening to people from different social and economic classes within particular societies, different genders, different religious affiliations, and different ethnicities in order to get a diversity of perspectives. As Grace has noted, a diversity of perspectives is good because it provides a rich resource or creativity.[49] It also reflects the plurality that is inherent in the ontology of natality. An anthropology of natality which argues that love is action on behalf of other natals and which assumes action in the public sphere as an inherent ontological characteristic of natals signifies that it is important to talk with activists and those engaged in social justice projects.

Grace goes further to note that these oppressions do not form one centre of oppression, but constitute matrices of oppression. These matrices of oppression constitute the fourth key aspect of the epistemological implications of natality which I consider for the development of this methodology.

In order to suggest how these matrices function, Grace explored the writings of Patricia Hill Collins. Rather than an 'additive approach to oppression' where factors like race, sex, class, and gender are seen as separate variables, Collins noted that these oppression based on intersections of these variables actually form dynamic 'interlocking systems of oppression' which form a 'matrix of domination' in which different forms of oppression are not separable from others but build upon, inform, and reinforce others.[50] An example of this would be how notions of race and class also depend on certain dominant gender constructions. Consequently Grace recognized that there are multiple forms of oppression and argued that people could inhabit more than one site of oppression, therefore one could simultaneously suffer oppression because of race, class and sexual orientation.

This matrix approach to oppression creates political space in which to observe how systems of oppression might work and how different people in the system,

---

49   Jantzen, *Becoming Divine*, p. 124.

50   Jantzen, *Becoming Divine*, p. 124.

or matrix, might be impacted by oppression. For instance it becomes possible to explore how one oppressed person, a white woman, might also be guilty of oppressing a black woman. It also makes it possible to look at the oppression of men who might not be oppressed according to their gender, but might be oppressed by virtue of their race, social class, or ethnicity. It also provides the means for overcoming the victim/oppressor binary inherent in the human rights advocacy narrative which occludes differences in oppressions by insisting that one side in the conflict is always the victim, a poor suffering and ennobled saint, and the other is categorically the evil monolithic powerful oppressor. Someone who is an oppressor in one instance, say in terms of belonging to the dominant race, might be a victim of oppression in another instance, say in terms of their social class. For instance, in the case of FGC, mid-wives who perform the surgeries, both undergo the surgeries themselves, but also are the ones insisting upon them. It is not just a case of powerful bad men oppressing helpless, but good women.

However, given the anthropology of flourishing, it is also important to consider that these matrices are not only ones of oppression, but are also ones of flourishing. It is possible for people's lives to have meaning in excess of how they are constructed by the dominant group. The insights of how people actively perceive what flourishing is to them and what it means to flourish in their context will also provide rich insights that will challenge the moral imaginary.

This is where I depart from Grace. She developed her feminist epistemology in terms of gaining knowledge solely through resistance to oppression. I think this is too limiting. In this sense she is still tied to the Western liberal feminist emancipatory framework which she is trying to escape. She does not seem to give enough weight to the resilience, the inner resources, or to the imagination and creativity of natals to do new and surprising things. To define people in terms of resistance still means their subjectivity is being worked out in opposition to what is considered normative. They remain, to an extent, defined by their oppression rather than being defined first and foremost as natals.

In this respect the work of Saba Mahmood, a South Asian anthropologist based in the United States, provides insights as to how women, but it need not be limited to women, can actively construct their subjectivities.[51] She brings the perspective of different cultural, religious and ethnic backgrounds to bear on the Western moral imaginary and begin to transform it.

One of the goals of Mahmood's research is to 'resolve the profound inability within the current feminist political thought to envision valuable forms of human flourishing outside the bounds of a liberal progressive imaginary'.[52] This goal is compatible with Grace's work and in fact it was Grace who first pointed out Mahmood's writings to me. Her challenge is one that must be taken seriously in terms of a politics of natality that is able to account for different visions of human flourishing across religious and cultural boundaries. Mahmood is more interested

[51]   Saba Mahmood, *The Politics of Piety* (Princeton, 2005).

[52]   Mahmood, *The Politics of Piety*, p. 155.

in how people actually inhabit norms rather than how they subvert them or resist them.[53] By decoupling the notion of agency from the goals of the progressive politics of liberal feminism, she is able to explore a different kind of agency and a different kind of flourishing; one in which desire is not always ready for freedom from domination. For instance, she looks at importance of the quality of docility, the willingness of a person to submit themselves to a set of practices to learn a set of skills, which is one of the values of these women. She argues that this quality is not a passive exercise of agency, but one in which people willingly submit themselves to a set of practices to learn a set of skills in the way that a virtuoso pianist does.[54] The binaries of subversion and resistance do not capture the desire of the women of the piety movement. Rather, this binary ignores 'projects, discourses and desires that are not captured by these terms'.[55]

For instance in the case of the women participating in the Cairo Muslim Piety Movement, their motivation for wearing the veil is based on their desire to become moral human beings. Mahmood argues what constitutes flourishing in this context is pious morality rather than a desire, as some feminists have suggested, to conform to a patriotic national identity in which Islam is one of the markers of patriotism to be asserted against a 'Christian West'. In fact these women speak out against 'political' Muslims who assert Islam as an identity, but who are not interested in becoming ethical, pious Muslims and who are not interested in living according to the moral lights of their religion.[56] Neither of their activities is best represented in terms of 'subaltern feminists' who are subverting the norms of patriarchal Islam through acts of 'resistance'; nor are they best represented, as they often are, as the 'Fundamentalist Others' of feminism's progressive agenda.[57] Mahmood does demonstrate, however, that their ethical actions do have unintended and unpredictable political consequences. The fact that State attempts to shut them down is the best evidence, according to Mahmood, that their actions threaten and transform secular Egypt.[58]

Mahmood concludes that there are other models of flourishing which do not view all of life in terms of subjection and resistance. She observes:

> It is quite clear that the idea of freedom and liberty as *the* political idea is relatively new in modern history. Many societies, including Western ones have flourished with aspirations other than this. Nor for that matter, does the narrative of individual and collective liberty exhaust the desires with which people life in liberal societies.[59]

---

53   Mahmood, *The Politics of Piety*, p. 123.
54   Mahmood, *The Politics of Piety*, p. 29.
55   Mahmood, *The Politics of Piety*, p. 14.
56   Mahmood, *The Politics of Piety*, p. 16.
57   Mahmood, *The Politics of Piety*, pp. 154–5.
58   Mahmood, *The Politics of Piety*, pp. 34–5, 37, 47–8.
59   Mahmood, *The Politics of Piety*, p. 14.

Consequently, it is important to consider how partial perspectives obtained from research of individuals from different marginal subject positions might inform and enrich one another in the analysis of this material. It is important to look at the interlocking nature of these perspectives and how they inform one another in a matrix of both flourishing and oppression. It is not enough to obtain only a few partial perspectives and then analyse them from the additive perspective in which race, gender and class exist as separate variables. These partial perspectives are dynamic and as such must challenge the blind spots as well as acknowledge the strengths of one another. In this regard, it is important to continually keep the question in mind as to how a more accurate picture of various issues of social injustice and solutions to resolve them might emerge through this dynamic engagement of partial perspectives.

A methodology that recognizes matrices of oppression and flourishing will be able to uncover the dynamic and different ways in which victims are sometimes oppressors, where oppressors are sometimes victims, within and between both sides of a social justice issue. It will also permit researchers to identify the ways in which people who are considered 'marginalized' find meaning in their lives that goes beyond mere resistance to oppression and are able to give meaning to their lives that flourish in creative ways in spite of the oppressions they suffer. Similarly, it will facilitate the exploration of ways in which people who are viewed in the conflict as 'the oppressors' also suffer or lack the fulfilment of their desires, something which is obscured by the false binary in which there are only oppressors and victims. It allows for the acknowledgement and recognition that victims can and do act in oppressive and unjust ways whilst 'oppressors' can often can and do act in very life-giving and flourishing ways.

In this respect, it will be important to ask questions which will elicit some notion of the past. What resources from their past histories are they mobilizing in order to flourish and how do they view their futures? How does the past inform the future? In this methodology it is important not only to examine where people have struggled against and have resisted, but look for where they are actively flourishing. To imply that only resistance and oppression characterize a person's existence, is to deny other ways in which people define their lives and ignores and denies that people are always already flourishing, an ontological state more in keeping with natality. People exceed their circumstances and their oppressions. They are capable of doing and are already are doing new things.

Grace also hints that these communities might also be places of more than resistance against injustice, but she does not develop how this might occur. While she does suggest that individuals in these communities also actively should come together and be actively attentive to what brings people love and joy in order to discover additional sources of creativity and imagination for transforming the status quo, she does not pursue this train of thought.

The ontology of natality as developed in this essay, claims that individuals can and do flourish in communities in ways that are not defined in terms of resistance to oppression. Therefore a politics of natality would insist that the partial perspectives can be developed out of the rich resources of how individuals participating in these communities flourish and see their lives apart from their active resistance to injustice.

Grace proposed, but did not operationalise, an epistemology, or a feminist methodological framework for exploring how epistemological communities might develop creative insights that could transform the Western moral imaginary in a direction that was more conducive for the flourishing of plural human subjects, particularly in her case, woman qua woman. In this very important sense, her project is incomplete. In her work, Grace does not take into account that such epistemological communities might already exist, albeit in less than the ideal form for which she is advocating. Instead she suggests that women should begin consciously forming these communities with the explicit intent of producing transformational insights to the religious discourse that helps to form the moral imaginary. She suggested that feminist theologians come together and deliberately form 'beloved communities' in which new insights and creativity could be birthed through action and dialogue that would create spaces for the development of a genuine female subjectivity.

However, I go one step further and argue that such epistemological communities already do exist in the form of transnational and local (or indigenous) nongovernmental organizations engaged in advocacy and other social justice activities like community development projects. They are forging insights at the grassroots that could potentially be transformative both at the international and grassroots level; however in order for these insights to be uncovered and truly be heard, they have to be decoupled from the Western liberal emancipatory ontological, epistemological and ethical frameworks in which these development and advocacy projects operate. I think these insights, once uncovered can be mobilized to begin to transform the current human rights discourse into one that is more genuinely democratic; that is, one that is more reflective of a diversity of subjectivities that respect but are not subsumed by religious, national, economic and sexual differences.

Therefore, in order to uncover creative insights, it would be important for researchers to interview individuals who are working on behalf of a wide range of secular, religious, feminist and non-feminist nongovernmental organizations which are involved in a range of projects aimed at resolving or transforming situations of oppression and injustice. It is a bit of a stretch to call nongovernmental organizations 'beloved communities', but they do form epistemological communities of individuals who are engaged and involved in social change.

In order to take Grace's theoretical insights as developed and built upon in this article further, the next step is to actually undertake the field research suggested in the final section of this article in order to discover what insights are currently being birthed through action born of love and natality. Then, these insights must be placed into a dynamic fluid dialogue with the theory and challenge where it is still a prisoner of the current moral imaginary. These insights will also serve to challenge and transform the prevalent human rights discourse as universal ethics which is the particular focus of this chapter in directions that cannot yet be anticipated at this point. Although Grace did not know the exact contours the new moral imaginary of flourishing and natality would take, she pointed the way. The challenge of her legacy is to take it a step further and begin fleshing out in more detail what a vision of human flourishing grounded in an ethics and flourishing might look like.

Bibliography

Abi-Kyles, Ayanna, *Interview, Oral History Project*, Candler School of Theology, Emory University, Atlanta, GA (10 November 2004).

———, *Interviews, Oral History Project*, Candler School of Theology, Emory University, Atlanta, GA (15–16 September 2006).

Agamben, Giorgio, *Homo Sacer: Sovereignty and Bare Life*, trans. Daniel Heller-Roazen (Stanford: Stanford University Press, 1998).

———, *The Time That Remains: A Commentary on the Letter to the Romans*, trans. Patricia Dailey (Stanford: Stanford University Press, 2005).

Althusser, Louis, *Lenin and Philosophy and Other Essays* trans. Ben Brewster (New York: Monthly Review Press, 2001).

Anderson, Benedict *Imagined Communities* (London: Verso, 1991).

Anderson, Pamela Sue, *A Feminist Philosophy of Religion: The Rationality and Myths of Religious Belief* (Oxford: Oxford University Press, 1988).

———, 'Correspondence with Grace Jantzen', *Feminist Theology* 25 (2000): 112–19.

———, 'Liberating Love's Capabilities: On the Wisdom of Love,' in Norman Wirzba and Bruce Ellis Benson (eds) *Transforming Philosophy and Religion: Love's Wisdom* (Indianapolis: Indiana University Press, 2008).

Arendt, Hannah, *The Human Condition* (Chicago: University of Chicago Press, 1958).

Asad, Talal, *Genealogies of Religion: Disciplines and Reasons of Power in Christianity and Islam* (Baltimore: The John Hopkins University Press, 1993).

Aschenbrenner, George A., *Stretched for Greater Glory: what to expect from the Spiritual Exercises* (Chicago: Loyola Press, 2004).

Badiou, Alain, *St. Paul: The Foundation of Universalism* trans. Ray Brassier (Stanford: Stanford University Press, 2003).

———, *Metapolitics* trans. Jason Barker (London: Verso, 2005).

Bald, J. C., *John Donne: A Life* (Oxford, London, New York, Toronto: Oxford University Press, 1970).

Barry, William A., 'Towards a Theology of Discernment', *Way* (Supplement) 64 (1989): 129–40.

Bechtle, Regina, 'Reclaiming the Truth of Women's Lives', *Way* (Supplement) 28 (1988): 50–59.

Belsey, Catherine, 'John Donne's Worlds of Desire', in Andrew Mousley (ed.), *John Donne* (Basingstoke and New York: Palgrave, 1999).

Berlin, Isaiah, *The Roots of Romanticism* (London: Pimlico, 2000).

Bernauer, James W., 'Michel Foucault's Ecstatic Thinking', in J. Bernauer and D. Rasmussen (eds), *The Final Foucault* (London and Cambridge, Mass: Massachusetts Institute of Technology, 1998).

Berry, Thomas, *The Great Work: Our Way Into the Future* (New York: Bell Tower, 1999).

Best, Ernst, *One Body in Christ* (London: SCM Press, 1955).

Blumenfeld, Bruno, *The Political Paul: Justice, Democracy and Kingship in a Hellenistic Framework* (Sheffield: Sheffield Academic Press, 2001).

Bunch, Charlotte, Antrobus, Peggy, Frost, Samantha and Reilly, Niamh 'International Networking for Women's Human Rights', in Michael Edwards, John Gaventa (ed.), *Global Citizen Action* (Colorado Springs, CO: Lynne Rienner Publishers, 2001).

Butler, Judith, *Bodies that Matter: On the Discursive Limits of 'Sex'* (New York: Routledge, 1993).

Byrne, Lavinia, 'Asking for the Grace', *Way* (Supplement) 64 (1989): 29–36.

Canters, Hanneke and Jantzen, Grace M., *Forever Fluid: A Reading of Luce Irigaray's Elemental Passions* (Manchester: Manchester University Press, 2005).

Carotenuto, A., *A Secret Symmetry: Sabina Spielrein, Between Jung and Freud* (New York: Pantheon, 1984).

Carrette, Jeremy and King, Richard, *Selling Spirituality: The Silent Takeover of Religion* (London: Routledge, 2005).

Carrette, Jeremy, 'Foucault, Monks and Masturbation', in Tom Baldwin, James Fowler and Shane Weller (eds), *The Flesh in the Text: Body, Flesh and Text in French Literature* (Oxford: Peter Lang, 2007).

———, *Religion and Critical Psychology: Religious Experience in the Knowledge Economy* (London: Routledge, 2007).

Castree, Noel, *Nature* (London and New York: Routledge, 2005).

Chappell, Louise, 'Contesting Women's Rights: The Influence of Religious Forces at the United Nations', paper given at Australian Political Studies Association Conference, University of Adelaide, 29 September–1 October 2004.

Chavel, Cécile, 'La Jouissance Féminine', unpublished conference paper at the University of Kent, *The Flesh and the Text*, 3 November, 2006.

———, 'Métapsychologie de l'acte théâtral, étude clinique sur la jouissance de l'acteur en scène avec son public' (Doctorat de Psychopathologie Fondamentale et Psychanalyse à l'Université Paris VII Denis Diderot, June 2002).

Collier, Diane, 'Gender Issues', *Way* (Supplement) 90 (1990): 97–107.

Cowan, Marian, and John Carroll Futrell, *Companions in Grace: A Handbook for Directors of the Spiritual Exercises of Saint Ignatius of Loyola* (Saint Louis: Institute of Jesuit Sources, 2000).

Creasey, M. A., '"Inward" and "Outward": a study in early Quaker language' Supplement No. 30, *Journal of the Friends Historical Society* (1962): 1–24.

Crosfield, G., *Friends and the Women's Movement* (London: Headley Brothers, 1911).

Crouch, Colin, *Post-Democracy* (Cambridge: Polity Press, 2004).

Dandelion, Pink, *A Sociological Analysis of the Theology of Quakers: the silent Revolution* (Lampeter: Edwin Mellen Press, 1996).

———, *The Liturgies of Quakerism* (Aldershot: Ashgate, 2005).

Davies, Tony *Humanism* (London and New York: Routledge, 1997).

DesBrisay, G., 'Jaffray, Alexander (1614–1673)', *Oxford Dictionary of National Biography* (Oxford, Oxford University Press, 2000) [http://www.oxforddnb.com/view/article/14582, accessed June 2007].

de Beauvoir, Simone, *The Ethics of Ambiguity*, trans. Bernard Frechtman (New York: Citadel Press, 1948).

de Lubac, Henri, *Corpus Mysticum: l'Eucharistie et l'Église au Moyen Âge* (Paris: Aubier-Montaigne, 1944).

Deleuze, Gilles, *Spinoza: Practical Philosophy*, trans. Robert Hurley (San Francisco CA: City Lights, 1988).

Desmond, William, *Hegel's God* (Aldershot, Burlington: Ashgate, 2003).

———, *God and the Between* (Malden, Oxford, Victoria: Blackwell, 2008).

Dixon, S., 'The Life and Times of Peter Briggins', *Quaker Studies*, 10 (2006): 185–202.

Donne, John, *The Sermons of John Donne: volume X* (eds) George Potter and Evelyn Simpson (Berkeley: University of California Press, 1962).

———, *Devotions Upon Emergent Occasions* (ed.) Anthony Raspa (Oxford, London, New York, Toronto: Oxford University Press, 1975).

———, *John Donne: The Major Works*, (ed.) J. Carey (Oxford, London, New York, Toronto: Oxford University Press, 1990).

———, *The Poems of John Donne*, (ed.) H. J. C. Grierson (Oxford, London, New York, Toronto: Oxford University Press, 1933).

Dyckman, Katherine, Garvin, Mary and Liebert, Elizabeth, *The Spiritual Exercises Reclaimed: uncovering liberating possibilities for women* (New York: Paulist Press, 2001).

Edwards, David L., *John Donne: Man of Flesh and Spirit* (London and New York: Continuum, 2001).

Elliot, Neil, Liberating Paul: *The Justice of God and the Politics of the Apostle* (Minneapolis: Fortress Press, 2005).

Ellis, Bret Easton, *American Psycho* (London: Picador, 1991).

Endean, Philip, 'Discerning Behind the Rules', *Way* (Supplement) 64 (1989): 37–50.

Fischer, Kathleen, *Women at the Well: feminist perspectives on spiritual direction* (New York: Paulist Press, 1988).

Fleming, David L., *Like the Lightening: The Dynamics of the Ignatian Exercises* (Saint Louis, MO: Institute Jesuit Sources, 2004).

Foucault, Michel, *The Will to Knowledge: The History of Sexuality, volume 1*, trans. R. Hurley (Harmondsworth: Penguin, 1978).

———, *The Use of Pleasure: The History of Sexuality, volume 2*, trans. R. Hurley (Harmondsworth: Penguin 1985).

Freud, Sigmund [1920], 'Beyond the Pleasure Principle', in *On Metapsychology* (London: Penguin Freud Library Volume 2, [1984] 1991).

———— [1933], 'Why War?' [Einstein and Freud] in *Civilization, Society and Religion* (London: The Penguin Freud Library volume 12, [1984] 1991).

Fromm, Eric, *The Crisis of Psychoanalysis* (London, 1970).

———— [1964], *The Heart of Man: Its Genius for Good and Evil* (New York: Harper Collins, 1980).

———— [1973], *The Anatomy of Human Destructiveness* (London: Penguin, 1977).

Fukuyama, Francis, *The End of History and the Last Man* (Harmondsworth: Penguin Books, 1992).

Fulkerson, Mary McClintock, *Changing the Subject: Women's Discourses and Feminist Theology* (Minneapolis: Augsburg Fortress Press, 1994).

Fyfe, C., 'Kilham, Hannah (1774–1832)', *Oxford Dictionary of National Biography* (Oxford, Oxford University Press, 2004) [http://www.oxforddnb.com/view/article/15526, accessed 22 November 2005].

Galama, Petronella Hedwig Herman Maria, 'Behold How I Love You: The Theology and Mystagogy of Julian of Norwich's Showing of Love' (PhD thesis, University of Bristol, 2005).

Ganss, George E., *The Spiritual Exercises of Saint Ignatius: A Translation and Commentary* (St Louis: Institute Jesuit Sources, 1992).

Gatens, Moira and Lloyd, Genevieve, *Collective Imaginings: Spinoza Past and Present* (London: Routledge, 1999).

Gill, C., *Women in the Seventeenth-Century Quaker Community: A Literary Study of Political Identities, 1650–1700* (Aldershot: Ashgate, 2005).

Gopin, Marc, *Holy War, Holy Peace: How Religion Can Bring Peace to the Middle East* (Oxford: Oxford University Press, 2002).

————, *Healing the Heart of Conflict: 8 Crucial Steps to Making Peace with Yourself and Others* (Emmaus, PA, Rodale Books, 2004).

————, Lecture, Emory University, Atlanta, Georgia (22 March 2007).

Gössmann, Elisabeth, 'The Image of God and the Human Being in Women's Counter-Tradition', in Deborah F. Sawyer and Diane M. Collier (eds), *Is There a Future for Feminist Theology?* (Sheffield: Sheffield Academic Press, 1999).

Graham, Elaine, *Representations of the Post/Human: Monsters, Aliens and Others in Popular Culture* (Manchester: Manchester University Press, 2002).

————, 'Feminist Theology: Northern', in William Cavanaugh and Peter Scott (eds), *Blackwell Companion to Political Theology* (Oxford and New York: Blackwell, 2003).

Graham, Elaine, Walton, Heather and Ward, Frances, *Theological Reflection: Methods* (London: SCM Press, 2005).

Gray, John, *Straw Dogs: Thought on Human and Other Animals* (London: Granta, 2002).

Green, Deidre, *Gold in the Crucible* (Longmead, Shaftesbury: Element Books, 1989).

Grey, Mary, *The Outrageous Pursuit of Hope: Prophetic Dreams for the 21st Century* (London: Darton, Longman and Todd, 2000).

———, 'The Spiritual Journey of Impaired Pilgrims', in Macquiban, Tim (ed.), *The Faith Journey of Impaired Pilgrims* (Salisbury: Sarum College Press, 2006).

———, *To Rwanda and Back: Liberation Spirituality and Reconciliation* (London: Darton, Longman and Todd, 2007).

Habermas, Jurgen, *The Structural Transformation of the Public Sphere: An Inquiry into a Category of Bourgeois Society*, trans. Thomas Burger (Cambridge: Polity Press, 1989).

Hardt, Michael and Negri, Antonio, *Multitude* (New York: Penguin Press, 2004).

Harris, Harriet A., 'Feminism', in Chad Meister and Paul Copans (eds), *The Routledge Companion to Philosophy of Religion* (London: Routledge, 2007).

Hassan, Rifat, 'Muslim Women in Post-Patriarchal Islam', in Paula M. Cooey, William R. Eakin and J. B. McDonald (eds), *After Patriarchy: Feminist Transformations of the World Religions* (Maryknoll: Orbis Books, 1992).

Hayek, Freiderich A., *The Road to Serfdom* (London: Routledge, 1981).

Hegel, Georg W. F., *Elements of the Philosophy of Right*, trans. H. B. Nisbet (Cambridge: Cambridge University Press, 1991).

———, *Phenomenology of Spirit*, trans. A. V. Miller (Oxford: Oxford University Press, 1997).

Henning, Brian, *The Ethics of Creativity: Beauty, Morality, and Nature in a Processive Cosmos* (Pittsburgh: University of Pittsburgh Press, 2005).

Hesford, Wendy and Kozol, Wendy S. (eds), *Just Advocacy? Women's Human Rights, Transnational Feminisms, and the Politics of Representation* (New Brunswick, New Jersey: Rutgers University Press, 2005).

Hollywood, Amy, *Sensible Ecstasy* (Chicago: The University of Chicago Press, 2002).

Horsley, Richard A. (ed.), *Paul and Empire Religion and Power in Roman Imperial Society* (Harrisburg: Trinity International Press, 1997).

——— (ed.), *Paul and Politics: Ekklesia, Israel, Imperium, Interpretation* (Harrisburg: Trinity International Press, 2000).

Hughes, Gerard W., *God of Surprises* (London: Darton Longman and Todd, 1985).

Ingstad, Benedicte and Whyte, Susan Reynolds (eds), *Disability and Culture* (Berkeley: University of California Press, 1995).

Ivens, Michael, 'Ignatius Loyola', in C. Jones, G. Wainwright, and E. Yarnold (eds), *The Study of Spirituality* (London: SPCK, 1986).

———, *Understanding the Spiritual Exercises* (Leominster: Gracewing, 1998).

Jaffray, A., 'A Word of Exhortation', in George Keith, *Help in the Time of Need from the God of Help. To the People of the (so-called) Church of Scotland, especially the once more zealous and professing, who have so shamefully degenerated and declined from that which their Fathers, the Primitive Protestants attained unto* (Aberdeen, 1665).

——— [1614–1661], *Diary of Alexander Jaffray* (London: Harvey & Darton, 1833).

James, Stanlie M., 'Reflections around Female Genital Cutting' in Stanlie M. James and Clair C. Robertson (eds), *Genital Cutting and Transnational Sisterhood* (Chicago: University of Illinois Press, 2002).

Jantzen, Grace M., 'Omnipresence and Incorporeality' (published under surname Dyck), *Religious Studies*, vol. 13, no. 1 (1977): 85–91.

——, 'On Worshipping an Embodied God', *Canadian Journal of Philosophy* VIII/3 (1978): 511–9.

——, 'Hume on Miracles, History and Apologetics', *Christian Scholar's Review*, vol. VIII, no. 4 (1979): 318–25.

——, 'Incarnation and Epistemology', *Theology*, vol. LXXXIII, no. 693 (1980): 170–77.

——, 'Human Diversity and Salvation in Christ', *Religious Studies*, vol. 20, no. 4 (1983): 579–92.

——, 'Do We Need Immortality?', *Modern Theology*, vol. 1, no. 1 (1984): 33–44.

——, *God's World, God's Body* (Philadelphia, PA: Westminster, 1984).

——, 'Human Autonomy in the Body of God', in Alistair Kee and Eugene Long (eds), *Being and Truth: Essays in Honour of John Macquarrie* (London: SCM, 1986), pp. 183–91.

——, 'Conspicuous Sanctity and Religious Belief', in W. Abraham and S. Holtzer (eds), *The Rationality of Religious Belief: Essays in Honour of Basil Mitchell* (Oxford: Blackwell, 1986), pp. 121–40.

——, *Julian of Norwich. Mystic and Theologian* (London: SPCK and New York: Paulist Press, 1987. second edn with new author's introduction, London: SPCK, 2000).

——, 'Reply to Taliaferro' (an exchange on *God's World, God's Body*), *Modern Theology*, vol. 3, no. 2 (1987): 189–92.

——, 'Epistemology, Religious Experience, and Religious Belief', *Modern Theology*, vol. 3, no. 4 (1987): 277–92.

——, 'Review Article: Recent Writing in Spirituality', *Theology*, vol. XCIX no. 743 (1988): 405–11.

——, 'Mysticism and Experience', *Religious Studies*, 25/3 (1989): 295–316.

——, 'Where Two are to Become One: Mysticism and Monism', *Royal Institute of Philosophy Lectures* 25 (1989): 147–66.

——, 'The Language of Desire', *The Way* (1990): 26–36.

——, 'Mysticism and Experience', *Religious Studies*, 25/3 (1989): 295–315.

——, 'Could there be a Mystical Core to Religion?' *Religious Studies*, 26 (1990): 59–71.

——, 'Connection or Competition: Personhood and Identity in Feminist Ethics', *Studies in Christian Ethics*, vol. 5, no. 1 (1992): 1–20.

——, 'The Legacy of Evelyn Underhill', *Feminist Theology*, no. 4 (September, 1993): 79–100.

——, 'Ethics and Energy', *Studies in Christian Ethics*, vol. 7, no. 1 (1994): 17–31.

——, 'Feminists, Philosophers and Mystics', *Hypatia*, 9/4 (1994): 186–206.

————, *Power, Gender and Christian Mysticism* (Cambridge: Cambridge University Press, 1995).

————, 'Healing our Brokenness: The Spirit and Creation', in Mary Heather MacKinnon and Moni McIntyre (eds), *Readings in Ecology and Feminist Theology* (Kansas City: Sheed and Ward, 1995).

————, 'Feminist Flourishing: Gender and Metaphor in Theology', *Feminist Theology*, 10 (1995): 81–101.

————, 'Knowledge and Gender: Sources of Religious Knowledge', *Literature and Theology*, vol. 10, no. 2 (1996): 91–111.

————, 'The Gendered Politics of Flourishing and Salvation' in Vincent Brümmer and Marcel Sarot (eds), *Happiness, Well-Being and The Meaning of Life* (Kampen: Kok Pharos, 1996).

————, 'What's the Difference? Knowledge and Gender in (Post) Modern Philosophy of Religion', *Religious Studies*, 32 (1996): 431–48.

————, 'Religion, Feminism and the Family', in Hugh Pyper (ed.), *The Christian Family: A Concept in Crisis* (Norwich: Canterbury Press, 1996), pp. 63–84.

————, 'Feminism and Pantheism', *The Monist*, 80/2 (1997): 266–85.

————, 'Power, Gender and Ecstasy: Mysticism in Post/Modernity', *Literature and Theology*, vol. 11, no. 4 (1997): 385–402.

————, 'Devenir Divin(e)s: La Raison, et les Buts d'une Philosophie Feministe de la Religion', in Elisabeth Hartlieb and Charlotte Methuen (eds), *Sources and Resources of Feminist Theologies* (Kampen: Kok Pharos and Mainz: Matthias-Grünewald Verlag, 1997), pp. 96–125.

————, 'Equal to Whom? Luce Irigaray', in Graham Ward (ed.) *The Postmodern God* (Oxford, Blackwell, 1997), pp. 198–214.

————, 'Disrupting the Sacred: Religion and Gender in the City', in Kathleen O'Grady, Ann L. Gilroy, and Jeanette Gray (eds), *Bodies, Lives, Voices: Gender in Theology* (Sheffield: Sheffield Academic Press, 1998), pp. 72–92.

————, *Becoming Divine: Towards a Feminist Philosophy of Religion* (Manchester: Manchester University Press, 1998).

————, 'Necrophilia and Natality: What does it mean to be religious?' *The Scottish Journal of Religious Studies*, 19/1 (1998): 101–21.

————, 'Reflections on the Looking Glass: Religion, Culture and Gender in the Academy', in *John Rylands Bulletin*, vol. 80, no. 3 (1998): 273–94.

————, *Becoming Divine: Towards a Feminist Philosophy of Religion* (Bloomington: Indiana University Press, 1999).

————, 'Nativity and Natality', in George J. Brooke (ed.), *The Birth of Jesus: Biblical and Theological Reflections* (Edinburgh: T&T Clark, 2000), pp. 111–21.

————, '"Canonized for Love": Pleasure and Death in Modernity', in Lisa Isherwood (ed.), *The Good News of the Body: Sexual Theology and Feminism* (Sheffield: Sheffield Academic Press, 2000), pp. 185–204.

————, 'Flourishing: Towards an Ethic of Natality', *Feminist Theory*, 2/2 (2001): 219–232.

Jantzen, Grace M., 'What Price Neutrality? A Reply to Paul Helm', *Religious Studies*, 37.1 (2001): 87–92.

———, 'On Changing the Imaginary', in Graham Ward (ed.), *The Blackwell Companion to Postmodern Theology* (Oxford: Blackwell, 2001), pp. 280–93.

———, 'Feminist Philosophy of Religion: Open Discussion with Pamela Anderson', *Feminist Theology*, 26 (2001): 102–9.

———, 'Before the Rooster Crows: The Betrayal of Knowledge in Modernity', *Literature and Theology*, 15/1 (2001): 1–24.

——— 'A Reconfiguration of Desire: Reading Medieval Mystics in Postmodernity', *Women's Philosophy Review*, 29 (2002) pp. 23–45.

———, 'Beauty for Ashes: Notes on the Displacement of Beauty', in *Literature and Theology*, vol. 16, no. 4 (2002): 427–49.

———, '"Barely by a Breath": Irigaray on Rethinking Religion', in John Caputo (ed.), *The Religious: Blackwell Readings in Continental Philosophy* (Oxford: Blackwell, 2002), pp. 227–40.

———, 'Birth and the Powers of Horror: Julia Kristeva on Gender, Religion and Death', in Phillip Goodchild (ed.), *Rethinking Philosophy of Religion: Approaches From Continental Philosophy* (New York: Fordham University Press, 2002).

———, 'A Reconfiguration of Desire', *Women's Philosophy Review* 29 (2002): 23–45.

———, 'Contours of a Queer Theology', *Literature and Theology*, vol. 15, no. 3 (2001): pp. 276–85; reprinted in Janet Martin Soskice and Diana Lipton (eds), *Feminism and Theology: Oxford Readings in Feminism* (Oxford: Oxford University Press, 2003).

———, 'The Horizon of Natality: Gadamer, Heidegger and the Limits of Existence', in Lorraine Code (ed.), *Feminist Interpretations of Hans-Georg Gadamer* (University Park, PA: Penn State University Press, 2003), pp. 285–306.

———, 'Eros and the Abyss: Reading Medieval Mystics in Postmodernity', *Literature and Theology*, 17/3 (2003): 244–64.

———, 'Death, then, how could I yield to it? Kristeva's mortal visions', in M. Joy, K. O'Grady and J. L. Poxon (eds), *Religion in French Feminist Thought* (London: Routledge, 2003).

———, 'Thanatos and the Passion for Transformation', *Temenos* vol 42, no. 1 (2006): 73–92.

———, *Foundations of Violence: Death and the Displacement of Beauty Volume 1* (London and New York: Routledge, 2004).

———, 'Choose Life! Early Quaker women and violence in modernity', *Quaker Studies*, 9 (2005): 137–55.

———, 'On Philosophers (Not) Reading History: Narrative and Utopia', in Kevin Vanhoozer and Martin Warner (eds), *Transcending Boundaries in Philosophy and Theology: Reason, Meaning and Experience* (London, 2007).

————, 'The Womb and the Tomb: health and flourishing in medieval mystical literature' in *Wounds that Heal: Theology, Imagination and Health* (ed.) Jonathan Baxter (London: SPCK, 2007).

————, *Violence to Eternity: Death and the Displacement of Beauty volume 2* (eds) Jeremy Carrette and Morny Joy (London: Routledge, 2008).

————, *A Place of Springs: Death and the Displacement of Beauty volume 3* (eds) Jeremy Carrette and Morny Joy (London: Routledge, 2009).

Jennings, J., *Gender, Religion, and Radicalism in the Long Eighteenth Century, the 'Ingenious Quaker' and her Connections* (Aldershot: Ashgate, 2006).

Jenson, Robert, 'Anima Ecclesiastica', in R. Kendell Soulen and Linda Woodhead (eds), *God and Human Dignity* (Grand Rapids: Eerdmans, 2006).

Jiseok, J., *Han Sokhon's Pacifism and the Reunification of Korea: a Quaker theology of peace* (Lampeter: Edwin Mellen Press, 2006).

Jonte-Pace, Diane, *Speaking the Unspeakable: Religion, Misogyny and the Uncanny Mother in Freud's Cultural Texts* (Berkeley: University of California Press, 2000).

Julian of Norwich (1978), *Showings* (Classics of Western Spirituality), trans. Edmund Colledge and James Walsh (London: SPCK).

Kantorowicz, Ernst Hartwig, *The King's Two Bodies: A Study of Mediaeval Political Theology* (Princeton: Princeton University Press, 1957).

Käsemann, Ernst, *Leib und Leib Christi* (Tübingen: J. C. B. Mohr, 1933).

Kaufmann, Walter, *Nietzsche: Philosopher, Psychologist, Antichrist* (Princeton: Princeton University Press, 1959).

Keller, Catherine, Nausner, Michael and Rivera, Mayra (eds), *Postcolonial Theologies: Divinity and Empire* (St Louis, Missouri: Chalice Press, 2004).

Kerr, John, *A Most Dangerous Method: The Story of Jung, Freud and Sabina Spielrein* (New York: Knopf, 1993).

Kilham, H., *Memoir of the late Hannah Kilham; chiefly compiled of her Journal* (London: Darton and Harvey, 1837).

King, Ursula, 'Mysticism and Feminism: Why Look at Women Mystics?' in M. A. Rees (ed.), *Teresa de Jesus and her World* (Leeds: Trinity All Saints College, 1981).

————, *Women and Spirituality: Voices of Protest and Promise* (London and Basingstoke: Macmillan, second edn, 1993).

————, 'Love – A Higher Form of Human Energy in the Work of Teilhard de Chardin and Sorokin', *Zygon: Journal of Religion and Science*, 39/1 (2004): 77–102.

————, 'Inspired by Julian – Seeking a feminine mystical way for the 21st Century', The 27th Julian Lecture 2007, The Julian Centre, Norwich (used here with permission).

Lacan, Jacques [1975], *On Feminine Sexuality: the Limits of Love and Knowledge* [Encore: Seminar XX] (New York: Norton & Co., 1999).

Lanzetta, Beverley, J., *Radical Wisdom: a feminist mystical theology* (Minneapolis: Fortress Press, 2005).

Lanzetta, Beverley, J., *Emerging Heart: global spirituality and the sacred* (Minneapolis: Fortress Press, 2007).

Laplanche, J. and Pontalis, J. B., *The Language of Psychoanalysis* (London: Karnac Books, 1988).

Latour, Bruno, *We Have Never Been Modern*, trans. Catherine Porter (New York: Longman, 1993).

————, *Reassembling the Social: An Introduction of Actor-Network Theory* (Oxford: Oxford University Press, 2005).

Lear, Linda, *Beatrix Potter: A Life in Nature* (New York: St. Martin's Press, 2007).

Lederach, John Paul, *The Moral Imagination: The Art and Soul of Building Peace* (Oxford: Oxford University Press, 2005).

Le Doeuff, Michèle, *Hipparchia's Choice: An Essay Concerning Women, Philosophy Etc.* trans. Trista Selous (New York: Columbia University Press, 1991; second edn, 2007).

————, *The Sex of Knowing*, trans. Kathryn Hamer and Lorraine Code (London: Routledge, 2003).

Lee, Michelle V., *Paul, the Stoics, and the Body of Christ* (Cambridge: Cambridge University Press, 2006).

Levine, Michael, 'Non-theistic conceptions of God', in Chad Meister and Paul Copans (eds), *The Routledge Companion to the Philosophy of Religion* (London: Routledge, 2007).

Lightfoot-Klein, Hanny, *Prisoners of Ritual: An Odyssey into Female Genital Circumcision in Africa* (New York and London: Harrington Park Press, 1989).

Lloyd, Genevieve, 'The Man of Reason', in Ann Garry and Marilyn Pearson (eds) *Women, Knowledge and Reality: Explorations in Feminist Philosophy* (London: Routledge, 1996, second edn).

————, 'What a Union!' *The Philosopher's Magazine*, 29 (2005): 45–8.

Lonsdale, David, *Listening to the Music of the Spirit: The Art of Discernment* (Notre Dame, IN: Ave Maria Press, 1993).

————, [1990] *Eyes to See, Ears to Hear: An Introduction to Ignatian Spirituality* (London: Darton Longman and Todd, 2000).

Lovelock, James, *The Revenge of Gaia: Why the Earth is Fighting Back – and How We Can Still Save Humanity* (London: Penguin, 2007).

Loyola, Ignatius, *The Spiritual Exercises of St. Ignatius, based on studies in the language of the autograph*, trans. Louis J. Puhl (Chicago: Loyola University Press, 1951).

Lunn, P., '"You Have Lost Your Opportunity": British Quakers and the militant phase of the women's suffrage campaign, 1906–1914', *Quaker Studies*, 2 (1997): 30–56.

Lux-Sterritt, Laurence, *Redefining Female Religious Life: French Ursulines and English Ladies in Seventeenth-Century Catholicism* (Aldershot: Ashgate, 2005).

McDermott, Amy Farrell and Patrice, 'Claiming Afghan Women: The Challenge of Human Rights Discourse for Transnational Feminism', in Wendy S. Hesford and Wendy Kozol (eds), *Just Advocacy? Women's Human Rights, Transnational*

Feminisms, and the Politics of Representation (New Brunswick, New Jersey: Rutgers University Press, 2005).

Macek, Ellen A., '"Ghostly Fathers" and their "Virtuous Daughters": The Role of Spiritual Direction in the Lives of Three Early Modern English Women', *The Catholic Historical* Review 90/2 (2004): 213–35.

Mack, P., *Visionary Women: Gender and Prophecy in Seventeenth-Century England* (Berkeley, University of California Press, 1992).

McLaughlin, Eleanor, 'Women, Power and the Pursuit of Holiness', in R. Ruether and E. McLaughlin (eds), *Women of Spirit: female leadership in the Jewish and Christian traditions* (New York: Simon and Schuster, 1979).

McNay, Lois, *Against Recognition* (Cambridge: Polity Press, 2008).

Macquiban, Tim (ed.), *The Faith Journey of Impaired Pilgrims* (Salisbury: Sarum College Press, 2006).

Mahmood, Saba, *The Politics of Piety* (Princeton: University of Princeton Press, 2005).

Maitland, Sara, *A Map of the New Country. Women and Christianity* (London: Routledge, Kegan and Paul, 1983).

Martin, Dale B., *The Corinthian Body* (New Haven: Yale University Press, 1995).

Matheron, Alexandre, 'Spinoza et la sexualité', *Giornale Critico della Filosofia Italiana* 8/4 (1977): 436–57.

Merriam-Webster OnLine, 'Beauty', Available at: www.webster.com, accessed 22 December 2007.

Mitchell, Juliet, *Feminism and Psychoanalysis* (London: Penguin, 1974).

Mol, Annemarie, *The Body Multiple: Ontology in Medical Practice* (Durham, NJ: Duke University Press, 2002).

Monks, Judith and Frankenberg, Ronald, 'Being Ill and being Me: Self, Body and Time in Multiple Sclerosis Narratives', in Ingstad, Benedicte and Whyte, Susan Reynolds (eds), *Disability and Culture* (Berkeley CA, London: University of California Press, 1995).

Moore, A. W., *Making Sense of Things: The Evolution of Modern Metaphysics* (Cambridge, forthcoming).

Moore, Mary Elizabeth, 'The Ethics of Institutions: Compassion, Critique, Creativity, and Form-Giving', in Theodore Walker, Jr., and Mihály Toth (eds), *Whiteheadian Ethics* (Cambridge: Cambridge Scholars Publishing, 2008).

Moore, R., *The Light in their Consciences: the early Quakers in Britain 1646–1666* (University Park, PA, Pennsylvania State University Press, 2000).

Moser, Michaela, 'A Good life for all! Feminist Ethical Reflections on Women, Poverty and the Possibilities of Creating a Change' (PhD thesis, University of Wales, Lampeter, 2008).

Muesse, Mark W., 'Religious Studies and "Heaven's Gate": Making the Strange Familiar and the Familiar Strange', in Russell T. McCutcheon (ed.) *The Insider/Outsider Problem in the Study of Religion* (London: Cassell, 1999).

Newman, Barbara, *Sister of Wisdom: St. Hildegard's Theology of the Feminine* (Berkeley: University of California Press, 1987, second edn, 1997).

Nussbaum, Martha C., *Sex and Social Justice* (Oxford and New York: Oxford University Press, 1999).

———, *Women and Women and Human Development: The Capabilities Approach* (Cambridge: Cambridge University Press 2000).

———, *Upheavals of Thought: The Intelligence of Emotions* (Cambridge: Cambridge University Press, 2001).

———, *Hiding from Humanity: Disgust, Shame, and the Law* (Princeton, NJ: Princeton University Press, 2004).

———, *Frontiers of Justice: Disability, Nationality, Species Membership* (Cambridge, Mass., Harvard University Press, 2006).

Nussbaum, Martha C. and Glover, Jonathan (eds) (1995), *Women, Culture and Development: A Study of Human Capabilities* (New York: Oxford University Press, 1995).

Nuth, Joan, *Wisdom's Daughter: The Theology of Julian of Norwich* (New York: Crossroad, 1991).

O'Connor, James, *Natural Causes: Essays in Ecological Marxism* (New York: The Guilford Press, 1988).

Oduyoye, Mercy Amba, *Introducing African Women's Theology* (Sheffield: Sheffield Academic Press, 2001).

Padgett, S. B., 'The Eschatology of Margaret Fell (1614–1702) and its Place in her Theology and Ministry' (PhD thesis, University of Durham, 2003).

Palmer, Martine E., *On Giving the Spiritual Exercises: The Early Jesuit Manuscript Directories and the Official Directory of 1559* (St Louis: Institute of Jesuit Sources, 1996).

Pencavel, Heather, 'An Urban Version of Isaiah 35', in Geoffrey Duncan (ed.) *Wisdom is Calling: an Anthology of Hope: an Agenda for change* (Norwich: Canterbury Press, 1999).

Pontalis, J. B., 'On Death-Work in Freud, in the Self, in Culture' in Alan Roland (ed.), *Psychoanalysis, Creativity, and Literature,* trans. Susan Cohen (New York: Columbia University Press, 1978).

Quaker Faith and Practice: the book of Christian discipline in the Yearly Meeting of the Religious Society of Friends (Quakers) in Britain (London: Britain Yearly Meeting, 1995).

Raimondo, Meredith, 'Intensifications: Representing Gender and Sexuality at the UN General Assembly Special Session on HIV/AIDS', in Wendy S. Hesford and Wendy Kozol (eds), *Just Advocacy? Women's Human Rights, Transnational Feminisms and the Politics of Representation* (New Brunswick, New Jersey: Rutgers University Press, 2005).

Rich, Adrienne, *Poems 1985–1988* (New York: W. and W. Norton, 1989).

Ricoeur, Paul, 'Autonomy and Vulnerability', in *Reflections on the Just*, trans. David Pellauer (Chicago: University of Chicago Press, 2007).

———, *L'unique et le singulier. L'intégrale des entretiens 'Noms de dieux' d'Edmond Blattchen* (Brussels: Alice Editions, 1999).

Riley, Mary Sharon, 'Women and Contemplation', *Way* (Supplement) 82 (1995): 35–43.

Robinson, John A. T., *The Body: A study in Pauline Theology* (London: SCM Press, 1952).

Rorty, Amelie, 'Spinoza on the Pathos of Idolatrous Love and the Hilarity of True Love', in Genevieve Lloyd (ed.), *Feminism and the History of Philosophy* (Oxford: Oxford University Press, 2002).

Rose, E. A., 'Alexander Kilham', in D. M. Lewis (ed.), *The Blackwell Dictionary of Evangelical Biography 1730–1860 vol. II* (Oxford: Blackwell, 2005).

Royal Canadian Commission on New Reproductive Technologies (RCCONRT) *Proceed with Care: The New Reproductive Technologies and the Ethic of Care* (Ottawa: Government of Canada, 1993).

Ruether, Rosemary Radford, *Sexism and God-Talk: Toward a Feminist Theology* (London: SCM Press, 1983; second edn, Boston: Beacon Press, 1993).

Santmire, Paul H. *The Travail of Nature: The Ambiguous Ecological Promise of Christianity* (Philadelphia: Augsberg Fortress, 1985).

Saunders, Ben, *Desiring Donne: Poetry, Sexuality and Interpretation* (Cambridge, Mass. and London: Harvard University Press, 2006).

Scarry, Elaine, *On Beauty and Being Just* (Princeton NJ: Princeton University Press, 1999).

Schmidt, Leigh Eric, 'The Making of Modern "Mysticism"', *Journal of the American Academy of Religion*, 71/2 (2003): 273–302.

Schmidt, T., *Der Leib Christi* (Leipzig: A. Deichert, 1919).

Scott, Peter Manley, *A Political Theology of Nature* (Cambridge: Cambridge University Press, 2003).

———, 'We have never been gods: transcendence, contingence and the affirmation of hybridity', *Ecotheology*, 9/2 (2004).

———, 'Anarchy in the UK? Political authority and the rioting of God', *Ecotheology*, 11/1 (2006): 32–56.

———, 'The End of Nature and the Last Human? Thinking Theologically about Nature in a Posthuman Condition', in David Albertson and Cabell King (eds) *Without Nature* (Fordham, 2009).

Scottish National Dictionary (Edinburgh: The Scottish National Dictionary Association, 1974).

Scruton, Roger, *Spinoza: A Very Short Introduction* (Oxford: Oxford University Press, 2002).

Sheldrake, Philip, *Befriending our Desires* (London: Darton, Longman and Todd (2001).

Sikkink, Margaret Keck and Kathryn, *Activists Beyond Borders: Advocacy Networks in International Politics* (Ithica, New York: Cornell University Press, 1998).

Sittler, Joseph, *Evocations of Grace: Writings on Ecology, Theology and Ethics* (Grand Rapids: Eerdmans, 2000).

Skene, L. [1667], 'A Warning to the Magistrates and Inhabitants of Aberdeen, writ the 31st Day of the First Month 1677', in J. Besse (ed.), *A Collection of the Sufferings of the People called Quakers* (London: Luke Hinde, 1753).

————, 'Lillias Skene's Poems 1665–1696', transcribed by W. Walker (Aberdeen, University of Aberdeen library, Special Collections, MS. 2774, c. 1850).

Sorokin, Pitirim A.([1954] 2002), The Ways and Power of Love. Types, Factors, and Techniques of Moral Transformation (Philadelphia and London: Templeton Foundation).

Spielrein, Sabina (1912), 'Destruction as the Cause of Coming into Being', *Journal of Analytical Psychology* 39 (1994): 155–186.

Spinoza, Benedict de, 'Tractatus Politicus', *The Political Works* (unfinished at his death) (ed.) and trans. by A. G. Wernham (Oxford: Oxford University Press, 1958).

————, *Ethics* (ed.) and trans. G. H. R. Parkinson (Oxford: Oxford University Press, [1661] 2000).

Stogdon, Katharine M., 'The Risk of Surrender: *Se Livrer* in the Life of Thérèse Couderc (1805–1885)', (PhD thesis, University of Manchester, 2004).

Stubbs, John, *Donne: The Reformed Soul: A Biography* (London, New York and Toronto: Viking, 2006; Harmondsworth: Penguin, 2007).

Tanner, S., 'Women's Suffrage', *The Friends' Quarterly Examiner* 42 (1908): 401–9.

Tarter, M. L., 'Reading a Quaker's Book: Elizabeth Ashbridge's testimony of Quaker literary theory', *Quaker Studies*, 9 (2005): 176–90.

Teilhard de Chardin, Pierre, *Toward the Future* (London: Collins, 1975).

Thompson, John B., *Studies in the Theory of Ideology* (Cambridge: Cambridge University Press, 1984).

Toner, Jules J., *A Commentary on Saint Ignatius' Rules for the Discernment of Spirits* (St Louis: Institute of Jesuit Sources, 1982).

————, *Discerning God's Will: Ignatius of Loyola's Teaching on Christian Decision Making* (St Louis: Institute of Jesuit Sources, 1991).

Tousley, N. C., 'The Experience of Regeneration and Erosion of Certainty in the Theology of Second-Generation Quakers: no place for doubt?' *Quaker Studies*, 13 (2008): 6–88.

Trevett, C., '"Not Fit to be Printed": the Welsh, the women and the Second Day's Morning Meeting', *Journal of the Friends Historical Society* 59 (2001): 115–44.

van Huysteen, J. Wentzel, *Alone in the World? Human Uniqueness in Science and Theology* (Grand Rapids and Cambridge: Eerdmans, 2006).

Vermes, Geza, *The Changing Faces of Jesus* (London, Penguin, 2000).

Walley, Christina, '"Searching for Voices": Feminism, Anthropology, and the Global Debate over Female Genital Operations', in Stanlie M. James and Clair C. Robertson (eds), *Genital Cutting and Transnational Sisterhood: Disputing U.S. Polemics* (Chicago: University of Illinois Press, 2002).

Walton, Izaak, *Lives* (Oxford, London, New York, Toronto: Oxford University Press, [1670] 1932).

Weale, Albert, Pridham, Geoffrey, Cini, Michelle et. al., *Environmental Governance in Europe* (Oxford: Oxford University Press, 2003).

Webb, Stephen H., *Dylan Redeemed: From Highway 61 to Saved* (London: Continuum, 2006).

Weldon, S. Laurel, 'Inclusion and Understanding: A Collective Methodology for Feminist International Relations', in Brooke Ackerly, Maria Stern, and Jacqui True (eds), *Feminist Methodologies for International Relations* (Cambridge: Cambridge University Press, 2006).

Whitehead, Alfred North, *The Aims of Education and Other Essays* (New York: The Free Press, 1929).

——, *Science and the Modern World* (Cambridge: Cambridge University Press, 1925).

——, *The Function of Reason* (Boston, Mass: Beacon Press, [1929] 1958).

——, *Adventures of Ideas* (New York: The Free Press, [1933] 1967).

——, *Process and Reality: An Essay in Cosmology* (New York: The Free Press, [1929] 1978).

Woods, Richard, *Mediaeval and Modern Women Mystics: The Evidential Character of Religious Experience* (Lampeter: Religious Experience Research Centre, Second Series Occasional Paper 7, nd).

Yorke, Gosnell L. O. R., *The Church as the Body of Christ in the Pauline Corpus* (Lanham, MD: University Press of America, 1991).

Žižek, Slavoj, *The Plague of Fantasies* (London and New York: Verso, 1997).

——, *The Puppet and the Dwarf: the Perverse Core of Christianity* (Cambridge: MIT, 2003).

Index of Names

Index of Subjects